PRODUCER

A MEMOIR

DAVID L. WOLPER

WITH DAVID FISHER

A LISA DREW BOOK

SCRIBNER
New York   London   Toronto   Sydney   Singapore

A LISA DREW BOOK/SCRIBNER
1230 Avenue of the Americas
New York, NY 10020

SCRIBNER and design are trademarks of Macmillan Library Reference USA, Inc.,
used under license by Simon & Schuster, the publisher of this work.
A LISA DREW BOOK is a trademark of Simon & Schuster, Inc.

For information regarding special discounts for bulk purchases,
please contact Simon & Schuster Special Sales at 1-800-456-6798 or
business@simonandschuster.com

Set in Caledonia

Manufactured in the United States of America

1   3   5   7   9   10   8   6   4   2

Library of Congress Cataloging-in-Publication Data
Wolper, David L.
Producer : a memoir / David L. Wolper, with David Fisher.
p.   cm.
"A Lisa Drew book."
Includes index.
"The Wolper filmography": p. 341.
1. Wolper, David L. 2. Motion picture producers and directors—United States—Biography.
3. Television producers and directors—United States—Biography. I. Fisher, David. II. Title.

PN1998.3.W645 A3 2003
791.43'0232'092—dc21
[B]   2002030654

ISBN 0-7432-3687-4

To my wife, Gloria,
who, through her spirituality and kind heart,
has taught me the true meaning of life
and for thirty-three years has been "the wind beneath my wings."

To my children, Mark, Michael, and Leslie, and their spouses,
who have been a constant joy to me throughout my life.

And to my grandchildren,
who, I hope one day, through this book,
will discover the comings and goings of their grandfather.

ACKNOWLEDGMENTS

No one person is responsible for the making of a film, in spite of the so-called auteur theory. It took a large number of people with individual skills to create over seven hundred films by the Wolper Company. I wish to acknowledge and thank those people for their talents and dedication.

My thanks to Charles Uy and Sona Basmadjian, curators of the David L. Wolper Center at the University of Southern California Cinema and Television School, for digging up material and information from the collection. And thanks to Steve Hanson, head of the Cinema-Television library and to the dean of the school, Elizabeth Daley.

To Ruben and Merci Corea, for clearing the decks at home so I could concentrate on my book.

To Andy Stuart, my book agent, whom I've known from birth, as he is the son of one of my top executives and creative producers, Mel Stuart.

Thanks to Janette Webb and Diane Thompson, for transcribing, organizing, photocopying, and recopying this book; and to Joan Koury Rhodes, for transcribing hundreds of hours of my thoughts from audio tapes to near perfection.

To Warner Bros., where I spent the last twenty-four years of my film career. To Charlie McGregor, Frank Wells, and Ted Ashley, who brought me in. To Bob Daly, Terry Semel, and Barry Meyer, who were always kind to me. And to Steve Ross, chairman of Time Warner, who, as one person commented, "His generosity exceeded my greed."

To my editor, Lisa Drew, whom I first met when I produced the miniseries *Roots*. She was Alex Haley's editor for his Pulitzer Prize–winning book. Thanks for teaching me what book editing is all about and getting rid of the superfluous material.

Thank you, Auriel Sanderson, vice president of my company, who has been my assistant for more than thirty years. Auriel has been with me through all the exciting moments of my career and has helped me keep all the balls in the air. I couldn't have done it without her.

Finally, to David Fisher, who was tough as he could be and kept me on the straight and narrow during the creation of this book. Thank you, David, for your friendship, caring, and talent.

CONTENTS

PART VI:
The Spectaculars

PART VII:
Sunset

I REMEMBER DAVID

ART BUCHWALD

I know a lot of people are going to say they gave David Wolper his start in the business, so I'd like to get my claim in early. David Wolper worked for me as my business manager on the University of Southern California's humor magazine the *Wampus* in 1947 and 1948. I was managing editor of the *Wampus*, and when I spotted David I knew immediately he had the talent and the drive to be a great business manager. For one thing, he had a car, which no one else on the staff did. For another thing, he seemed to know more pretty girls than the rest of us, and for a third, he wore a tie to school, which gave our publication a great deal of class.

Our operation was small and our sales staff consisted of about ten sorority girls, all selected by David. We also ran a Coed of the Month, and since David was the only one who owned a camera, he got to pick and photograph her. I'm not telling how David posed his girls, but had he stuck to publishing, Hugh Hefner might never have gotten off the ground.

David was also a publicity man for the USC varsity show that I
wrote, and his greatest stunt was crashing the Academy Awards presentation at the Shrine Auditorium with a man dressed as a gorilla. The
gorilla had a sign on him saying "If you think this is good, see *No Love
Atoll.*" No one bothered to stop David or the gorilla at the door, and they
had about ten minutes walking up and down the aisles before someone
decided to throw them both out. It was David's finest hour at USC.

In 1948, I decided to go to Paris. I asked David what he was going
to do.

"I'm going into television," he said.

"You're crazy," I said, "it's just a fad. You'll never make a go of it."

But David was determined: "Maybe I'll never make any dough at it,
but it's a great art form, and besides, I hear it's a swell way to meet girls."

Well, I went off to Europe and David went off into television, and
that's the last I ever heard of him. I guess to this day he's sorry he didn't
take my advice.

ABOUT DAVID L. WOLPER

MIKE WALLACE

Back in May of 1958, a rather unimposing, blondish, slight, and pale young man came into my office at Channel 13 in New York City to tell me he had exclusive rights to some Soviet space footage that had never before been seen in the United States. What he had in mind, he said, was to make a documentary he intended to call *The Race for Space*, detailing the long and previously little known history of space exploration; he intended to focus especially, he said, on the competition between the Soviet Union and the United States for primacy in space. He wondered if I might be interested in reporting the story, doing the interviews, and narrating the film.

I was skeptical that he did in fact hold the exclusive rights he'd mentioned. If they were available, the television news networks would surely have them. But as we talked and he began to elaborate on his vision, I found him more persuasive. David Wolper sneaks up on you; there's no bombast, no bells and whistles. He is quiet, logical, credible, and before you realize it, you are his coconspirator. I've known him almost forty years now and I don't remember him ever raising his voice, or making extravagant promises, or going back on his word.

Following *The Race for Space,* I worked with him on a series of hour-long documentaries, biographies of various sports figures mostly, out of which grew the original Wolper *Biography* series; a new version is now a popular staple on A&E. Back then, we profiled all manner of public figures. This was the early sixties and the profiles were syndicated on four hundred TV stations around the world.

It was David who first led me to understand the meaning of the word *producer.* He didn't write, he did little of the film direction, he didn't supervise the research or butt excessively into the work of the men and women he hired to do those things. He had a vision, he organized, he was there from conception to delivery, every time. It was his clairvoyance, his engagement, his encouragement, that made a Wolper production a joy to work on. Once he'd hired you, he let you do your job, encouraged your comments and contributions, gave you a sense of collaboration that has to be at the root of every successful enterprise. And I marvel at the variety of enterprises that have borne the David L. Wolper name, undertakings of quality, prestige, compassion, and distinction.

He deserves to celebrate his half century of magnificent accomplishment.

PART I

Sunrise

With my mother and father,
Anna and Irving Wolper (late 1930s)

NEW YORK, NEW YORK

With Frank Sinatra (1943)

In the meeting, this is what I might have said: "Now just imagine this, this is a story that's got murder, humor, and sex, includes the most extraordinary true adventures and events from the conquest of the North Pole to the greatest Olympic pageant in history. It's got a Russian invasion and a terrorist attack. It's got a bomb squad searching for what might be an explosive set to blow up a crowd-filled stadium, and it's got the strangest end of a basketball game in history. It takes place just about everywhere from the deepest point on earth to the farthest reaches of outer space. Characters? Name them, it's got them all: Jesus, Abe Lincoln and Jack Kennedy, John Wilkes Booth and Hitler, Napoleon and Picasso, Orson Welles and Brando, Marilyn Monroe, Princess Grace, Jacques Cousteau, Elvis and John Lennon. It's got animals, insects, aliens, and monsters; it's got reality and fiction, science and mythology. And it combines the grandeur of *Roots*, the passion of *The Thorn Birds*, the intrigue of *L.A. Confidential*, and the whimsy of *Willy Wonka*."

That's probably what I would have said sitting in the office of a television network executive trying to sell the miniseries of my life. But I doubt the executive would have believed me. I've spent a half century making films, and if someone were telling this story to me, even I wouldn't believe it. But it's true; I lived every word of it.

I'm a producer. I do whatever is necessary to turn an idea into a finished product. That means that at different times I've been a salesman, director, film editor, casting director, creative consultant—I've even driven the bus. The only role I haven't played is actor. "David L. Wolper Presents" is me and several thousand talented people who, in four decades, created thousands of hours of TV programming, Oscar-winning motion pictures, and spectacular outdoor live events. I was involved in three major Americana events of the last half of the twentieth century. In 1976, I was chairman of the President's Commission to Celebrate the 200th Anniversary of the United States. In 1984, I produced the opening and closing ceremonies for the 1984 Los Angeles Olympic Games. And in 1986, I was chairman, executive producer, and creator of Liberty Weekend—the four-day celebration of the one hundredth anniversary of the Statue of Liberty. While my name is only vaguely familiar to people outside the entertainment industry, billions of people throughout the world have seen my work. For television I have produced movies, miniseries, documentaries, sitcoms, music and dramatic specials. Of the fifty highest-rated programs in the history of television, I've produced ten of them. My company produced the two highest-rated miniseries of all time, *Roots* and *The Thorn Birds*. We helped modernize, and popularize, the long-staid documentary form by applying entertainment values to it and produced television's highest-rated documentary—and I brought to television the great adventures of Jacques Cousteau aboard the *Calypso*.

Television and I were born two days apart. I came first, being born at Polyclinic Hospital New York City on January 11, 1928. I was delivered by my uncle, Dr. Arthur Stoloff. Two days later, in Schenectady, New York, the General Electric Company broadcast the first hazy picture to home receivers. Later that same year, twenty-seven-year-old William Paley founded the Columbia Broadcasting System, Mickey Mouse and Amos and Andy made their debuts, the Daven Corporation of Newark, New Jersey, began selling TV sets for $75, the first talking picture, Al Jolson's *The Jazz Singer*, played on Broadway, and in December, the Newsreel Movietone News—history recorded on film—first appeared in motion picture palaces.

I grew up all over New York City. My first real home was between the "els," at 223 East Fifty-second Street between the Second Avenue (demolished in 1942) and Third Avenue (demolished in 1955) elevated trains. My father was . . . perhaps the best way to describe my father is to acknowledge that Donald Trump referred to *him* in his book as "one of the greatest bullshit artists I'd ever met"—while admitting that my dad had taught him much about the art of the deal. Irving Wolper was a complicated man. During the Depression he had what was perhaps the toughest of all jobs—he was a bill collector for Finley Strauss, a large jewelry store. On occasion I would go with him to collect on an overdue debt. I can remember people screaming at him, threatening him; I remember wondering why people were so angry with him. I remember waiting outside a house in a car watching my father come running out the door, pursued by a man throwing things at him.

Eventually he began selling real estate. Selling property in the Depression was only slightly easier than collecting on jewelry. But, because the buildings were so big, the commissions were substantial. Infrequent, but substantial. Whenever my father made a large sale, we'd move to a nicer neighborhood, but several years later when the money began running out, we'd have to move again.

After my father died I discovered that he'd kept a scrapbook containing all the newspaper clippings announcing his deals. It's the record of a lifetime. For a time he worked for William Zeckendorf, the real estate developer who eventually bought the Empire State Building. Some years after my mother died, he took a job managing a large apartment complex in Cincinnati for Fred Trump. The complex was not doing very well. About half of the twelve hundred apartments were rented when my dad went to work. He did such a good job that Fred sent his son, Donald, to work with him. My father planted ten thousand flowers and trees. He installed twenty-four-hour security and upgraded maintenance. When Fred Trump worried that the kids in the buildings would destroy the flowers, my father solved that problem by paying the kids to clean up. And when tenants were late paying the rent, he would collect it himself. "He'd ring the doorbell," Donald Trump wrote, "and when someone came to the door he'd go crazy. . . . It was an act, but it was very effective. Usually they paid the rent right there."

Donald Trump joked that they paid Irving Wolper "$50,000 and all you can steal," but admitted, "there was no better manager than him." Eventually, through his efforts, the complex was 98 percent rented, and Trump sold it for double what he'd paid for it.

I suspect that both Donald and I learned from my father the value of bravado. He always had a weakness for a beautiful woman, and apparently, while living in Cincinnati, he had flirted with the wife of a construction worker. Trump was with him when this 240-pound monster burst into the room with murder in his eyes. "I expected Irving, if he had any sense, to run for his life," Trump reported. "Instead he verbally attacked the man, flailing and screaming and chopping his hands in the air: 'You get out of this office or I'll kill you. I'll destroy you. These hands are lethal weapons. They're registered with the police department.'"

The man eventually left, but, as Trump wrote, "Irving probably saved his own life by showing no fear. That left a very good impression: you can't be scared."

A lesson well learned. Like my father, I was a salesman, and my primary product was myself. Throughout my childhood I was always looking for something to sell. When I was in grade school, we lived on the eleventh floor of a building and I grew radishes in a flower box—which I sold to my mother for a penny each. As I got older, I worked in a record store, I worked as a waiter, a delivery boy for Christos and Koster's Flowers on Madison Avenue, an usher at the legendary Astor Theatre. I set pins in a bowling alley. I worked as a busboy at Birchwoods Hotel in the Catskill Mountains, I taught rumba as an Arthur Murray dance instructor. When I was a teenager, I delivered sealed envelopes all over the city for some of the wise guys who hung around the famed Copacabana lounge. Officially, I never knew what was inside, I never opened one of them, but as these men were big gamblers, I was pretty sure I was delivering cash or betting slips. My pay was "take a cab and keep the change." I always had a job; I was always working, always hustling.

My mother was a wonderful woman with a drinking problem. An alcoholic. But that never interfered with her job as wife and mother; there was always a hot meal on the table when my father came home. For a time, when money was a little tight, she worked at Bloomingdale's and I spent hours at the Boys Club. She died of a ruptured appendix in her late thirties.

I was a smart kid but not a great student. I was too busy learning about life to worry about an education. My father had sold a large building just as I was ready for high school, and he sent me to the famed Columbia Grammar School. It was New York's oldest high school, founded in 1763. Among my classmates were future Nobel Prize winner in physics Murray Gell-Mann; the great concert pianist Byron Janis; Steve Ross, who would create Time Warner; George Kaufman, who made a fortune in real estate and opened the Kaufman-Astoria Studio; Dr. Ion Gresser, who was involved in the discovery of interferon; and my best friend, Jimmy Harris, who later formed my first company with me and then became the producing partner of legendary director Stanley Kubrick. Of course, we also had a classmate who became a big gambler and was murdered when he failed to pay his debts. We were a wild class, but we had an English teacher, Albert Field, a tall skinny guy who taught us poetry. Nothing could be more valuable to a young man than a great teacher. From that moment I was interested in poetry and have written it my entire life. It always reminds me of the story when President Roosevelt invited John Steinbeck to have dinner with the president and Mrs. Roosevelt at the White House. Steinbeck's response went something like this: "Dear Mr. President, it is a great honor that you asked my wife and me to join you for a private dinner, but it just so happens that on that date, August 15, there is a dinner to honor my high school English teacher. In my life I have met five great presidents but only one great English teacher."

I don't know when I first knew I wanted to be in show business. It seems like I've known that forever. Somehow, some way, I would do it— end of discussion. The closest anyone in my family came to show business was my uncle, David J. Wolper. He was an attorney, and among his clients was gangster Mickey Cohen's glamorous moll, Virginia Hill. To settle a 1942 bill, Virginia Hill gave my uncle, the lawyer, the famed Hurricane nightclub on Broadway.

Which is how the Wolper family first got into the entertainment business. My uncle began producing shows for his club. Duke Ellington played there, as did the great bandleader Ted Lewis. Eventually, my uncle began producing Broadway shows, among them the hit musical *Follow the Girls* with Gertrude Neison and Jackie Gleason and *Glad to See You,* a musical revue written by Julie Styne and Sammy Cahn and staged by Busby Berkeley. For a time my uncle was very successful, but that time ended. It's one of those stories relatives whisper in the next room, but apparently he sold more than 100 percent interest in *Glad to See You*—a scam later to be immortalized by Mel Brooks in *The Producers.* As a New York City assistant attorney general announced, "The means of raising revenue were most unique and novel in the theater and financial circles."

Welcome to show business.

I couldn't sing, dance, or act. But I could dream. And I could talk. And I could sell; I could always sell. It was obvious I was going to be a director, an agent, or a producer.

I started my career by producing my high school junior prom. Normally, the junior prom is a small event. Normally. But this junior prom was going to be a David L. Wolper—as opposed to my uncle David J. Wolper—production. It was held in a hotel ballroom and I managed to talk Ted Lewis and his entire orchestra into playing for a greatly reduced rate. I don't remember exactly how I did it; I might have convinced him that he would get a tremendous amount of publicity for appearing at our junior prom. Or I might simply have pleaded with him.

Based on that success, Jimmy Harris and I decided to form the New York City high school band, consisting of the best high school musicians in the city. We were sure the big theaters like the Paramount and the Roxy would be interested. We sent our press release to all the high school newspapers and actually received hundreds of responses. But, as hard as we hustled, no theater was interested in booking it. We just couldn't sell it.

As a producer, I never invested too much emotion in a single idea. As much as I might have loved it, as a producer I understood that its real value was only what someone else would pay for it. So I tried to sell whatever the buyer wanted to buy. I remember once going to a network sales meeting with the producer-director Mel Stuart, who was with me almost from the day I formed the Wolper Company. Mel and I went into that meeting to sell a specific program and left with an order for something entirely different. Mel was astonished. "We went in there to sell them apples," he said, "and they bought oranges. We don't know anything about oranges."

"We do now," I told him.

Jimmy Harris once explained that I always had the ability to take no for an answer—meaning that I didn't let a negative response defeat me or embarrass me, nor did I persist in trying to convince the other person he or she was wrong. Instead I accepted it and kept moving forward. I always had a lot of guts, which I suspect I inherited from my father. To collect money during the Depression you had to have guts—although mostly, you had to be very big. My father was over six feet and weighed over two hundred pounds.

No guts, no glory, no Wolper. I have never been easily intimidated. That is an extremely valuable trait for a producer. For example, growing up, I was a big Frank Sinatra fan. One night in 1939, as we were driving up to the Catskills to my busboy job, my parents stopped at the Rustic Tavern just over the George Washington Bridge on Route 9 in New Jersey, and a very young Frank Sinatra was singing with the Harold Arden Band. I was absolutely enthralled. So, long before he became *Frank Sinatra*, long before he was the Chairman of the Board, I was a fan. In fact, after his legendary engagement at the Paramount Theatre in New York in 1942, I stood outside watching as they took down his huge wooden likeness over the marquee and followed the truck transporting it out to a dump on Long Island. I quickly bought a saw and cut off Sinatra's head. It was more than five feet tall and hung over my bed for the rest of my adolescence.

Many people would have been satisfied with Sinatra's head, but it wasn't enough for me. I wanted to meet him. He was appearing at the Waldorf, and I and my friend Frankie Military—who eventually became a top executive at Warner Music—decided we were going to meet him. Although people waited hours in line just to catch a glimpse of him leaving the theater, we were determined to get our pictures taken with him. We got all dressed up, took my camera, and marched into the hotel as if we belonged there. After finding out where he was staying, we went to his floor. When he came out, I asked if he would pose for a picture. It's a wonderful photograph. Sinatra is looking at me as if I'm slightly crazy, and rather than looking at him, I'm looking directly into the camera and smiling proudly. I knew I could do it.

While I was in high school, and shortly thereafter, I began hanging out with show people on Broadway. I'd go to the restaurants and the jazz clubs and became friendly with a lot of young performers. I knew all the hip comedians: Alan King, Joey Bishop, Red Buttons, Jack Carter, Phil Foster, Jan Murray, Larry Storch, Gary Morton, Sid Gould, Buddy Hackett, Fat Jack Leonard, Lenny Gaines, as well as Manischewitz's ubiquitous wine salesman, Peppy Wiener. We'd all hang out at Bird in the Hand, at Lindy's, and go to Chandlers late at night to see disc jockeys Barry Gray or Symphony Sid at Birdland or Jack Egan at the Copa Lounge. I worked summers as a waiter at Birchwoods Hotel in the Catskills and also after meals as an Arthur Murray dance instructor teaching the rumba. The assistant social director was a kid named Don Rickles. That was when I almost discovered him.

During the week, Rickles would do stand-up. Even then he was doing insult humor. I thought he was funny—and incredibly brave. So I called my uncle and told him I'd found a comedian who'd be perfect for the Hurricane. "Bring him down," my uncle said.

In retrospect, perhaps I should have described his act. Just imagine meeting Don Rickles without knowing that the insults were his act. I vaguely remember my uncle standing there with his mouth hanging open in stunned silence as Rickles went to work on him. What I remember clearly is my uncle's response: "Get out of my fucking office, both of you."

I was a kid who was much better on Broadway than in the classroom. My academic career might best be described as, well, he's no Murray Gell-Mann. When I graduated from high school, I wanted to go to the University of Southern California. Only one thing prevented me from doing that—the University of Southern California. My grades weren't good enough. So I stayed in New York for a year, working as a salesman in a record store and as an agent. Not exactly an agent, more like a shepherd.

In the late 1940s, athletes had few promotional opportunities, beyond the front of a box of Wheaties. A man named Bill Robbins ran a division of the large talent agency Columbia Entertainment called Sports Stars, which had been formed to represent the most famous athletes. Bill hired me to escort his clients around New York. Among them was the lovely Florence Chadwick, the first person to swim the English Channel both ways, an incredible feat. She was on the front page of every newspaper. New York City welcomed her with a ticker-tape parade. All the major television shows wanted her, and my job was to see that she arrived on time. When she appeared on the *Jackie Gleason Show*, I traveled with her to Florida. While there, we had a brief affair. Everything I'd dreamed about show business was coming true.

TWO

BUCHWALD AND USC

Art Buchwald and I with some USC coeds (1947)

After spending a year in New York in 1946, I enrolled at Drake University in Des Moines, Iowa. I was halfway to USC—geographically, at least. Drake was a great college for me. I worked hard there and made excellent grades—and signed my first business contract. A talented collegiate playwright named John Poister agreed to let me represent the play that he'd written. I probably mentioned all the right words: *New York, Broadway, money*. And I was bluffing about the money. I tried everything I could to raise funds to stage the show in Des Moines. I even went "downtown" to meet the gangsters running the local clubs, but I couldn't find any investors. The play was never produced.

In 1947, I was accepted by the University of Southern California, where I majored in cinema, journalism, and extracurricular activities. In addition to working as a photographer for the campus newspaper, *The Daily Trojan*, I was publicity manager for the school show, the agent for a student dance band, a relief pitcher who provided no relief on the Trojan baseball team, and the business manager of the campus humor magazine, the *Wampus*. The editor of the *Wampus* was Art Buchwald, and we immediately became close friends and business partners. While we received no salaries, each year the editor and business manager bought from the previous editor and business manager the advertising agency that sold all the ads in the magazine—which means Buchwald and I got a 15 percent commission on every ad we sold. I did everything I could to help sell copies. I convinced Jane Russell to pose for us supposedly reading it. Long before Hugh Hefner, I created the vitally significant pictorial centerfold USC Sweetheart of the Month, which allowed Buchwald and me to reach two important objectives: to meet every pretty girl on campus, and to sell more advertising.

Of my many achievements at USC, perhaps most memorable was bringing a gorilla to the Academy Awards ceremony. Buchwald had coauthored a musical comedy entitled *No Love Atoll*, which took place on an island in the South Pacific, and asked me to promote it. The first thing I did was issue a serious press release announcing that a savage woman—I named her Ngaya—captured on a remote Micronesian island would be exhibited at a lecture by the president of the International Anthropology Society. I mentioned that she was so wild that, for safety reasons, she would have to be kept in a steel cage. The loud complaints from other campus organizations—slavery, they called it—resulted in even more publicity. At noon, March 19, 1948, a large crowd gathered in front of Hancock Hall and I presented my "wild woman"—who was actually a student wearing a rented gorilla outfit with a sign taped on his back that read "See *No Love Atoll* coming soon!"

I had rented the costume for three weeks, so I intended to take advantage of it. At that time, the Academy Awards were being held at the Shrine Auditorium, which bordered the USC campus. I rented a limousine and pulled up right in front just like all the other stars. Except that, when the door opened, a gorilla got out of our limousine. The security people obviously assumed we were part of the show because they let us walk right inside, right down the wide red carpet—me and a gorilla with a sign taped to its back publicizing the show.

We walked down the center aisle, creating a sensation and scaring poor Ginger Rogers, who turned around casually just in time to see the gorilla approaching her. The reporters and photographers loved us; in fact, the next day the picture of the gorilla being escorted out of the Academy Awards ceremony by police officers appeared in all the newspapers.

About the only publicity that equaled that was our ad campaign that claimed the show featured "fifty beautiful native girls wearing forty-nine lovely sarongs."

Perhaps the final thing that convinced me that my future was in show business was my ability as a baseball player. Our manager at USC was the legendary Rod Dedeaux, who coached USC to five national championships and eventually coached the 1984 U.S. Olympic baseball team to a gold medal. I was a relief pitcher, although in truth I provided no relief. I pitched in one preseason game, gave up three runs, and got nobody out. When coach Dedeaux came out to the pitcher's mound to take me out of the game, he told me honestly, "Tiger"—he called everyone Tiger—"I'm going to save your life. If you're planning to take up baseball as a career, you're going to starve to death. The only way you're gonna get anybody out is if they bat out of order." So ended my baseball career.

Television and I started maturing at just about the same time. As I learned in a Wolper documentary, the concept of television was discovered in 1922 by a fourteen-year-old Idaho farm boy named Philo Farnsworth. According to the legend, Farnsworth was an inventive young man fascinated by electricity. One day, as a shadow moved over a cornfield, the rows and rows of cornstalks seemed transformed into a face. He realized that an image could be created by combining dots— each cornstalk was a dot—and that dots could be transmitted electrically. The day he applied for his first patent, January 7, 1927, is officially considered the day television was invented. Utilizing a completely different technology using revolving disks, Farnsworth's competition, Bell Labs, had transmitted a live picture of Herbert Hoover answering questions in Washington, D.C., to a room on West Street in New York City the previous April. But eventually, that broadcasting system proved unwieldy.

The first image Farnsworth broadcast was a horizontal black line painted on a glass slide. To prove the picture was actually being broadcast, the slide was moved up and down. A few years later, Farnsworth broadcast the first program, Walt Disney's cartoon *Steamboat Willie*, to his own home for his son to watch. The first public demonstration of television was held in Philadelphia in 1935. Philadelphians lined up for blocks to see themselves on TV. In this case the monitor was the bottom half of a ten-gallon jug, while a second receiver showed a variety of entertainment programming.

I saw television for the first time at an exhibition at the 1939 World's Fair. I don't remember the programming, but it was certainly more entertaining than a black line. While, at that time, most people considered TV more of an oddity than the harbinger of the most powerful medium in the world, I was incredibly impressed.

My father bought our first television set right after World War II ended. It had a very small screen, probably about seven inches in diameter. It was so small it came with a large round magnifying glass screwed to its front. When we got that television, I insisted my eighty-year-old grandfather come to our house to see it. For some reason it was important to me that he see this miracle at least once before he died.

While I was at USC, I kept my close friendship with Jimmy Harris. He was in the army, stationed somewhere in the Nevada desert, at a place he never talked about very much. As I later learned, that was because they were testing atomic bombs. But some weekends we'd meet in a dinky town named Las Vegas, where gambling was legal. We stayed at Bugsy Siegel's brand-new hotel there, The Flamingo.

By the late 1940s, television was booming. By 1949, more than 1 million television sets were in use, many of them in bars and restaurants. Within three years there were 17 million sets, most of them in private homes, and America had changed forever. The time of small, isolated towns was finished; television helped turn America into one large small town.

Broadcasting stations were beginning to open in every city in America. There were no television networks providing a full schedule of programming, so these stations had to fill time as best and as cheaply as possible. One of the biggest stars in television was Bishop Fulton J. Sheen on the DuMont Television Network. Bishop Sheen would simply sit in front of the camera and tell religious stories. People were so fascinated with the concept that they would have watched anything. People actually did watch the test pattern, a simple lined diagram identifying the channel, which was broadcast when the station closed for the night.

DuMont had put Bishop Sheen on the air to counter the huge success of comedian Milton Berle. Berle used slapstick and wisecracks and generally outrageous behavior for that time to become TV's first superstar. He is still credited with selling more TVs than any other person or show in history. Everybody had to see "Uncle Milty."

This is when I made my first money in television. As new stations opened, the demand for product increased tremendously. In those early days, guild regulations prohibited television stations from showing reruns. They recorded their live programming on kinescope, which was like poor-quality tape, for distribution to affiliates in other cities. But the kinescopes had little other value. As far as the networks were concerned, they were just taking up valuable warehouse space. So they threw them out or burned them. Much of the best programming from the early years of television was just destroyed. The first presidential broad-cast, Harry S Truman addressing the nation from the White House, was destroyed. The first six months of Berle's *Texaco Star Theater* history was destroyed. Coverage of the 1948 election, the first presidential election reported on television, gone. Just imagine what those programs would be worth today in terms of real dollars as well as television history. Iron-ically, for a brief time in the late 1940s, Jimmy Harris and I burned kinescopes for NBC. We'd bring the kinescopes to a building my father represented on the Upper West Side of Manhattan and toss them in the furnace. We were being paid to destroy television history.

I was still a student at USC when Jimmy Harris got out of the army. One summer we decided to go into the film distribution business. We purchased the American distribution rights to an Italian movie entitled *The Miracle at Monte Casino*. We retitled the film *Fear No Evil*, and rather than showing it to critics in a screening room, we invited the crit-ics to Jimmy Harris's apartment. It was not exactly a gala premiere. Lunch was catered by Jimmy's mother in the living room. We showed the film on a 16mm home projector and had to stop in the middle to change reels. But critics from the major newspapers came to this screen-ing and gave the film decent reviews. We opened and closed it in a small art theater, and except for sympathetic relatives and supportive friends, nobody wanted to see it. It was definitely a failure.

At about that same time, Jimmy's father, Joe Harris, who ran an insur-ance brokerage company, bought a series of old short travel films, which he had originally intended to sell to schools, but they were so boring no one would buy them. I don't remember who suggested it, but Jimmy and I, Joe, and a friend of Jimmy's brother named Sy Weintraub, formed a company to sell these films directly to television stations around the country. We named our company Flamingo Films after Bugsy Siegel's Las Vegas hotel, where we had stayed one weekend and won a few bucks. I left school to become a film distributor. Art Buchwald also left before he graduated, so I have proof he's no smarter than I am.

THREE

THE LONELY ROAD

Jimmy Harris, singer Tony Martin, and I in Vegas
at the Flamingo Hotel (1947)

We opened an office in New York at a swanky Fifth Avenue address. The
rent was cheap, but we found out why. We were over Stouffer's Restaurant and the odors found their way to our offices day and night. Jimmy
Harris and I left for the road to sell the films. He went south, and I went
north.

My very first stop was WJAR in Providence, Rhode Island. I was there
July 10, 1949, the day they opened the doors. Over time, I probably wit-
nessed eighty stations going on the air. I was in Omaha, Nebraska, on
September 1, 1949, when KMTV went on the air. Later I found out that a
performer named Johnny Carson was also there that day. I was in Havana
when CMQ television went on the air—showing my travel shorts with
someone doing a voice-over in Spanish. Literally, this was the beginning
of television and I was right there to sell them these terrible films. The
best of them was *Let's Visit the Orkney Islands,* which are somewhere off
the Scottish coast. After a few weeks I hated the Orkney Islands. I used to
have to dig my fingernail into my hand to keep awake, so my hands would

end up cut and bruised. In Pittsburgh, I remember, after watching one of these films, the program director started shouting at me, "You cheap son of a bitch, trying to sell this crap to us. You got some nerve trying to sell that shit." I was so tired, so young, and so upset I started to cry. I was crying! What was he yelling at me for? I didn't want to visit the Orkney Islands. Truthfully, I wasn't that thrilled to be in Pittsburgh.

But that was unusual; most of the time quality didn't matter. There were about sixty-five TV stations in the entire country and they were desperate for product. Desperate. Even the Orkney Islands. After my slow start, I sold them everything I had, and the station managers practically begged me for more. The programs they wanted most, Hollywood feature films, were not available. None of the studios would sell their pictures to television. The executives were terrified TV was going to wipe out the movie industry, so they weren't going to assist in their own demise. But Joe Harris knew a producer named Sam Bronson, who had independently financed a film entitled *The Adventures of Martin Eden.* Bronson sold him the TV rights for $2,000 and we set out to sell it. *The Adventures of Martin Eden* with Glenn Ford and Evelyn Keyes was the first feature film ever broadcast on television, and we sold it to countless stations.

One of the first places I tried to sell it was Kansas City, where the owner of the *Kansas City Star,* Roy Roberts, was opening the new television station, WDAF, on October 16, 1949. Before buying the film he wanted to see it. So I went into his office with the program manager, Bill Bates, and set up the screen, and we sat there for an hour and a half watching this movie. As we did, I thought, geez, if we ever get ten or twenty features, I'll be sitting in Mr. Roberts's office for two weeks.

But when the film ended, the owner of the station was ecstatic: "It's a lot of fun watching films in my own office. I never did that before." He bought it for the station. Fortunately, most station managers bought it without watching it.

We were helping lay the foundations of the television industry. After that, we knew we could sell just about anything we could get. An independent distributor, Sam Krellberg, sold us *Meet John Doe* with Gary Cooper. An independent film distributor from Boston named Joseph L. Levine sold us a package of very old feature films, among them semi-classics like *East Lynne* and *Gaslight Follies.* We sold them all. It was soon obvious that the real star of television was television. Nobody cared about quality as long as it was on television.

My territory kept expanding. I sold *Meet John Doe* to Klaus Landsburg, general manager of KTLA in Los Angeles for $5,000, the most ever paid for a feature film. That success convinced Joe Harris to buy the rights to every film available. The studios still adamantly refused to sell us their old movies. The situation was so ridiculous that in 1950 I actually offered the seven major studios $10,000 for the TV rights to their movies on the moon, Mars, and Venus. When they didn't respond, I limited my $10,000 offer to television rights just for the moon. I was twenty-two years old and I was trying to buy TV rights to the moon. One executive told me that the studio just couldn't sell the rights that cheaply. Obviously it was a gimmick, but I was serious: I could just envision the publicity when I announced that Flamingo Films had bought the rights from MGM to exhibit its films on the moon.

The lack of salable product just about forced us to start producing original programming. The first show we did was a cartoon series called *The Funny Bunnies*. We had nothing to do with the actual production; we made a deal with a production company and distributed the series. Jimmy Harris produced a show in cooperation with major league baseball called *Baseball Hall of Fame*. It was just a lot of old footage stuck together and narrated by Marty Glickman.

In May 1951, we signed a $30 million, thirty-one-year deal with Harry Donnefeld, president of National Comics, for the TV rights to *Superman*. Three years earlier Buchwald and I had been selling ads at space rates in a humor magazine, and suddenly at the age of twenty-three I was involved in a $30 million deal. We produced twenty-six shows in 1951 at $20,000 per episode, but it took us two years to find a sponsor. Eventually I sold Kellogg's cereals the show and they syndicated it, meaning they bought time on individual stations around the country, rather than placing it on one of the major networks. *Superman* was produced by Robert Maxwell, and eventually we shot 104 episodes. In those days almost everything you did was the first time it had been done on television. To save money, we filmed scenes from several episodes at the same time on the same set, which is why Clark Kent— played by George Reeves—Lois Lane, Perry White, and Jimmy Olson wore the same clothes week after week. While I always thought the special effects were a little corny, and at times Superman's indestructible costume looked wrinkled, almost half a century later the show is still being run. To the entertainment industry that is the real definition of indestructible.

Initially, it was produced in black and white, but within a couple of years we were shooting in color. There was no color TV at that time, but we believed it was inevitable and wanted to be ready for it. *Superman* might have been the first film series produced in color.

In October 1948, the FCC decided to stop licensing any new television stations while it developed its blueprint for a fair and efficient distribution of service among the states and cities. So, until July 1952, the number of television stations in America was frozen. When it was lifted, I was there for the opening of the first station after the freeze in Denver, Colorado—selling and selling and selling.

We sold every film we had and still the demand increased. New stations were opening every day. As the studios accepted the inevitability of television, old B movies became available. Flamingo Films eventually merged into the legendary Manny Fox's Motion Pictures for Television, which owned the films produced by a low-end studio named Allied Artists, and I moved to Los Angeles as head of our small West Coast office. The merger gave us the rights to a package of feature films that we sold to the New York television station WCBS. They began showing the movies at night after the local news, the first time television programming extended into the late night. *The Late Show*, which ran for decades, was created to show our films.

Other B-picture studios such as Monogram and Eagle-Lion quickly followed Allied Artists, and we got the distribution rights to classic cowboy films starring Johnny Mack Brown, Bob Steele, and Red Ryder. We got some Sherlock Holmes, and we got some exploitation films like *Hitler—Dead or Alive*.

But the major motion picture studios still didn't understand television. In the late 1950s, Jack Warner sold the Warner Bros. film library to television for about $15 million and thought he'd made a great deal. Several decades later, after those movies had been shown on television countless times, Ted Turner paid $1 billion for the rights, which he used as the foundation of two cable networks, Turner Classic Movies and Turner Network Television. A billion dollars!

Product came from everywhere. We bought cartoons made in Russia from the Soviet film distribution company Artkino Films and added an English narration. In cartoons, Russian mice looked very much like American mice. We had British short subjects. We had a beauty series and a cooking show. Universal Pictures had made fifteen-minute serials for the theaters—one cliff-hanging episode showed each Saturday morning—under a license from King Features. Although Universal was supposed to have destroyed the negatives when the license expired, we discovered that they had not. We purchased the rights to Flash

Gordon, Buck Rogers, and Don Winslow of the Navy from King Features and we bought the negatives from Universal. Putting the two together, we brought these serials to TV and to a whole new generation.

Flamingo Films became one of the biggest distributors in television. It wasn't that we were so much better than everyone else; at that time there just weren't that many people in the business. When we started attending the annual National Association of Broadcasters convention in the early 1950s, we were treated terribly. Distributors were considered peddlers. Some years the organizers didn't even let us stay at the convention hotel, so we stayed as close as possible and used gimmicks to lure buyers to our suite. One year I had seven gorgeous women in bathing suits on stands, each one representing a different program. We had Miss Features, Miss Flash Gordon serials, Miss Baseball Hall of Fame, Miss Funny Bunnies . . . and the model would give a strong sales pitch about the program she represented. At another convention I created a sensation by hiring a Marilyn Monroe look-alike and whisking her through the lobby to our suite; people thought Marilyn Monroe was in our suite and came to see her.

The most unusual promotion was not from Flamingo Films, however. Stations used to go off the air before midnight and often ended the day with a little homily or a little slice of Americana—something that left viewers feeling content. One company was selling a series of short Bible stories to end the day, and to get station managers to buy their Bible stories, they were supplying prostitutes.

In only a few years I had learned a tremendous amount about selling. I was always low-key. And my sales technique was based on a story I'd heard about a dry cleaner. The first time a new customer left a suit or jacket with this dry cleaner, when that customer picked it up, the dry cleaner would tell him, "Oh, by the way, you left this dollar bill in your pocket." The dollar bill came from the cash register, but invariably the customer was so impressed by the dry cleaner's honesty that he would return. So it cost the dry cleaner a dollar to get a customer for a lifetime.

I discovered that, if I began by telling the truth about the worst thing I was selling, the buyer would trust me about everything else. "I've got some great shows," I'd begin, "but I've got to tell you, this one is a real stinker. I don't want you to watch it and get upset with me. The rest of the shows though . . ."

I spent almost two full years on the road, basically living out of my car, selling from city to city. It was tough, lonely. But I met so many people; I had so many wonderful experiences. Often one of the young comics I knew from New York was working in the city I was visiting and we'd spend time together, and after a while I became friendly with executives from the local TV stations. But for two years I was never in the same place longer than a few days. Ironically, while I was certainly one of the most successful distributors of TV programming, I didn't even own a TV. And few hotel rooms had them. Even though I didn't drink, I spent a lot of time in nightclubs waiting for my show-business friends to finish their act.

I didn't drink then and I don't drink now, probably because my mother was an alcoholic. I am one of very few people who would be sitting in an elegant restaurant or a fancy bar and order iced tea—or milk. I was the permanent designated driver long before that term became popular.

This was also the early days of commercial aviation, and as my territory expanded, I found myself spending a considerable amount of time on airplanes. As there were no coast-to-coast flights, I made a lot of landings and takeoffs. Coming into Buffalo one windy afternoon, the plane almost flipped over on its side. On another flight we lost one of our two engines. But the flight I remember most was the landing in Salt Lake. Not Salt Lake City, *the* Salt Lake. I was on a DC-3, probably the best airplane ever built. As we made our approach into Salt Lake City, the pilot announced that the wheels would not come down and we were going to land on the lake. I was petrified. Some things in this life are worth dying for, but *The Funny Bunnies* is not one of them.

The decision made sense. The Great Salt Lake is the densest lake in the world. It's a hard surface, but not nearly as hard as a concrete runway. And the salt makes the lake so buoyant the plane wouldn't sink. It was the best water landing I've ever experienced—meaning we survived. There were no serious injuries. Rescuers took everyone off the plane in boats.

Only four years later, I got right back on an airplane again. And the only reason I did that was because I had to be in New York for an important sales meeting and missed my train connection in Chicago. A plane was my only option that day—but before I got on that airplane I had my first real drink. And my second.

In those days I was young and single, making a good living—and I had an expense account. While living in Los Angeles, I met some wonderful women. I married one of them, a gorgeous former-Copa, six-foot-tall showgirl and cabaret singer named Toni Carroll. We had a pleasant marriage and I supported her singing career. One night I found myself sitting in a nightclub in Bakersfield listening to her sing—she was the opening act for Peter Marshall and Tommy Noonan—and I realized that I did not want to spend the next few years of my life sitting in nightclubs listening to my wife sing. Toni was a terrific person, but our marriage wasn't working and both of us knew it. Divorce was less common in the 1950s, even in Los Angeles, and California law required specific grounds for a divorce. As United Press reported, "Actress-singer Toni Carroll came up with new grounds for divorce today—her husband's 'insults' made her stutter." Only now does it occur to me that the song she should have tried singing was "K-K-K-Katie . . ."

I married my second wife, a beautiful and charming young woman named Dawn Richard, who, when I met her, had just finished being choked by the werewolf in the famous scene in *I Was a Teenage Werewolf.* We were married for twelve years and had three children. When we divorced, she moved to Greece, remarried, and had another child. We still remain friends to this day. Later, when my divorce to Dawn was in the works, I happened to look out my office window on the MGM studio lot and saw this lovely young woman. She walked by every day at about the same time. As men do, I began to look forward to seeing her. My mystery woman. Finally, one day, I followed her into an elevator and introduced myself. Her name was Gloria Hill. She was an actress and gym instructor working as a secretary between jobs. I called her and we began dating. Winning the affection of an extraordinary woman is tougher than selling any kind of film. There is always another buyer for a film. But there was no one else like Gloria. Of all the sales I've made in my life, this was the best one. We married in July 1974 and we've spent the rest of our lives together.

In 1954, I decided to leave the distribution business. When I did, to my surprise, I discovered that my 25 percent ownership of Flamingo Films had somehow become 2.5 percent. What a difference a decimal point makes. I was stunned. I had considered Joe Harris my second father. That experience transformed me into a tough businessman. Maybe too tough sometimes, but I had a demanding teacher. The price of that lesson, to my calculations, was 22.5 percent of a very successful distribution company.

I CAN'T BELIEVE I'M A BANKER!

Baseball manager Leo Durocher
donated one of his trophies
to the Dodger Museum (1956)

I didn't know what I really wanted to do with my life. So, naturally, because of my background in TV distribution, in 1956, I accepted the position of executive vice president and treasurer of a new bank. I was responsible for TV contract approvals.

In those days in California, anything was possible. Actually, the Continental Thrift Bank intended to make substantial loans to TV distributors using their contracts as collateral. It was a great idea; there were always cash-flow problems in the business. I knew most of the TV stations; I knew who would pay right away and who would be slow to pay. So the president of the bank hired me to advise the bank on these loans.

I don't know where creativity comes from. I've always believed it to be that place in the mind where curiosity, intellect, and necessity meet. But, throughout my life, I've been able to find ways to bring excitement and attention to my projects, whether it was the opening of the Olympics or the opening of a bank. Ideas have always just flowed from my mind, and I've found that when I get excited about a concept, other people have always responded to them.

We were a new bank in competition with established giants. We needed publicity. At that time, the Brooklyn Dodgers had revolutionized major league baseball by announcing they were moving to Los Angeles, the first team to relocate to California. It was a huge news event in L.A. In some sociological ways it knitted the state to the rest of the country. It occurred to me that, as a promotion for the bank, we should open a Dodger Baseball Museum.

It was a beautiful match. The Dodgers wanted to promote the team and we wanted to promote the bank. The Dodgers were agreeable, so long as I did all the work. People had not yet put price tags on baseball history, so I called different players and collected about thirty items— including the first baseball pitched in a major league game in California. The value of those items was postage—today they would be worth a fortune. The promotion was successful for everyone—the Dodgers are still in Los Angeles, and for years, I kept that baseball. But when my friend Bob Daly, the former head of Warner Bros., bought a piece of the team and decided to run the Dodgers in 2000, I gave him that baseball, as a gift.

FIVE

SHADES OF JERRY SPRINGER

Dr. Paul Popenoe (1956)

I wasn't suited to be a banker. David Gerber, a lifelong friend who was then an agent at General Artists, knew that. "You're not a banker," he said, "you're born to be in the entertainment business." In those early days of television the talent agencies held the real power.

Gerber introduced me to two of his clients who had a concept for a show entitled *Divorce Hearing*. Dr. Paul Popenoe, of the American Institute of Marital Relations, acted as a mediator for couples considering a divorce. He took this show seriously. He really wanted to help people. It was one of the first reality programs. We would advertise in local newspapers for couples who had filed for divorce and pay them $150 to appear on the show. I don't know where our guests came from, but I suspect some of them had filed for divorce just to get on the show. Looking back, I believe that in the great history of the medium, this surely ranks as one of the strangest shows ever televised.

Dr. Popenoe would sit at a judge's bench and the couple would stand in front of him, separated by a railing. Theoretically, each of them would explain to him the problems in their relationship, and he would try to help them bridge gaps, solve their problems, and save their marriage. The stated goal was to keep couples together. In reality, we really wanted them to fight for the camera.

We brought the people into the studio by separate entrances and kept them apart until we were on the air. Each of them was briefed by one of my coproducers, Ralph Andrews and Harry Spears, whose job it was to remind that person why he or she was so angry. Sometimes, the first time they'd seen each other in person in months was on the show. We wanted confrontation, and often we got it. One husband, I remember, got so angry with his wife that he suddenly reached across the set and took a swing at her. She hit him right back. Our crew leaped in to separate them, but they knocked over the set and pieces started falling. This couple is fighting, the set is falling, while in the background Dr. Popenoe was banging his gavel and saying calmly, "Come on now, come on. Let's come to order here. Let's be adult about this."

There have been very few moments in my career of which I'm not proud. Most of them occurred on this show. One couple I'll never forget was separating because the husband was always drunk and the wife was always complaining. The day of the show, the husband did a terrible thing—he came in sober. Harry and Ralph took the guy to Diamond Jim's, the bar next door, listening sympathetically as he bought drinks for him. By the time the show started, the guy was smashed. Seeing him that way, his wife became irate. They started screaming at each other, and the future was secure for Jerry Springer and all those other shows that exploit human relations.

PART II

The Documentary Years

Jacques Cousteau and I (1966)

SERENDIPITY

Directing host Mike Wallace in *The Race for Space* (1958)

I worked on *Divorce Hearing* while still working at Continental Thrift. I was desperate to get out of the bank. I knew I wanted to be in the entertainment industry, but I didn't know what it was that I really wanted to do. One afternoon in 1957, as I walked along Sixth Avenue in New York City, I ran into the American representative of Artkino Films, the Russian company from whom I'd bought cartoons and short subjects for Flamingo Films. During our brief conversation, he told me that he'd recently received some exciting footage from the Russian space program that he wanted to sell to one of the networks.

I don't remember his precise words, although they changed my life. Basically, he told me that he had exclusive footage of the Russian space program that no one in America had seen. I knew nothing more about the space program than any other American who read the newspapers. This was at the height of the Cold War and the battle to control outer space—and with it perhaps the ability to put terrifying weapons into space—was raging. The Soviet Union appeared to be in the lead. The Russians had stunned the world in October 1957 by launching the first satellite, *Sputnik*, into outer space. They then shot a dog into space and brought him safely back to earth. The American space program, as seen on the news, seemed to consist primarily of rockets rising a few feet, then falling over and exploding. Maybe I didn't know much about the space program, but I knew that people were interested in it.

I could feel the excitement of discovered possibility just surging through my body. The timing could not possibly have been better. Only a few months earlier the networks had been caught rigging quiz shows, providing answers to popular contestants to ensure their return. In response to this scandal, the networks announced they would begin providing more public interest programming. That meant more educational shows—and more documentaries. What subject could be more in the public interest than the battle for control of space with the Soviet Union?

I made a decision as we stood on Sixth Avenue. Using money I'd gotten from the sale of Flamingo Films, as well as what I'd saved, I bought exclusive rights to the Russian space footage for $10,000. I was going to make a documentary.

I really knew little about documentaries. Growing up, I had seen documentaries in school. They were usually dull educational films about animals or foreign lands, but I remembered them. I learned from them. The impact of a film shown in the classroom—on me—was extraordinary and permanent.

But I didn't intend to make a tedious informational documentary. The battle for supremacy in outer space was a great story, and I knew that if I could tell it in an exciting way, I could find an interested audience. Once I'd made it, I felt certain I would have absolutely no problem selling it to a sponsor or one of the three networks.

I knew little about the history of documentaries, which, in retrospect, was beneficial. I was not bound by the earlier conventions of documentary filmmaking. I didn't know "the rules," so I couldn't follow them. As I later discovered, the first films ever shot were documentaries. A kiss, a sneeze, girls dancing, a horse running, workers leaving a factory in 1895, lady fencers, a heavyweight boxing match. In 1894, Thomas Edison captured on film celebrities like Buffalo Bill, Annie Oakley, and Sando the Strong Man. "The Washington Navy Yard" was shot in 1897. There was no editing in these films. The cameras were turned on to capture the action or the subject and turned off when it was completed. One of the first true documentaries, in which actual footage was combined with historically accurate re-creations, was about the 1898 assault on San

Juan Hill by Teddy Roosevelt and his Rough Riders. The popularity of that film, when it was exhibited, enhanced Roosevelt's growing legend and helped elect him president. Travel films that showed unusual and exotic worlds from London, England, to darkest Africa—though probably not the Orkney Islands—fascinated a population to whom a twenty-mile trip was a daylong journey.

Documentaries were shown in small theaters or on bedsheets hung in halls and attracted a small audience of curiosity seekers. The addition of the newsreel to a movie theater program that often included two features, coming attractions, and cartoons allowed people to see current events for the first time.

Early television introduced documentaries to a massive audience. The networks loved them. They were inexpensive to produce because they consisted mostly of available footage, and they satisfied the FCC's desire that networks broadcast some educational programming. They were spliced together and a narration added. The NBC series *Victory at Sea* added Richard Rogers's music to World War II navy footage to produce dramatic documentaries. Walter Cronkite's *The 20th Century* took advantage of existing footage to document history, and eventually, Edward R. Murrow produced several classic social documentaries, among them *Harvest of Shame* about the exploitation of migrant workers, that brought harsh reality into American homes.

It was an illustrious history. But initially, my interest was not in adding to it; I just wanted to do a television program that I could sell to a network. I left the bank and rented a small office. I began reading everything I could find about rockets. A friend of mine, Jack Haley Jr., son of the famous actor who'd played the tin man in *The Wizard of Oz*, was in the army and stationed nearby. He usually got off duty about three o'clock, and I hired him to work for me. I heard about a young film-research company in New York called Film Finders, run by Mel Stuart, who had been working for Cronkite's *20th Century* and then with a friend opened his own company. I hired him to find the film I needed. I invested $50,000, just about my life savings, and convinced Joe Harris to loan me another $20,000 at substantial interest.

There was not enough Russian footage for an entire show, so I decided to tell the complete story of the race for space supremacy between the United States and the Soviet Union. As I learned, it was a fascinating history. Few people had heard of the American space pioneer Robert Goddard, who had begun developing rockets just after World War I. He held more than two hundred rocket patents. Goddard had died in 1945, but I located his widow. She was a lovely lady. I asked to interview her and then, almost as an afterthought, asked if she had any personal footage. She told me she'd filmed her husband's experiments in Massachusetts and New Mexico on an 8mm home camera. That was incredible. This was the only existing footage of the birth of the American space program. Nobody had ever seen it. Nobody knew it existed. Why hadn't anybody seen it before? "No one ever asked," she explained. I paid her a small amount for the film and she agreed to be interviewed on the show.

As I learned, German rocket scientists had based much of their research on Goddard's work—which they had obtained legally from the U.S. Patent Office. With Nazi support, they had built a rocket program and were targeting London with Vengeance rockets, the well-known V-1 and more sophisticated V-2. Their research was invaluable, and when the war ended, both the Americans and the Russians were desperate to capture German rocket scientists, particularly the head of their rocket program, Wernher von Braun. Operation Paperclip, the American effort to find and bring these scientists to the United States, had been headed by General Holger N. Toftoy. He explained that a lot of powerful Americans wanted to put von Braun and other Germans responsible for the rocket program on trial with Nazi leaders at Nuremberg, but he had convinced them instead to let him bring 100 scientists to the United States and establish our space program. He asked permission for 300 men, but was limited to 100. Eventually Toftoy gathered 127 essential individuals, among them Wernher von Braun, and brought them across the Mexican border—somehow managing to sneak in the extra 27—into Texas, where the American space program took root. Toftoy agreed to tell this story on my show.

We got film from everywhere. I went to Washington and convinced the Department of Defense to give me official government footage. We got captured German film from the Library of Congress Alien Property Department that showed V-rockets being launched.

The American government was cooperative. While we were making this film, the Department of Defense invited me to the rocket-engine testing grounds in the Santa Susana Mountains in southern California to witness test firings of large rocket engines anchored to the ground. This was a lot more exciting than handling loan applications. Before going to the site, I had to sign a paper saying I wasn't affiliated with any of "the below organizations." On the top of that list was the Communist Party. It was that time in America. Someone gave me a pair of rubber pants and told me to put them on under my underwear. I didn't know why, but I did as told.

When the incredibly powerful rocket engine was ignited, the earth trembled. It was unbelievable. A tremendous shock wave rolled right over us. It was so overwhelming that I literally . . . learned why I was wearing rubber pants. Obviously other people before had learned this same lesson.

As I was not a documentarian, I didn't know my film was not supposed to be entertaining in addition to being informative. To make it more exciting as well as appealing to the networks, I signed the famous film composer Elmer Bernstein to write the music—rather than paying him a salary I bought him a boat—and hired a controversial young reporter named Mike Wallace to report and narrate the show. Wallace had his own program on a local station in New York and was gaining a reputation as a tough interviewer. When I first approached Wallace, he refused to believe that I had beaten the networks to exclusive footage of the Russian space program. But when he saw what I had, he agreed to host the show for $5,000.

I worked on every frame of that film. I produced it and directed it. I helped Laurence Mascott with the writing and I helped Phil Rosenberg with the editing. While we were cutting it, I practically lived in the office, sleeping on the couch.

This was the beginning of my education in filmmaking.

I was proud of the final product, which we named *The Race for Space*. "You are the first Americans to see the launching of *Sputnik I*," the program began in dramatic fashion. I'd paid $10,000 for that footage; I intended to squeeze as much publicity out of it as possible. In addition to telling the history of the space race, we also criticized government policy that had prevented the United States from beating the Russians into space. When it was done, Jack Haley Jr. and I headed to New York to meet with network executives and potential sponsors. With the space program on the front page of the newspapers every day, I expected to be able to quickly sell and get on the air a program that included never-before-seen, exclusive footage of Soviet rockets being launched.

My education in network television was about to begin.

SEVEN

DAVID VS. THE GOLIATHS

I was born a salesman. I not only understood the art of selling, I loved it. I also believed that a deal is only a good deal if all the participants are satisfied. When I had to, I could sell a bad film like *Let's Visit the Orkney Islands,* but when I went to New York to sell *The Race for Space,* I knew I was selling a wonderful program. My plan was to find an advertiser to sponsor the show and then place it with one of the networks. I was confident that the three networks would be bidding against each other for it.

From somewhere, I obtained a model rocket about ten feet long that I intended to use in my sales pitch, and Jack Haley and I took our rocket to New York. When we changed trains in Chicago, Haley hoisted the front of the rocket on his shoulder and I picked up the tail and we walked casually through the station. People stared at us as if they had never seen two guys in business suits carrying a big rocket before.

The first people to see the show were—now television legends—Lee Rich and Grant Tinker of the advertising agency Benton & Bowles. Haley and I walked in and put down our rocket on the table in front of

34

us. Instantly they were intrigued by our show. After screening it they thought it would be a good buy for IBM and gave me a $1,000 option. Eventually, IBM decided not to sponsor it. We pitched the program to anyone who would meet with us. After several weeks of fruitless meetings, I could no longer afford to keep both of us in New York, so Jack returned to L.A. and I kept trying to find a sponsor. Finally, Frank Carpenter, vice president of the Shulton Company, the maker of Old Spice toiletries, bought it. We had our sponsor. Shulton would pay the network for the broadcast time—and pay me all my money back. The hard part was done, I figured; now all Shulton had to do was decide which network it wanted to broadcast the show.

Shulton wanted to be on CBS. From the days of early radio, CBS News was considered the finest news reporting organization in broadcasting. So I went to CBS. Dick Salant, the head of CBS News, turned it down because the network didn't produce it.

I was stunned. What did that mean, I asked, CBS didn't produce it?

The network policy was explained to me: Public affairs shows had to be produced by the network. They would not buy work from outside producers. I was furious. What are you talking about? I practically screamed. Are you saying there is something wrong with it?

It had nothing to do with content or quality, I was told. CBS simply would not broadcast public affairs programming it had not produced. CBS also objected to the inclusion of music in a documentary. Music? The score was by Elmer Bernstein! Music is no different from narration, I tried to explain to them; when done properly, it explains a sequence just as surely as does writing—but it does so emotionally. It enhances understanding. Look at *Victory at Sea* on NBC.

CBS policy did not allow music to be used in documentaries. Period. CBS took its documentaries very seriously.

I warned them that if they turned me down, I would go right to NBC. I did—and the result was pretty much the same. Bill McAndrew of NBC told me, "Our policy is that we do not broadcast public affairs programs produced outside the network."

Policy? What policy? No advertising agency had ever heard of that policy. No producer knew about it. Newspaper reporters were not aware of it. It was as if NBC had decided, starting that day, that had always been their policy.

McAndrew did like the show well enough to offer me a job—producing documentaries at NBC. So, while I was good enough to work there, they still wouldn't broadcast my show.

I received the same rejection at ABC. I was stunned. My total investment by that point was probably close to $100,000. If I couldn't get that show on the air, I was going to be stuck with the most expensive home movie ever made. Either that or I was going to have to start hanging bedsheets in halls and charging two bucks a head.

I didn't set out to break the hold the networks had on television, it just turned out that way. I was desperate. All my experience in television had been as a syndicator, selling programs to individual stations. I knew how that business worked. It occurred to me that I could set up my own network consisting of one station in each market. I could place *The Race for Space* city by city. The more I thought about it, the better it seemed. Network ratings varied from city to city and from time period to time period. If I set up my own network, I could pick the station I wanted in each city as well as the time period. But to accomplish this, I needed the support of Shulton. It would be slightly more expensive than a network broadcast because I'd have to supply a print of the show to each station, but if it was done correctly, the result could be substantially higher viewership.

This had never been done before. That challenge appealed to me too. "There are about one hundred and forty stations in the NBC network," I told Shulton. "If I place it on one hundred and eight top stations market by market, most of them on the same week, will you take it?" Shulton agreed.

I had a huge advantage. During my years on the road with Flamingo Films, I'd developed strong relationships with most station managers. I couldn't possibly screen the program in every city, so I asked two men I knew well, Dick Moore, the head of KTTV in Los Angeles, and Fred Thrower, at WPIX in New York City, to look at the program. If they liked it, they would send a telegram affirming the quality of the show to every station manager in America.

Armed with this telegram, Shulton's advertising agency, Wesley Associates, began building my one-week, one-show network. Originally, I had been aiming mostly at independent stations, but I discovered that, in most cities, network affiliates were willing to preempt regularly scheduled network programming to show *The Race for Space*. Their contract with the network allowed them to preempt network shows for public affairs programming. It was wonderfully ironic. The networks had turned down my show because they would not broadcast public affairs programming that they did not make, so they could not claim that this wasn't public affairs programming. The deal was very profitable for the stations too. Shulton was paying full rate, three times as much as the networks paid affiliates for the same time. In fact, it was so profitable that in certain cities we actually bought time on several stations for the same night. In New York, for example, we placed the program on three independent stations, at 9, 10, and 11 P.M. Eventually, we cleared 109 stations—including 40 CBS stations, 34 NBC stations, and 25 ABC stations. I delivered 109 prints, allowing each station to screen the show for the local newspaper critics and other opinion makers before the broadcast. The result was a tremendous amount of publicity. In New York City, for example, critic Marie Torre of the *Herald-Tribune* wrote, "The rejection [by the networks] is akin to a literary magazine turning down an Ernest Hemingway original because he is not a member of the magazine staff. Nothing the networks have done on the subject of space flight tells the story with the simple thoughtfulness and perspicuity of *The Race for Space*." We were definitely ready for prime time.

After one of the prebroadcast screenings for friends and critics in New York, I got a call from Jack Gould, television editor of the *New York Times*, who wanted to do a story about the creation of my network. On Saturday, I went up to his house in Westchester. He told me the story would appear on Monday. At midnight, Sunday night, I was standing outside the Times building waiting for Monday's paper. As soon as I got it, I turned to the television page—there was no story. Very disappointed, I went back to my hotel, got into bed, and started reading the rest of the paper. And there, on the front page of the *New York Times*, was the story: "Fourth TV 'Network' Assembled to Show a Film Others Barred." Page one. The best publicity imaginable.

The show ran the week of April 24, 1960. It was a tremendous success. Critics across the nation raved about it. We entered it in competitions and it won honors at film festivals throughout the world—and eventually became the first television documentary nominated for an Academy Award as the Best Documentary Film.

This was my film. The one the networks turned down.

It also resulted in a tremendous controversy about the responsibility of the networks to broadcast a diversity of programming. In 1960, there existed three powerful networks and many much less important local stations. Cable television did not exist. The three networks were located in New York City and really had a monopoly over television. They controlled television journalism. Their executives—every one of them at that time living and working in New York City—decided what the nation, as a whole, would have the opportunity to see. Their parochial point of view, and only that point of view, would be expressed. They all went to the same parties, ate in the same restaurants, read the same newspapers, had the same friends, and were affected by the same thinking. Maybe a documentary produced by somebody in another city such as Los Angeles would bring fresh thinking to the news business. In later years, Fox News and CNN came from different cities and definitely changed the news media.

Several years later the Federal Communications Commission held hearings about the way the networks used their power. The real focus of these hearings was network pressure; the networks were demanding, from independent producers, a percentage of each program they broadcast or they wouldn't show it. I was subpoenaed about my dealings with the networks. In my testimony I pointed out that, if independent producers were unable to find a place on network television for documentaries, they would be forced into making westerns, detective stories, and other potboilers. I understood that the networks had to retain final approval on the suitability of a program, but it seemed to me both desirable and logical that some stretch in their policy could be arrived at that would preserve their safeguards yet make room for the contributions of independent documentary producers. "Several independent producers of documentaries are struggling on the fringes of the business," I explained, "because of the refusal of the networks to allow outside products. If the networks would open the window, you'd find that a lot of fresh new ideas would blow onto the television scene and the public would get the advantage of this exposure to some new and exciting programming."

CBS vice president Dick Salant explained that the networks had to retain control to ensure fairness and balance, and to guarantee that sponsors did not interfere or participate in the development of news and public affairs programming. Salant then added, referring to Mike Wallace, who had previously done commercials for a cigarette company, "We think it's quite inappropriate to have the newsman in a program measuring the missile gap be one who is identified with the measurement of the quarter inch by which the Parliament cigarette filters are recessed. I think that alone justifies the wisdom of our policy if television journalism is to fulfill its role as a responsible journalistic source."

Of course, that was said several years before Mike Wallace became one of CBS's biggest stars as a trusted correspondent on *60 Minutes*. For years, Mike Wallace refused to believe Salant had said that—until I showed him the quote from the *Congressional Record*.

CBS also claimed that its policy of not broadcasting independently produced public affairs programming was well known, and to prove it provided a copy of a letter that had been sent to advertising agencies thirty-one years earlier—on October 17, 1939—before some of the agencies even existed. I have a tremendous regard for Dick Salant, who later became a good friend, but I would have to describe his testimony in these hearings as the biggest crock of horseshit I'd ever heard.

My career, in addition to most of my savings, was riding on the success of *The Race for Space.* I had no backup plan, nor did I have a specific plan for moving forward. I had no idea what I was going to do next. *The Race for Space* proved I didn't need the networks to survive. Not that I didn't want to work with them, I did, but I didn't need them. But that program had practically dropped from the sky, or at least from a chance meeting on a New York street. I knew I wasn't going to be that fortunate a second time.

EIGHT

A PHONE CALL IN THE NIGHT

Mike Wallace, Rafer Johnson, and Mel Stuart (1961)

The night after the show played, the reviews were quite impressive. I was in my New York hotel room—it was after eleven o'clock—when Mike Wallace called: "Hey, what are you doing?"

"Actually I'm in bed, Mike."

"Get over here right away," he ordered.

"Here" was a party where there was someone he wanted me to meet. Mike introduced me to Bob Foreman, president of the advertising agency BBD&O. Foreman told me that the Schaeffer Brewing Company of New York City, one of his clients, was trying to reach a black audience and had decided to produce two shows about black American athletes. He didn't quite hand me the order that night, he just asked me for some suggestions, but it was obvious he wanted me to make those films.

Doing documentaries about black athletes, in 1960, was a brave thing to do, for Schaeffer beer. This was at the very beginning of the civil rights movement. Much of the country was still segregated. It had been only slightly longer than a decade since Jackie Robinson had broken baseball's color barrier, and professional sports teams still had unwritten quotas on how many black players they could field. But in the 1960 Olympics in Rome, Rafer Johnson became a national hero by winning the decathlon. I decided he would make a fine subject. And people I knew with the Dodgers told me a rookie named Willie Davis was going to be a major league star, and I thought it would be fascinating to follow him through spring training in his first year in the major leagues.

When Schaeffer Brewing accepted my proposal, I began building my first real company. One of the few people who didn't really like *The Race for Space* was my film researcher in New York, Mel Stuart. He wrote me a long, intelligent letter describing in detail what was wrong with it. While, obviously, he was completely wrong, it was an impressive letter. So I offered him a job working with me at $200 a week. Mel Stuart was doing most of his work for Burton Benjamin and then producing Cronkite's *The 20th Century*. When Stuart informed him that he was moving to California to work for David Wolper, Benjamin was incredulous: "David Wolper? He's a rug salesman."

Mel disagreed, telling him confidently, "No, he's got an office and a staff and we're going to do a lot of films."

Benjamin looked at him skeptically. "What films?"

Okay, perhaps that question stumped Mel: "He didn't tell me, but I'm sure he's got a lot of stuff."

What I did have was a lot of ideas, a small two-room office, me, Mel, and Jack Haley, the deal for two shows for Schaeffer, and a lot of optimism.

I received an Oscar nomination, an almost impossible feat to duplicate, for *The Race for Space*, my first film. But I realized that, if we were going to build a company, we couldn't do the same solid, craftsmanlike documentaries being produced by the networks in New York. We had to do better. I wanted the films for Schaeffer to be entertaining. I wanted them to be dramatic, as well as informative. And I wanted them to have star power. At that time, the most famous cameraman in Hollywood was Academy Award winner James Wong Howe, who'd begun his career in silent films working for Cecil B. DeMille. It occurred to me that Howe had probably never worked in television and had almost certainly never shot a documentary. I knew if I could get him I could get publicity for my films. His involvement would make them special.

Mel Stuart thought I was crazy. This was the first of many times he would think that. He was in the room when I got James Wong Howe on the phone. "Mr. Howe," I said politely, "I would like to talk to you about shooting my documentary film."

"Documentary?" he responded. "I don't do documentary. I do feature. Feature, only feature. Documentary shit, shit, shit."

"Well, we'd really love you to do this. With your name attached to it—"

"No. No documentary. No."

I persisted. "Mr. Howe, how much do they pay you a week when you're shooting a movie?"

"I get two thousand dollars a week," he said proudly. That was a substantial amount of money in those days.

I didn't even hesitate: "I'll pay you three thousand."

"I do documentary," Howe said. The most respected director of photography in Hollywood would shoot my television documentary.

That was way over my budget for a cameraman. I had to make it up somewhere. I figured if James Wong Howe was shooting my film, I didn't need a particularly strong director.

As long as I got the footage I needed, the documentary would come together in the writing and editing. Mel Stuart offered to produce and direct it. Except for the fact that Mel had never produced or directed a film in his life, this seemed reasonable. But I knew how smart he was, and I knew he worked as hard as I did. I decided to take a chance with him. This was the filmmaking equivalent of a battlefield promotion. I made him the producer-director while I became executive producer.

The result was surprising. Mel Stuart did a fine job and James Wong Howe was terrible. He was impossible to work with. He drove everyone crazy with his demands. Fortunately, he brought with him a young assistant, a Latvian named Vilis Lapenieks, who had escaped from both Hitler and the Communists. Vilis did everything from loading the camera to shooting second-unit, or background, material. Howe didn't even know how to load the camera, and he was always screaming at Lapenieks, "You never get in guild, you lazy . . ." Meanwhile, Vilis is a blur. We never see him standing anywhere for longer than a few seconds. The footage James Wong Howe shot was static; he'd set up his camera so far from the field that it was barely possible to see the players, while Vilis was practically in Willie Davis's pocket. We ended up using more footage shot by Vilis than the Academy Award–winning Howe.

Eventually, Vilis Lapenieks made about fifty films for the Wolper Company. He was a remarkable cameraman. When shooting, he'd look through the lens with his right eye, but his left eye was also open so he could see what was happening around him. He had the knack for being in the right place at the right time—all the time. When Robert Kennedy was shot, Vilis was right there, and in the midst of chaos, he kept his camera rolling. Unfortunately, the man holding the lights dropped them, so the film shows an eerie blackness, punctuated by the bright snaps of flashbulbs exploding, while on the sound track people are screaming and crying.

Like all great cameramen, Vilis always put himself in position to get the best shot. We were shooting a rodeo once, and he decided to get inside the barrel clowns use to distract wild bulls. Unfortunately, this barrel attracted the wild bull—the bull came right out of the chute and went directly for the barrel. Vilis got a black eye and a slight concussion.

In making these films, we used techniques not normally used in documentaries: telescopic close-ups and tracking shots to enhance the dramatic story we were telling. Instead of the familiar talking head, a shot of a person speaking into the camera, we used voice-over narration. Willie Davis was seen running the bases, but his voice was heard describing his days in school. It's possible other documentaries had used voice-over narration from the participants before we did, and it has certainly become a staple of nonfiction television, but no one was doing it at that time. It was new and exciting. It gave the film a reality that simply didn't exist with a third-person narration. Obviously, we still used a narrator to bridge scenes—Mike Wallace narrated the Rafer Johnson film—but the voice-over technique made our films distinctive.

We believed in using in our documentaries all the tools available to filmmakers. That included music and sound effects and camera effects, the storytelling techniques used to enhance drama in feature films that one network had practically banned from documentaries. And sometimes, I'm sure to the absolute horror of purists, we even included— humor!

Just before I delivered the shows to Bud Stefan at BBD&O in New York, he called to ask me if I drank a lot of liquor and was occasionally drunk. I told him I didn't know what he was talking about. Actually, I didn't drink liquor or wine. He told me privately that an organization called Channels had investigated me, as they do for everybody at BBD&O, and had come up with this report. This was a continuation of the Red Channels group. You wonder how accurate they were in charging people as being Communists during the McCarthy era.

The Rafer Johnson Story and *Biography of a Rookie* were well received—although many Southern stations refused to broadcast them. I didn't have time for a battle. I didn't think it was my battle. Mostly, I thought those stations were silly. It is difficult to believe that documentaries about black athletes excelling could be called controversial, but rarely, if ever, at that point had successful black men been the subject of a documentary. My objective was not to make a racial or political statement. Throughout my early career that was rarely a goal. I wanted to make good shows and build a company. Documentarians were usually considered serious people, even noble, who had strong beliefs in their subjects and wanted to make a statement. That wasn't me, I admit. While I've participated in the making of hundreds and hundreds of documentaries on an extraordinary variety of subjects, I've always admitted that the only two subjects on which I consider myself an expert are the founding of America and the making of a documentary. Later in my career, whenever I was asked by a reporter why I chose to make a particular film, I would reply honestly, "I made this film to pay my bills, feed my children, and pay for their education. I'm in the business of making films—much the same way you're being paid to ask that question."

NINE

HOORAY FOR HOLLYWOOD

With Bette Davis (1961)

I had learned an important lesson with *The Race for Space.* Freedom of the press, it has been said, belongs to the people who own the presses. But in the 1960s, television belonged to the three networks. My option was to continue fighting them or to make shows that they would run. I decided to take the decision away from network news departments and instead deal with programming. Entertainment. I'd do something few people were doing at that time: I'd make entertaining documentaries. They would have the look and feel of documentaries, but they would not be about current events. They would not compete with network news departments.

President John Kennedy gave me the subject of my next program. Speaking in Boston's Faneuil Hall, known as the Cradle of Liberty, he stressed that the greatness of this nation lies in its appreciation of our history. He said that knowing and understanding our past was vital to our success in the future. As I listened to him, it occurred to me that there existed an official history of almost all the significant industries: the automobile industry, the steel industry, the labor unions. But one had been completely ignored. Incredibly, there had never been a documentary about the history of the motion picture industry. No one was documenting the cultural history of the United States. It was like getting hit over the head with a movie camera. As soon as I had this idea, I knew I could sell it.

The television industry loved the movie business. And the movie industry had reached an uneasy truce with television. While in the first decade of television movie attendance had declined and theaters were closing, the revenue generated by the studios from selling movies to television had more than compensated for it. It seemed to me that doing a television show about the movies would attract TV viewers while serving as advertising for the movies. Everybody benefited. Especially the growing Wolper Company.

My problem was getting the rights to use the film clips I needed—and getting them inexpensively enough to make it possible to do the show. In 1960, I met with the board of directors of the Motion Picture Association of America, a group consisting of representatives from all the major studios, and made an impassioned plea. I evoked the image of John Kennedy standing proudly at Faneuil Hall, emphasizing the importance of our history. "There are many films about the history of our country," I pointed out, "but there is no history of our own industry. Imagine that there isn't a single film about the history of the film industry." I explained that I wanted to do a history of the movie business beginning with silent films, "to create a permanent record for our industry." I wanted footage from all the studios and in return offered to donate 10 percent of my profits to the Motion Picture Home.

I felt that free was about as inexpensive as I might hope to get the film I needed. I would still have to lay out my own money to make this film, but this arrangement would make it possible. The studios gave me the footage. In less than a decade the movie industry had gone from fighting to keep films off television to using TV to tell its history. I produced and directed, and Jack Haley, who'd grown up in Hollywood and knew everybody in the industry, was the associate producer. *Hollywood: The Golden Years* was the history of the motion picture industry from its birth to the first talking pictures. In retrospect, it seems difficult to believe that the networks had never done documentaries as entertainment programming, particularly because it was precisely this type of documentary that, years later, enabled cable channels to prosper. We were expanding the documentary form. And while the subject might not have been as significant as the exploitation of migrant workers or as newsworthy as the race for outer space, we treated it no different from a more serious subject.

Every documentary begins with an intensive search for existing film. While we had the cooperation of the studios, only a portion of what we needed was owned by them. We bought film from film libraries and private collectors. We advertised in newspapers, and many of those papers did feature stories about our search. To my great surprise, we discovered that many of the stars of silent films had been smart enough to retain ownership of their films. From D. W. Griffith's estate we got footage from his classics *Birth of a Nation* and *Intolerance*. Director Harold Lloyd and the legendary actress Mary Pickford controlled the rights to all of their films. We searched the world. From Kooperative Filmavdeling of Stockholm, we got footage of a chunky Greta Garbo modeling in bakery commercials years before coming to the United States.

Hollywood: The Golden Years included scenes from twenty-three silent movies and cameo shots of more than sixty early movie stars, both on and off camera. We had the original chariot race scene from *Ben-Hur,* a remarkable piece of filmmaking. We had Chaplin's *The Gold Rush,* Valentino in *The Sheik,* and Buddy Rogers in the film that won the first Academy Award, *Wings.* But to tell the story of this era we also included historical footage, such as the hotel sign declaring "No Dogs or Actors Allowed," and the mobs of hysterical women at Rudolph Valentino's funeral. We found some extraordinary footage of the stars at play. There was a great clip of Douglas Fairbanks and Charlie Chaplin behind the studio. Fairbanks leaped over a chair—and Chaplin just crashed right into it.

While putting together a show like this might seem simple, in reality it is tremendously complex and time-consuming. It is far more difficult to cut and paste footage from numerous sources to make a compilation film than to actually film material. Every frame of footage had to be analyzed to determine who owned it and to be sure permission to use it had been obtained. For those films owned by Mary Pickford, I negotiated by charm. Mary Pickford was still living in Pickfair, perhaps the most famous of the great Hollywood mansions. Kings, presidents, and the most famous had dined there. It had been built when she was married to Douglas Fairbanks. Now she lived there with her husband, Buddy Rogers. As I drove up to the front door, it was like arriving in the past. A white-gloved doorman opened the door for me and led me into a small room off the vast living room. I'm rarely nervous, but meeting Mary Pickford made me very nervous.

She was delightful. She began by telling me the most wonderful stories about old Hollywood. At one point, as she was describing her romantic escapades with Rudolph Valentino, she knelt down beside me and took my hand in hers and kissed my hand to demonstrate his charm. As she did, I thought, this is incredible. Here's this little Jewish kid from the East Side of New York sitting in Pickfair with Mary Pickford kneeling in front of him kissing his hand.

She gave me permission to use footage from her films under one condition—she wanted to see the finished cut to make sure everything we said in the documentary was accurate. That seemed quite reasonable to me.

When we had completed a rough cut of the show, which included a temporary narration, I returned to Pickfair, this time with Jack Haley, to screen it in the living room, which had been converted into a screening room. Buddy Rogers joined us, but we had to wait for Mary. And suddenly, from the top of the stairs, I heard her voice: "Buddy, are our friends here yet?"

She appeared at the top of the stairs in a gown that went down to the floor, her hair cascading down over her shoulders. This was the great star of motion pictures Mary Pickford making an entrance. It was a scene from one of her movies.

She had known Jack Haley's parents quite well and sat with Jack as we screened the film. As we did, she provided her own narration: "Wasn't Douglas handsome . . . Oh, that scamp, Charlie . . ." And always, "Mr. Griffith." When the film ended, I waited for her response, but Rogers spoke first: "Mary, wasn't that wonderful? I thought it was terrific."

I thought to myself, "Thank you, Mr. Rogers, thank you." Whatever Mary really thought, she agreed with him. On the phone the next day, she told me, "I think your project is fabulous and I want to help you any way I can." I was extremely pleased. I'd won her with my charm. And then she added, "All I want is one thousand dollars a minute."

So much for negotiating by charm. We'd never paid half that much for footage. No wonder she had been shrewd enough to keep the rights to her films. Obviously, I had no choice; it was not possible to do the history of silent films without including Mary Pickford. So I negotiated a deal for her footage: I paid her what she asked.

Gene Kelly was the narrator. Elmer Bernstein wrote a powerful score, and Malvin Wald wrote the script. It was Wald, incidentally, who invented the word *filmmaker* when his former partner, actress Ida

Lupino, asked him for a term describing the people who write, direct, and produce motion pictures.

At the conclusion of a screening of the finished documentary, Wald found Mary Pickford standing outside the theater sobbing. "Was my script so bad it made you cry?" he asked.

"Oh, no, my dear," she responded, "it's because they're all gone. Mr. Griffith, my own dear Doug . . . all of them . . ."

"No," Wald said, "no, they're not. Douglas Fairbanks and Griffith are still alive in this film. And when it plays on television, millions of people will see them and love them just like you do."

"Thank you," she said, then kissed him and departed.

Producer Jack Warner, of Warner Bros., also wanted to see the completed film. I was excited about that. By this time, many people had seen the movie and loved it, so I was feeling pretty confident. But when the lights went on, Warner was somber: "You've got to cut out all that stuff about sex and the Hayes Office." The Hayes Office was the first official censor and played an important role in the development of Hollywood.

"I can't cut it out, Mr. Warner," I said, "it's part of the history of the business."

I don't think Jack Warner appreciated that he couldn't change history. For so many years, he'd been inventing Hollywood, it was probably difficult for him to accept that he could no longer shape it as he desired. He continued to insist that I take it out, and I continued to remind him that I didn't need his permission. In the end, the segment remained in the film and I never heard from Jack Warner again.

Having personally financed the entire film, I had to get it on the air. The first people I showed it to were Lee Rich and Grant Tinker of Benton & Bowles. Lee Rich was a rough, tremendously intelligent man, and because he represented General Foods and Procter and Gamble—the two largest advertisers in television—he was one of the most powerful men in the industry. The networks owned the time, but he had the money. Both Lee and Grant Tinker loved the film. "Okay," Lee told me, "I'll buy it. I've got a sponsor for you." Then he added, "Can you do two more segments?"

I wanted to jump into the air and throw my hands up with joy, but that would have been unsalesmanlike. Instead, I calmly nodded and said, "Sure I can." But remembering my futile efforts to sell *The Race for Space*, I asked, "Can you get it on a network?"

Basically, if Lee Rich couldn't get a show on the network, the networks would soon be reduced to running test patterns. Lee set up a screening for David Levy, NBC's head of programming. I was sitting in the back of the screening room. Levy liked it as much as Grant Tinker and Lee Rich and decided to run it on NBC.

"You think you'll have any problems with the news department?" Tinker asked.

"No, this isn't hard news," Levy said, "this is entertainment. There won't be any problems."

I couldn't believe it; I was finally going to get a show on the network. I was tremendously excited.

"Great," Lee Rich said, "then I want the *Wagon Train* time period."

I couldn't believe what I was hearing. *Wagon Train* was one of NBC's highest-rated programs. There was no way they would give up that time slot for my little documentary. I was sitting in the back thinking, don't do this, Lee.

To my surprise, David Levy seemed to be considering it: "I don't know. I have to get an okay on that. I don't think I can clear *Wagon Train* . . ."

After he was gone, Rich said in a booming voice, "You look nervous back there, Wolper. Don't worry about it, he'll clear it for me." And he did.

We were fortunate. The American Dental Association had just given Crest toothpaste permission to advertise, right on the box, that it was the first toothpaste to receive the association's seal of approval that it helped fight cavities. Crest wanted to get that message out before its competition also got approval. So it bought all three of my shows.

Of which, one was completed, and two existed only in my head.

Hollywood: The Golden Years, the first independently produced documentary to run on network television, finished eighth in the weekly ratings. It proved that entertaining documentaries, properly promoted, could compete with regular programming.

The other two shows, *Hollywood: The Great Stars* and *Hollywood: The Fabulous Era,* were more contemporary and, admittedly, were not as good. They were clip shows. We used footage owned by the studios. *The Fabulous Era* was about the early talking pictures and *The Great Stars* was a compilation of brief biographies of the biggest stars in the business, which enabled us to use clips from their most popular movies.

We had collected an enormous amount of film while producing these shows and had used only a small percentage of it. We'd established important contacts at all the studios and we had a staff in place—and we'd proved there was a sizable audience for TV programs about the movie business. So, I sold a series of thirty-one half-hour shows, *Holly-wood and the Stars*, to Timex and Purex and placed it on NBC. This was the first independently produced documentary series to be shown by a network in prime time. We were making television history by making programs about movie history. But I really didn't care much about that. What it really meant to me was that the company was planting roots. We had been surviving program to program. This gave us at least the whis-per of stability.

The series was narrated by Joseph Cotton, and there we encountered the first of many problems. Between the time Cotton did the pilot and got ready to do the first real show, he had had his teeth fixed. Badly. Every *s* sound resulted in a whistle. Naturally, it took us quite some time to discover this—the first line of the first show was "Certain stars have a certain charisma," which came out something like, "Ssscchhertain sssstars . . ." Every time Cotton opened his mouth, it sounded as if he had a canary in there. The sound engineers were going crazy. They couldn't figure out what was wrong with their equipment—until some-one asked Cotton to read the line again, and he answered, "Ssssure."

We did not have the technology we needed to remove that *ssss*-sound. Discovering that the famed actor we'd hired to narrate the entire series couldn't talk was admittedly a setback.

Of course, Cotton didn't undersssstand what we were telling him. He thought he sounded great. We finally sent him home and waited several weeks until he got used to his new teeth.

Obtaining clearances for the footage was a nightmare. We had to get permission from every actor in every scene. We also had to buy rights to use the music sound tracks. It was endless. And expensive. In our cow-boy show, "They Went That-A-Way," for example, we wanted to use one of composer Dmitri Tiomkin's classic scores. But he was difficult. We just couldn't get the rights, but somehow the music got in the show. Tiomkin was furious and could have sued for several hundred thousand dollars. Eventually, we paid him about $25,000 for a few seconds of music.

When we did the Rita Hayworth show, we wanted to use a scene with her and Glenn Ford that had a full orchestration behind it. But if we had, we would have had to pay both the music publisher and the orchestra. Instead, Rita Hayworth actually came into our studio and reread her lines, and we fit that into the film without the music.

Ironically, one of the few movies we were never able to get permis-sion to show was *The Wizard of Oz*—costarring Jack's father.

Generally, those stars still alive were pleased we were doing this series and very accommodating. Rita Hayworth had never been on television when she agreed to do our show. I would have loved to have done her real story. As was revealed years later, when she was younger, she traveled with her father as a dance team—and he was sleeping with her, claiming she was his wife. But when Rita Hayworth eventually saw the show, she lamented, "I wish they'd used more of the footage they took on the golf course. I had a great tee shot and my pitch to the green was very good."

Kim Novak agreed to appear in an episode about her career entitled "Portrait of an Actress." She had pretty much retired and was living in a large house up in Big Sur. She was a lovely woman, smart and cooperative. I don't know why she agreed to do it, but as we proceeded, it became obvious she was having doubts. Late one night, she reached the breaking point. She was working in the office with writer Al Ramrus and our producer, Jack Haley Jr. She suddenly wondered, "Why am I doing this? I don't want to do this damn show." To make things worse, Ramrus questioned her like Mike Wallace: Novak was about to start a remake of *Of Human Bondage* and Ramrus wondered whether she thought she could follow Bette Davis in the role. Novak began to get nervous. She was wearing a reversible coat, which, on one side was cheerful, but on the other was black. Without a word of warning, she turned it to the black side, walked to the window, and looked out suspiciously. The office was on the second floor, but the drop was steep enough to be fatal. Ramrus was terrified. He looked around for Haley, who had run out of the office. He remembers seeing the newspaper headlines flash in front of his eyes: *Movie Star Commits Suicide in David Wolper's Office. Writer Held for Questioning.* Eventually, she turned back and the episode was never mentioned.

Mel Stuart did the program about Natalie Wood. According to people who were there when she saw a rough cut at a screening, she wasn't particularly pleased with it. She asked Mel to make some changes and he refused, explaining, "Listen, I'm captain of the ship and what I say goes."

To which Natalie Wood responded, "Well, Mel, the ship just sank and there are no survivors. Now I'm going to tell you how it's going to be done."

We didn't get every star we wanted. When we asked Stan Laurel to be interviewed for our episode on the great comedians, he wrote back that his ill health made that impossible, then wondered, "How come you didn't contact me for 'The Great Lovers' program?"

The series received mixed reviews. We were criticized by some people for doing too much of one subject, and by other people for doing too little of the same subject. But it was commercially successful. Timex and Purex were satisfied, and it helped put us in the series business.

T E N

"D-DAY"

Visiting Normandy Beach

David Levy, the NBC program chief, was so pleased with the three original Hollywood specials that he actually ordered shows from my company for NBC. Sponsors still bought time periods in large blocks rather than spots, just as had been done on radio, and *The DuPont Show of the Week*—which Levy had created—had a spot to fill in their schedule. They wanted to do a documentary about the greatest battle of World War II, D day, the Allied invasion of Normandy. It was perhaps the greatest drama of our lifetime. Within a few hours, on June 6, 1944, men experienced every possible emotion. Thousands of men died. There were countless acts of extraordinary bravery and sacrifice. And there were miracles—events for which there was no rational explanation. Telling the whole story of the invasion in one hour was a challenge, particularly when the men who had lived through it would be watching. Yet it was a documentarian's dream. Thirty years later, Steven Spielberg told some of it in his film *Saving Private Ryan*.

The D-day film took almost a year to make. We collected tens of thousands of feet of official army footage—and we started getting film

from soldiers who had been in France. At the same time, producer
Darryl F. Zanuck was making a multimillion-dollar movie about the
invasion called *The Longest Day*, featuring a long list of major stars.
Apparently, Zanuck was afraid that our little film was somehow going to
detract from his feature, because the day we announced our film, he told
reporters that no film had been shot during the actual invasion, and that
we were using fake material that had been shot a day or two after the
invasion. "I have no intention of cheating the public," Zanuck said. "I
will not use library footage claiming to be D-day combat coverage
because no such films exists. . . . No film camera covered the assault. I
have had three editors go through all available material with a fine-tooth
comb and they found nothing of an authentic nature."

He needed a better comb. Old film finder Mel Stuart found footage
showing a movie clapboard reading: "Sub: Invasion, Loc: On the Beach,
Date: 6/6/44." In response to Zanuck's statement, I took an ad in the
trade papers showing that clapboard and stating, "To Darryl Zanuck,
David Wolper's production of 'D-Day' will include footage shot on the
beach on D day."

The footage was incredibly dramatic. Almost all of it was shot from a
distance. But in one segment it's possible to see a soldier moving toward
the beach being shot, falling to his knees, and collapsing in death. I've
looked at millions of feet of film in my career, but I've never seen anything else quite like these few frames. The cameraman had captured the
moment of death, and it was chilling. But we realized it was an integral
part of our story. So we took those frames and blew them up as large as
possible—just like taking a small section of a photograph and blowing it
up, making it look like a close-up.

In later years, I've seen this same piece of film used in other documentaries. I know it was taken from our film, without payment or
credit, because we discovered it and enlarged it ourselves. Ironically, the
most difficult materials to find are scenes showing historic figures doing
ordinary things, particularly speaking on the telephone. We found
another segment of rare footage that we used in "D-Day": President
Franklin Roosevelt and General Dwight Eisenhower sitting in a car eat-
ing sandwiches. It was extraordinary for its normalcy.

"D-Day" ran on NBC and received tremendous reviews. No one complained that it had been made by an independent producer. *Time* magazine named it one of the year's ten best television shows, raving, "It
makes Hollywood war movies look like so much stagecraft." We had
found our niche; we were going to make nonfiction entertainment. We

would stake out areas then being ignored by the networks—history, nature, interesting lives, and adventure—the subjects that subsequently became the source of reality-based programming. This was a vein of gold that nobody else was mining. We would leave to the network news departments those areas of national debate: civil rights, poverty, the Cold War, national defense, and within a few years, the war in Vietnam. At least that's the way we started.

We were unique: we were just about the only documentary film-makers making entertainment programming. Wolper Productions was growing rapidly; even the unions didn't know how to classify us. In Los Angeles there was no union category for documentarians. While we could afford to pay the same rates as the networks were paying people in their news divisions, we couldn't afford to pay the Guilds network salaries for entertainment programming, so the unions tried to put us out of business. They were on strike against Wolper Productions for three years before finally agreeing to create a new category, documentary films, with realistic fees. By that time my company was producing hundreds of hours of television programming and employing hundreds of very talented people.

We had endless subjects from which to choose. Network documentary makers were people who saw the world as journalists. We saw the world through a poet's eyes; we were just trying to satisfy our curiosity by exploring subjects of interest and fascination, while making a profit. Our objective was to make films of lasting value, films that would live on television forever. While there were many other wonderfully talented documentary filmmakers, such people as Bruce Hershenson, Richard Leecock, Emilio DeAntonio, Albert and David Maysles, and D. A. Pennybaker, their films were mostly issue-oriented, which put them in competition with the networks' news divisions, or so quirky—like the Maysles film about Bible salesmen, *Salesman*—that the networks weren't interested.

Ideas for programs came from everywhere, from me as well as a kid delivering pizza. Everybody participated. We were always making lists of subjects that might interest the networks. The ideas came from books and newspapers and magazines, feature films, TV and radio—in other words, the world. I would meet with the networks or advertisers to sell our ideas, but I would always ask if there was a subject in which they were interested. If an ad agency account executive told me a client was interested in saving endangered species, we'd outline a program about endangered species. We didn't only make films in support of our beliefs or politics, we also made the films that people would pay us to make. At that time, I was a Democrat. Yet the Republican Party hired the Wolper Corporate Films division to make films about Richard Nixon for their convention. We made a corporate film for General Motors about automotive safety after the publication of Ralph Nader's highly critical book about the auto industry, *Unsafe at Any Speed.* Actually, I was quite surprised that General Motors was able to find stations in every market to broadcast this corporate film—until I realized that automobile dealerships were among the biggest advertisers in local television. The credo of the Wolper Corporate Films division was simple: absolutely everything we portrayed had to be true. We wouldn't lie, but the basis of every corporate film was the point of view of the client.

ELEVEN

BIOGRAPHY—WE WERE FIRST

With Alan Landsburg, Mel Stuart,
and Jack Haley Jr. (1962)

The success of *The Race for Space* and the Hollywood films enabled me to syndicate three half-hour series, *The Story of . . .*, *Biography*, and *Men in Crisis*. No longer were we surviving one film at a time; we were in the entertainment business. What made these series even more important was that it marked the first time in my career that I was able to secure outside financing for my projects.

Because of these three series, I was able to bring in a group of new and young documentary filmmakers, film editors, and writers: Nick Noxon and Irwin Rosten, who would later produce the National Geographic series; Alan Landsburg, who would become one of the top producers and officers of my company; Jim Brooks, who worked in *Men in Crisis*, and became an Emmy award–winning television and Academy award–winning motion picture producer/director/writer; Fouad Said, who worked on *The Story of . . .*, and later created his own motion picture equipment company and became a billionaire financier in Hong Kong; Wally Green, a major television and movie writer; and Al Ramrus, Syd Fields, David Vowell, Jack Kaufman, Larry Neiman, John Soh, Mel Shapiro, William Cartwright, Ed Spiegel, and David Blewitt, all joined the Wolper Company and developed their craft under these three television series.

The Story of . . . took viewers inside fascinating lives. We told the stories of people with unusual professions at a climactic point in their careers. It consisted almost completely of original footage that we shot using cutting-edge filmmaking technology—cutting edge in the early 1960s consisted of lighter and more mobile handheld cameras with telescopic sights and portable microphones—which enabled us to get closer than ever before to our subjects without being intrusive. At one point, to save money, executive producer Mel Stuart sat Vilis Lapenieks in a wheelchair with a handheld camera and pushed him around to create our own dolly shots—instead of being forced to lay tracks and use bulky equipment to "dolly" or move along with a subject. We did thirty-eight *The Story of . . .* programs over two years, among them a test pilot, a bullfighter, an artist, a jockey, a pro wrestler, a folk singer, a dancer, a prisoner, a gambler, a pro football player, a marine drill sergeant, a writer, an intern, an actress, a beauty contest contestant, even a professional tiger hunter.

The first show we did was "The Story of a Matador," Mexican bullfighter Jaime Bravo. I decided to personally produce the first episode to help set the tone I wanted. When we crossed the Mexican border into Tijuana, we were stopped by the police, who demanded our permit. This was the first I'd heard about any permit. Oh, yes, I was told, we had to have a permit—and the only person who could issue that permit was the chief of police, who was on the golf course.

They took me to meet him there. We walked behind a large trailer and I asked politely, "How can I take care of this, sir? Can I give you the money for the permit?"

Admittedly, I was not surprised when he agreed to that. "It will be five hundred dollars for the permit."

I handed him $500 in cash and we shot the program without further problems.

The quality of each show depended almost completely on the person we selected to profile. When we focused on someone interesting and provocative, the show was wonderful. For "The Story of an Artist," producer-director Bill Kronick selected a controversial young Los Angeles artist named Ed Kienholz, who turned junk, things Californians had thrown out, into art as he prepared for his first one-man show.

Critiques of his work ranged from brilliant to . . . junk—although he eventually became famous and successful. But this show gave viewers an intimate glimpse into the life of a struggling artist, and Kienholz's engaging personality made it work. Kienholz described his art by explaining he would be one of very few people to see a nuclear war as an opportunity. "When the atom bomb wipes out most of the world," he said, "I'd probably be the best guy to be around because I'd be able to take all that blown-up shit and make something out of it."

When he died of a heart attack in 1994, his embalmed body was wedged into the front seat of a 1940 Packard coupe. With a dollar and a deck of cards in his back pocket and the ashes of his favorite dog in the backseat, he and the car were wheeled into a large hole on a mountain in Idaho. In spite of this eccentricity, he had become so respected that two years later the Whitney Museum in New York staged a retrospective of 120 of his works.

Biography was the complete opposite of *The Story of . . .* We used a compilation of stock footage to tell the life story of our subject; we shot no original film. *Biography* was a syndicated show, sold market by market rather than to a network. Jack Haley was the supervising producer for the sixty-five half-hour episodes in the series, which were, once again, narrated by Mike Wallace. Mike made sure everything we said was consistent with his journalistic standards—meaning it was true.

We used two basic criteria to select our subjects for *Biography:* we began by picking well-known people of interest to viewers throughout the world, and from that group we tried to pick people who had been filmed extensively. We did Hitler in two parts because we had a lot of film and Gandhi, Admiral Byrd, Babe Ruth, and the presidents of the United States. We did Winston Churchill, Charles de Gaulle, Charles Lindbergh, the Windsors, Grace Kelly, world leaders, movie stars, artists, and athletes. We profiled Thomas Edison, Will Rogers, and Helen Keller. We did the famous and the infamous, people from around the globe. If we could find sufficient footage, we did the show.

We wanted to do a show about famed war correspondent Ernie Pyle, but just couldn't find enough film. When we tried to do a show about the greatest female athlete of all time—and just maybe the greatest athlete, male or female—Babe Didrikson Zaharias, the footage we needed was owned by her husband, who demanded $50,000 for it. That was more than twice our budget to produce the entire show, so we couldn't do it.

Most of the time, though, we found what we needed. In the Library of Congress, for example, Bill Edgar found a remarkable piece of film made in 1921 in which Helen Keller, the extraordinary woman who overcame being blind and deaf to become a writer and world-renowned inspiration, played herself in a movie about her life while actors portrayed the other significant characters. For a *Biography* show on Eamon de Valera, a leader of the Irish rebellion, we found an organization in Dublin that had more than a thousand feet of historical film that no one even knew existed. It was the Irish rebellion, in black and white, as if it had been shot a few days earlier. We took great pride in mining these jewels of history.

It was while producing *Biography* that I first had to deal with pressure. Sometimes it was simple. When we did a show about Senator Huey "Kingfish" Long of Louisiana, his son called me at six in the morning and claimed we had misrepresented his father. Everything we said in the show was true. We got that kind of complaint all the time.

But when we did a show about Spanish dictator Franco—pointing out that he had spent millions of dollars to build a monument to himself—Franco himself took action. One of our sponsors in New York was Chemical Bank, which held a substantial amount of funds from the Spanish government. To punish the bank, the government removed its deposits. The bank could do nothing about it; the episode had already been broadcast. But the distributor of the show was Official Films, and to prevent Official Films from offering this program to the educational market, the Spanish government warned that the company would not be allowed to release any films in Spain if it did.

Unlike Chemical Bank, which did business with the Spanish government, Official Films couldn't be hurt by this threat and continued to offer the program in its catalog. That was my first up-close encounter with a pressure group, but even I could not have imagined what was to come.

It took us about three months to produce a *Biography* show. Our budget was $25,000 a show, which resulted in about a $5,000 profit. Those were well-made programs and they still play all over the world. A&E bought our original series and, after exhausting it, began making its own biographical programs. A&E's *Biography* has been running for several years and they are running out of both deserving subjects and footage. I often watch their shows in amazement, thinking these people deserve the Emmy Award for guts. They do entire programs with only a dozen photographs and a small amount of film, filling the rest of the hour with period footage—New York City in the 1930s, for example—and interviews with other people. You rarely see the subject. If the Jews at

Masada had been able to stretch their supplies the way these programs squeeze their footage, they would still be up there fighting. Eventually, A&E is going to run out of deserving subjects and they'll end up doing the biography of John Travolta's barber! Or Madonna's manicurist.

We were producing so many films about so many different subjects that it made sense to me to form my own distribution company. I opened offices in New York, St. Louis, and Pittsburgh. The first show we made specifically to be sold by that division was called *Men in Crisis. Men in Crisis* was the story of historic confrontations, Mao vs. Chiang, Stalin vs. Trotsky, Rommel vs. Montgomery—but mostly, it was product for the distribution company. Most of the footage was recycled from earlier shows and it was done by the same writers and editors working on the other shows, which made it inexpensive to produce.

Only a few years earlier, I had been unsuccessfully banging my head against the network door, but by 1962, an article about my company in the Show Business section of *Time* magazine referred to me as "Mr. Documentary."

TWELVE

WOLPER UNIVERSITY

Time magazine stated, "The three largest producers of documentaries for television are NBC, CBS, and David Wolper. At thirty-four, Wolper is the youngest and often most vigorous of the three. His offices on the Hollywood strip have grown in the past three years from a five-man shop to a two-hundred-employee corporation with forty cutting rooms crammed with 8 million feet of film. . . .

"The secret of these gains is not something magically created from David Wolper's particular genius, but rather a thorough-going capacity for careful research and intelligent selection. . . . Excellent fiction may be the highest matter that TV can offer, but so much TV fiction is so blatantly phony that a crisp edited set of authentic film clips about anything from a war to a horse race seem stunningly original."

We were a rapidly growing success. A very rapidly growing success. We were forced to continue expanding just to keep pace with the work coming into the shop. There had never been another company like Wolper Productions. We rented every available space in the neighborhood, eventually occupying space in seven buildings on one block, "one of them," *TV Guide* explained, "a converted bungalow that can be entered only through the bathroom. Scurrying up and down the street, in and out of alleys, shortcutting through a basement garage and bounding up and down a frightful collection of stairways are more than 190 employees."

We added people as rapidly as we added working space. We hired talented young people who wanted to make documentary films and gave them a real-world education and corresponding responsibility almost immediately. Some of them thrived, others failed. "Wolper University" became known in the industry as a place where you learned how to make a film under just about any condition. You learned how to make it good, make it honest, make it cheap, and how to overcome every problem imaginable to deliver it when it was due, whether you had five days or five months.

The Wolper Organization has been called one of the greatest incubators of talent in the history of the TV industry. I hired mostly young people because they had the drive, the creativity, and the enthusiasm—and because they worked cheap. That's all we could afford. Documentary buyers only paid so much money. Experience came with a price we couldn't afford to pay, so we depended on ambitious young people.

Our learning curve was more of a sharp angle, and those who couldn't keep up were quickly let go. But those who survived prospered. After spending only a few months as a film researcher, for example, people might find themselves producing a half-hour documentary. A month later they would be writing a show, and then we would send them somewhere to produce and direct a show. They had to learn fast. A twenty-three-year-old kid producing U.S. government documentaries, Nick Noxon, sent us a film he'd made about migrating herring. We didn't have a specific job for him, but he was obviously talented so we hired him. A month later he was making segments for *Biography*. Not too long after that he was working on a special for National Geographic that was to be narrated by Orson Welles. Nick had progressed from migrating herring to Orson Welles in only months.

Orson Welles had a magnificent command of the English language, and no one was more aware of that than Orson Welles. Welles was a huge man; Noxon was a little guy with horn-rimmed glasses. This was Noxon's first major opportunity to show his ability, and obviously, he was excited and nervous. He flew to Europe and went to work at a recording studio in Paris.

In his great mellifluous voice, Welles began, "The man went down the mountain—"

"Uh, Mr. Welles," Nick interrupted, and asked softly, "could you, um . . . go down on that point because we're trying to—"

"*What* did you say?"

"That one line, maybe you could just go down a little bit . . ."

Welles continued reading his narration. Perhaps three lines later Nick pressed the button again. "Uh, Mr. Welles, um, would you mind speaking just a little faster. We've only got eight seconds there and it has to fit. . . . Okay, let's start again."

Welles read another few lines and Nick stopped him once again. He had the courage of his youth. But Welles had had enough. "Young man," he boomed, "I am Orson Welles. I know what the fuck I am doing and you do not. There is only one correct way to read these words. I will read this narration from the beginning to the end and it will be correct. I assure you that nobody will do it better than me. Thank you very much."

Welles then read the entire narration. Nick was mortified, but he could do absolutely nothing but sit there, listen, and figure out how he was going to explain to us why the narration did not fit the film. We had to recut the footage to fit Welles's reading. Welles did many more shows for us over the years, and Nick went on to make many films for us before leaving to become executive producer of the acclaimed National Geographic series.

The roster of young people who began their careers at Wolper Productions is long and distinguished. Ten of them would eventually win Academy Awards, among them writer-director Jim Brooks, who won three Oscars and created the *Mary Tyler Moore Show;* Billy Friedkin, whom I brought to L.A. from Chicago after the William Morris Agency showed me the film he had made about a condemned prisoner, was named Best Director for *The French Connection;* film editors Verna Fields and Neil Travis; and documentary producers Terry Sanders, Frieda Lee Mock, Arnold Shapiro, and Wally Green, were all Academy Award winners. Among the many others who went on to great success were Alan Landsburg, who created and produced classic nonfiction television series such as *That's Incredible* and *In Search of . . . ;* writer David Seltzer; producer Bob Guenette; Vilis Lapenieks, who started as James Wong Howe's assistant; a salesman in the distribution company, Charles McGregor, who eventually became president of Warner Bros. Worldwide TV Distribution; Irwin Russell, whom I brought from New York to serve as our in-house attorney, became a board member of the

Disney Company; and even the great writer Theodore H. White, who started his TV writing career at Wolper U. My close friend Julian Ludwig, who started to work for me in the Flamingo days, remained many years as a producer at my company.

Three future billionaires started there at entry-level salaries: entertainment mogul David Geffen worked as a film editor; Irvine Company owner, real estate magnate Donald Bren worked in the shipping department; and Oscar-winning cameraman Fouad Said made his fortune in international finance.

These people learned from each other, they competed with each other, they became friends and grew together. There was little formal structure in the office. I set the tone—I wore slippers all day, all the time. I did, I suppose, because I could. I was the boss. It could be a pretty raucous place. It became pretty obvious that our greatest resource was this collection of talent, so when anyone screened his rough-cut film, I had whoever was in the office that day sit in—and then we'd discuss it. Everybody looked at everybody else's films. Is there anything more intimidating for a young filmmaker than knowing that a dozen people who know how to make a documentary will be watching his film? Most of the time that screening room was not a pleasant place to be. A lot of screaming and yelling went on. One producer described these screenings as "inquisitions blended with a touch of Dante's Inferno, with just a hint of a radiologist examining your soul." Another producer compared it to "wild dogs attacking bait on an African plain."

But it was always professional. It was never personal. It was about filmmaking, about making better films. People never argued about the size of their office or their expense account, but they would be brutally honest about a scene that didn't work. And they would do so knowing that their turn would eventually come. Billy Friedkin called me "the bullshit detector." My greatest talent was being able to look at these films through the eyes of our viewer. I'd looked at a lot of film, I'd done every part of the work myself, and I knew how to tell a story dramatically. I had a facility for spotting the extraneous crap that inexperienced filmmakers invariably included in their work.

Bill Friedkin joined us with a reputation as something of a young genius. We assigned him to a show we were making entitled *The Bold Men*, produced by Julian Ludwig, which featured people attempting extraordinary feats such as breaking the land speed barrier or jumping out of an airplane without a parachute. We let Friedkin travel all over the world to make this film, and finally he was ready to screen it.

I would not describe the rough cut as bad; it was much worse than that. *Awful* is probably more accurate, and I, being aware of the sensitive nature of a young man's personality, responded kindly. I believe this was the only time in my career that I actually threw something at the screen. I took off my slipper and threw it across the room. I was enraged. As Friedkin remembers it, I fumed, "There comes a time when the white-hot light goes on and the bullshit falls away like bricks on the ground. You're ruining me. This is the worst piece of shit I've ever seen. What a piece of garbage!" And then I really got angry.

What Friedkin had yet to learn was that this was how the process worked. This was tough love in the filmmaking business. We had a lot of *artistes* coming into the shop, and they had to learn how to make films for a mass audience, not for a small group of critics. And as rough as I could be, when Mel Stuart, who had become a vice president of my company, got on a roll, he was so much more . . . everything . . . than me.

What made this kind of behavior acceptable was the incredible camaraderie and respect for each other that we shared. No one was afraid to express an opinion because there were no penalties for it. I learned early that the best way to stifle creativity is to have a lot of rules; our only rule was that we didn't have a lot of rules. I ran a loosely structured organization. So loose that, on occasion, things got very much out of control. Bud Friedgen remembered his first week as an assistant editor. We were already becoming known as a creative, pro-fessional shop, and he was excited to be there. "Jack Haley and Julian Ludwig started throwing cores, the center of film reels, at each other. That battle expanded quickly to include just about everybody else in the place. It suddenly dawned on me that these people were nuts. Someone grabbed the fire extinguisher and opened fire. It was about that time, I remember, that Haley put the garden hose through the window. Some-one came down the stairs and started yelling—Haley turned the hose on him and drove him back upstairs." That was Bud Friedgen's initiation to Wolper Productions.

I never minded things like that, even if I had known about it, which I did not. They would clean up well. They had some good fights down-stairs, especially late at night. And there were a lot of late nights. We once made a list of the top ten reasons to work at Wolper Productions. Num-ber six was "the chance to see the sun go down from the door of the edit-ing room," and number five was "the chance to see the sun come up from the door of the editing room." Filmmakers are artists, and like artists they often worked without regard for time. To people who love it, making documentaries isn't a job, it is a passion—which did enable us to keep salaries decently low. Our people would often work right through the weekend, and in many cases, it affected their lives. We were beginning to see a lot of separations and divorces. The wives of our employees referred to themselves as "Wolper widows" because their husbands were always at the shop.

Producer-director Marshall Flaum says, "I'll never forget the day my wife said to me, 'Seth wants to play the violin for us.'

" 'Seth wants to play the violin?' I asked. Seth was our seven-year-old son. 'What do you mean? Since when does Seth play the violin?'

" 'He started his lessons seven months ago,' she said. My son had been taking violin lessons for months and I wasn't even aware of it. That really bothered me."

Finally, we had to make one of our rules: if you come in Sunday, don't come in Monday. We locked the office on Sunday; anybody who came to work on Sunday would be fired. That was the only way I could keep them away from the Moviola.

We were locked into a delicious cycle: to complete the series we had to hire additional people; to keep those additional people working, I had to sell more shows; to complete these additional shows . . .

Most of the shows we were doing were film compilations. But we weren't just pasting together footage, we were telling the stories of history. In a sense, we were creating art just like artist Ed Kienholz. We were taking bits and pieces, adding substantial production values, and making something original and exciting. But we were dependent almost completely on existing film. We were, arguably, the largest users of existing film in the world. In 1963, Paramount put up for sale its newsreel library, which consisted of more than 10 million feet of film covering just about every historic event that had taken place since 1927. Before there was television news, the major studios did weekly newsreels for theatrical release, basically the pictorial history of the times. For a company like ours, the Paramount Library was the equivalent of discovering the Holy Grail—if we could make a deal. I opened the bidding at $300,000, an enormous sum for the company. Someone else bid $350,000. We couldn't figure out who was bidding against us, but we bid $400,000. The mysterious other bidder raised me $50,000. I countered to $500,000.

I don't know how much higher I would have gone, but I didn't have to find out. Just as, one day, while walking down the street I'd met the representative of the Russian film agency, I was walking along New York's Madison Avenue when I bumped into Sherman Grinberg, the owner of the Grinberg Film Library, from whom we bought a consider-able amount of the footage we used. Sherman Grinberg was a fine man. "What are you doing?" I asked.

"Bidding on a film library," he replied.

I really should spend more time walking. I should have realized that he was bidding on the library because that was his business, but he would never have suspected that I was the other bidder. We agreed that I would purchase the Paramount Library for $500,000, and after several years I would sell it to him for the same $500,000, retaining rights to use the footage in my films. It turned out to be a great deal for both of us. That library proved to be a tremendous resource and served as the foundation for numerous shows.

In the early 1960s, stock footage was affordable. People were happy that someone actually wanted to buy their old film. That changed drastically when the lawyers got involved. The estate of Albert Einstein claims rights to all footage of Einstein. Martin Luther King's family claims it owns the rights to his famed "I Have a Dream" speech, which was made at a public event, on public grounds, and was printed, without a copyright, in hundreds of newspapers and books. Both claims are ridiculous. Nobody owns the moments of history.

Most of our film came from film libraries, but when we were doing a specific show, we would advertise in newspapers or plant feature stories about the show. When we were doing *Four Days in November*, the story of the assassination of President Kennedy, we put an ad in all the Dallas newspapers offering to buy any footage of the Kennedy motorcade. We got about seventy pieces of film that people had shot with their home movie cameras, enough to enable us to put together an entire sequence of Kennedy's ride through Dallas.

While researching the Humphrey Bogart *Biography* film, we found a writer who had Bogart's first film, a two-reeler called *Broadway Is Like That*, and bought it from him.

Normally we paid about $500 a minute for film, but there was no standard rate. We paid whatever we had to for what we needed. A man named Herman Axelbank, for example, owned a vast collection of pre-revolutionary-Russian footage. If we needed film of the tsar swimming in the Baltic, the only place to get it was Axelbank. So every time we did a show about Russia, we went to him. Herman Axelbank was slightly crazy. You had to look at his stock in his office. In most film libraries, after finding what you were looking for, you would order several hundred feet of film, then make a rough cut to determine precisely what you needed.

You'd pay for what you used. That was not the way Herman Axelbank worked. He sold his film by the frame, for about fifty cents a frame. If you needed four feet, three frames, he would go into his lab, cut it right out of his original footage, and hand it to you.

History has been recorded; it's just a matter of finding the footage. At times we found the most incredible film. When we were doing *China: Roots of Madness,* Teddy White told us that prior to 1911 the Chinese wore their hair in pigtails. We had some still photos, but never expected to find film. We found a travel film the famous documentarian Burton Holmes had shot in Beijing at the turn of the century—and there were these men with pigtails. Teddy White kept telling us it was impossible, that film couldn't exist.

The oldest piece of film we used was quite well known, "The Kiss," filmed by Thomas Edison. The kiss is just a kiss, five seconds long at most, but it is the earliest known footage.

Probably the most unusual footage we found was color footage of Adolf Hitler. One day a reel of 16mm color film arrived in the office— footage of Hitler near Stalingrad. The existence of this film was a big surprise to us. Without a doubt we made more films about Nazi Germany and Adolf Hitler than any other subject. We must have made at least fifty films covering nearly every conceivable angle. We did a miniseries based on the best-selling book *The Rise and Fall of the Third Reich.* We did numerous biographies of Hitler. We did war stories. We did the *Trial at Nuremberg.* We did *The Plot to Murder Hitler* twice, once as a drama for a TV movie and once as a documentary for which we created our own period footage with an actor playing Hitler.

Almost all of the footage we used had been shot by the Nazis. The Nazis were efficient, they recorded everything. At the end of World War II the Allies captured the German film libraries, tens of millions of feet of film, and brought it to the United States. This was the entire visual record of a nation gone insane. It included everything from a 1929 rally in which people brought Nazi flags to Hitler and he would put his hand on the flags and bless them, to the huge piles of corpses of the Holocaust. All that film was sitting in the Alien Property Department of the Library of Congress—until Congress voted to give it back to the Germans. I fought that decision; this was an extraordinary historical record and I didn't know what the Germans would do with it once they gained control. But the U.S. government returned it as a gesture of goodwill.

The Holocaust footage, and films shot inside the Warsaw ghetto, were the most horrifying things I've ever seen. People dying in the streets, piles of bodies, corpses being transported in wheelbarrows. These films had been sitting in a vault in Washington, D.C. With the exception of a few clips, the public had never seen them. I didn't want to give back this record to some of the people responsible for these atrocities, but I could do nothing about it.

There was one thing I could do, though. The head of the American Nazi Party, George Lincoln Rockwell, spoke to students at Berkeley and claimed the Holocaust had never happened, that it was a creation of Jewish propaganda. After being made aware of his remarks, I asked to speak at the university, and I showed some of these films to the students, who were stunned. People were screaming in the theater, they ran out in tears. When the film was over, I said simply, "This is my answer to George Lincoln Rockwell."

Most of this footage was too strong for television. So when we used it, we picked representative segments; when we showed a pile of bodies, it was a quick shot. The point was well made.

Once we found a strong piece of film, we would use it in many different programs. As far as documentary filmmaking was concerned, we were the major studio. We were churning out more hours of nonfiction programming than anyone else in the industry, and we were always trying to sell more. We produced good films about any subject in which people were interested, from *Day of Infamy,* about the December 7, 1941, Japanese attack on Pearl Harbor, to *The Really Big Family,* the story of the biggest family we could find in America. We were doing historical documentaries, human-interest stories, and personal stories. If a sponsor or a network was interested in it, we could do it. I remember sitting in the office of a network executive trying to sell him a show about the sex symbols of Hollywood. He misunderstood me and thought I was pitching a show about Marilyn Monroe. He thought that was a great idea. From that moment on, as far as I was concerned, I had always been trying to sell him a show about Marilyn Monroe.

I had tremendous support. During a meeting in New York someone would spark an idea and I would claim that we were already working on it. As soon as the meeting ended, I'd call the office on Sunset and get my research team under the direction of Christine Foster working on a proposal—and deliver it the next day.

THIRTEEN

SO POWER PASSES

With Theodore H. White (1969)

While the studios had long been turning novels into movies, no one had transformed a best-selling nonfiction book into a TV documentary. It seemed like a good idea. When Theodore H. White's Pulitzer Prize–winning chronicle of the 1960 presidential campaign, *The Making of the President,* came out, I called White's agent, the eminent Swifty Lazar. "I'd like to buy the television rights . . . for a documentary on *The Making of the President, 1960.* What will that cost me?"

Lazar didn't hesitate. "Mr. Wolper, the asking price for that book is two hundred and fifty thousand dollars."

"I can't pay that, Mr. Lazar," I said. "This is a documentary. I only have twenty-five thousand dollars for the rights."

"Mr. Wolper, you have a deal."

While I was spending my own money, I was confident I could sell this to one of the networks or a sponsor. This was not a controversial issue, this wasn't a policy issue, this was the story of an election that had been decided two years earlier. What I did not know was that producer

David Susskind had previously optioned the rights and had tried unsuccessfully to sell a one-hour special based on the book to the networks.

But I was no longer at the mercy of the networks; if I had to, I could put back together my own network. I decided to make a ninety-minute documentary; the $475,000 budget was one of the largest ever for a documentary in TV history. I assigned Mel Stuart to produce it. Elmer Bernstein wrote the original score. The book was so beautifully written that I asked Teddy White to write the script. He'd never written for television, but he immediately became one of the finest documentary-film writers I had ever known.

The other writers were in awe of him. When he would leave the office at night, a couple of the young writers would rummage through his wastebasket to read what he was throwing away. Teddy White once said that the script-writing experience had been frightening for him, because the medium can easily invite men to rearrange visible truth into historical lies—that unless goodwill and conscience dominate the entire production, what the viewer sees may actually be untrue.

"Rearrange visible truth into historical lies." I have often thought about that warning, particularly many years later when I saw Oliver Stone's perversion of truth, the movie *JFK*.

By the time Teddy arrived in California we had collected more than five hundred hours of film from every conceivable source—even the network news departments. We looked at more than a million feet of film and tape—knowing that we would use only twenty-five hundred feet. We were not able to find footage of some of the important scenes from the book, including John Kennedy's magnificent speech in Houston, Texas, in which he confronted the religious issue, making a plea for religious tolerance that changed American politics forever. But we did have wonderful amateur film shot on Kennedy's airplane, and we found candid footage of Kennedy and Richard Nixon taken as they prepared for their historic first debate. We worked by assembling the film from an outline and then writing the narration to fit it. Eventually, editor Bill Cartwright cut it into a two-hour film. Then the real making of the program began as we fought to find just the perfect balance between these pictures and Teddy White's words.

At that point the cutting gets tough. People fight for scenes, for a few seconds of film. When the ninety-minute rough cut was finally assembled, it was obvious we needed a strong closing line. The film ends with a freeze frame of President Eisenhower shaking hands with Kennedy.

"Teddy," Mel told him, "we've got to have something to go over this last image." Mel rambled on for about a half hour, explaining that he wanted to finish with some thoughts about the office of the presidency, the tradition, the majesty of the moment . . .

"Okay, how many words do I have?" Teddy had learned to write to time.

"Three," Mel said.

Teddy was incredulous. "You expect me to finish a ninety-minute program with three words?" Try, we told him, try. He disappeared into his office.

Perhaps an hour later, I was meeting with Mel and several writers about another show when Teddy walked into the room and handed me a sheet of paper. On it he had written the perfect ending. At the inauguration of John Kennedy, former president Dwight Eisenhower and Kennedy shake hands. The narrator says, simply and beautifully, "So power passes."

I went to New York with the film under my arm and $475,000 at risk. Xerox agreed to sponsor the show. The first place I tried to sell it was CBS, for whom Teddy White served as a political adviser. The election was long over; I figured Teddy was a CBS consultant. They couldn't possibly object.

They objected. They would not use public affairs programming made by an independent producer. NBC turned me down. ABC turned me down. A network executive told a reporter that President Kennedy had participated in re-creations of scenes from the book, which was beyond absurd. The networks just didn't want it. Just as I got ready to sell it market by market, a friend of mine arranged for ABC president Leonard Goldenson to see the show. Goldenson and his wife loved it. He overruled John Daly, president of ABC News, insisting ABC broadcast the program. Not too long afterward John Daly left ABC, perhaps because of this incident.

The show was scheduled to run in February 1964. Elmer Bernstein was recording the final score, with a forty-man orchestra, on November 22, 1963. We felt that there were too many violins and we wanted the music to be more exciting, less romantic. I was sitting in my office when someone came in and told me the president had been shot. It was a stunning time, and my memories of those days seem to flow together. At some point, Teddy White called and we discussed how best to proceed. I didn't know what to do. Tear the film apart, or leave it as it was finished before his death? Was it fair to show Kennedy young, raw, and vibrant? Was it fair to show Lyndon Johnson, Richard Nixon, and Hubert Humphrey attacking him in the heat of the 1960 campaign? "There's only one answer, David," Teddy told me. "John Kennedy loved the battle of a campaign and he loved history. This is both. He would have wanted an honest picture of the fight, not a compromise. We shouldn't change a word."

We were concerned that whatever we did might look as if we were exploiting this tragedy. But no one could ever accuse Teddy White of that. While researching his book, he had become close to the Kennedy family. Days after the president's death, Jackie Kennedy sat with him for an interview for *Life* magazine. Just before the memorial service, she told Teddy that she regretted having put her bloodstained wedding ring on her husband's finger at Parkland Hospital in Dallas: "Now I have nothing left." That night, at Bethesda Naval Hospital in Washington as JFK was being prepared for burial, Kennedy aide Kenny O'Donnell slipped into the room where the president's body was lying and brought the ring back to her. After waiting more than a week, I called Xerox and ABC. Both the sponsor and the network agreed with Teddy. The only change we made was to add a prologue, in which Teddy White appears on camera and says, "John Fitzgerald Kennedy loved American politics. The story you are about to see tells of one of its greatest clashes. This film was finished shortly before his death. We have left it as it was then, believing that the noble profession of politics and the men who aspired to lead us are greater in candid recollection."

White asked ABC to run it in December, rather than in February as originally scheduled. "The longer we wait," he said, "the more we might be inclined to revise it, and there was nothing to be revised. Pull one emotional thread and you can unravel the whole fabric." We got the finished prints three days before it was going to be broadcast, and someone realized the copyright date in the credits, 1964, had to be changed. Ben Bennett sat at a splicer with a needle stuck in a paintbrush and by hand scratched a 3 over the 4 on every frame of every print.

The Making of the President was broadcast on Sunday, December 29, 1963, 8:30 to 10:00 P.M., to rave reviews. Several months later, we were nominated for Emmys in four categories, including the highest honor the Academy of Television Arts and Sciences can award, Program of the Year. We all went to the Emmy Awards: Teddy White, Elmer Bernstein, Mel Stuart, and Bill Cartwright. We had already won three Emmys for music, editing, and best documentary when it was time to name the best television program of the year. Also nominated in that category were

NBC's *The American Revolution of 1963;* CBS's "Blacklist," an episode of the series *The Defenders;* NBC's *The Kremlin;* and CBS's *Town Meeting of the World.* When Jack Benny announced the winner in Los Angeles, *The Making of the President, 1960,* Mel Stuart and I went up to the stage together. In my mind I kept thinking, "Screw 'em, screw 'em, we beat them." It was a great moment for me. For the first time in history an independent documentary producer had beaten the networks. What sweet revenge.

The next day in the *New York Times,* critic Jack Gould wrote, "To Mr. Wolper the award was undoubtedly particularly satisfying. His efforts to prove that an independent producer should have a place in news and public affairs had been cold-shouldered by both CBS and NBC. It remained for ABC to decide that quality is where one finds it and that a network did not compromise its final editorial control by entertaining a freelance contribution."

This was the beginning of my long friendship with Teddy White, a truly remarkable man. He worked with the Wolper Company on several shows after that, including *The Making of the President, 1964* and *1968* and *China: Roots of Madness.* As much as he loved American politics, he loved China equally. As *Time* magazine's Far East correspondent, he had been with Mao in the mountains and knew Chiang Kai-shek and Chou En-lai. He was endlessly fascinated by Chinese history. It was his major in college. Once, he said, trying to explain the way the Chinese thought, he had been invited to dinner by Chou En-lai. It was a feast and with great fanfare the main course was served, a large suckling pig with an apple in its mouth. Teddy politely told his host, "I cannot eat the pig. It is against my religion to eat pig."

To which Chou En-lai responded, "But, Teddy, it's not a pig. It's a chicken."

Teddy White wrote history with more insight than anyone else I've ever read. But in 1968 he almost caused it to be changed. In addition to buying footage for the *Making of the President, 1964* and *1968,* we had our own crews filming the campaigns. In 1968, while I was in Most, Czechoslovakia, filming the feature *The Bridge at Remagen,* Mel Stuart was with Vilis Lapenieks and two assistants in the Ambassador Hotel filming Robert Kennedy for the TV Special *The Making of the President, 1968.* Stuart and Lapenieks had been upstairs with Kennedy and filmed him coming down through the kitchen and out into the ballroom, where he gave his victory speech. As he was talking, Mel moved into another area and started shooting the speech on a television set. They didn't know by which exit Kennedy was going to leave the ballroom. They wanted to be in front of him, filming him as he accepted congratulations, and go with him into the lobby. But instead Kennedy turned and went back through the kitchen. So Mel and Vilis were behind rather than in front of him. "I've never stopped thinking about what might have happened if I'd waited for him behind the podium," Mel says. "If we had been in front of him when he left, Sirhan Sirhan would have had to climb over the four of us and all our equipment to get a shot at Kennedy."

The Making of the President, 1960 was the last time I had to finance my own production. After that, everything we did was presold to a sponsor or a network.

FOURTEEN

JOHNSON, NIXON, NADER, PEROT, AND OLIVER NORTH

At the White House
with President Lyndon Johnson (1964)

The Wolper Company continued to expand. In addition to the television distribution department, I opened two music firms and added an educational, corporate, and political film division. I received some criticism for making corporate films and political campaign films as well as documentaries, as if making films for hire somehow tainted my integrity.

Idealism is a wonderful thing. But so is being able to pay the salaries of more than two hundred employees. I made films not to champion causes but to tell good stories. I made documentaries for both Democrats and Republicans. I made films for the U.S. Army and for major corporations through my Corporate Films division. These weren't my films, they didn't represent my point of view, they were jobs. *Destination*

Safety was made for General Motors in response to Ralph Nader's book. I met with the chairman of GM, who told me the corporation wanted to respond to charges leveled against it. Any reluctance I might have had about making the film disappeared after an executive pointed out to me that GM had a right to present its point of view, just as Nader had done, and wanted it to be done professionally.

In 1964, I was invited by Arthur Krim, chairman of United Artists, to go to the White House. This had nothing to do with my personal politics. I met President Lyndon Johnson and his aide Jack Valenti, who was to become a close friend. They wanted me to make two films for the 1964 Democratic National Convention. The first film, I was told, would be about President Johnson and his policies, and the second film would be a tribute to the slain president, Kennedy.

I assigned producer-director-writer Alan Landsburg to both films, and just before completion I sent them to Washington for review. Lyndon Johnson was a stickler for details—he even personally selected the color of the seats in the convention hall in which he would be nominated. After viewing his film, he approved it, but he decided not to screen the Kennedy film because he didn't want any responsibility for it. He left it to the Kennedy family to approve it or suggest changes.

Originally the Kennedy film, *A Thousand Days*, was scheduled to be shown to the convention and a national television audience on the second of the three nights, but after Jack Valenti screened it, he went right to Johnson. "I think it would be wise if we moved the film to the last night," he said.

"What are you talking about?" Johnson wondered.

"Well, Mr. President," Valenti explained, "the film *A Thousand Days* is so strong that I'm afraid if we show it before we select the vice president, there might well be a groundswell from the floor for Bobby Kennedy."

The last thing Johnson wanted was to have Bobby Kennedy forced on him as his vice president. After watching the film, he moved it to the final night of the convention, where, dramatically, it was much more effective as the grand finale. Bobby Kennedy introduced it, and when the lights went back on he—and the film—received a four-minute standing ovation from a teary-eyed audience. Ironically, after all my problems, a Wolper documentary was shown on all three networks simultaneously.

Seven years later I was asked by Peter Daley and Bill Carruthers of the November Group, an advertising unit established for Richard Nixon's 1972 reelection campaign, to make several films for the Republican National Convention. Nixon had seen and enjoyed *The Making of the President, 1960.* At the White House, I met with Nixon associates Dwight Chapin, deputy assistant to the president, Jeb McGruder, head of the Citizen's Committee for the Reelection of Nixon, Bob Halderman, Herb Klein, and Dick Moore, a friend of mine who ran a television station in Los Angeles. They told me they were thinking of having filmmaker Bruce Hirshenson make the film, but they liked the documentaries I made better. Dick Moore said at the meeting, "This is the gentleman who is responsible for *The Race to Space,* which was a great film." Bob Haldeman asked me a number of questions, one being, "Is there anything the president could do that would prevent you from finishing these films?"

It was an interesting question. "There's really only one thing I can think of. If the president came out against Israel, I think I'd have to drop out of the film or turn it over to someone else."

"We don't have to worry about that," Halderman responded. "President Nixon is one hundred percent for Israel and that will never change."

Incidentally, our first assignment was to accompany Nixon on his groundbreaking trip to China as the official film crew for the United States.

Although several people in the administration didn't trust me because we had produced the Democrat's films, eventually my Corporate Films division was hired to produce three films for the reelection campaign: a personal film about Nixon, a film about his achievements, and a short film about Pat Nixon. We were given specific directions: "The first film should project the president as a man of the people, an uncommon common man, a man whose personality has been shaped by . . . his less advantaged small-town boyhood, his toughness shaped by his trials and football . . ."

Unlike Lyndon Johnson, Richard Nixon never viewed his film before it was shown to the convention. But when producers Ed Spiegel and Alex Grassoff screened it for his aides, they called me and requested that one scene be removed. This was a conversation in which Nixon came out strongly against committing millions of dollars to build a commercial supersonic airplane. "Let's take it out," Halderman said. "Why make it an issue in the campaign when it isn't?" So it was cut out of the film.

Talk about irony, the Johnson film was titled *Quest for Peace,* while the Nixon film was called *Change Without Chaos.* Both films proved to be completely backward. There was no peace during Johnson's administration and Nixon's presidency dissolved in chaos.

Almost two decades later, in June 1992, I was invited to Dallas, Texas, to meet with Ross Perot to discuss making a biographical film for his presidential campaign. I had previously spent considerable time on the phone with the leaders of his campaign, and they had drawn up an outline complete with storyboards. The boards were hung on the walls of Perot's campaign headquarters. When Perot finally arrived, we shook hands and he began looking at the boards. Ed Rollins, who was running the campaign, began explaining it to him. About five minutes into this, Perot stopped him: "I'm sorry, fellas, but I'm not going to spend a penny of my money on this. Thank you, Mr. Wolper, for coming." And then he left. Everybody was stunned. Within minutes I was on my way to the airport.

The Corporate Films group made films for many different organizations, but I will never forget one that we did not make. In the 1980s, I was asked by the Reagan White House to come to Washington for a meeting. I was met at the airport and driven to a private home in a suburban Virginia neighborhood. There I met Oliver North, who asked if I would be willing to make a documentary from the contras point of view about the war being fought in Nicaragua.

"Who would I be making it for?" I asked.

"We don't know that yet," he said, "we'll get the funding from somebody."

I was given a thick briefing book, which included everything from published articles to National Security Agency reports. It included a resource paper about groups called the Nicaraguan Democratic Resistance. There was a complete book with photographs of Nicaragua, people being beaten and tortured, and a report from the State Department and Department of Defense, dated March 1985, about the Soviet-Cuba connection in Central America. There was a report on the prosecution of black Nicaraguans dated July 20, 1984, and photographs showing tools for the torture of young kids who looked as though they were fifteen. They found secret plans to bomb civilians and kids and torture people. I took it all and returned to California. Like most Americans, I knew little about the war in Nicaragua between the Sandinistas and the contras—except that supporters of both sides were certain they were right.

It turned out that North was hoping I would make this film on my own, using materials given to me by his group. That wasn't possible, I told him, knowing I couldn't sell it anywhere. If he wanted it done, he would have to find someone to pay for it. I never heard from him again.

FIFTEEN

THE WOLPER WAY

I lived in the world of practicality. The first questions I asked myself about any idea were: can I sell it, can I get a sponsor for it, and can I get it on the air? I never saw the value of investing considerable time, money, and passion on a film that few people would ever see. Traditionally, documentaries had not been produced for the mass audience. We weren't competing against other documentaries, we were competing against entertainment programming, from sitcoms to movies. We had to be able to attract that mass audience by finding subjects that would be of interest to millions of people, then produce films with the same production values that the audience had come to expect from entertainment programming. My concept from the first day was to inform and entertain—not just inform.

No matter what the subject of our films, we always attempted to tell the truth in story form. In every film we made, we tried to tell a dramatic story through the lives of the people involved, whether it was the making of the atom bomb or the life and death of Marilyn Monroe. Certainly, a major difference between the films we were making and traditional documentaries is that most documentarians tried to tell their stories dispassionately.

They did not want sentimentality to color their story, while we always looked for the emotional content in a story. I knew that, if we could make people laugh or cry, they would become involved with our picture.

One method we used to heighten that emotional response was music. Music is the expressed language of the emotions, and all of our documentaries had strong scores. Elmer Bernstein, who scored twenty of our films, once demonstrated the impact of music on a scene. He showed the same film clip twice: a telephone rings, a man answers and speaks for a moment, then hangs up. The first time Elmer accompanied the clip with bright, bouncy, cheerful music, making it obvious this was an ordinary phone call. But the second time he used dark, ominous music—and suddenly the scene took on an entirely different tone. The footage was exactly the same, but the meaning of the scene had completely changed.

Beginning with *The Race for Space*, we used the finest composers in the industry for our documentaries: Bernstein, Henry Mancini, Lalo Schifrin, Walter Scharf, Gerald Fried, Arthur Morton, Lyn Murray, Ruby Raskin. Most of these people were expensive, but we were buying their reputations as well as their talent. Their names, as well as their music, were important to potential sponsors of these films. We were buying quality. We owned so much wonderful music that I opened two music companies to control the rights, and at times, we issued albums of our scores.

Only once did I ever have a problem with a composer, but not in a documentary, and that was many years later, when we were making *Roots*. To write the score, I hired Quincy Jones, certainly one of the greatest musical geniuses of our time. Quincy wanted the music to be perfect, so he spent a tremendous amount of time learning about African music. So much time that he fell behind schedule. He wrote the main theme, but was late with the rest of the score. I found out he was sidelined with a medical problem. The airdate was approaching rapidly and we still didn't have our music. Finally we met in my office. This was an incredibly difficult day for me; I was firing perhaps the greatest black American composer and arranger and hiring a white Jew, Gerald Fried, to finish the work. I knew how much completing this score meant to Quincy, but I had absolutely no choice. "I've got to have it by . . ." I told him the date.

"I can't deliver it that fast," he said.

"Quincy, I don't have a choice. I've got to bring in somebody else." It was an awful moment. I went around the desk and hugged him. There were tears in both our eyes.

"I wanted it to be perfect," he said. So, I brought in Gerald Fried to finish the score—but we based it on the theme Quincy had composed. We remain friends, and when we speak of it, our eyes still redden.

Our use of music—and sound effects—in documentaries offended some network news executives. When we were making *The Yanks Are Coming*, our second Academy Award–nominated documentary, the story of the American involvement in World War I, I found an early gramophone and some old cylinders in an antiques store. These turned out to be patriotic songs from that period, and we used them—in addition to an original score—in the documentary. We also added the thunder of guns to the battle scenes. Fred Friendly, then the head of CBS News, objected to the addition of sound effects to footage of the fighting. I thought that was ridiculous, and I said so: "There certainly was sound when the battle took place, but they didn't record it. The addition of sound effects does not affect the accuracy of our program. The facts of the battle remain exactly the same, this is actual footage, but we felt sound effects would make it more exciting. Fred Friendly did a show about World War I and he had music behind battle scenes. There certainly wasn't an orchestra playing that day. Mr. Friendly added music to heighten the effect of the scene, I used sound effects."

No company ever made the range of films that we did, and the changing economics of television and the motion picture industry makes it almost certain no one ever will again. But no matter what each film was about, our goal was always to make films that would endure. We were trying to make films that would be watched for decades. History doesn't disappear. History doesn't get old. Unlike entertainment programs, which age quickly, a well-told story about a historical event should never become dated. For many years, for example, I tried to sell the mythical story of Ulysses—an important part of world cultural history—as a television movie. At one network I gave a great pitch: I told the entire Trojan horse story, the soldiers sneaking out in the middle of the night. It really was a strong sales job. And when I finished, the network executive looked at me and asked, "But, David, do you think the story will hold up?"

I looked right at him and said softly, "It's held up for three thousand years. I think we can make it through one more television season." Eventually someone produced it and it received excellent reviews and ratings.

SIXTEEN

THE CREATIVE INTERPRETATION
OF REALITY

With Israel's founder, David Ben-Gurion (1964)

The documentary film we made most replete with emotion was *Four Days in November,* the story of the assassination of John Kennedy and the days of mourning that followed. It would have been impossible to make that film without a strong emotional content. The emotional toll on the entire nation was an important aspect of that story. For people who lived through those four days, the facts have faded, but the memories remain forever. Even four decades later it remains extremely difficult to view the film without tears. Originally, I brought this film idea to Arthur Krim at UA, who decided immediately to make it a theatrical release—meaning it would play in movie theaters rather than on television; this was our first such film.

I sent Mel Stuart to Dallas within weeks of the assassination. He filmed interviews with many of the people who had crossed Lee Harvey Oswald's path on November 22. This is history told by the people who made it. We interviewed the cabdriver who drove Oswald, the police officers who were involved in the investigation, coworkers who were in the Texas Book Depository with Oswald that day and talked with him. We interviewed his housekeeper, and the friend who drove him to work that morning and told of his carrying a long, slender object covered with a blanket that Oswald claimed was curtain rods. We got amateur footage of the entire motorcade. We even had still pictures of Oswald standing proudly with his rifle. We also re-created some moments using the people who were there, and showing the action from their point of view. The camera ran down the same staircase that Oswald had used after the shooting, we drove into the city with his friend who had driven him with that long, slender object perched in the backseat. Every scene was historically accurate.

I have seen this film innumerable times, yet there is one scene to which I will always react. It's filmed from outside Parkland Hospital. As the camera slowly pans across the exterior of the hospital from our room to another, writer Ted Strauss explained that "Kennedy aide Kenny O'Donnell walked slowly from the emergency room, where Kennedy had just died, to the waiting room, where Lyndon Johnson was sitting. To Lyndon Johnson he said, 'Mr. President, the president is dead.'"

It still makes my eyes well with tears. He didn't have to say that second part, did he? In those two words, "Mr. President," the story is told.

For the premiere of the film in Washington, D.C., in 1965, we had invited members of the Kennedy and Johnson administrations as well as major Republican leaders. It was an important event. Wisely, early in the afternoon, Mel Stuart decided to look at this picture one final time to check the sound, to see how it looked on the theater screen. And suddenly, in the middle of the film, a western goes on. A western! Someone had mixed up the reels. Mel sat there in disbelief for only a few seconds. Then he got on the phone. Within the hour someone was flying to Washington from New York hand-carrying the correct film. These many years later, I still shudder to think what might have happened that night had Mel not, on the spur of the moment, decided to screen the film.

Four Days in November was nominated for an Academy Award, though we lost to a film made by a French scuba diver named Jacques Cousteau. Millions of feet of film exist about those four terrible days, but

I believe that this film stands as the definitive piece and summarizes one of the most significant events of the century.

We did have one significant advantage over other television production companies: while they had to make up new stories every week, we had all of history from which to pick the best stories. Between 1962 and 1968, we made thirty historical documentaries. When beginning each film, I found an acknowledged expert on the subject and hired him as our consultant. We were experts on making documentaries. We needed a historical adviser to make sure our story was accurate.

History can be interpreted many different ways, particularly when dealing with complex and often controversial subjects, as we did in *The Rise and Fall of American Communism* or in *The American Woman of the Twentieth Century,* on the women's movement. Our dependence on advisers and experts enabled us to respond to criticism by explaining, this isn't what David Wolper says about the end of the Civil War in *The Surrender at Appomattox,* this is what Pulitzer Prize–winning historian Bruce Catton says. We used the most respected scholars in the country, men like James McGregor Burns or Arthur Schlesinger Jr. or William Shirer. We hired the people who had been present when history was made, or who had spent their lives researching a subject, people like Teddy White, Jacques Cousteau, Betty Ford, Mrs. Robert Goddard, Karl Menninger, M.D., Senator John Glenn, or Jack Valenti. We took very seriously our obligation to be as historically accurate as possible.

And in so doing, we got to tell some truly wonderful inside stories. For example, our expert adviser for *Ten Seconds That Shook the World,* the story of the atom bomb, was *New York Times* science reporter William Lawrence. Long before anyone knew of the existence of the Manhattan Project, Lawrence had practically been kidnapped from the campus of Columbia University and taken to meet President Roosevelt, who offered him the opportunity to live in Los Alamos and record the history of the making of the bomb—and even be there when, and if, the decision was made to use it. And in fact, several years later, Lawrence was on the plane that dropped the second bomb. The Nagasaki bomb.

It was Lawrence who told us a great story that became an emotional centerpiece of our film. Early in World War II, the secretary of war invited the CEOs of five major corporations to Washington for a meeting at which they were asked to make one piece of a secret project. A briefing book was put in front of each of them, and all they were told was that the government needed the help of their companies. "The details of the entire project are in that book, and you're entitled to know the secret. But President Roosevelt would prefer you not open it. He'd prefer that your companies do the work for us without knowing what it's about. You'll all be paid a fair price for everything you do. If you agree not to open your book, please pass it to me."

All of them passed the books forward. They completed the job without ever knowing that they were building the atomic bomb.

Ten Seconds That Shook the World is shown regularly at the National Atomic Museum in Los Alamos, New Mexico.

We went to great lengths to ensure historical accuracy. When we were making *The Crucifixion of Jesus,* for example, we used three biblical experts—a Protestant, a Catholic, and a Jew. These three men had to approve everything—the artifacts, the clothing, the sets, the decorations, and every word in the script—before we started filming. That all went well—although it took them a long time to reach an agreement on how to deal with the blood of Jesus. The entire show was filmed in Jerusalem wherever possible, at the actual sites where the events took place. There was one scene, though, in which we knew we were probably historically inaccurate, but we did it for a reason.

The Last Supper was re-created in the room over the Tomb of David, where it is believed to have taken place. We originally shot the scene with everyone sitting at a round table for the Passover seder, as our experts told us was accurate. But everyone who saw the scene—particularly the sponsor, Timex, and the network—was disappointed because everyone was familiar with Leonardo da Vinci's painting in which everybody was sitting side by side at a long table. As far as most people are concerned, that is reality. They had expected to see that painting come to life in our show. So, reluctantly, we agreed to reshoot the scene that way. To my knowledge, in all the documentaries we did, that is the only time where we, knowingly, were probably historically inaccurate.

Television at that time had not yet become a slave to the numbers. Networks and sponsors didn't test concepts with focus groups before deciding whether to proceed. It was seat-of-the-pants programming. People made decisions based on their gut feelings. We even made one important movie that, to my surprise, I learned the sponsor didn't really care how many people actually watched. We had a long and good relationship with Xerox, who sponsored ten of our programs. In 1965, Xerox sponsored *Let My People Go,* the two-thousand-year history of the Jewish people culminating with the creation of the state of Israel. This compelling story had never really been told on television, at least not the way we wanted to tell it. Because Xerox sponsored this program, its products were banned in Arab nations for many years.

Generally, when I met with a potential sponsor, I brought with me a list of programs that might be appropriate for them and went down that list one by one. I sold this show as the dramatic story of a people, the Holocaust, fighting the British, the war for creation of the state, rather than the story of a religion.

Xerox was just beginning to build its corporate image as a company that made high-quality products. Their strategy was to sponsor prestige programming—*The Making of the President, 1960,* for example—just as Hallmark has subsequently done over the years, to reinforce that image. Additionally, while they were successfully selling copiers to large companies, they were less successful selling them to small businessmen—many of whom were Jewish. Based on my one-page proposal, they felt this program would help them reach this thus far elusive customer.

I had a sponsor, but I didn't have a network. And even with the financial power of Xerox, I wasn't sure I could sell it to one. But Xerox didn't care. As a corporate executive explained to me, the number of people who actually watched the show made little difference to Xerox. What mattered was that they could take full-page ads in major newspapers to make sure people associated the company with intelligent, quality programming.

This was corporate advertising. Brand-name building.

Rather than even going to a network, we decided to reprise my *Race for Space* strategy, placing the program in all the desired markets. Xerox wanted only prime-time slots any night but Friday, because that is the Jewish Sabbath. More importantly for Xerox, because we had to deliver a print to every station, in many cities the stations held advance screenings for Jewish organizations, local business clubs, civic leaders, and newspaper editors, which was never done for network programs.

Eventually *Let My People Go,* which was produced and directed by Marshall Flaum, was broadcast on 107 stations, becoming the third-highest-rated documentary of the television season. Xerox did an amazing thing—they felt the show was so strong that it ran no commercials, just long spots at the beginning and the end. That was a bold statement and resulted in even more publicity. In addition to winning a Peabody Award, one of journalism's highest honors, it was nominated for two Emmys and the Academy Award as Best Documentary Feature. The third year in a row for a Wolper Company film.

Admittedly, not every documentary we did in those early days was significant. Some might generally be termed human-interest programming. These could most accurately be summed up as pretty much anything that I could sell to one of the networks.

No matter how serious or how frivolous the subject, we produced every documentary with the same dedication to quality as we did when making historical programs. Few personalities in any field have ever been so idolized by the American public as Marilyn Monroe. So, when she died, I decided we needed to have film of the funeral. I had no plan, at that time, to do a documentary about her life, but it seemed like footage we would eventually use. Only later did I decide to do a documentary about Marilyn Monroe—and we did it completely on spec, meaning I paid for it. We could have done a clip job, just pasting together scenes from movies, but that was not the way we worked. We hired Elmer Bernstein to do the music and John Huston—who had directed Marilyn in her first important role and her last picture—to narrate it. This was long before the sad details of her private life had become so publicly known; the legend was still very much intact, and Terry Sanders directed, produced, and cowrote, with Ted Strauss, a very human, touching documentary.

We found material that had never before been seen: an early TV commercial she'd made for Union Oil, footage from private collections. The Democratic Party loaned me the only known footage of Marilyn singing "Happy Birthday" to President Kennedy at his birthday party; we had boxes of never published still photographs. We needed to show the famous nude calendar that had first made her famous, but the censors would not allow nudity on TV; we solved that problem by showing the negative rather than the photo. Viewers could see a nude figure, but without any detail—and there was nothing the censor could do to stop it.

One of the people we interviewed was her first husband, Jim Dougherty, a policeman who had met and married her when she was still Norma Jean Baker. I called him myself and convinced him to do the interview. He was remarried and reluctant, but I told him that it was an important part of her life and had to be told. Finally, he agreed. We paid him for it. During a conversation one day, I asked him what he thought about Marilyn Monroe, and he replied, "You don't understand. I never knew Marilyn Monroe. I knew Norma Jean Baker."

When the interview was finished, Dougherty told me, "Now be sure and don't tell anybody I did this. If my wife ever gets wind of it, she'll kill me."

Terry Sanders and I promised him that we wouldn't tell anyone. I knew that 50 million people were going to see this on television, but personally, I never breathed a word of it to anyone—nor did Terry.

Marilyn's mother had never been filmed. We found her living in a sanitarium. She was senile and could not be interviewed, but we got permission from the state to photograph her. We set up hidden cameras and took considerable footage, and she never knew we were there. During the production, Terry got permission from the estate to examine Marilyn's stored belongings. Opening the locked door to an old, dusty storage bin at the Santini Brothers facility in New York was like walking into the middle of her life. Among her possessions, Terry found a white piano that she had been given as a child by her mother. That white piano was the only possession she had kept her entire life. It was our Rosebud.

It took us nine months to complete the film, and when it was done, I had great difficulty selling it. It had cost more than $200,000, but I was confident we would eventually find the right place for it. A year later, ABC broadcast it to rave reviews, and Sanders and Strauss received an award from the Writers Guild for the script.

I had a very difficult time finding a sponsor for the film *The Really Big Family*. Someone suggested we find the biggest family in America and document their lives, which sounded like a great idea to me. UPI columnist Vernon Scott announced it and we got letters from across the nation. The Duke family of Seattle, Washington, consisted of the father and mother and their eighteen natural children. The father worked at Boeing and his wife stayed home. Well, with eighteen kids she didn't have much time to leave the house. The father supported the family on his salary by finding ways to economize, and that was our problem. They never bought brand-name products, only generic brands. They didn't shop at supermarkets. When they needed meat, the father would buy half a cow, slice it himself, and freeze it.

As they used no name-brand products, we couldn't find a sponsor. The film sat on the shelf for a long time, and I finally sold it to individual markets. The one brand-name item they owned was a car; there are no generic cars. And that car company sponsored the film on a local basis. While I lost money on this film, it was nominated for an Oscar as the Best Documentary, our fifth in a row, but once again, we lost.

Some smart studio executive saw this on TV and turned it into the motion picture *Yours, Mine and Ours* starring Lucille Ball and Henry Fonda, the story of a married couple trying to deal with their . . . eighteen children. We didn't get a dime for it.

Two decades later, we tried to make a second film about the Duke family to see what had happened to the eighteen kids. The answer was everything. Some of the kids had succeeded, others were living in poverty, and they just didn't want the attention.

Without doubt, the most unusual stunt we ever filmed appeared in Billy Friedkin's documentary about risk takers, *The Bold Men*. Friedkin was always on the cutting edge of technology and innovation. For his documentary about professional football, *Mayhem on a Sunday Afternoon*, he shot with seven cameras and sewed microphones inside players' jerseys, producing the most realistic footage ever done of pro football. And to emphasize the erratic beauty of the game, he used an original jazz score by organist Jimmy Smith. It was a great piece of creative filmmaking.

The Bold Men was the forerunner of all the stunt reality shows, in which people risked their lives, that later appeared on TV. In addition to a land speed racer chasing the sound barrier, Friedkin did a piece on a fourteen-year-old sharpshooter named Mickey Luguin Jr. Using the facet of a diamond ring as a mirror, he could look over his shoulder and shoot an apple off his father's head or shoot a cigarette out of his mouth. He could do the same stunts bending over and shooting through his legs. It was an incredible stunt—but still not the most amazing stunt we ever filmed.

Billy found a man who would jump out of an airplane without a parachute. The plan was that another sky diver would jump before him and be waiting in midair with a second parachute. This was definitely a bold man.

Everyone thought Friedkin was crazy for even considering this stunt, but Friedkin persisted. Finally, several people came to see me. "This is insane! We really shouldn't do this. We're throwing a guy out of an airplane. He could get killed! I'm sure there are laws against doing things like this."

I sat there, just thinking about it. I don't know where my response came from, but I replied, "So, we'll do it over Mexico!"

Friedkin was elated. As they left, I remember shouting after them, "Now make sure you do it over Mexico, but I don't want to know anything about it."

What we didn't know until later was that the sky diver had had an affair and married the wife of the other sky diver, the man who would be waiting for him with a parachute. Friedkin always thought that would have made a wonderful plot for an Alfred Hitchcock movie.

Setting it up was a logistical nightmare—somebody had to film it in midair, and we really needed to make sure we had someone shooting from the ground in case it failed. And we did argue with the sky diver about insurance. He wanted $500 and we only wanted to give him $250.

It turned out that putting on a parachute while free-falling is more difficult than the sky diver imagined. By the time he got it on, he was too close to the ground, and when he landed, he broke his foot. And we did break some laws. The pilot's license was suspended. And the man who jumped without a parachute was heavily fined—apparently the law is pretty clear that, when jumping out of an airplane, you must have two chutes, not zero. And we got in some difficulty for allowing this to happen.

While Friedkin was under contract to us, he was offered the opportunity to direct a feature starring Sonny and Cher, then the hottest act in the business. Although I had brought him to Hollywood and given him his start, I released him from his contract with the provision that, at some future time, he would direct a feature film for me for $10,000.

I still have that contract. Still unused. But I haven't forgotten it. And when the right project comes along . . .

Of all the 798 shows I made, of the thousands of hours of television programs and motion pictures we created, of the millions of feet of film we shot, one show stands out as the worst I ever made—*Do Blondes Have More Fun?* I make no excuses for it. I sold out. I admit selling out. This was the selling out of all time. But it was perhaps the easiest sale I ever made. Clairol wanted to do a show that would promote its hair products. Clairol's slogan was "Is it true blondes have more fun?" I gave them back their own slogan as the title of a documentary about blondes. How could they not like it? It did have a wonderful opening, though. The camera is on the back of a woman, with long blond hair, walking down the street. She has a great figure and her face is left to the imagination—but it is pretty easy to imagine that she is beautiful. She passes several men, and as she does, each one turns and watches her. Finally, at the conclusion of the credits, as the title comes up again, the woman turns around—it was comedienne Phyllis Diller, whose unattractive appearance was part of her act. Phyllis winked and said, "Blondes do have more fun!"

Not a beautiful sight, but proof that blondes do get more attention. That was the high point of the show.

It was always exciting to come to work. I ran the place, but even I didn't know what to expect when I showed up in the morning. We did it all, from the stories of the greatest moments in world history to daredevils jumping out of airplanes without a parachute. We did it all. And as it turned out, that was only the beginning.

SEVENTEEN

NO SUCH WORD AS *NO*

With my company's vice president
Auriel Sanderson (1977)

The most unusual sales pitch I ever made occurred in the office of Bud
Stefan, a vice president at the ad agency BBD&O, where I was speaking
on the phone to a top executive named Lymon Dewey at DuPont. I was
trying to convince him to sponsor the voyages of the underwater explorer
Jacques Cousteau and his ship, the *Calypso.* I began my pitch at 4:45 in
the afternoon and continued until 5:15. I stressed the mystery and the
beauty of the world beneath the oceans. I emphasized the value to a great
corporation, such as Du Pont, of being associated with a great explorer
like Cousteau. I sold the excitement of the great killer sharks, giant
whales, and giant squid. This was a classic pitch. And finally, after ram-
bling on for more than a half hour, I paused to ask, "So what do you think,
Mr. Dewey?"

A strange woman's voice responded, "Hello, Mr. Wolper?"

"Yes? This is Mr. Wolper. Where's Mr. Dewey?"

"Oh, Mr. Dewey left fifteen minutes ago."

"What? What do you mean he left? Didn't he hear my pitch?"

"He heard some of it, but he left at five o'clock."

"Yes, but I was talking," I said.

"I understand, but it was five o'clock and Mr. Dewey always leaves the office at five o'clock."

Right in the middle of my brilliant sales pitch, this executive had quietly put down the telephone and left. He walked out on a telephone call!

I put down the phone and started laughing. I couldn't stop laughing. I had never heard anything like that.

As it turned out, Du Pont did agree to sponsor half the shows, which, obviously, made complete sense because he'd heard only half my pitch.

It would not be possible to define my job at the company. Basically, I turned ideas into films. But in five places during production, I specifically exercised control: I worked on the original theme outline, the shooting outline or script, the rough cut, the final cut, and the final script. Nothing went out the front door until I was satisfied it represented the best work we could do. I did whatever else was necessary from negotiating contracts to soothing damaged egos. I helped select narrators. On occasion, I pitched in to work with the film editors. I motivated. I supervised. And I knew when to get out of the way.

Obviously, I didn't do it myself. I have the ability to pick the right people. Like Mel Stuart, who was crazy as a loon, but a terrific producer. Jack Haley, who kept the strangest hours of anyone I knew, but, somehow, always got done what needed to be done and was a storehouse of Hollywood information. Alan Landsburg, who could put a show together as well as anybody in the business. And men and women who wrote, filmed, directed, edited, scored, and did the technical work on all the shows.

But I got most of the publicity. Every program that we did had my name on it, and because of that, some people criticized me, at the time, for taking credit on all of our shows. I thought that was unfair. We were selling a brand name and that name was David L. Wolper Productions or "Presents" or "Company" or "Incorporated," but it was always David L. Wolper. The way we built the company was by promoting that name.

I earned the right to put my name big and bold on the building. When I produced and directed my first documentary, *The Race for Space,* I gambled everything that I owned that I could sell it. When we made *The Making of the President, 1960,* we went way over budget. If we hadn't sold it, I was bankrupt. I spent money that sometimes was very tight—

money that didn't really need to be spent—to produce a program that was acceptable to my standards. The Wolper style, I called it. Make a program that entertains and informs.

I have heard people claim there was no such thing as "the Wolper style," that I was fortunate enough to have hired talented people who did quality work. Yes. I did hire talented people, and we received nine Oscar nominations for films done by seven different producers. Although they were all Wolper shows, seven producers received nominations. That was either some great coincidence or I actually had something to do with those shows. In fact, every one of those films had the same overall dramatic feeling, as well as the same dedication to accuracy and quality.

The Wolper name, eventually, became synonymous with top-quality work. When someone left the company, having the name Wolper Productions on their résumé made a huge difference. Almost inevitably, they got a job right away. I knew how valuable the name was. I knew it because I paid for it. In 1964, I sold the company to John Kluge at Metromedia. That gave us the funding support of a major corporation. When I left several years later to form an independent company, I paid Metromedia $500,000 for the rights to the name Wolper Productions. And I thought it was a bargain, because I was buying a respected brand name. My own.

But the whole system depended on my ability as a salesman. And I could sell. The great producer Stan Margulies once said with respect, "David can sell anything—even if it's good!"

Sometimes, when I was selling, I would be so focused that I didn't even realize what I was saying. One night, I remember, I was watching a documentary about Paris, and it occurred to me that a musical tour of Monaco, hosted by Princess Grace, would make a great television special. That Grace Kelly had retired from show business and never appeared on TV did not deter me. If I could get her to do the show, I, certainly, could sell it. Rupert Allen, her public relations man, set up a meeting with Her Serene Highness for me and Jack Haley at the palace in Monaco. We met with Princess Grace and Prince Rainier in a small salon. "Your Highness," I told her, "I'd like to do a musical tour of Monaco and Monte Carlo, and I would like you to lead this tour. It would be great publicity for Monaco. You wouldn't have to do any singing or dancing. You'd really just be the host."

As I was talking to her, Prince Rainier was talking quietly with Jack Haley. Haley was reputed to know every beautiful woman in Hollywood.

At the time, the hottest club in the world was the Daisy, and Prince Rainier wanted to know all about it. "There are many beautiful women at the Daisy, are there not?" he whispered to Haley.

I didn't hear a word of that conversation. I was selling Princess Grace: "It wouldn't take long, only a few days of your time over a two-week period . . ."

Meanwhile: ". . . and you know many of these beautiful women?"

Princess Grace was reluctant. Finally she asked, "David, do you really believe an American audience will appreciate this show? Will people watch this show?"

"Your Highness," I responded confidently, "when they see this show, they'll drop their pants."

Perhaps, as Haley claimed, the foundations of the entire monarchy did shake when I said that. As we drove back later, he scolded me. "You actually told the princess people would drop their pants!" were his exact words.

"Well," I said, not quite understanding his problem, "they will, won't they?" But, in fact, I didn't even remember saying that.

Princess Grace asked a lot of questions, most of which I answered. Finally she said, "If the script is acceptable, and the performers are acceptable, I think I would be prepared to do it."

I was thrilled. "Your Highness," I said, feeling quite benevolent, "I would also be prepared to donate one hundred thousand dollars to your favorite charity."

"Well, David," she replied softly, "my favorite charity is me."

And then Prince Rainier added, smiling, "Wolper, do I get scale?"

Her Highness was a tough negotiator. There is nothing like a beautiful princess explaining that she wanted a piece of the profits. Fortunately, I convinced her to take a net profit; not gross. She got 50 percent.

For several years, I was represented by the William Morris Agency. An agent there convinced me I could make a lot of money producing TV situation comedies. He introduced me to a brilliant young writer named Jimmy Komack. Together we produced two television sitcoms, *Chico and the Man* and *Welcome Back, Kotter. Kotter* was created by Alan Sacks and comedian Gabe Kaplan. It was the story of a teacher, returning to the neighborhood in which he had grown up, to teach a group of tough kids. Komack cast all the roles, including Kaplan, and a young actor named John Travolta, and we made a pilot. The networks make hundreds of pilots each year, but few of them get on the air. That was my job.

At ABC, Fred Pierce was one of the executives who made that decision. Each year he would come to L.A. for staff meetings, then return to
New York to screen all the pilots, meet with executives and producers,
and begin to plan the following season. Producers stood in long lines to
see him for five minutes. Getting an appointment with him to pitch a
pilot was almost impossible, but I had my own plan. I found out exactly
when he was flying back to New York and I booked the seat next to him
on the plane.

Well, imagine my surprise when I, casually, got on that plane and
discovered I was sitting right next to Fred Pierce. The very man I was
going to New York to meet. I had his complete attention. For four and a
half hours I sold this show—young people will relate to it, the music is
going to be great, it's everybody's favorite teacher great-looking boys
the girls will love. Pierce was listening to me, or he was in a complete
daze. But by the time we got off that airplane, I was confident that ABC
was going to put *Kotter* on the air.

Which is exactly what happened.

On occasion, I did have to make a great sacrifice to sell a program.
But when necessary, I had a valuable assistant, my wife Gloria. She is a
very smart and charming woman, and just as important, resourceful.
One year, she and I planned to have our yacht in New York for the selling season. The yacht was the gimmick. We hired a talented chef and
made plans to have top network executives to dinner on our yacht
every night for almost two weeks, as we circled Manhattan. Unfortunately, the day we arrived in New York our chef quit.

We had dinner plans with the most important people in TV for
eleven consecutive nights and nobody to cook dinner. This was beginning to shape up as an episode of a bad sitcom.

It was hard to find a chef. Good chefs are very much in demand. We
finally hired someone, but we really didn't know much about his ability.
Gloria taught him how to cook lamb chops with green peas and a baked
potato, a salad, chocolate pudding and make coffee. She worked with him
until it was perfect. And for the next eleven nights—every night—we ate
lamb chops with green peas and a baked potato, a salad, chocolate pudding, and drank coffee. Every night.

Everyone who came aboard loved the dinner. However, they didn't
have to eat it eleven nights in a row. That was the kind of sacrifice I made,
willingly, for my business.

EIGHTEEN

NOBODY'S PERFECT

Me with Betty Freidan (1981)

I must admit, I didn't sell every idea. I have a long list, a very long list, of unsold ideas and concepts that I remain convinced would make wonderful programming. Some I didn't sell for obvious reasons: One network executive asked if I had a story about a handicapped person and I said, "Boy, I have the greatest story of all for you. Helen Keller."

Helen Keller, who was born blind and deaf, overcame those handicaps to become a noted writer. This executive looked at me and asked, "Who's that?"

On another occasion, I was having lunch with Ted Turner and suggested a show about the Ten Commandments, showing how each had affected someone's life.

I knew I was not going to sell that series to him when he replied, "I don't believe in God."

I had the National Spelling Bee under contract and, unsuccessfully, tried to sell it as a special for several years. In 1972, I almost sold a weekly series entitled *Chess with Bobby Fischer.* A show I was certain I would be able to sell was *Miss Television USA,* a weekly half-hour beauty pageant in which we would stage contests in each state and then bring the winners together for a two-hour special culminating in the selection of Miss Television USA. For some reason, I couldn't sell it.

In 1970, I signed a three-year exclusive contract with America's fifty active astronauts to produce a series of specials. Among the programs I had planned were *Apollo 11: The Eagle Has Landed* and *Apollo 13: The Day the World Was One.* No matter how hard I tried, I couldn't sell that series. This was less than two years after we'd landed on the moon, but nobody was interested in space stories. I was never able to sell it.

I made twenty-nine movies for television. But several movies I developed never got made. I bought the rights to the book *One Hell of a Gamble: The Secret History of the Cuban Missile Crisis* between John F. Kennedy and Nikita Khrushchev. It was written by Yale historian Timothy Naftali, who tells the American side, and for the first time, what went on on the Russian side is told by Aleksandr Fursenko, a member of the Russian Academy of Science and one of the Soviet Union's leading historians. The book moves back and forth between Kennedy and Khrushchev. The book even had a great villain, Fidel Castro, who was apparently urging Khrushchev to bomb the United States. It is one of the most dramatic stories I've ever read. The world could have ended October 22, 1992.

Maybe I should have tried to show the networks that the end of the world would have been good for their business, because they just weren't interested in this project. My failure to sell it is one of the two biggest disappointments I've had in the TV business.

I was equally disappointed by my inability to sell Gerald Posner's book detailing his investigation into the assassination of President Kennedy, *Case Closed.* Posner was an investigative journalist who had been hired by a major publisher to examine in depth all the Kennedy assassination theories. He persuasively argued that Lee Harvey Oswald acted alone. This well-researched, highly detailed book served as a response to the intellectually dishonest garbage produced by Oliver Stone. But when I tried to sell it, all three networks told me it was just too boring if there was no massive plot to kill the president. Posner seemed to have made one big mistake—he debunked all the conspiracy theories. Basically, the networks were saying there was no story if there was no story. So I decided to make it as a documentary. But no one was interested in it as a documentary either. For years, I have heard people say, knowingly, that we will never know the truth about the Kennedy assassination. The truth is, we already know the truth. But it is more fun to believe there exists some great mystery that will never be solved.

I bought the rights to several best-selling books, certain that the networks would be excited about turning them into prestigious motion pictures, among them Betty Friedan's classic thesis on the role of women in America, *The Feminine Mystique*. This was the book that launched the feminist movement. I figured this was a slam-dunk sale; sponsors crave a large female audience, and this movie certainly would deliver that. The way I envisioned this movie, every woman in America was going to want to watch it.

Sponsors reacted to *The Feminine Mystique* with about the same enthusiasm as a vampire has for sunlight. In the book, Betty Friedan complained that advertisers reinforced the image of the subservient woman by always portraying her in the home, happily preparing meals, waiting on her family, and cleaning the house. Friedan wondered why female lawyers couldn't be depicted in commercials arguing in front of a judge in a courtroom, for example. Well, as I discovered, the answer to that was that sponsors did not believe female lawyers bought laundry products or breakfast cereals or soaps and cleansers. The only women's movement the agencies were interested in led directly to the super-market.

I tried for years, without success, to sell that book. In February 1965, ABC agreed to broadcast it. They announced, "TV cameras will . . . attempt to capture the opinions of American women . . . women will be able to tell the cameras what their role in life and the country should be." But sponsors did not want to be told what women wanted, they wanted women to continue wanting their products. Betty Friedan, one of the great people I know, became a good friend. She would, on occasion, go with me to meet a potential sponsor. But still no luck. Later, in an article in a major magazine, she mentioned me as one of the top ten men who understood what the women's movement was all about.

Admittedly, not every idea was perfect. A writer named Clifford Irving claimed to have met with reclusive billionaire Howard Hughes and collaborated with him on his autobiography, which he sold to a publisher for a small fortune. This was a major news story. Hughes hadn't said a word in public for many years. Even *Life* magazine bought an excerpt. But Hughes came forward in a telephone hookup to major news organizations and denied ever meeting Irving. The whole thing was an elaborate hoax. Irving was convicted of fraud and sentenced to two and a half years in prison. But the book was still a great read, so I optioned it and attempted to sell it as fiction. *The Billionaire—the Untrue Story of Howard Hughes* would have made a wonderful movie, but apparently I was one of the few people to believe that, because I couldn't sell it.

I optioned two books and planned to produce them. I brought them to two major writers and I believe they stole them. One was an unpublished book called *All the Conquerors,* by Howard Livingston, about an automobile family from their early lives to the building of a giant company. I asked Harold Robbins to work on the television show with me, and shortly thereafter he wrote *Betsy.* Another book I optioned was *The Great Endurance Horse Race* by the great western writer Jack Schaffer. It was about a horse race across the country. I presented it to the great action writer-director Richard Brooks. Years later he did a film about a great cowboy race. It may be coincidence with both, but I never believed it.

It took me a long time before I gave up on what I believed was a good idea. I spent almost four decades trying to sell *The Encyclopedia of the 20th Century in Sight and Sound,* the complete visual record of the century. Over the years I tried to convince Charles Bluhdorn of Gulf and Western, Charles Benton, whose father owned the *Encyclopaedia Britannica,* and Steve Ross at Warner Bros. In the 1980s, I met with everyone from Warren Buffett to a top executive at a small company named Microsoft. I knew it was a good idea, and every time I went back to the idea pile, it was right there on top

Time passed and history kept happening, making it more expensive to produce. But we made technological leaps to VCRs, cheap cassettes, and DVDs, making it less expensive to distribute. The concept changed, it expanded, and it evolved. I persisted. Although it took the turn of the millennium for people to understand how valuable this could be, more than thirty years after coming up with the idea, three divisions of Warner's joined with me and Bob Guenette to produce *Celebrate the Century,* a ten-hour program featuring the greatest events of the twentieth century—many of which hadn't yet occurred when I first tried to sell it. In addition, we produced another ten-hour miniseries, *Legends, Icons & Superstars of the 20th Century,* about fifty great people.

I didn't only fail to sell many programs, I also turned down the Beatles and Graceland. When the Beatles were making their first tour of America, their manager, Alan Epstein, asked me to document it. Unfortunately, he wanted it to be work-for-hire, meaning he would own the film. I turned down that offer.

In 1981, we were making a full-length theatrical documentary, *This*

Is Elvis. As there existed almost no footage of his early life, we did a lot of re-creations, filming extensively in the actual locations. Producer-directors Andrew Solt and Malcolm Leo auditioned hundreds of Elvis impersonators, although sometimes it seemed like thousands.

I had worked out, with Colonel Tom Parker and Priscilla Presley, that we would be the first people permitted to film inside Presley's house, Graceland. They had not yet opened Graceland to tours, so it was pretty much exactly as it had been the night he died. Elvis's underwear was still in his bureau; the shag carpet was still on the floor of the bathroom in which he died. While we were there, one of the coexecutors of the estate approached producer/writer Andrew Solt and asked him, "Do you think Mr. Wolper would like to buy Graceland?" Andrew Solt thought he had misheard the question, but the man continued, "We're definitely thinking about selling it. We have a major problem with the finances. There's no income. We can't even pay the taxes on the house."

They were looking for $10 million. It seemed like a lot of money for that house, but it was a cultural landmark. I immediately called my former classmate from Columbia Grammar Steve Ross, the chairman of Warner Communications.

Steve Ross turned it down, one of the few mistakes he made in his career.

"We're not in the amusement business," he told me, "it doesn't work for us." I didn't push him hard. One of the biggest mistakes I've made in my career was not buying it myself. The value of Graceland is incalculable, but if you had to calculate it, it has earned at least a quarter billion dollars.

NINETEEN

A COMPANY IS KNOWN
BY THE COMPANY IT KEEPS

Meeting with famous historians, including Daniel J.
Boorstin, Dr. James McGregor Burns, Dr. Bruce Catton,
Dr. John Garraty, Dr. Eric Goldman, Mr. Walter Lord,
Dr. Richard Morris, Dr. Arthur Schlesinger, and
Dr. Barbara Tuchman (1973)

In spite of a few miscalculations, I sold enough shows and films to keep the company in business. Among the early lessons I learned in selling to the networks was the value of associating myself with respected entities. It was a lot easier to sell a show about the history of flight, for example, if it carried the name and stature of the Smithsonian Institution. I did a series of specials in partnership with the National Geographic Society, the Smithsonian Institution, Time-Life, American Heritage, and Reader's Digest. Those organizations brought with them a presold audience, credibility, and respect.

In 1964, the National Geographic Society approached me to form a partnership to produce a series of nature and travel documentaries.

The Geographic had been sponsoring research expeditions to the most exotic and unusual places on earth for almost a century. They had an extensive film library, but didn't know how to turn it into programming. This was adventure from the top of Mt. Everest to the bottom of the ocean.

I knew it would be hard to sell it to the networks. This was the closest I had yet come to the traditional nature and travel documentaries. Network executives reacted to words like *nature* and *travel* with only slightly less excitement than they reacted to phrases like *big losses* and *no audience.* And if we did them the way they had long been done, the networks would be right. But I thought, if I could inject the form with real drama, we could produce something exciting. At CBS, a young executive named Fred Silverman was becoming head of programming, and he understood the potential. He also realized he had little to lose; to serve their duty to the public—and avoid all fears of being branded monopolies—the networks occasionally ran documentaries produced by their news departments. And almost always, the ratings were dismal. So, Silverman and CBS president Bob Wood decided to take a chance.

I was able to find two sponsors for the series, the *Encyclopaedia Britannica* and Aetna Life Insurance, so the network was not taking a financial risk. These programs were the first reality-based nature documentaries to be broadcast in prime time. My partnership with the Geographic lasted ten television seasons, and together we produced twenty-seven specials, including some of the most awe-inspiring—and entertaining—documentaries ever done. They were popular. CBS broadcast the first Geographic, "Americans on Everest," September 10, 1965. Eventually, they began running on the Public Broadcasting System, and our final show together, "The Incredible Machine," an exploration into the human body, was the highest-rated program in PBS history—attracting more than a third of all viewers.

National Geographic was more of an adventure series than nature documentaries. True-life drama in documentary form. There were moments captured on film that I will never forget. One of the first shows we did was "Miss Goodall and the Wild Chimpanzees," the extraordinary story of naturalist Jane Goodall, who lived among the chimpanzees in East Africa. The program chronicles her attempts to make contact with these animals. Finally, in one scene, she puts out her hand, and in response, a chimp puts out its hand and touches its finger to hers. It is a powerful scene, strongly bringing to mind the detail from Michelangelo's Sistine Chapel ceiling in which God's touch brings Adam to life and mankind is born. Jane Goodall had earned the trust of these animals. Few things I have ever seen in my life had the emotional content of that footage.

There were similarly powerful scenes in "Dr. Leakey and the Dawn of Man," in which famed anthropologist Dr. Louis Leakey and his wife, Mary, searched for evidence of human evolution, for more than thirty years, in the mountains of Africa. In July 1959, Mary was poking around on a cliff and brushed aside some scrub. And there she found a human skull and two teeth. She cried out with joy, believing that she had discovered links to mankind's distant past.

These fragile pieces were sent to the University of California at Berkeley, where geologists used a carbon dating process, normally employed to determine the age of rocks, to determine the age of these fragments.

The Leakeys are seen waiting by the telephone for news that could, quite literally, change all the theories of evolution. Finally, the test results are reported: Mary Leakey's discovery is nearly three times older than any other proof of human existence previously found, dating back 1.75 million years. It is an extraordinary moment of triumph and relief, and both Louis and Mary Leakey collapse in tears of joy and disbelief.

Some of the shows we made caused considerable controversy. We did a show for the Geographic entitled "Journey to the Outer Limits," about a group of twenty teenagers in an Outward Bound program who learn important lessons about life while climbing a mountain in the Peruvian Andes. A brief article appearing in *Ms.* magazine, quoting a young woman featured in the show, claimed, "The crew decided that none of the females would be filmed at the top because a shot of a woman making the ascent would diminish the difficulty of the task. Instead [she] was asked to fake a scene in which she was forced to stop because the climb made her dizzy."

For reasons I never understood, *New York Times* television critic John O'Connor actively disliked most of the work we did. I felt, as a journalist, he was irresponsible. I never objected to legitimate criticism, but too often his was inaccurate or based on misleading information. Without checking the accuracy of the story in *Ms.* magazine, O'Connor became critical of the whole program. In fact, the story wasn't true—it was absolutely false. No one was held back, and later, the woman claimed she was misquoted. She denied it completely. Other young women on the trip came forth and said the story was not true. But we were criticized for it, and even after the truth came out, John O'Connor never retracted a word. The show was nominated for an Oscar in the feature documentary category.

One Geographic film we made did turn out to be completely false— as we and the National Geographic Society were hoodwinked by one of the great scientific hoaxes of the twentieth century. In 1971, a hunter on the island of Mindanao supposedly made the greatest anthropological discovery of the century when he walked into a clearing and encountered the Tasaday tribe, the last vestige of the Stone Age. The tribe consisted of two men, six women, and fourteen children living deep in a rain forest in the Philippines. These gentle people had never been exposed to civilization. They had no words in their primitive language for war, weapon, or enemy. They were living as their ancestors did, six thousand years ago, wearing loincloths, making fire by friction, using primitive tools of stone and bamboo.

It was truly an amazing discovery. To protect this tribe from being exploited, the Philippine government of President Ferdinand Marcos created a forty-six-thousand-acre preserve, which included extremely valuable timber and mining lands, guarded by the army. National Geographic did a long cover story about the Tasaday in the magazine, then filmed with us a remarkable documentary about this fragile link to prehistoric times, "The Last Tribe of Mindanao." The documentary was supported by study guides for students and quite a bit of publicity. Newspapers and magazines around the world did stories on the tribe.

And except for the fact that the whole thing was a fraud, it was a wonderful story. In 1986, after the fall of the Marcos government, a Swiss journalist named Oswald Iten discovered the tribe living in frame huts, sleeping on beds, wearing Western clothing. They confessed that they had been paid to pose as a Stone Age tribe. The whole scam had been set up to allow Manuel Elizalde, a minister of the Marcos government, to wrest control of the valuable timberland for private business interests. Elizalde escaped to Costa Rica with $35 million. Eventually, he squandered the money and died destitute. The National Geographic Society had been hoodwinked.

Initially, executives at the Smithsonian Institution were reluctant to make a full commitment to television. While in 1974 we made three successful documentaries with the Smithsonian, we had a fundamental disagreement over our programming objectives: we wanted to attract as large an audience as possible, they wanted to impress academia.

The Hope Diamond, which carries with it a curse that misfortune will befall the person who possesses it, has been in the Smithsonian since 1958. It has a wonderfully colorful history, dating back to 1642, which includes Louis XIV and Marie Antoinette. We planned a show entitled "The Curse of the Hope Diamond." It took twenty-eight meetings and a Smithsonian committee before they agreed to the format of the show—and insisted we change the name to *The Legendary Curse of the Hope Diamond.*

The third show we did together was *Monsters! Mysteries or Myths?*, an investigation into the existence of the Loch Ness monster, the Abominable Snowman, and Bigfoot. The Smithsonian did not want us to make this documentary—these monsters don't exist, end of story. Producer Bob Guenette convinced them that these creatures were an important part of cultural fascination with unsolved mysteries. Reluctantly, they agreed, and we did a balanced show: we offered enough support for those people who wanted to believe these creatures existed and debunked their existence for those people who did not.

We did a lot of interviews with people who believed they had seen these monsters; we investigated photographs and amateur footage. We were able to explain almost every sighting—but not every one of them. While we knew it was a well-made show, even we never anticipated the audience reaction. Narrated by Rod Serling, *Monsters! Mysteries or Myths?* remains the highest-rated documentary in television history. And with the fragmenting of the audience because of cable stations, it will never be eclipsed. We had an incredible 44 share—meaning almost half the people watching TV that night saw this show. Those would be very strong numbers for an entertainment program, but it was amazing for a documentary.

But at least one person didn't really like it much. Bob Guenette got a phone call from a Bigfoot hunter in Oregon warning us that a man who considered himself the expert on Bigfoot was on his way to Los Angeles to kill both of us. He felt we had distorted the facts to prove Bigfoot did not exist. Whether Bigfoot existed or not, this man had a gun and was supposedly driving to Los Angeles. It was difficult to make the police understand that someone might be trying to kill us because we'd cast doubt on the existence of a monster, but in any case he never showed up.

Perhaps the most famous theatrical documentary series ever produced was Time Inc.'s *The March of Time.* From 1935 to 1951, Louis de Rochemont produced two hundred short, timely documentaries, almost 10 million feet of film, which were shown in movie theaters. They were approximately twenty minutes in length and were a combination of newsreels and re-created scenes based on real-life events that were performed by people who looked like the political figures, scientists, artists, military leaders, and other celebrities selected for these issues. The name of the series was ingrained in American culture, and I thought we could bring it to television. In 1965, in collaboration with Time-Life, and under the direction of Alan Landsburg, we produced eight one-hour programs on subjects ranging from pop science to great adventure. But we did not use the same re-creation technique that *The March of Time* used because, for the moment, re-creations were not an acceptable form for reporting or for documentaries on television networks. We explored research into brain function and mind control in "Frontiers of the Mind," and we told the history of the automobile in the "Odyssey of the Automobile," and the history of flight in "The Epic of Flight." At one point, I had a great idea: I remembered that a newspaper had sent Stanley into the jungles to search for Dr. Livingston, and I found no reason filmmakers shouldn't conduct a similar search. Except, in our case, we decided to send filmmaker Wally Green into the jungles of Paraguay to search for infamous Nazi Dr. Joseph Mengele.

"The Search for Vengeance," the attempt to track down escaped Nazi officials, had Wally Green working for months following rumors, hints, and leads in search of Mengele, finally tracking him to a small town. Wally managed to get only a brief shot of someone identified as Mengele escaping back into the jungle in a small boat. Just a few feet of film. That footage was used many times without our permission by news organizations and other filmmakers and was always identified as Mengele. Years later we discovered that the man was probably not Mengele but, rather, a local doctor. However, as the program was as much about the continuing search for escaped Nazis, rather than the capture of one man, it was still a valid story.

George Plimpton was the cultured, extremely articulate founder of the literary magazine *The Paris Review,* who gained fame by going through training camp as a quarterback with the Detroit Lions football team and describing it in the best-seller *Paper Lion.* This upscale Walter Mitty format, the sophisticate-out-of-his-cravat, worked extremely well, so it occurred to me that we should let Plimpton sample other unusual occupations.

We began with a special in 1967 for Bell Telephone, *The Musical Life of George Plimpton,* in which he played the triangle for Leonard Bernstein in the New York Philharmonic. His participation allowed viewers to learn what life is really like inside a great orchestra. This was the human side of music—the cellist had eleven kids, the piccolo player once starred in a rodeo with cowboy star Hoot Gibson—and it worked beautifully. In the concert, Plimpton only had one note to play. When Leonard Bernstein pointed to him, he was to hit the triangle. Unfortunately, in rehearsals, Plimpton never got it perfect. He was always a split second too early or too late. While most viewers or listeners would never notice it, in the mind of a genius like Bernstein, that split second was crucial. Bernstein was frustrated. But during the concert, Bernstein pointed at Plimpton and he hit his note perfectly. We concluded with a wonderful shot of Bernstein with a big smile on his face.

We did seven specials with Plimpton over four years from 1968 to 1972 under the direction of William Kronick. These shows were armchair adventures: Plimpton as the football player who gets buried by huge defensive linemen in his one play, Plimpton as the circus acrobat who does a somersault on the flying trapeze, Plimpton as the bad hombre in the movie western *Rio Lobo* who gets beaten up by John Wayne, and Plimpton riding a race car in the Baja 500. The only show we didn't do is Plimpton doing something really dangerous—like being a bill collector for a retail jewelry store during the Depression.

TWENTY

THE OLD MAN AND THE SEA

With Jacques Cousteau

As advanced communications and transportation made the world smaller and smaller, it became more difficult to find new places to explore. Through the years, we did many shows re-creating the adventures of explorers from Cortés to Peary. But the very few true explorers, those people who risked their lives to go places where humans had never been before, were running out of earth. One of the few people who spent his entire life exploring an uncharted world was the magnificent Jacques-Yves Cousteau.

Few people are aware that Cousteau was a filmmaker many years before he coinvented the Aqua-Lung. He started making films underwater with a home movie camera in the 1930s, staying beneath the surface as long as he could hold his breath. Then he tried breathing underwater through a pipe, and when that proved inadequate, he adapted a regulator, used to control the flow of cooking gas to automobiles during World War II, to feed oxygen to divers. With his coinventor, Emil Gagnan, Cousteau tested the unit in January 1943 in a river just outside Paris. After a modification, they patented the Aqua-Lung. Now, with the Aqua-Lung, Cousteau and Gagnan had opened up the vast underwater world to human exploration.

"We first met the peaceful Mediterranean fish," Cousteau once explained, "and it was much later that we encountered our first sharks and barracudas. By that time, we were already at ease in the sea. We knew there were no monsters. I thought life under the sea would be even easier than on land. We were the aliens there and, as such, would not be recognized as prey, especially with our rubber suits. We were nonviolent, and very early on, we dropped our weapons. We had only a piece of wood we called a shark bully, to push sharks a little farther off if they came too close, and it worked very well."

I had met Jacques Cousteau when we did a documentary with him for the National Geographic Society, *The World of Jacques-Yves Cousteau*. While not yet famous, he was known for his Oscar-winning documentary about life under the ocean, *World Without Sun*. When the National Geographic documentary we produced with Cousteau was broadcast, I was watching it at home with my wife, Gloria. It was stunning. "Look at that," I said. "On TV, the fish look like they're in a fishbowl. This would make a great series."

I never wanted to do just one show with anyone; I was always trying to create a series of shows. By the time I met Cousteau again, I'd come up with the perfect concept for him: explore the entire world underwater.

He took me to visit his ship, the *Calypso*, a converted minesweeper that had once belonged to the Royal Navy during the reign of King George V, but had been given to Cousteau in 1951 by Lowell Guinness, of the beer company. I am rarely less than honest in business; the job of the producer is to get it right, not to win a popularity contest. "Jeez," I said, as nicely as possible when I saw this boat, "it looks like shit." If you're going to do a television show, I explained, you have to create exciting visual images. The ship has to look exciting. The dive suits can't be all black because they can't be seen underwater, and the equipment needs to be high-tech. I told him he needed to jazz up the whole world of Jacques Cousteau.

Cousteau was as smart and clever as any man I've ever known. He understood immediately what I was talking about and began making plans. "But this is very expensive, David," he told me. "You're going to have to sell twelve shows."

I was always the most optimistic person in the room, but . . . a dozen specials? "Let me try to sell four," I suggested, "with an option for eight more."

Cousteau was adamant: "For four shows, I can't even get going." To modernize the *Calypso* and his equipment, he needed a substantial amount of guaranteed money.

I returned to New York and found sponsors for twelve shows—including Lymon Dewey at DuPont. But I had to find a network to broadcast those shows. NBC wasn't interested, they had not heard of Jacques Cousteau; and CBS would only take six. Coincidentally, when Cousteau and I had lunch at the St. Regis Hotel in New York to finalize our deal, Tom Moore, the president of ABC's entertainment division, happened to be sitting a few tables away. Moore was a member of the Explorers Club of New York, so he was well aware of Cousteau. He invited us to have dinner with him at the club that night, and the club members seemed quite excited to meet Cousteau. Weeks later, after some difficult negotiations, Moore offered me the kind of deal that makes television history: He was on the Explorers Club committee to find a speaker for the annual dinner. If Cousteau agreed to speak at their big dinner, he'd broadcast all twelve shows. The ultimate example of food for thought. "Give me an hour," I told him.

It was the middle of the night in Monaco. I woke Cousteau and outlined the deal for him. He immediately agreed. And that is how we brought Jacques Cousteau to American television and the world. The first program on sharks premiered January 8, 1967.

Maybe I got him the opportunity, but Cousteau beautifully exploited it. He refitted *Calypso* to make it a state-of-the-art wonder—including a helicopter landing pad. He designed new dive masks and added a bright yellow stripe to his dive suits. He developed exotic submersibles to enable divers to move easily and rapidly under the sea, and all kinds of new equipment. He made scuba diving appear to be a safe and beautiful adventure.

Cousteau took *Calypso* on a three-year journey around the world. Alan Landsburg produced the first of the shows we did together. I'll never forget the day Alan screened the rough cut of the first show for Tom Moore and the head of programming, Len Goldberg. ABC was very much the third network at that time; it did not even have in-house facilities for screening two-track film, so we rented a dubbing room. What we didn't know was that this place specialized in dubbing X-rated films. It was the smallest, shabbiest, smelliest room Landsburg had ever been in. The room itself was X-rated.

The equipment was as bad as the room. The sound track was completely out of sync with the picture. Landsburg tried three times to get the audio in sync with the footage, but just couldn't do it. Tom Moore was furious. This thing is a disaster, he said, and stormed angrily out of the screening room.

When Alan reported this to me, he said, "I swear to you nothing is wrong. Just put out the fires and let me finish the show." A week later, Alan delivered the finished show. After ABC screened it, Moore wrote a nice note of apology.

I only did the first four specials with Cousteau. After completing those shows, I ended my arrangement with Metromedia, and with that went the rights to the Cousteau series. But the shows I did laid the ground-work for the many years of programs Cousteau would produce through-out his lifetime. In those programs we did, we always went for drama, for adventure. But one show about life on a coral reef seemed too tame. It wasn't terrible, but nothing exciting was happening on the screen. We didn't know how we were going to attract an audience, but Landsburg came up with the solution: we titled the show *The Savage World of the Coral Jungle*.

I had great admiration and respect for Jacques Cousteau. He was exactly as he appeared to be on the screen, a brave man who believed, passionately, in what he was doing and loved the oceans of the earth. He poured most of the money he earned from the shows back into *Calypso* or his museum or his expeditions. He was among the first people to bring attention to the terrible damage we are inflicting on the oceans and spent the rest of his life leading the crusade to save this environment.

Cousteau was a tough guy. He was a tough businessman, tough on the people who worked for him, even tough on his own family. Who knows what drives people. He was a taskmaster. He wanted things done when he wanted them done, and he wanted them done correctly the first time. We got along well because we were equals with the same objective. And we also had much the same philosophy. "I find poets closer to the truth than mathematicians or politicians," he once said. "They have visions that are not only fantasy; they are visions that for some reason they cannot explain are an inspiration that guides them and brings them, by hand or pen, closer to the truth than anybody else. I believe we should follow poets more than anybody else in life. It's the light, it's the star we should be guided by."

Eventually, Cousteau did more than seventy specials, becoming one of the most respected adventurers—and environmentalists—of the century. And when he was inducted into the Television Hall of Fame, I was extremely proud that he asked me to introduce him.

Cousteau's own crew produced most of the footage used in the specials. The film was delivered to the office and one of his assistants, usually his son Philippe, worked with editor John Soh and my staff from the beginning of postproduction to the day it was broadcast. But my crews also shot the footage for the shows we did—often under the most difficult circumstances. Few people have more courage than a committed documentarian. The cameramen, the producers in the field, these people were dedicated to telling the story and were willing to endure whatever was necessary to get the footage they wanted. They traveled to the ends of the earth, literally.

Of all the films I've made, the Jacques Cousteau specials have been seen by more people in more countries throughout the world. These shows are certainly nonpolitical. They don't require a tremendous amount of translation, and people everywhere are intrigued by the world beneath the sea.

Many years later, Philippe Cousteau was killed as his helicopter crashed rising off the deck of the *Calypso*. The loss of his son affected Jacques Cousteau for the rest of his life. He never got over it. Had Philippe lived, the adventures of the *Calypso* might have continued when his father died. But with Jacques Cousteau's death the *Calypso* went into port, where it sits, rusting, today. Unfortunately, Cousteau's heirs were involved in many lawsuits over his name and assets.

To re-create Admiral Peary's race for the North Pole for our Appointment with Destiny series, we took a crew to the Arctic Circle—in December. The whole expedition was extremely well planned, down to the last detail. Unfortunately, the last detail was that there is little daylight at the Arctic Circle in December. At most, they had two hours of acceptable lighting a day. With the windchill factor, the temperature hovered between eighty and one hundred degrees below zero. The actors and crew had to watch out for each other, and at the first sign of frostbite, filming stopped immediately. So, in the best of circumstances, they had less than two hours a day to shoot.

We had hired several Eskimos, who knew how to live in this environment, to work with the crew. At one point, producer-director Bob Guenette asked one of the Eskimos if they had problems with anything. "Sure," the Eskimo replied, "it's fucking cold up here. That's what we have problems with."

During Peary's trek to the North Pole, several members of his team had been separated when an ice floe broke off and began floating away.

We had to re-create this dramatic moment. We decided to use dynamite to break off a large piece of ice. Guenette's crew used ropes and hooks to make sure they could maintain control of the newly created iceberg. "It never occurred to us," Guenette recalled, "that we didn't have the slightest idea what we were doing with these explosives. We put our actors and dogs at the edge of the ice, blew off a large piece, and started filming as it drifted away. Fortunately, we were able to pull it back. No one got hurt, but I think we were very lucky."

The less predictability there was, the more these filmmakers seemed to enjoy it. Most of them wanted to be in the middle of the action. While shooting *The Story of a Fireman*, Vilis Lapenieks strapped himself to the front of a fire engine as it raced through the streets to capture the feeling of racing to a fire. For the climax we set fire to an old house—Lapenieks put on a protective uniform and went inside to shoot the firemen coming inside. The fire raged out of control, and at the last minute, the firemen grabbed him and pulled him out the window into a bed of foam. The footage was incredible—but getting it almost cost our top photographer, Lapenieks, his life.

It has often been said that Ginger Rogers had to do the same difficult dance steps as Fred Astaire—but she had to do them backward and wearing high heels. Documentary crews have to endure the same hardships on an expedition as everyone else—while transporting and caring for equipment, which in those days was big, bulky, and heavy. For the Geographic's "Journey to the Outer Limits," our crew had to climb a mountain—lugging cameras and equipment with them. At about fifteen thousand feet everybody got sick—and an Outward Bound instructor went berserk. He literally went mad, declaring himself the producer-director of the program, screaming, "I'm running the show, I'm running the show." They had to tie him up for an entire day until he calmed down. When they came down from the mountain, he was diagnosed as suffering from oxygen deprivation due to the altitude. During one of the Geographic specials, our film crew was taken captive by rebels in southern Ethiopia. All their equipment was stolen, and they were held for weeks. We tried to get the U.S. government to help us, but no one could do a damn thing about it. Fortunately, they were finally released.

TWENTY-ONE

A NIGHT TO FORGET

The last photo of some of the Wolper crew who were lost
in a plane crash (*l to r*): Anthony Mazzola (obscured),
Al Kihn, Dennis Azzarella, Robert and Janos Prohaska
(March 13, 1974)

Considering all the productions we did, all the risks taken by all the
filmmakers, we suffered only one great tragedy. But the enormity of that
disaster was overwhelming. On March 13, 1974, I attended an American Film Institute dinner honoring James Cagney. I'd left a little early
and had just gotten home when famous entertainment columnist Army
Archerd called. "David, have you heard?" he asked. "A plane with all
your people aboard crashed into the mountains."

In this way began the worst night of my life, as well as many other
lives. I immediately went to the office. Other people from the company,

having heard the news, began wandering in. I think everybody just needed to be there.

The details followed quickly. Thirty-one members of our crew shooting an episode of a series called *Primal Man* had been killed when a Sierra Pacific airliner crashed into the top of a foothill in the White Mountains near Bishop, California. *Primal Man* was a four-part series about the evolution of mankind. Ironically, they had just completed principal photography for an episode entitled "The Struggle for Survival." The plane had taken off from Bishop Airport on a clear, moonlit night, climbed smoothly and seemingly without difficulty into the black sky, and for some reason no one will ever know crashed into the mountain and exploded.

The plane missed clearing the mountain by no more than thirty feet. That's all, thirty feet. This remains the most devastating accident in the history of the entertainment industry. All of us were in a daze that night. It wasn't just that we knew all these people—they were each of them part of each of us. This crash affected everybody in our industry.

The first decision I made when I got to the office was that I would make all the phone calls to the families, except in those few instances where someone had a personal relationship with that family. I was told, by either the National Transportation Safety Board or the FAA, not to do anything until it was verified that there were no survivors and we knew with certainty the names of the people on that flight—and then I was to call the next of kin. "What do I say?" I asked. I had never been at a loss for words in my life. We had to find the phone numbers of the families that night, and a whole group of individuals, headed by Auriel Sanderson, my assistant, were calling friends and prior colleagues. Information supervisors were looking for names of parents of film crew members whose friends only knew they came from Florida on the Gulf coast. The operators checked every name in every beach town until we located the right family. The staff worked on getting me numbers all night and through the next morning, without a break.

Make sure you're speaking to the right person, I was told, don't give any information to anyone until you are certain you are speaking to the next of kin. Then, without delay, I was to identify myself, then tell them the facts. I was told that most of them would ask "Are you sure?" I was to respond that I was positive. The worst thing I could do would be to hold out any hope.

It was awful, terrible. We learned that one member of the crew had missed the flight, and we had to wait hours to identify that person before making any calls. Waiting, having nothing to do but anticipate the reaction to these calls, made it even more difficult. Once we knew for sure who had survived, I picked up the phone.

Nothing I've done in my life was more horrifying than calling a wife or a husband or parent to tell them that their spouse or their son or their daughter was dead. "This is David Wolper," I said, is this . . . ? I'm afraid I have the sad task of telling you that your child has been killed in an airplane crash this evening."

Inevitably, they screamed. I still hear the screams. Then, just as I had been warned, they asked if I was certain. "Yes," I said, "I'm certain, there's no hope."

I spoke to each person as long as they wanted to talk, then hung up and dialed the next number. Person after person. Scream after scream. Tear after tear. After each phone call, I leaned back in my chair and tried to catch my breath. I wanted to make the calls as rapidly as possible, to get done with this as quickly as possible, yet I had to rebuild my resources before making each call. Knowing what response to expect made the task even more difficult. How do you wake someone up in the middle of the night to tell him or her that his or her life will never again be the same? That a person they loved will not be coming home?

Meanwhile, we were receiving calls from different agencies. One agency needed dental records to assist in identification of the bodies. The FBI called; because *Primal Man* was about the evolution of mankind, the bureau wanted to know if we had received any threatening letters or phone calls from fanatical religious groups. They just wanted to make sure this was an accident and not sabotage. We had received no such letters.

We stayed there until four in the morning. Feeling totally helpless.

The next few days remain a blur of activity. Tributes to these people poured in; we received more than five thousand letters and telegrams. We held two memorial ceremonies and tried to work, but it was tough, very tough. The first memorial service was held at Forest Lawn, and we invited a reporter from KTTV, Larry Atterberry, to speak at the service. He had written an unusual, poignant piece the day after the crash: "Those of us who have the high honor and responsibility to report the news sometimes treat the tragedy in a rather professional, detached manner. We give the facts and figures, names and hometowns, and go on to the next story with hardly a second thought.

"[But] this was not just another plane crash. This was a personal story. The thirty-one members of the Wolper film team were members of my profession and . . . each one of them had touched my life and yours through their talent. As I talked with the other newsmen and women at the scene . . . it turned into a sort of family meeting. Comments of 'Oh, my God, I worked with her last year,' or 'He was one of the finest cameramen in the business,' or, 'I can't believe it. His baby is just three months old.' That scene was repeated in my office and at other television stations and production houses and movie studios all over town. Suddenly, it was clear to me that, not only those of us in the business had lost, you have too. The wonder of the National Geographic specials, the Wolper magic in showing life as it is, the humor of a dancing bear and a thousand other shows. Each of us has been enriched by their enormous talent. We may not know their names or even what they did, but all of us, anyone who goes to the movies or watches television, suffered a big loss. A lot of fine talent died on White Mountain last night."

Amen. Even all these years later, amen.

After the crash, producer Malcolm Leo wanted to go up to the site just to see it. He was going to be our own reporter. I don't know what we expected to know, but we needed to know it. He flew to the top of the mountain in a helicopter. The entire fuselage had been destroyed by fire—with the exception of the tail section. Apparently, when the plane hit the mountain, it had flipped over and the tail section had separated and been tossed forward, spewing what appeared to be a trail of debris. But it was luggage and personal effects. Malcom Leo began collecting these items—and as he did, he discovered equipment that had been in the compartment. He found viewfinders, camera equipment, and rolls of unexposed film still in the metal cans. He found film cans three hundred, four hundred feet from the crash site. One film can was found hanging on the side of the mountain caught in a bit of cactus; another was just hanging over the edge of the mountain. He brought it all back.

We didn't know what we had, whether it had been damaged. But not one frame of film was damaged. Every frame was intact. Everybody died, but their work survived. Looking at that footage was chilling. The last shot, taken just for fun, showed the whole crew going down the hill in massive snow tractors—waving good-bye to the camera. It was impossible to look at that film and forget, even for an instant, that, with only one exception, everyone pictured had died suddenly and tragically.

The cause of the crash was thoroughly investigated. The captain had flown in and out of this airport several times and was familiar with the terrain. Toxicology tests on the crew members revealed absolutely no evidence that they were in any way impaired. The engines were working well. "Therefore," concluded the National Transportation Safety Board, "it is difficult to conceive of any problem with the aircraft that could have caused the flight to deviate from a safe flight path. . . .

"The NTSB is unable to determine the probable cause of this accident. The reason the flight crew did not maintain a safe distance from hazardous terrain, during night visual flying conditions, could not be established."

We finished the film and broadcast it with a tribute to those people. In many ways it was a tribute to all of the documentarians who have, so willingly, risked their lives to record the truths of life.

These are the men and women who died on the White Mountains that night:

Rick Ackerman	William Miller
David Ayvazian	Howard Perlman
Dennis Azzarella	James Phillips
Ronald J. Brandt	Giovana Piazza
Irene Burnde	Irving Pringle
James H. (Rusty) Carter III	Janos Prohaska
Gene Darval	Robert Prohaska
Ronald J. Dickson	Lorin Raymond
Jay Fishburn	Joel Rosen
Alan Hoffman	William J. Savoy
Donald H. Jacob	Mary Skolnick
Robert Jones	Steve Solon
Al Kihn	Charles Sorkin
Billy Lucas	Gary Spero
Anthony Mazzola	Jackie Tang
Rolf Miller	

TWENTY-TWO

LET'S NOT KILL THE POLAR BEAR

Baby polar bears in the film *Say Goodbye* (1971)

Not shooting a polar bear became one of the most controversial things I've ever done. Or didn't do. And perhaps changed the history of documentary television.

At one of our concept meetings, someone suggested we do a documentary about endangered species. We realized immediately it was a strong idea. Animals sell. People love animals. People like to help animals. That entire species of animals were being threatened with extinction was a worthwhile—and commercial—concept to report on. Personally, I knew little about endangered species. On occasion, I went to the zoo with my three kids, Mark, Michael, and Leslie, and that was about the extent of my knowledge of wild animals.

Say Goodbye, as it was titled, was developed in association with the World Wildlife Fund. Quaker Oats agreed to sponsor the program and distributed considerable supporting material explaining what individuals could do to save the species being destroyed by the actions of mankind. It was a powerful film. The message is clear, as composer Dory Previn wrote in our title song: "share this world or say good-bye." We showed films of prairie dogs being shot, baby seals being clubbed to death, pelicans dying, horses being killed—and polar bears being shot by hunters flying in helicopters. Every fact in the film was absolutely true. Among our sources was *American Heritage* magazine, which warned, "For the past few years, light planes, boats, and snowmobiles have been taking hunters to the polar ice cap in such numbers that the polar bear may be threatened with extinction. The animal is being killed as never before."

When I read in the outline that hunters were shooting polar bears from the air, I knew it would be extremely dramatic footage—but as we discovered, that footage did not exist. Hunting polar bears from airplanes is illegal—and no one dared to be filmed committing a crime. We were told that the only way we could photograph it was to actually do it, actually shoot a bear. So, I was in the paradoxical position of having to shoot a polar bear to make a film against the shooting of polar bears.

My response was considered: Are you out of your fucking mind? No one in the Wolper Organization is going to kill a polar bear to provide footage for a TV documentary. Not only was it illegal, it was ridiculous. Someone suggested that we demonstrate it. We could shoot the bear with a tranquilizer dart, and it would look as if it had been shot by a rifle. But within several minutes, the bear would recover and it would be perfectly fine, and we would have the dramatic footage we needed. This would demonstrate an illegal act without committing the act ourselves.

The plan worked. We didn't even have to do it ourselves. We researched and found existing footage of a polar bear being shot with a tranquilizer. Seconds after being shot, the bear collapsed. Its two cubs looked sadly into the camera, turned, and started running. It was as if Bambi had been killed.

Say Goodbye ran on NBC. At the end of this four-minute segment, narrator Rod McKuen said, "Polar bears have two advantages over other threatened animals: they have nothing we need and live where we can't. For them, life is good. At home in the hostile climate, the polar bear has, for centuries, taken for granted its freedom in the Arctic—but, no more. No other creature on earth kills for less—a fur rug for the den, a head mounted over a bar. Grieve for them—and for us."

After the film was broadcast, the National Rifle Association attacked us with its arsenal—and few organizations have more weapons than the NRA. Nowhere in this film did we say, or even imply, that we were against hunting or in favor of gun control. I met with an executive of the NRA—at their request. At this meeting this executive told me the NRA hated, absolutely hated, Walt Disney, because his movies gave personalities to animals, it made them seem to be all warm and cuddly. Finally, gun clubs suggested hunters boycott Quaker Oats because they had sponsored the film.

When the NRA learned that we had used footage of an anesthetized polar bear rather than an actual killing, it had the ammunition it needed to attack the credibility of the entire film. The National Sportsmen's Club announced that its proposed boycott of all Quaker Oats products would remain in effect until the company publicly initiated efforts to repair the damage done by its biased, one-sided, emotionally phony presentation.

As famed naturalist Roger Caras wrote, "The special interest groups, hunting lobbies specifically, have attempted, through an incredible campaign of insinuation, to discredit the entire presentation. . . . They are attempting to insinuate that, because of one four-minute sequence that was reenacted, the entire fifty-three-minute film was false. . . . *Say Goodbye* told a larger truth than its detractors care to deal with."

The resulting controversy was not about the fact that hunters were using aircraft to track down and kill polar bears, but rather that we had sullied the documentary form and destroyed our own credibility by re-creating this event. If there was a moment that long-established conventions about making documentaries ended forever, this was that time. People had come to believe that documentaries pictured actual events as they occurred, rather than simply reflecting reality. That had never been true. With the birth of the network news departments, they had set rules about no staging. But they were doing news events. Documentaries do not have to be, necessarily, news events. Throughout the long history of documentary filmmaking, reporting the truth had often required staging events. That didn't make the events depicted less accurate.

More than a century ago, documentary filmmakers had combined actual footage with staged footage to tell the story of the assault on San Juan Hill by Theodore Roosevelt and his Rough Riders during the Spanish-American War—and helped elect Roosevelt president of the United States. The staged footage didn't make Roosevelt's heroism any less true; it simply captured events that could not be filmed as they occurred. Re-creating events necessary to the truthful telling of a story became an accepted convention of documentary filmmaking. Cinema verité, which, by definition, uses only real-time footage, is only one form of documentary filmmaking.

Even the legendary documentarian Robert Flaherty re-created

events. He basically told the Eskimos he was filming, "Remember how you made that fire yesterday? Do it again today—but this time, I'm going to photograph you doing it." In *Nanook of the North* he paid Eskimos to perform actual rituals for his cameras. He filmed hunting parties and insisted they use harpoons, though Eskimos, by this time, were using rifles rather than spears. As intrusive as the camera sometimes seems, it simply can't be everywhere at all times.

Some of the most dramatic moments ever filmed turned out to be re-creations. When General Douglas MacArthur waded ashore in the Philippines, fulfilling his dramatic pledge "I shall return," there were no cameras on the beach. So, MacArthur turned around and returned again—this time for the cameras of history.

Incredibly, the gun lobby was able to muster enough support to cause the Special Committee on Investigations of the House of Representatives to hold hearings. Even these many years later, this remains a terrifying memory: Congress investigating filmmaking. I was handed a subpoena, which ordered me to produce just about everything relating to the making of the film, every piece of paper, every frame of footage. At just about the same time, another congressional committee was investigating CBS for its documentary *The Selling of the Pentagon*. Neither CBS nor NBC complied with the subpoena, claiming First Amendment rights. But I did give to Congress all the material relating directly to the polar bear sequence. "*Say Goodbye* is a cinematic documentary essay," I explained in a letter to CBS president Frank Stanton. "It is not a news report or a news documentary." If it had been, I wouldn't have given them even a used gum wrapper.

In another letter, this to Ken Mason of Quaker Oats, I wrote, "We are also dedicated to the view of John Greerson, one of the world's most highly respected documentarians, who invented the word *documentary*, and who declared, 'The purpose of the documentary is to make observation a little richer than it was by the creative interpretation of actual reality.' The techniques used in this film were also used in Walt Disney nature films . . . and a host of other distinguished nature productions."

This was clearly an attempt to exert enough pressure on the networks to prevent them from showing controversial programming. It didn't work. The networks were completely cleared and no action of any kind was taken against my company. In fact, while outdoor writers, meeting at the annual trade show of the National Sporting Goods Association, voted *Say Goodbye* "the worst conservation film of the year," Quaker Oats and Wolper Productions received more than fifty thousand letters from viewers supporting our position and requesting additional information. As a topper, it won an Academy Award nomination for Best Feature-Length Documentary. Even the Oscar nomination proved controversial, and hunting groups organized to have it rescinded. That failed. We didn't win—but even receiving the nomination was a great victory.

As a result of this controversy, from that time on every nature documentary on NBC and the other networks concluded with a statement saying, generally, "This is a documentary film essay. Whether actual or created, all the scenes depict authenticated facts."

We were extremely careful when re-creating reality to make certain it was reality. I have always been aware of the power of film to shape opinion, record history, create knowledge. But it can just as easily be used to distort history—create false knowledge—and still shape opinion. Moving images can be dangerous when manipulated by talented people to further their own beliefs. Leni Riefenstahl's *Triumph of the Will*, the story of Adolf Hitler's visit to Nuremberg, is perhaps the greatest propaganda film ever made. Events picturing hundreds of thousands of cheering people were staged for her cameras. The documentary form carries with it the unstated premise that what the viewer is watching is an accurate reflection of reality. To use this form to create false impressions is the basis of propaganda and is clearly intellectual fraud—and something we never did.

PART III

Changing Directions

Actor Billy Fricke in our docudrama
The Plot to Murder Hitler (1972)

TWENTY-THREE

ROOTS OF THE DOCUDRAMA

On the set filming "Showdown at O.K. Corral" (1972)

Looking for a new way to tell a story, we decided to use the techniques of documentary filmmaking to depict the great events of history, and to take the techniques of television documentary storytelling to a new level. We knew we would be criticized, and we weren't disappointed.

The concept was simple: In a decade of documentary filmmaking, we had practically exhausted the best sources of stock footage, so it occurred to me that we should create our own. We would use re-creations to fill the gaps in a story, to tell the stories of history where no film existed.

The plan was to do entire pictures as if they had been filmed in real time by cameras on the scene. For example, the true story of an actual robbery by John Dillinger was filmed as if it were being recorded by a security camera inside a bank. As far as we knew, no one had ever attempted anything like this before.

Bob Guenette and I worked out the entire first script. Our original concept was to tell the story of jewel thief "Murf the Surf" and the heist of the "Star of India." In New York I pitched the concept to the advertising agency representing Quaker Oats. It was obvious during our meeting that they liked the concept but not the idea of Murf the Surf. I had to come up with an alternative idea on the spot. Afterward, I called Bob Guenette and told him I had good news. "We sold the concept, and the first show is the murder of President Lincoln."

"They've Killed President Lincoln" became the basis for a series entitled *Appointment with Destiny,* in which we told historical stories as if cameras had been present to film them. We were making new "old" documentaries. We were not the first company to present history as it might have been seen if television cameras had been present. Walter Cronkite's *You Are There* series did it live, actually stopping historical figures in the middle of the action for brief interviews. Our shows and our concept—what cameras would have seen—made them seem much more like traditional documentaries than TV shows. We were simply documenting events as would have happened if the technology had been available at that time.

Our objective was to re-create the suspense of history as it had been lived, with complete credibility, vividness, and factual authenticity. So, once again, we hired experts—this time leading historians—as advisers. For the Lincoln show, Pulitzer Prize–winning author Bruce Catton—the acknowledged expert on the Civil War—served as our consultant.

Eventually, we did seven *Appointment with Destiny* specials, ranging from "The Crucifixion of Jesus" to "The Last Days of John Dillinger." Where actual newsreel footage was available, we used it, then matched the quality and texture in our new footage. In most cases though, there wasn't any existing film. So, to make these documentaries seem more realistic, we altered or damaged the film stock to give it the appearance of age or misuse. When we did the Lincoln show, for example, we wanted to make it look as if someone might have found some footage in an old trunk in the attic of his house in Springfield, Illinois. That film would be scratched, dirty, and slightly decayed. So we dropped the footage on the floor and stepped on it, we used a sharp stylus to scratch it; instead of being careful with this film, we were intentionally careless. People thought we were crazy; even people inside the company objected. In addition, we used other techniques to age our film. For the Lincoln story, we colored all the film sepia; for the Crucifixion film we gave it a golden hue—religious gold we called it. Once, we got lucky. When filming "Peary's Race to the North Pole," producer Bob Guenette had problems with one of the cameras and the footage was blurred. For any other show it would have been useless, but we decided it looked as if we were shooting in a snowstorm and added that "snow" to other footage.

We made up our rules in the beginning and followed them rigorously. Our first rule was that these shows had to be filmed as if they were being shot by a newsreel cameraman on the scene. If a camera couldn't have been in a place in real life, we couldn't go there. Cameras certainly would not have been allowed in Lincoln's White House, for example, so when we wanted to shoot a scene of Lincoln speaking with his wife, we shot it through a window. It looked as if the camera were eavesdropping on them, rather than a simple staged scene.

We used every technique we could devise to duplicate newsreel footage. When we filmed "The Showdown at O.K. Corral," the story of the dramatic shoot-out between the Earps and the Clanton gang, we had the cameramen film it as if it were being shot from the window of a building right next door.

Sometimes it took real guts to do it this way. In 1944, several of Hitler's trusted officers tried to assassinate him by exploding a bomb in a Quonset hut. Hitler was wounded but escaped death. For the filmed assassination attempt, we actually blew up a Quonset hut with stuntmen inside. When the bomb went off, they were to come running out of the building. The cameraman wanted to focus on the hut when the explosion was detonated. This was the climactic scene, but director Bob Guenette insisted that the cameraman be shooting in another direction, and "as soon as it blows, you're going to whip around and grab the shot, as if you didn't know it was going to happen."

Guenette did not intend to film the actual explosion, explaining there was no justifiable reason a newsreel cameraman would have been focused on it. We had no second chance; it would be too expensive to rebuild the hut simply to blow it up again. The cameraman objected, suggesting that we use a second cameraman to "cover" the explosion. Guenette refused, saying that if we had that shot, somebody would insist on using it and that would destroy the concept. So, he didn't shoot it. We didn't have it. We couldn't use it—and the footage of the attempt to kill Hitler looked remarkably real.

As often as possible, we filmed at the actual site of the historic event. General Robert E. Lee's surrender at Appomattox to General U. S. Grant was filmed right at the Appomattox courthouse. Lincoln's assassination was filmed in the actual box in Ford's Theatre in which the president was sitting, at the precise moment in the play, *Our American Cousin*, at which he was shot. We even covered the street outside the theater with dirt so our carriages would be driving on dirt roads. The killing of gangster John Dillinger, for "The Last Days of John Dillinger," was reenacted right in front of Chicago's Biograph movie theater—on the thirty-seventh anniversary of his killing, on the same spot. To properly set the scene, we not only hid all the television antennas and restored the marquee of the theater—*Manhattan Melodrama* starring Clark Gable and William Powell was playing—we even changed the prices in the window of the local grocery store. The day Dillinger was shot, eggs were twenty-nine cents a dozen, rib roast was twenty-two cents a pound, and milk was ten cents a gallon. "The Showdown at O.K. Corral" was filmed where the Earps and the Clantons shot it out in Tombstone, Arizona.

Where historical facts weren't known, we made educated guesses. For example, no one knows how the citizens of Jerusalem, who lined the Via Dolorosa to watch Christ bearing the cross, were dressed. We did not know how to costume our extras. So, we gave cloth to our extras and let them make their own costumes—just as people did in Christ's time. When we filmed "Cortés and Montezuma: Conquest of an Empire," the story of the confrontation between cultures that changed the course of history, we had no idea what sort of costume the Aztec emperor Montezuma might have been wearing when the Spanish conquistadores landed in Mexico. We assumed it was elaborate and extremely colorful. One of our production assistants solved the problem: he found a gorgeous cape with colorful feathers being worn by a drag queen in a striptease parlor. We rented it for almost nothing—and Montezuma had his robes.

One of the first and most important decisions we had to make was whether the actors should speak. Many people felt strongly that these films would be boring if the actors never spoke. Then, someone wondered aloud, "What kind of accent did Christ have?" His point was made. Seeing Hitler argue with his generals in English would have destroyed the sense of reality. Finally, we decided the actors would not speak; the story would be told by a narrator and "man-in-the-street" interviews. This allowed us to cast, in leading roles, actors who looked closely like the historical figures. If they had no lines, we didn't really care if they could act or not.

We used a substantial amount of actual historical footage in "The Plot to Murder Hitler," which was mixed with the scenes we filmed, so our Hitler had to look identical to the real one. The resemblance between our Hitler, actor Billy Fricke, and "Der Führer" was incredible. Frightening really. When we filmed in Hitler's home at Berchtesgaden we had to put up ropes to keep back German tourists. People wanted to get their picture taken with him, or they wanted the actors dressed as SS troops to be photographed holding their babies. One older woman literally flung herself at Fricke and started crying hysterically, screaming, "*Mein lieber Führer, mein lieber Führer.*" She clung to him and would not let go. It was chilling.

After we finished filming, our "Führer" approached me with an unusual idea—he wanted to do a porno film starring as Hitler. I had no doubt there would be an audience for that film, but I wasn't going to make it.

We actually did too good a job making our film look realistic. It was so difficult to tell the difference between Adolf Hitler and our actor that we opened the program with a disclaimer: "The program you are about to see is a dramatized reenactment. All eyewitness characters identified by caption are actors, filmed at actual historical locations wherever possible in the style and technique of the period in order to match existing black-and-white newsreel footage. The official SS logo on film sequences is provided for dramatic purposes and does not denote authenticity."

We did such an exceptional job matching actual wartime footage that, several years later, I was watching a show about Hitler—and discovered that they had used our footage. They stole our created footage—but identified it as actual Nazi film.

This was precisely what critics were concerned about when these programs were broadcast. Obviously, no one was going to believe that our footage of the Crucifixion was filmed at that time, but with contemporary events—such as the attempt to assassinate Hitler—the line between reality and fiction was more easily blurred. We weren't trying to fool anyone, but obviously we did. And, the audience responded well to these films.

Our nemesis, *New York Times* critic John O'Connor, seethed with puritanical anger: "The area is something the producers have dubbed 'the re-created documentary,' and aside from the idea itself being pointless, the techniques employed are highly questionable, even dangerous. What is a re-created documentary? It is, in fact, pure fiction masquerading as reality. . . .

"*Appointment with Destiny* is a model of deception presented in the grainy black and white of old newsreel film. . . . In one scene . . . the real Hitler was juxtaposed with the fake Hitler anxiously poring over table maps." Unfortunately, O'Connor had no idea what he was writing about—the "fake" footage was actually real Nazi film.

I was furious with O'Connor because he never contacted us. He wasn't interested in learning what we did to ensure that every scene was historically accurate. Our adviser for the Hitler program was William Shirer, the author of *The Rise and Fall of the Third Reich.* Shirer had spent years in Germany covering Adolf Hitler and is certainly one of the world's most respected historians. Shirer approved every scene, every word, in our film. We didn't lie, we didn't cheat, and not one false sentence appeared in any of these programs.

O'Conner never considered the positive aspect of what we were doing by bringing history to life. Most of human history predates the camera. Even in modern times, many of the most significant moments of recent history were not filmed or the film was lost or destroyed. Yet the contemporary audience has become accustomed to receiving information visually. By focusing on the drama of history, rather than simply reciting the facts, we were telling exciting stories and attracting a new audience. Some of the documentary purists assailed us for daring to break convention, but television had created a new audience, and the old formats simply did not appeal to them anymore.

Many other critics understood completely and applauded our efforts. Cecil Smith of the *Los Angeles Times* wrote, "The creation of factual history in the theatrical language of television, by its very nature, could be a powerful and effective art form."

Eventually we won numerous awards for these shows. The *Appointment with Destiny* programs shattered forever the rigid historical documentary format and were the bridge to a new type of filmmaking, which became known as the docudrama. At one point these stories were being referred to as "historical dramas," or "theater of fact," but I always believed docudrama was an appropriate term. The docudrama was a natural extension of the re-created documentaries we had been doing, and it was a creation of the Wolper Organization. Probably the best definition of a docudrama is that it is a dramatization of a real incident or life of an actual person. It's a story based entirely on fact, reality in a dramatic format. The purpose of a docudrama is to convey the emotional feeling of what it might have felt like to be present at a moment in history. When people need dates and minutiae, they have always gone, and should go, to the more detailed written word.

Television is entertainment for a mass audience, and we tried to make programming that would attract as big an audience as possible. And as a by-product, we educated those people. We didn't make them experts, we didn't include every detail, we simply brought them information about a subject of which they might not have been aware. While being entertained, the audience learned about a piece of history or social life. They discovered what life was like at different times throughout history.

The docudrama had its origins in radio, which did reality-based programming like *Famous Trial Stories* and *The Big Story*, which relied on actual police, government, and journalistic case files. *The Armstrong Circle Theatre* brought dramatized history to television in 1955. According to producer David Susskind, this sixty-minute weekly series attempted to "combine fact and drama, to arouse interest, even controversy, on important and topical subjects."

But no one in TV history had ever done historical dramas with the care—and the budgets—that we had available to us. There were no guidelines, no rules, and no boundaries; we really made up the technique as we went along. We obviously were not the first people to make films about historical events or the lives of famous people; biographies had long been a staple of the Hollywood studios. But there were several significant differences between what we were doing and what previously had been done, the biggest one being that we insisted on historical accuracy. The studio-made pictures were, for the most part, melodramas produced for theatrical distribution, and they often included fictional events and characters added to enhance the story. The stories of people like Alexander Graham Bell, Thomas Edison, Lou Gehrig, Louis Pasteur, Émile Zola, and even Napoleon were only vaguely historically accurate.

We were accurate. We occasionally made mistakes, and when we did, viewers caught them. When we made "The World Turned Upside Down," the story of George Washington at the Revolutionary War Battle of Yorktown in 1781, for example, Washington was wearing a uniform that would not be designed for another half century. And in "Napoleon and Josephine" we mistakenly decorated a set with a Victorian chair.

We didn't pretend that we were telling history exactly as it happened. We knew we were making art. Filmmaking is subjective, not objective. This was the creative interpretation of reality. Every decision we made changed, in some way, the impact of our story. To tell a person's entire life literally would require a lifetime. We only had a few hours of airtime, so we had to select those moments and create scenes that would enable us to tell the story we chose to tell to the best of our creative ability. Our honesty in telling that story was based on our integrity. We had to hire actors and direct their performance, we had to light sets and add music, we had to write dialogue for scenes in which no one except the actual participants knew exactly what was said.

Creating dialogue is always difficult. If only two people are in a room, they are the only people who know what is said there. But, based on the result of that meeting, as well as historical documents, it is possible to speculate on the conversation. Through this means, we were able to capture the spirit of that conversation. We always did as much research as possible to get it right. And while we couldn't possibly re-create the precise conversations, we were always true to the impact of those conversations and history.

TWENTY-FOUR

BETTY FORD . . . NEZ PERCE . . . AND GOD

With Betty Ford (1987)

One of the most difficult but rewarding television movies we made was *The Betty Ford Story*, the story of President Gerald Ford's wife, who courageously admitted publicly that she had breast cancer, and then that she was addicted to alcohol and pills and had voluntarily checked herself into a rehabilitation clinic. Who knows how many lives she saved by courageously telling her story to the public.

It took me six years to obtain the rights to Mrs. Ford's story. Every year I tried to buy them, and every year my efforts were rejected. Finally, I wrote a long letter to her listing the reasons this film should be made. Paramount among them was that a movie focusing on her battle against addiction could help thousands of people fighting the same struggle. A year later she finally agreed.

This was not a pretty film. It depicted this elegant woman slobbering all over herself and embarrassing her family. But she insisted that we make it as accurate as possible. She wanted it to be perfect. The most important scene in the film showed the intervention—the night the Ford family, in the presence of a medical team, confronted the former first lady with her behavior. One by one the kids related incidents at which their mother was drunk and embarrassed them. Then the president described a political rally at which she had embarrassed him. The purpose of an intervention is to break down a person and make her accept that her behavior is out of control.

This was a powerful—and painful—scene. But Mrs. Ford insisted that we get it exactly right. As painful as it was to her, she wanted the dialogue to be accurate; she did not want us to create any phony story matter. Some people, I suppose, might legitimately criticize us for allowing our subject such involvement in this film. The danger is that the subjects can revise history to portray themselves in the most favorable light. In this case I didn't feel that way. This was her story, and she was probably rougher on herself than a dispassionate writer would have been. I readily admit we made some changes in our script to satisfy Mrs. Ford—and I don't regret it at all. The result was a powerful film detailing the descent into addiction and the recovery of a remarkable woman. To me, Betty Ford is a hero. I gave her the right to make changes; I wasn't interested in making a film that would hurt her. In fact, if I had been forced to choose between including material that would have been less than faithful to her story and satisfying the network, I wouldn't have made the film. Fortunately, I never had to make that choice. For her portrayal of Mrs. Ford, actress Gena Rowlands received an Emmy Award.

Working with Betty was difficult. In her zeal to make sure we told the true story—she did not want to be portrayed sympathetically—she was a pain in the ass. I spent countless hours with her discussing the most minor points. Ironically, in those arguments she was usually pressing for a more realistic, less favorable portrayal. She had agreed to make this film because she wanted other people to seek the help they needed, and to accomplish that, she wanted it to be as brutally honest as possible. She is a great lady and I admire her very much. She later referred to our battles as "constant bugging." And as her husband, former president Gerald Ford, wrote me, "It wasn't an easy project, but we feel the film will help others."

The docudrama format gave television filmmakers dramatic access to the greatest stories in world history. Television began creating a visual library of history, scouring the past to find sometimes forgotten but fascinating stories. The American Indian, for example, had rarely been the subject of reality-based programming. Most of the knowledge people had about Indians came from grammar school textbooks and Hollywood films portraying Indians as one-dimensional people who painted their faces and attacked wagon trains. Little had ever been done that reflected Indian culture.

Like many other people, I had a passing interest in the subject. Then my head writer came to me with the story of Chief Joseph of the Nez Perce, who had tried in vain to lead his people off the reservation to freedom and safety across the Great Plains, while battling the U.S. cavalry. The words of his surrender came to symbolize the defeat of the Native Americans by European settlers: "Hear me, my chiefs. I am tired. My heart is sad and sick. From where the sun now stands, I will fight no more, forever."

I Will Fight No More, Forever embodied the culture of a nation and served as an epitaph for a proud people.

The original concept to tell the Nez Perce story on film was suggested by writer Ted Strauss, a former *New York Times* reporter who had studied the subject for twenty-five years and had traveled most of the "trail of tears," the route the Nez Perce had followed when fleeing the U.S. Army. This was obviously a fresh, exciting, and potentially important project. We proposed it to ABC, and the network was as excited about it as we were. Strauss and Jeb Rosebrook wrote a wonderful script. We were in preproduction, meaning we were hiring the crew, casting the actors, finalizing the budget, and deciding where to film, when we were contacted by representatives of the Nez Perce. They had read about the project and were upset that the tribe had not been consulted. They wanted to be paid for the rights to the story.

The rights to history? I didn't know how to respond. We invited a representative of the tribe—a tribal elder—to Los Angeles to review the script. I made no promises, but I explained that we wanted the story to be accurate and would make whatever changes were necessary to accomplish that. I also suggested that we would cast some American Indian actors and that the tribe could make the costumes and supply the artifacts we needed. The tribal elder agreed. After the script had been read, I received a letter outlining their complaints. Among them: "(1) The fictitious names and portrayal of cultural practices are not acceptable. Historical errors are noted and should be corrected. (2) The movie is being filmed in a foreign country [Mexico], away from the actual sites that were involved in the conflict. (3) The majority of actors and extras are not Nez Perces." The letter also complained that the non-Indians were being portrayed too sympathetically.

We immediately corrected only historical errors. I explained that we had to film in Mexico because it was prohibitively expensive to shoot the movie in the United States. Obviously, I couldn't use Nez Perce in the leading roles because I needed professional actors; and I defended the portrayal of the non-Indian characters in the story as being historically valid.

Then the phone rang again. Another member of the tribe was calling. When I explained that we had reached an agreement with the tribe, I was told, "No, that was the Christians." The tribe had split long ago, and this person was representing the other segment of the Nez Perce.

I didn't know what to do. Finally, I told this person that we were willing to have one representative of the tribe on the set as an adviser—but only one person. The two sides settled on George American Horse, the founder and president of Native American Research Consultants, who worked with us while we were making the film. We also consulted other leading scholars on Indian history and culture to make sure our script was accurate.

In the middle of all these discussions with both sides of the Nez Perce tribe, Marlon Brando called me. I had never met him. He told me that he had learned of my problems with the Nez Perce and wanted to meet with me. I was delighted. I felt I had done as much as possible to satisfy the tribe.

Several days later, Marlon came to my office with Indian activist Russell Means. I was blunt with him. I told him I would use as many Indian actors as possible, including Indians from all tribes. I told him that I could not afford to shoot the movie on Nez Perce lands. I told him which experts had been consulted for the script. Brando and Means listened politely. They asked me to use as many Indians as possible on my production crew, and I told them to give me a list of Indians in the unions and I would try to use them. I doubt they were completely satisfied when they left, but I think they believed I was sensitive to the needs of the Nez Perce.

For the first time in an American film, the roles of Indians were going to be played primarily by Indians. Previously, Indians had been played by men with dark makeup and contact lenses. The key role, obviously, was Chief Joseph. The producer, Stan Margulies, finally narrowed his choice to three Indian actors. "We gave each of these men three scenes to study," Margulies remembered, "a scene with his wife, a scene in which he negotiated with the cavalry, and the scene in which he made his famous speech, which ends, 'From where the sun stands, I will fight no more, forever.' The first two actors were okay, but didn't knock us out. The third actor, whose mother was a member of the Blackfoot tribe and his father was Mexican, did the first two scenes nicely, but when he started to read Chief Joseph's speech, his eyes teared and he had to stop. He took a deep breath and then started again. This time when he reached the final words, he began crying. He paused again, apologized, took a moment to regain his composure, and started once more. When he reached the final line, he broke down in tears; he was so embarrassed he ran out of the room.

"I just sat there. I was stunned. Like every other kid, I'd grown up watching cowboy-and-Indian movies. I'd seen them all—and yet it had never occurred to me that an Indian would cry, could cry. I had grown up believing Indians were stolid, stoic, savages. I suspected most of America felt that way.

"The actor's name was Ned Romero. He returned to the room, read the part splendidly, and we cast him on the spot."

For Ned Romero this wasn't simply an acting job, this was his heritage, being portrayed in a realistic manner for the first time. Those words of Chief Joseph's weren't just rhythmic on the ear, they impacted his heart. If ever we needed a reminder than we had a responsibility to be accurate, this was it.

I Will Fight No More, Forever was sponsored by Xerox, which also supplied related study materials to schools and educational institutions. It was enormously successful, receiving a 45 share—making it one of the highest-rated TV movies ever to be broadcast on television. I think it also marked the beginning of a new understanding of the Native American way of life.

Naturally, critic John O'Connor found fault with it. He wrote that he had received letters complaining about inaccuracies. One letter he quoted was from the features editor of a college newspaper, who had written about Chief Joseph and was incensed by some of the "outrageous distortions" and added, "with questions of factuality mounting." Mounting? They were not even mole-hilling. The only questions about the facts were being asked by O'Connor, and he was simply repeating the claims of a college student without doing any research of his own. He didn't even bother to pick up the phone and call us to ask what proof we had, or what research we had done. Who knows what his motive was, though it was obvious that this letter supported his feelings that docudramas were potentially dangerous.

Screenwriter Ted Strauss responded to O'Connor with a letter of his own. It concluded, "I do believe that . . . I felt a far heavier obligation to the truth than did Mr. O'Connor, who on the basis of a minor detail from a college student, and on misinformation, impugned the entire film in his reckless and intemperate review."

We also contacted the *Times* and complained to several journalistic organizations. We didn't have to, the picture was clearly successful, but we had a reputation to protect. If it was suggested by a major periodical that we were careless with the facts, other projects might suffer.

In retrospect, it seems hard to believe that the introduction of the re-creations and docudrama caused such controversy. For a time, the networks adamantly refused to allow their news and documentary departments to use re-creations. Change was slow, but complete. Re-creations and docudramas became an important part of programming. The networks finally accepted that re-creations can be done honestly and are an important means of communicating information, and they began using them on their newsmagazine shows such as *20/20* and *Dateline*. It's just another means of telling a story.

O'Connor was right about his essential point: an inherent danger in the docudrama form that it can be exploited by irresponsible filmmakers. Oliver Stone proved that with his film *JFK*. Perhaps because I'd spent my entire career making sure my films were historically honest, I was outraged by the film. Stone is a talented filmmaker with questionable ethics. Thanks to *JFK*, impressionable young people may well grow up believing the government conspired to kill President Kennedy in a complicated plot involving the CIA, the FBI, and the Mafia, which is sheer nonsense. Numerous facts in this movie were simply wrong. The case Garrison presented was so weak that the jury deliberated less than twenty minutes—and only took that long because two members had to use the rest room—before dismissing all of Garrison's absurd charges. Garrison knew he had no case and was not even in the courtroom to cross-examine his key witness.

In 1975, *I Will Fight No More, Forever* was among the first original movies for television that we produced. The first original movies for television were broadcast in 1964 by NBC as part of a program called Project 120, which consisted of a series of two-hour movies—120 minutes—produced by Universal Television. It was considered a daring experiment at the time because conventional wisdom stated that people watched TV by themselves and it was highly questionable that anyone would be willing to sit in front of a TV set for two hours.

The first film produced originally for television was *The Killer*, starring Ronald Reagan, Lee Marvin, and Angie Dickinson. But when it was screened for NBC president Robert Kintner in his apartment, he decided it was too violent to broadcast. So a suspense film entitled *See How They Run* became TV's first original movie, running on October 7, 1964.

NBC remained the leader in world-premiere movies, as they were then known, for several years. In 1969, ABC aired *Seven in Darkness*, a drama starring Milton Berle as a blind plane-crash survivor, which introduced a new phrase to television—*the movie of the week*. ABC's *Movie of the Week* was the first regularly scheduled show consisting of a movie made for television. TV movies began exploring social issues in 1970 with NBC's *A Clear and Present Danger*, a film about the dangers of air pollution, and *My Sweet Charlie*, which focused on racial prejudice.

One of the first television movies we made—this was a "back-door" pilot, a TV movie that eventually became a series—was *Get Christie Love*, which turned into one of the most unusual situations in which I have ever been involved. Throughout my career I had worked with thousands of actors, and I believed I had heard of just about every possible problem—until we made this picture. Christie Love was a black policewoman and this was an action-adventure picture. The great actress Cicely Tyson was to play Christie Love, but two days before we were scheduled to begin shooting, I got a call from her agent, Norman Brokaw of the William Morris Agency, telling me that Cicely couldn't do the picture.

She wanted to explain her reasons to me personally, so I drove out to her home at the beach to meet her. "David," she told me, "I was standing right here, fixing this window, when I fell off the ladder and hurt my leg. I know that's a message from God telling me not to do the show."

Salesman that I am, I asked, "How do you know that it wasn't a message from God that you should do the show? I mean, it all depends on how you interpret it, right?"

Her interpretation was that God didn't want her to do this movie, and nothing I could say would change her mind. It's tough arguing with a message from God, especially when it isn't written down. A William Morris agent I could easily argue with, but God?

It was hopeless. Cicely was very nice about it. "I owe you one," she told me, but she was not going to do the picture. We had to find a replacement immediately, and we hired Teresa Graves, a wild, sexy, vibrant, beautiful woman who had become famous for having her body painted on the popular TV show *Laugh-In*. Teresa was thrilled to play the leading role and was wonderful as a policewoman. As played by Teresa Graves, Christie Love was a sexy, hip, black cop who also happened to be an expert in karate and a deadly shot. The movie was a big success, and ABC decided to turn it into a weekly series. Everyone was positive the show was going to be a hit.

While we were in series preproduction, with most of the scripts already written, Teresa Graves called and asked to meet with me. I had no idea what she wanted to talk about.

She had joined the Jehovah's Witnesses, she said, "And I can't do anything with blood or guns."

"What are you talking about?" I asked incredulously. "This is a police show."

She explained that the Jehovah's Witnesses have rules they must follow. There wasn't anything I could do about it—the network had bought the show with Teresa Graves. So, we agreed to a long list of rules for her character, among them: "There will be no obscenity or obscene speech in the body of the teleplay. There will be signs posted to warn performers and crew members that we will not abide obscenity or excessive language on the set. There will be no excessive violence, no sexual involvement, no use of homosexuality and lesbianism, and no portrayal of politics as the main theme of the teleplay. You will be given time off for Bible studies. You will not be asked to perform a blood transfusion, and you will not be asked to kill a person." And finally: "The end product will be considered for the positive force and the positive effect that it could have on viewers and that is the aiding of the needy and downtrodden, the moral lesson that crime does not pay and evildoers suffer."

Obviously, the story of a TV policewoman who would not resort to violence, who hesitated to use a weapon, was not a big hit with viewers. Clearly this series was going to be extremely difficult to do. So, I sold the property to Universal, and they produced the show for the one season it was aired.

Apparently God did not want me to do this movie, and He did everything possible to stop me. Well, either God or the devil. I guess the only real question I had was, Why didn't he stop me from doing *Blondes Have More Fun*?

One of the most important issue-oriented films we made was *The Morning After*, the story of a successful corporate journalist, played by

Dick Van Dyke, whose life is destroyed by alcoholism. What I did not know, when I sent the script to Dick Van Dyke, was that he was basically portraying himself—he is a recovering alcoholic. I remember that, after reading the script, he confessed to director Richard Heffrom he felt "like someone had been following me around." For his performance, Dick Van Dyke was nominated for an Emmy.

Perhaps the most unusual problem we dealt with was how to survive after your husband has assassinated the president of the United States, the subject of *Fatal Deception,* the story of Marina Oswald. When I'd first met Marina Oswald she—like me—believed that her husband had been the lone assassin. But by the time we completed the movie two years later, someone had convinced her that her husband had been a player in a conspiracy.

Eventually, television movies reached the point at which if the whole world wasn't threatened with extinction, nobody cared. *Without Warning* begins as an ordinary TV romantic comedy starring Loni Anderson and Ed Marinaro. Suddenly, we interrupted that movie for a special news bulletin—featuring journalists Sander Vanocur, Bree Walker, and Sandy Hill—that reported the approach of three giant meteorites threatening to crash into the earth. We had first pitched the concept of doing a television show on the world coming to an end to ABC twenty-five years earlier. They had liked the idea, and David Seltzer wrote the screenplay—but it didn't get made. Every few years I'd pitch it again to the networks, and finally, all these years later, CBS bought it. The script was rewritten and updated, but the basic idea remained the same. We made this as close to the actual broadcast of an impending catastrophe as technically possible, even interrupting satellite feeds from Europe with static as the asteroids came closer to earth. Although CBS ran a disclaimer every fifteen minutes, emphasizing that this was complete fiction, the network received hundreds of anxious telephone calls. Commenting on the gullibility of the American public, *Variety* wrote, "One would think that viewers should have become a bit more suspicious when the show kept breaking away in the middle of apocalyptic threats for toothpaste commercials. I mean, if the world was really coming to an end, they would have scrapped the commercials, wouldn't they?"

Television without commercials?

What surprised me most of all was that people didn't just simply turn the channel to confirm their fears. What did they think when they turned on ABC and saw it was televising *America's Funniest Home*

Videos? As someone suggested, they must have thought, "Oh, look, ABC's not covering the end of the world like CBS."

Most of our movies for television were based on true stories, many of them almost forgotten moments in history. *The First Woman President,* for example, was the story of First Lady Edith Wilson, who literally took over the duties of the presidency when her husband, Woodrow Wilson, became desperately ill. This movie was as much a tribute to Mrs. Wilson as a warning as to what is possible under our laws.

Certainly one of the most important two-hour films for television we ever made was *Murder in Mississippi,* the story of three young men, Mickey Schwerner, Andrew Goodman, and James Chaney, who went to Mississippi, in the summer of 1964, to join the campaign for civil rights and were murdered by Ku Klux Klan members. These killings shocked the rest of the nation into paying attention to the freedom marchers. *Murder in Mississippi* was written, originally, as a theatrical picture— meaning a big budget, major stars, and a release in movie theaters—but Gene Hackman's feature film *Mississippi Burning* was set during the same period. So Warner Bros. decided not to make it. I took the script to NBC; *Mississippi Burning* had reminded people of this tragedy, so the network decided, immediately, to make *Murder in Mississippi.*

How times change. We were invited to make this film in Meridian, Mississippi, where the murders had taken place. By now, the South was not trying to bury its past but rather to document it as part of its history. A lot of the things we made were basically product—they fit a need, they filled network time, they earned a profit—but I was extremely proud of this film. This was an important story, well told. As one reviewer wrote, "It is a heart-pounding film that climaxes with one of the most chilling scenes ever seen on television."

We were always searching for the drama in real life, and we found it in the courtroom. Stanley Kramer, who had produced and/or directed such classic films as *High Noon, The Men, On the Beach,* and two films about classic trials, *Inherit the Wind* and *Judgment at Nuremberg,* came to me with an idea for a series of movies about great trials. At that time, cameras were not permitted in the courtroom, and he wanted to dramatize socially significant trials using the actual transcripts. Eventually, ABC agreed to broadcast three films. The show was called *Judgment,* and each of the three two-hour films was directed by Stanley Kramer. The subjects were the court-martial of Lieutenant William Calley, the story of a twenty-seven-year-old army officer charged with murdering 102 men, women, and children in Vietnam; the trial of Julius and Ethel Rosenberg, who were convicted and executed for passing the secrets of the atom bomb to the Soviet Union; and the court-martial of the "Tiger of Malaya," Japan's General Yamashita, who became the first person prosecuted for war crimes, by the United States, for mass murders committed during the occupation of the Philippines in World War II. The scripts were actually edited transcripts of trial testimony. The Calley trial, in particular, was extremely controversial, as the Vietnam War had just ended but the nation remained bitterly split. To make sure we presented the case for both sides fairly and accurately, we hired the attorneys for the government, and for Calley, as consultants. Both sides approved the script.

Just to make the program a little more controversial, at the end Stanley Kramer made a statement in which he said, "Lieutenant Calley is guilty of what he did. But isn't it possible that all of us who oriented him, sent him into what was the violence of that place—all of us must share a little bit of what was the atrocity of Vietnam?" While we were making the Calley show, I remembered a conversation about the Vietnam War I'd had several years earlier with Teddy White. To win a guerrilla war, he'd said, when you go into a town, you have to be prepared to kill everybody there, and America just wasn't ready for that.

The Rosenberg trial remains one of the most politically controversial in our history, as many people still believed that the Rosenbergs were innocent. Later, information discovered in the Soviet Union proved their guilt. I don't think anyone ever believed *Judgment* was going to be a big ratings winner, but it was a fascinating look at history.

By the mid-1970s, just about the only kind of programming I hadn't produced was TV's most popular format—the half-hour situation comedy. We had even done sports programming, producing *This Week in the NBA* and *The NBA Game of the Week* for the National Basketball Association. But, until 1975, I'd never done straight comedy. Perhaps because of my background, it was just not a form that interested me. But, as I learned, a successful sitcom that runs long enough to be sold for syndication is the most lucrative form of programming. While I was fortunate enough to love what I was doing, I was also a businessman. If sitcoms were profitable, I wanted to be in the sitcom business.

TWENTY-FIVE

TWO HITS AND A MISS

With Freddie Prinze (1976)

One thing I have always been smart enough to know is my limitations and the limitations of my staff. I knew we needed the guidance of an experienced writer-producer to get into the world of comedy. The William Morris Agency suggested I team up with Jimmy Komack, who had written, produced, and appeared as an actor in several hit shows. Komack was terrific. We hit it off right away. He walked into my office with a list of forty ideas for sitcoms. One of them was the story of a nasty old white man whose Los Angeles neighborhood is being taken over by Chicano immigrants, and whose life changes when he hires a young, hip Mexican-American to help him operate his rundown service station.

Chico and the Man was Jimmy Komack's idea. The timing for it was perfect. America's ethnic complexion was changing. Hispanics were beginning to play a more prominent role in politics and culture; in a sense, this was the California version of *All in the Family,* in which Carroll O'Connor created the bigoted character Archie Bunker. Komack was also a good salesman, and together we made a formidable team. We pitched it to NBC and they bought it.

Casting the part of Ed Brown, "the Man," was pretty simple. Academy Award and Tony Award winner Jack Albertson, who had costarred in my film *Willy Wonka and the Chocolate Factory*, as well as my television version of the George Gershwin musical *Of Thee I Sing*, was an absolute natural for the role. Komack agreed right away. But finding the right Chico was much more difficult. We interviewed forty-one actors, many of them Mexican-Americans, Chicanos; we auditioned five of them and actually screen-tested three. Fourth on our list was a nineteen-year-old comedian named Freddie Prinze, who was just beginning to become known. One evening he appeared on Johnny Carson's *Tonight Show*, and he just blew away Komack. Jimmy called me right after the show screaming, "That's the guy, that's Chico." The next day I looked at the tape and agreed; more than agreed. Few people have ever been more perfectly suited to the role of the lovable Hispanic rogue than Freddie Prinze. The honesty and a joy in his humor just burst from his whole being. While some wonderful black comedians had poked fun at the different races, until Freddie Prinze began performing, the closest thing to a successful Hispanic comedian had been Bill Dana as José Jimenez— and I've wondered how funny Hispanics really thought he was.

Komack and I were convinced Prinze was our Chico. Now all we had to do was convince NBC that a nineteen-year-old kid, yet to be widely known, could carry a network sitcom. Komack arranged a screening for network executives and told me I had to come with him because, as he explained, "You can con them better than I can."

Serendipity entered my life again. During the screening, Dave Tebbet, an NBC vice president, happened to walk by and quietly ducked into the back of the screening room. Tebbet had a reputation as being able to spot young talent, so when he spoke, the network listened. When the lights went on, I got ready to make my pitch for Prinze, but before I could say a word, Tebbet asked loudly, "Who is that terrific comic? That guy's great, can we get him for NBC?"

Less than a year after graduating from New York's High School of Performing Arts, Freddie Prinze had his own series. He was so good the only real question was why it took so long.

The casting was announced and we began preparing to go into production. Everyone was excited about the show. Then my phone rang: the following day an organization of Mexican-Americans was going to protest the casting of Freddie Prinze. Prinze's mother was Puerto Rican and his father was Hungarian, making him, as he said, "a Hunga-Rican." The next day, Mexicans started picketing NBC. With so many real Mexican-American comics, they wondered, why did we have to cast a Puerto Rican? So many Mexican-American comics? Maybe there were more Mexican-American comics than there were Jewish quarterbacks, but believe me, there weren't many capable of carrying a television series.

It seemed as if every show we did that involved an ethnic minority resulted in a problem. What I did not know was that the difficulties I had with the Nez Perce and Mexican-Americans were little more than a rehearsal for what was to come.

I responded to the complaint by explaining that we had hired Freddie Prinze because he was the funniest guy we could find, and that, rather than criticizing our choice, they should at least appreciate that a Hispanic actor was starring in a major show. I didn't think it should make any difference what country he was from; he was Hispanic. And I pointed out again that, once the show got on the air, there would be many supporting roles for people from the barrio. If the show was canceled, those roles would disappear.

One of the people who seemed to agree with the protests was an associate producer at the Wolper Organization named Ray Andrade, a bright man and a Chicano. "I think the character of Chico is cheap and demeaning," he said. "I think the show has great potential and I am seventy percent happy with it, but there's a lot to explore in terms of authenticity. . . . The way Prinze is doing the role is part Jewish, part Italian. . . . Freddie is too servile to Albertson, he is looking for the white father." It was very confusing; this Puerto Rican–Hungarian was acting too Jewish and Italian to be a believable Mexican-American. And all I wanted to do was make a funny television show.

There was no way we could compromise. I understood their point; I just had to deal with reality. The networks simply ignored the protests. At that time there were only the three networks, and they were so powerful they were not subject to pressure. They were going to conduct their business and make their shows; protests just didn't affect them.

The show was an immediate hit. A huge hit. It was NBC's biggest show. Number four overall. The number one new program. Still, several Mexican-American organizations continued to protest the show, claiming the show "demeaned our Chicano youth and Chicanos in general by presenting the character 'Chico' in a serf-master relationship to Anglo-America as personified by 'The Man.'"

This was a situation comedy. A comedy. It wasn't a summit conference. There was nothing serious about it. It was about two people breaking down the barriers of age and ethnic differences to form a loving relationship.

Fame came fast to Freddie Prinze. He quickly became a major star, opening in Las Vegas for $25,000 a week on the same bill as Diana Ross. He was a smart, good-looking kid, and naturally, there were always women around him. As a major Hispanic star, the demands on his time were extraordinary, and it became impossible for him to satisfy everyone. I remember him complaining once, "I don't have time to breathe."

The show ran four seasons. Who knows how long it might have run if Freddie Prinze hadn't committed suicide. I didn't know him well enough to even suggest the reasons he put a gun to his head and shot himself. Who knows what goes on in the mind of someone so young, so talented, facing the kind of pressure he faced. But one day the phone rang and I was told Freddie Prinze was dead. It was a tragedy, a terrible, terrible tragedy. We tried to continue the show for another year—saying in the show that Chico had died. A twelve-year-old boy named Raoul ingratiates himself with Jack and becomes his personal resident alien. He was a new Chico and the Man, but it only lasted for a season. *Chico and the Man* died with Freddie Prinze.

Television is like a vacuum, it sucks up product as fast as it is produced—and then it needs more, and more. After a respectful few hours the business moved forward to make more product, to make new stars.

One of television's biggest hits resulted from a ten-page outline titled "Gabriel Kotter at P.S. 166 Again," created by Alan Sacks, one of our writers, and comedian Gabe Kaplan. It was a sitcom about a teacher who returned to the high school in Brooklyn from which he had graduated to teach the Special Guidance Remedial Academics Group, a class that became known and loved as "the sweathogs." Kaplan attended the equivalent of James Buchanan High School in Bensonhurst, Brooklyn, and had been a student in a remedial class. He credits a Miss Shepherd as the teacher who inspired him and led him indirectly to *Welcome Back, Kotter. Kotter* was the show I spent the entire flight from Los Angeles to New York pitching to ABC's Fred Pierce.

My involvement in these shows was to sell them, handle all the financial deals, and keep the network away from Jimmy Komack and the writers. Jimmy Komack brought Kotter and the sweathogs to life. Gabe Kaplan played Kotter, the teacher who employed some pretty unusual teaching methods to get through to his students. For the role of Barbarino, a tough-talking sweathog, he cast an unknown young actor named John Travolta.

Welcome Back, Kotter was also a big hit. And rather than receiving complaints from an ethnic group, this time it was the entire PTA, the Parent-Teacher Association, that found fault with the show. Every year the PTA selected the best and worst programs in television—and every year *Kotter* was near the top of the worst list.

Just as *Chico* launched Freddie Prinze, John Travolta emerged from the ensemble cast to become a major star. While the show was on the air, he spent two summers making two movies, *Grease* and *Saturday Night Fever.* Both of them were huge hits, and suddenly Travolta was the hottest actor in show business. He could have demanded $1 million a picture—and I had him under contract at $1,000 a week. I had been in show business long enough to know exactly what was going to happen— Travolta was going to try to get out of that contract.

I waited for the call from his agent that I knew was coming. I expected to be told that some quirk on page thirty-two of his contract claimed that when the sun rose in the east on three consecutive days when the temperature was over . . . he was required to be released from his contract.

Eventually the phone rang, but it wasn't Travolta's agent calling—it was John Travolta himself, who wanted to come in alone and talk with me. We really didn't know each other well. Friendly, but not friends. He knew I was the Wolper whose name was on the building. I knew he was the young superstar who wanted to break his contract. I was ready for the fight.

John Travolta came in by himself, no agent, and no entourage. He sat across my desk from me and suggested, "Let's try to solve this without any agents. I'm being offered a lot of money to make feature films, which I'd like to do, so let me make this proposal. I'll continue to do *Welcome Back, Kotter* at a thousand a week, but I'd like to do all my scenes within an eight-week period. You shoot all my scenes during those two months and give me the rest of the year off, and I'll do the show at the same salary until it goes off the air."

I was almost stunned. That's not the way things usually worked in show business. I reached across the desk and shook his hand. "You're a real gentleman," I said, "and we've got a deal." I had no intention of holding him back, I knew we would reach some sort of compromise, but this was much more fair than anything I could have suggested. In a half hour, we'd resolved a problem that might have taken months of legal fighting to settle. I think the only people who were unhappy with that agreement were the lawyers. Now, there is a real man, in my mind.

Travolta did exactly as he promised, showing up when scheduled and doing his scenes until the show went off the air. Surprisingly, the person we had some problems with was Gabe Kaplan. Several times on the set, Kaplan and Jimmy Komack almost got into fights. Our lawyers had to send Gabe Kaplan warning letters to make sure he reported for work.

Welcome Back, Kotter became part of television history. It was on the air from 1975 to 1979. I don't think I realized its true value. Eventually, I sold my company to Warner Bros., and with it went the rights to those shows. Warner Bros. Television sold *Kotter* into syndication for what, at that time, was the highest price ever paid for a series. Warner's probably made more money on syndicating *Kotter* and *Chico and the Man* than it paid for my entire company.

I retained only a small interest. More than two decades later, I was still receiving payments.

Two shows, two big successes; I felt confident I understood the world of series programming. Many of the close friends I had made early in my career continued to be successful, eventually reaching positions of great power in television. Grant Tinker and I became friends when he was still working at an advertising agency. Many years later, we were vacationing together on our annual visit to the south of France when he mentioned casually to my wife, Gloria, and me, "Tomorrow it's going to be announced that I'm the new chairman of NBC."

Long after Grant Tinker had taken charge at NBC, *60 Minutes* did a wonderful piece on the Humphrey Bogart–Ingrid Bergman film *Casablanca.* It is arguably the best-known film in movie history. More people can recite lines from *Casablanca* than any other film ever made: "Of all the gin joints in all the towns in all the world, she walks into mine." "Play it, Sam. You played it for her, you can play it for me." "Round up the usual suspects." "We'll always have Paris." And perhaps the most famous line of all: "Here's looking at you, kid." Like so many other people, I have always loved that film; but unlike most people, I had the clout to do something about it. I decided I wanted to do a TV series called *Casablanca.* It would be set in Rick's Place, the bar owned by Humphrey Bogart, and we would use all the characters decades of people had come to love. I knew I could get the rights because Warner

Bros. owned them. In 1955, *Casablanca* was part of a television series called *Warner Bros. Presents,* along with a series made from their movies *Kings Road* and *Cheyenne. Kings Road* and *Casablanca* were eventually dropped and the series came to be known as *Cheyenne.*

Sometimes, when I get an idea that I think is so exciting, I have to act on it immediately. This was one of those ideas. Rarely have I called upon a friendship to get a project done. This time I did. I called Grant Tinker and told him we just had to do this show. Grant was reluctant, but he agreed because of my long and successful track record.

NBC's head of production, the wonderful Brandon Tartikoff, did not like the idea at all—but since Tinker and I wanted to do it, he wasn't going to stand in the way. So, we obtained the rights and went into production. We got the original plans for the set of Rick's Place and rebuilt it almost exactly. We got the original doors, the original chandeliers, some of the original lamps, even the original bar. In homage to the film, I wanted to do the series in black and white, but the network turned me down and instead we shot in muted colors. We hired filmmakers who had been working in that era; our cameraman, Joe Biroc, was eighty years old and had shot fifty major films. Our makeup man was in his late seventies and had worked on *Citizen Kane.* The art director, Preston Ames, was also in his late seventies and had done *An American in Paris.*

For the role of Rick I picked David Soul, a tremendously underrated actor who had starred in *Starsky and Hutch.* Scatman Crothers was cast as Sam; Hector Elizondo would play Renault, the Vichy French police officer with an independent heart. As the stories would be set before Ingrid Bergman showed up in Casablanca, we didn't need to cast that role at all.

The stories were all straight drama—intrigue, smuggling, spying, love, moral decisions, human sacrifice, and romance. It certainly wasn't a typical TV show, and just about everybody thought I was crazy.

As it turned out, just about everybody was right. Everything about the show seemed almost perfect to me, everything except the scripts. The stories were terrible. I was bitterly disappointed. It wasn't quite Rick being threatened with eviction by his landlord, but they were not too much more exciting. The critics hated the show, and this time they were correct. That was my fault, I picked the producer, I approved the scripts, and so I take full responsibility. We did about five shows, and even my long, close friendship with Grant Tinker wasn't enough to keep it on the air. I agreed with him to close it down.

I felt terrible about it because this was a project I really loved. And I remain convinced it would have worked if the scripts had been better.

That was the last time I tried to do a television series. Instead, I stuck closely to those things with which I had been successful, the things I loved to do. Besides, I would pioneer a new television format, the miniseries.

PART IV

The Movies

Willy Wonka (Gene Wilder) and I (1970)

TWENTY-SIX

THE DEVIL'S BRIGADE

With William Holden (1966)

Many people grow up dreaming about making motion pictures. I was not one of them. I began making feature films in 1965 because it was a natural progression from the documentaries we were turning out—and it made good business sense. An agent sent me the manuscript of a book scheduled to be published a year later entitled *The Devil's Brigade.* It was the true story of the amazing World War II exploits of the First Special Service Force, consisting of elite Canadian troops and a bunch of American misfits, led by Robert Frederick. At thirty-seven, Frederick was the youngest American general at that time and, with nine Purple Hearts, the most wounded general of the entire war. It was a terrific story and I made a deal with United Artists to produce it.

A year earlier, I had sold my company to Metromedia, John Kluge's rapidly growing group of television stations, for $1 million in cash and substantial Metromedia stock. In addition, I became a member of Metromedia's board of directors. It was a good deal. A clause in my contract gave me a percentage of the profits of all films, both theatrical and television, made by the company. Since I was the major production arm, it made great sense at the time. But while I was working on *The Devil's Brigade*, Kluge initiated negotiations to buy United Artists. Then somebody realized that, if the deal was concluded, I would own a piece of every single film made by United Artists. Not just my films—every film.

That huge loophole gave me the opportunity I needed, and wanted, to reopen my own company. So, I negotiated a new deal with Metromedia in which I would leave the company and purchase, for $500,000, the rights to the name Wolper Productions. I would also retain ownership of all feature and movie properties in development. In return, I would give up my percentage clause and stay out of the television production business for one year. I opened up new offices—at MGM—and began making features.

"What they did to each other," boasted ads for *The Devil's Brigade*, "was nothing compared to what they did to the enemy!" During World War II, a joint Canadian-American force was created to accomplish an almost impossible objective—to climb a mountain under German fire and capture an artillery installation on a plateau at the peak. The Canadians sent some of their best soldiers, while the Americans sent a bunch of independent troublemakers. The movie told the story of how they learned to work—and fight—together. By the time the unit was disbanded, it had participated in three invasions, led the Allied liberation of Rome, and captured Axis strongholds in the French and Italian mountains. In the assault on the artillery installation that was holding up the entire American Fifth Army, they had to climb a three-thousand-foot mountain, the last thousand feet at a sixty-five-degree angle, at night, in freezing weather, in total silence, carrying full packs. It was estimated the assault would take three days—the German stronghold was captured in two hours. Of the 2,500 men assigned to the unit, 477 were killed in action and more than 1,800 were wounded. The name Devil's Brigade came from the Germans, who referred to them as "the devils in baggy pants."

This was my first feature, but I was not the slightest bit intimidated. To portray General Frederick I signed William Holden, then added Cliff Robertson and my close friend Vince Edwards. Having just completed playing the title character in the top-rated medical series *Ben Casey*, Edwards was the hottest of the three. The film was directed by Andrew McLaglen, son of the famous character actor Victor McLaglen.

We shot the film just outside Salt Lake City, Utah, and in Italy. Through my old contacts at the Defense Department, I was able to get the complete cooperation of the Utah National Guard. They provided everything we needed. They even built a road to the top of a mountain for me to get a great location to film the mountain capture. The shoot in Utah went smoothly. For the most part, producing feature films was no more complex or difficult than producing a television program—just a lot more expensive.

Holden could not have been more cooperative. On the first day of shooting, when we broke for lunch, Robertson and Edwards went right to the head of the service line. Holden took his place at the back and shouted loudly, "I think the actors should be last in line because the crew has to get back to work before we do." The embarrassed Robertson and Edwards moved to the rear. I had been warned that Holden had a drinking problem, but in Utah he drank only wine. Sober, he was a quiet man, although when he was drinking, he became gregarious—but always cooperative and nice. Only once in Utah did the alcohol affect his performance. We had to reshoot one scene, ironically, in which he had to berate his troops for participating in a drunken brawl. As one actor remarked, "Bill was the only one in the scene who really was drunk!"

Only after the production moved to Italy did Holden's drinking get out of control. One day, I got to the set only to discover that Holden was missing. He'd left the hotel in his Rolls-Royce and had not been seen again. I checked every place I knew he liked; he didn't seem to be anywhere. So, I got in my car and started driving back to the hotel. As I passed a really dingy bar on the side of the road, I saw his Rolls-Royce in the lot and went in. He was absolutely crocked; he didn't just fall off the wagon, he fell off the whole wagon train. Because I didn't drink, I didn't know how to deal with a drunk. "Bill," I said, "everybody's waiting for you. They're making this movie . . ."

Unfortunately, that day the admiral in charge of the Mediterranean Fleet and his wife were visiting the set—and wanted to meet Bill Holden. We were still quite dependent on the cooperation of the military; the last thing I wanted to do was disappoint the admiral. I snuck Holden into his trailer and we poured coffee down his throat. "I'm okay," he said, "I'm fine," although, truthfully, it sounded more like "Ishkay, m'fne . . ." But Holden was a fine actor—he knew how to act sober. He was a perfect gentleman with the admiral and his wife.

That day, we were filming a key scene in which a small platoon slogged through a waist-deep river that led into the town, the one route the Germans never expected the soldiers to follow. In this scene, they had to wade through the frigid water holding their rifles high above their heads. Hundreds of people from nearby towns had come to see us shooting this movie, and they lined both sides of a hill overlooking the river. They were not in the way at all.

But as Holden struggled through the water, he looked up and saw all those townspeople and shouted, "What the fuck are you staring at?" And then he opened fire on them with his submachine gun.

The townspeople dived for cover. Holden was firing blanks, but they didn't know that. And he continued cursing at them. I guess he was pleased, when he finished firing, that there wasn't a person in sight. I had to apologize to an entire town, explaining that it was all part of the scene and somehow he'd gotten the lines wrong.

I didn't know what to do. I had lost control of my star. I called Ilya Lopert, a famous producer then working at United Artists as head of European operations. He had worked with Holden before, so I asked him for advice. There was a woman in Paris, he explained, who knew how to take care of Holden in these situations. He advised me to get her down to the set as quickly as possible. We flew her to this small town and she stayed with him day and night for several days getting him into shape to go back to work. After he sobered up, he felt terrible about what had happened. He apologized to everyone. Holden was a wonderful man with a terrible problem. But finally we managed to finish the picture.

The Devil's Brigade turned out to be a terrific film. It was a wonderful story, the acting was excellent, and the preview audiences and critics loved it. Unfortunately, it came out just a few months after the release of the *The Dirty Dozen*, which was the same kind of story. It was a big hit and it killed us. We got lost in the wind.

But I had survived my first picture. I was a movie producer. I'd had my baptism under fire—although, admittedly, it was prop fire. I was ready to make more movies.

When I left Metromedia, I took with me the rights to all feature films in development. One of them was the *Bridge at Remagen,* a World War II story of the battle for the only bridge over the Rhine that the Germans failed to destroy during their retreat. Another was a comedy—*If It's Tuesday, This Must Be Belgium.*

If It's Tuesday was the story of a group of American tourists barreling through the continent. I had seen a CBS documentary about a bus tour and loved it so much I bought the title for $5,000. The advertising line basically summed up the entire picture: "Europe sent us Dutch elm disease, German measles, and heartburn. We sent them Whirlwind Vacation Tour #225. Now we're even!"

As I was busy with the war film in Czechoslovakia, I hired Stan Margulies, who had just finished producing a film in Europe, to produce *If It's Tuesday*. It was the first time Stan and I worked together and marked the beginning of a long, prosperous, and wonderful relationship. I wanted my friend Richard Crenna to direct it, but he was more interested in acting. We had a tight budget, so I decided this was the perfect opportunity for Mel Stuart to direct his first feature. Mel had done every other job about as well as it could be done, and he was smart and talented as hell. And, as he said, "he worked cheap."

The film starred Suzanne Pleshette, Ian McShane, and a lot of familiar character actors who fell into the category of 'There's what's his name again. I really like him.' I also hired a lot of major stars to make cameo appearances, including Anita Ekberg, Senta Berger, John Cassavetes, Ben Gazzara, and the great Italian filmmaker Vittorio De Sica. I met him with his son-in-law to ask him to be in the picture. It was a comedy, I explained, about Americans. His son-in-law translated every word. De Sica spoke only Italian, but apparently he thought that Americans were funny because he agreed to be in the picture. Only after he showed up on the set did we learn he spoke perfect English—he just wanted to listen carefully when we made the deal.

We filmed in seven countries, practically rewriting the script as the tour plowed through Europe. The budget for that film was slightly more than $2 million, so small we basically arrived in a city, set up the cameras, did the shot, got back on the bus, and drove to the next city. There was no time for luxuries, such as rehearsals. In one scene in Venice, for example, Sandy Baron was supposedly escaping from an Italian family, so he jumped out of a second-story window into a dirty canal. The scene went perfectly—except that, just after Baron made his leap, the principal cameraman reported to Stuart, "Okay, I'm ready. Let's shoot it."

We had to live with a long-distance shot filmed by another camera.

The only real disagreement I had with Mel was whether to bring the twenty extras, who were sitting behind the principals in the bus, for the entire shoot or hire local extras in each country, which would save a great deal of money. Mel insisted that we bring the extras with us, otherwise the audience would notice different people were on the bus in each country.

Mel, I told him, if the audience is looking at the people behind the stars, you're fired as the director because they are not looking where they're supposed to. Mel saw the wisdom of my argument. The only extra

we used for the entire shoot was the writer David Shaw, who was trav-
eling with the film to make script changes to fit the situation. If anybody
doubts Mel Stuart did a fine job in his first directorial effort, the proof is
that nobody ever noticed the extras.

TWENTY-SEVEN

I WAS A SPY FOR THE CIA?

Czech officer shows me an article accusing me
of being a CIA agent (1968)

We really had only one major problem while making *Bridge at Remagen*—the Russian invasion of Czechoslovakia.

In 1945, during World War II, the original bridge over the Rhine River, near the town of Remagen, had been bombed by the Germans ten days after the Americans had captured it. But, during those ten days, the Allies moved thousands of troops and tons of equipment into Germany. The story centered on the capture of the bridge and the fight to hold it.

The actual bridge had been replaced, long ago, by a modern one, so before beginning the film, I spent several months searching Europe for a bridge that resembled the original. We found one in the town of Davle, Czechoslovakia, which was not far from Prague. With the construction of towers at either end, it was almost a perfect match for the Remagen bridge.

This was a good time to be in Czechoslovakia. Although it was still a member of the Soviet Communist bloc, under the rule of Alexander Dubček the country was experimenting with a rudimentary form of democracy, a period known as the Prague Spring.

One of the freedoms in which the Czechs were already expert was the art of the bribe. I could get anything I wanted done—as long as I paid for it. The head of the Czech film industry told me I could hire soldiers from the Czech army as my extras for about a dollar a soldier—if I deposited $5,000 in American dollars in his Swiss bank account. We also made deposits in Swiss banks for some of the army officers. For one stunt, we needed a horse to leap off the bridge into the river—it was supposedly blown off by an explosion. We had difficulty renting a horse because everyone was afraid it would be hurt. Finally, our stunt director, the great Hal Needham, was able to rent a horse for about $25—but only after posting a $1,000 bond, payable if anything happened to the horse. The owner then put the heaviest iron shoes he could find on that horse's feet. It took six men to get it out of the river. I have never seen anyone so disappointed to get an animal back safely.

Because we were shooting the film in a Communist country, the Pentagon would not give us any assistance. We rented uniforms from costume rental agencies in Europe. We rented all the military equipment we needed—the eight tanks, trucks, and thirty other vehicles—from the Austrian army, which had purchased them as war surplus after World War II. Everything was shipped without incident into Czechoslovakia. I moved into the top floor of a lovely hotel in Prague and began preproduction.

The Czechoslovakian film industry was small but very good. We hired a Czech crew. One person I remember well was the special effects expert. I was told he was as good at safely creating mayhem as anyone else in the film business. But what I remember most about him was that he had only three fingers on one hand and four on the other.

Perhaps because the Czechs were used to working at a different pace than Americans, they didn't know unique ways of saving money. One shot, for example, was of a long line of tanks coming down a road. Simple enough, except we didn't have the road. Director John Guillermin wanted a black tar road with a white stripe down the middle. Although it was only for that one shot, the Czechs thought they would have to build it, which would be time-consuming and expensive. Instead, an American special effects expert solved the problem in about ten minutes. He simply spray-painted the dirt black and put a white line on it. It looked perfect—as long as the wind didn't blow too strongly. The tanks destroyed it when they drove over it, but that didn't matter because at that point it was no longer visible. And they did it in one take.

Painting a road was a simple effect; destroying an entire town was a lot more complicated. We needed to stage a major battle scene in a town, which would be devastated in the fighting. The Czech government could not have been more cooperative. Rather than have us build sets, the government actually sold us an entire town to blow up. It was named Most, in northern Czechoslovakia. This old industrial city was apparently of so little historical value that the government was planning to knock it down to allow expansion of neighboring coal fields. The residents had already been moved out. This could never have happened in a capitalistic country, never. We would have been negotiating deals for centuries. But in a Communist country they just decided to replace the town and that was the end of the argument. We paid $20,000, which was considerably less than it would have cost us to build sets to blow up.

The film starred George Segal, Robert Vaughn, and Ben Gazzara and was directed by John Guillermin. The first hint of the problems to come appeared in an East German newspaper article, which alleged that the military equipment I had brought into Czechoslovakia was not for a movie, but, rather, was being smuggled in by the CIA to support a subversive movement. 'Russian Discovery of U.S. Arms Cache in Czechoslovakia," read the headline. Among the weapons found, the story reported, were World War II rifles, machine guns, and tanks. I was called a CIA operative and my crew was accused of conducting counterrevolutionary activities. Of course we laughed at the story.

I'd brought my family with me to Europe. That summer my friend Bud Yorkin was making a film in England, and we rented houses in the south of France. Ironically, Yorkin's film was a comedy entitled *Start the Revolution Without Me.*

We began filming in June 1968. On the very first day, some members of the Czech crew were late and Guillermin screamed unmercifully at them. He was using that opportunity to establish his authority, but he was heavy-handed about it. Finally, one of the crew members told him if he ever insulted them again, the entire crew was walking off the picture.

At that time I had worked with few feature-film directors, so to say Guillermin was the most difficult director with whom I'd ever worked wouldn't mean much. So, it is probably better to say he was a real pain in the ass. One afternoon, while we were shooting a battle scene on the bridge, he told me that it was going to be so complicated that I couldn't come on the set.

"Excuse me?"

"I don't want you on the set today," he said.

My answer to that was simple: "You're fired."

"What?"

"That's right, you're fired, get off the set. I'll pay for your room for two days and then you're on your own."

When he realized I was serious, he apologized, so I rescinded his firing. But I wasn't kidding. Without that apology, he would have been gone. I had learned early that, as a producer, you have to be tough and you have to be tough right away. My name was on the picture; my name was on the deal with United Artists. I was responsible for everything that happened. "Directorial bullshit," I believe, is one of the causes of the great damage that has been done to the motion picture industry.

We shot for two months. The picture was proceeding well. We blew up the town and completed about half the filming on the bridge. It was an exciting time to be in Czechoslovakia. The residents of Prague were testing the boundaries of their new freedoms. There were, however, some ominous signs. When we began shooting outside Prague on July 22, Russian troops began maneuvers just across the border. The set was buzzed by Russian helicopters and MiGs, "just to let you know they are nearby," I was told. Believe me, this was still the middle of the Cold War—I didn't need to be warned the Russians were nearby.

On July 29, *Pravda* reported discovery of an arms cache in Czechoslovakia. An East German news agency, AMG, reported "unusual armaments" in the Remagen filming.

In early August, East German newspapers again reported that the movie was a CIA-created cover-up to move arms into Czechoslovakia and that I was a CIA agent. The paper claimed that the presence of our movie in Prague was "a grave and serious threat to the security of the Communist bloc." If I had been a CIA agent, I was the most overcovered undercover agent in history, because I answered questions from anyone who asked them. In response to the article, the Czech police temporarily confiscated our explosives and put our arsenal under guard.

On the morning of August 20, I flew to Italy where *If It's Tuesday, This Must Be Belgium* was filming. Just before leaving, I'd met with Alois Polednik, the director general of the Czech film industry, to discuss the situation. He'd reassured me that everything was fine and offered to issue a denial of all false charges if necessary. I left Czechoslovakia confident the problem was resolved.

When I got to my Italian hotel, I was informed that Russian troops had just invaded Czechoslovakia. The Prague airport had been closed minutes after I'd left and Dubček had been arrested. I tried to call Prague. The phones were not working, but I was able to communicate with my crew by telex. On the first day, they decided to keep filming. They filmed inside the studio all day while, in central Prague, the heroic Czechs were beginning to resist the Soviet invasion.

The Russians surrounded the International Hilton, where the crew was staying, and confined everyone to the hotel. Everybody got nervous. Rumors spread that the crew was going to be arrested and charged with spying. Obviously, it was impossible to work. The production report, the summation of what happened each day, read, "No shooting today because of shooting."

Finally, the crew took a vote whether to stay or to leave. With the exception of three votes, Guillermin's and two stuntmen's, everyone voted to get out. On the twenty-third, I told Milton Feldman, our production supervisor, to evacuate. I told him to hire every taxicab he could find and drive to the Austrian border, where I would meet them with buses. With the assistance of the U.S. embassy, a taxicab caravan was organized and the eighty-person crew made a dash for the border.

Before I left Rome, the United States Information Agency asked me to appear on Radio Free Europe to reiterate that I was not a CIA agent and my movie was not funded by the CIA to get arms into Prague. "This is a movie," I said, "these are famous actors, not spies." I couldn't believe this was happening. I was making a movie about World War II and people were accusing me of trying to start World War III. The closest anyone in the movie had ever been to spying was Robert Vaughn, who had starred in *The Man from U.N.C.L.E.*

I flew to Vienna and booked every hotel room I could find. I rented buses and drove to the border to meet the taxis. They weren't there. I began to get nervous—and I was on the safe side of the border. I wondered if the Russians had arrested my entire movie crew. Finally, somebody told me that a group of about one hundred Americans were waiting at the next checkpoint. I raced there with my buses. The crew carried their luggage across the border, and we went back to Vienna in a bus caravan. About an hour after my crew was safely out of the country, the borders were closed.

The media descended upon us. We repeated, over and over, that we were not government agents. We were actors and film crew. The crew was safe; the problem became what to do about the movie? We still had many scenes to shoot on the bridge, and the European production head, Ilya Lopert, came to Vienna to meet with me and I convinced United Artists that we could complete the picture. I have no idea how I did that because I had no idea how we were going to do it. UA gave me three weeks to get reorganized, believing that its insurance company would cover any losses. Incredibly, the insurance policy did cover an invasion—but the insurance company claimed that this wasn't an invasion. The new Czech government said it had asked the Russians to enter the country. From an insurance standpoint, if a country wouldn't admit it had been invaded, it wasn't invaded. Eventually, the claim was settled, I believe, for a substantial but not complete payment.

The immediate problem we had to solve was how to rescue the film and equipment we'd left behind in the dash to freedom. Hal Needham offered to take five stuntmen and sneak back into Czechoslovakia to retrieve the essential items. I was considering it seriously—until he asked me to get him some automatic weapons. The situation inside the country was chaotic enough; we had already been accused of being CIA operatives—if my people went in with guns and got caught, it would've created an international incident.

Fortunately, the Russians also wanted our military equipment out of the country as quickly as possible. They were afraid the Czechs would use it against Russian soldiers. In my mind, I could almost see on the front page of every major newspaper in the world the photographs of American tanks with the U.S. Army star insignia firing on Russian tanks.

I met with a Russian general and a representative of the Czech film industry who had flown to Vienna to resolve our problem. We agreed that I would send a train of flatbed railcars to Prague, where our equipment would be loaded and returned. With the aid of the Austrian government, who also wanted their tanks back, I rented a train and retrieved all our equipment. The Czech crew that had remained behind had protected our belongings. Nothing had been touched, nothing. Even cash left in a desk drawer in the prop truck was still there.

We scouted desperately for locations that we could match to the film we'd shot. We needed to shoot some scenes under a bridge, and we found a bridge in Hamburg, Germany, that, from the bottom up, might pass for the bridge in Czechoslovakia. We rented studio space in Germany. We found a location in Castel Gandolfo, Italy, the pope's summer residence, that resembled our old location. Because we had filmed our "army" fighting halfway across the bridge in Czechoslovakia, we only needed the other half of the bridge, so we decided to build half a bridge. But, to do so, we had to buy or rent three pieces of property on the shores of Lake Albano. We quickly reached an agreement with the owners of two of them, but an old woman who owned the piece in the middle refused to sell. She spoke only enough English to make it clear she wasn't interested in selling her land. We tried everything to convince her to sell, but she refused. I'd negotiated with many tough businessmen, I'd put together extremely complex deals, but this elderly Italian woman was either one of the great negotiators of all time, or she was serious. Without her land we couldn't shoot there; if we couldn't shoot there, I didn't know where we would go. Someone suggested we try one of the best negotiating tools—a suitcase full of cash. What a good idea! So I filled six briefcases with lira—probably about $10,000—and met with her. Cash is an excellent negotiating tool. She accepted the suitcase. Until she saw the cash, she could not fathom $10,000 worth of lira. It was that day I understood the difference between capitalism and Communism. For $25,000 I could blow up an entire Communist town, but it cost me $10,000 to buy a small piece of land in Italy.

While we were filming under the bridge in Hamburg, and construction crews were building half a bridge in Italy, our second-unit director, Bill Kronick, went back to Prague with the permission of the new Czech government and, under the very watchful eyes of Russian troops, simulated the blowing up of the bridge. With everything that had been going on, the Russians were wary of even simulated warfare. Using special effects, and shooting only long shots, Kronick "blew up" the bridge.

The half bridge in Italy was completed in weeks. It was a perfect match. The completed film is an extraordinary example of movie magic. The actors get on the bridge in Czechoslovakia, remove explosives from under the bridge in Germany, and get off the bridge in Italy. That's some impressive bridge. But it is done seamlessly. It's impossible to see the difference.

We completed principal photography in ninety-three days, a brief time considering that it included an invasion. The picture premiered in August 1969. Perhaps it was not the best idea to distribute a film about war and heroism at the height of the war in Vietnam. The film received mixed reviews. It was criticized for being both too realistic and not realistic enough. One reviewer even pointed out that we had not even used the actual bridge, failing to mention that it had been destroyed in 1945. The picture could absolutely not be judged on its merits in that political climate. Given the circumstances, I think it is a fine picture, and it plays quite often on television.

TWENTY-EIGHT

THEY WILL
TAKE OVER THE WORLD

(1971)

Having survived a Russian invasion, I was confident I could deal with any situation. I made a movie once that a New York critic described as "a showman's dream. It's full of sex, violence, and has a cast of tens of millions and is ideal and ingenious family entertainment." It was called *The Hellstrom Chronicle,* and basically, it was a feature-length documentary about insects taking over the earth.

In 1966, we'd done a show about insects for the National Geographic, and I remembered that some of the footage had been much too gruesome for television, so we'd cut it. The insect world is fascinating, brutal, and violent. There are no "anger-management courses," they just kill and eat each other. At that time I was very much involved with making feature films, and it occurred to me that the sight of microscopic insects on the giant screen would be surrealistic, and incredibly frightening. As I learned, there are more than six hundred thousand species of insects, and as many as three thousand new species are discovered annually. Insects account for 80 percent of all living things on earth. I knew it would make a great movie.

I immediately hired Wally Green to produce and direct it. Whenever we had a concept that required going someplace nobody wanted to go, doing things nobody wanted to do, we called Wally Green. Nobody enjoyed a quiet day in the jungle more than Wally. He loved the idea.

We didn't give the picture a title; we called it Project X so no one would know what we were doing because, as Wally once explained, "People would think Wolper had lost his mind." Not quite: before starting the project I'd presold the TV rights to Brandon Stoddard at ABC for $600,000—which covered almost the entire budget. It turned out to be a difficult shoot. We had to have cameras modified to our needs, which included special microscopic lenses and side-mounted motors so Wally could shoot from ground level. We had to use stroboscopic cold lighting—synchronized to pulsate with the camera at speeds up to ninety frames a second—because the heat generated by normal lighting would have fried our actors. When we needed faster film we used aircraft landing lights to focus a beam, making it possible to shoot up to five thousand frames a second, fast enough to film a bullet leaving a gun.

We filmed everything from the courting flight of the mayflies that emerge once a year over four days and live only a few hours on the Mississippi River in Minnesota, to the courage of driver ants, who willingly sacrifice their lives for the survival of the colony. Ants are fascinating creatures, the only known insect that uses other species as slaves or servants. We filmed in fourteen countries on four continents. We had crews shooting in Africa and Australia, in Japan and the United States.

One of the most difficult sequences to shoot was the army ants forming a living bridge over water to enable other ants to reach safety. At a remote location in Africa, Wally and his crew located as many as fifty ant colonies. Initially when the crew tried to film them, the ants would crawl over everything—inside camera cases and clothing, in their hair, in their equipment; ants were certainly taking over our world. Wally hired Africans to do nothing but brush away ants. These were not biting ants, but they were incredibly irritating. Finally, the crew decided to wear only bathing suits when they worked, just to keep the ants out of their clothing.

Eventually, Wally decided the ants were in the wrong location for our needs. The only solution was to move the entire ant colony. There are no professional ant movers, so Wally had to figure out how to do it himself. The crew covered the entire nest with a large tarp, knocked out the ants with CO_2 gas, vacuumed them up, and put the entire colony in a large plastic garbage bag, flew to a small island in the middle of a river, dumped out the ants, and began filming. A few ants got loose on the airplane, but not enough to make a difference.

On the island, the ants built their bridge to land. They made long columns, and when some of them drifted away in the current, others immediately replaced them. It was a remarkable sequence.

It would probably be inaccurate to claim "No ants were hurt in the making of this film," because many thousands gave up their lives for our art.

When Wally was making a film, it became his life. Once, I remember, my wife, Gloria, and I went to his house and he took us into his backyard to show us his insects. Locusts in California! "Where'd you get those?" I asked incredulously. "Aren't they illegal?"

"I needed some really good close-ups," he explained, "so I snuck them into the country."

I wondered what the penalty was for starting a plague in southern California. I stood there watching until every last locust had been destroyed.

We ended up constructing our own sets on a large table in the office. We decided to film the fatal mating sequence of the black widow spider, but as we discovered, our black widows had to be virgins. The only way to ensure that they were virgins was to breed them. I didn't know about this until early one morning when I walked into associate producer Sacha Schneider's office and found jars of black widow spiders all over the place. What was worse, locusts in Malibu, or black widow spiders in my office? Get them out of here! I screamed. Now!

I bought a small building on Wilshire Boulevard in Beverly Hills and set up a studio for the insect photography we had to do. We built big tanks and used time-lapse photography. "Stage 1," for example, was a large table.

It was a difficult picture to make. It seemed as if people were con-

Bertha and Isaac Fass,
my maternal grandparents.

Vera and Max Wolper,
my paternal grandparents.

Dr. Max Wolper Dies; Practiced Here 59 Years

East Side's Doctor Put Fire Gong on Buggy to Speed Delivering 10,000 Babies

New York Times, June 25, 1949.

Me at about two with my "security dog."

Me at four with my mother, Anna.

My father and I loved fishing together
(late 1930s).

I loved baseball (late 1930s).

Football wasn't my sport (1941).

Dig those abs (1940s).

Studying at the Boys Club in the Bronx
(late 1930s).

All dressed up for my job
delivering flowers
(1930s).

My mother and father, Irving and Anna
Wolper, on their honeymoon
in Niagara Falls (1927).

At the 1939 New York World's Fair,
where I saw television for the first time.

School	Boro.	Entered Mo. Da. Yr.	Class	Terms in School	Present	Absent	Late	Conduct	Work	Not Proficient in	School	Boro.	Entered Mo. Da. Yr.	Class	Terms in School	Present	Absent	Late	Conduct	Work
54	M	11.1.33	Kg⁴	PM	53	4	0	C	a		73	X	6.24.38	5B³	10	76½	13½		C	B
		1.31.34	K.09	1	72	22½	0	B	a				1.31.39	6A³	11	77½	19½		B	B+
		6.29.34	1B	2	75²	28	0	B	a				6.30.39	6B²						
		1.31.35	2Q³	3	48²	7½	0	B+	B	Sus. 5.3.35 11?	6	M	9.11.39	6B³	12	68½	23½	0	B	B
54	M	5.27.35	2C³	3	70²	8½	6	C	A				1.31.40	7A³		–	–	–	–	–
		6.28.35	*89	4	12	0		B	A		6	M	2.8.40	7A³	13	83½	18½	0	C	B
135	M	9.27.35	2B	4	78	2	1/4.4.27.35	B	a		6	X	6.28.40	7B³	14	80½	11½		B	B
		1.31.36	3A		14	4	5	C	B+ Sus3.10.36				1.31.41	8A³						L
		5.7.36	3A		5³16½			C	E		6	M	3.18.41	8A³	15	66	3	0	a	B
		6.30.36	3B										6.27.41	8B³	16	85½	6½			
73	X	9.14.36	3B⁴		77½	15½	1	C	B				1.31.42			COLUMBIA GRAMMER				
		1.28.37	4A³		91½	6½	2	C	B+											
		6.30.37	4B³	8	74½	13½	0	C	B											
		1.31.38	5C²	9	84⁴	7½		C	B											

* Give Number, Street and Boro. if New York City is

My NYC Public School report card from kindergarten,
1933, through grade school, 1942. Notice my grades were okay
but my conduct and attendance were a little shaky.

In 1944, during World War II, I worked as a volunteer greeter
at the Stage Door Canteen. Visiting were Jane Wyman and her husband,
Captain Ronald Reagan.

My wife, Gloria, in the 1960s. How could I resist that beautiful face?

Marrying in Hawaii at sunset, July 11, 1974. The best thing I ever did.

Gloria and I with sons Mark and Michael. Our annual two-week boat trip.

Gloria and I off the coast of Maine. We both love boating.

(*L to r*) My son Michael, daughter-in-law Tara, daughter, Leslie, son-in-law, Theo, son Mark, and daughter-in-law Amy. I'm really proud of that beautiful group.

The grandchildren (*l to r*): Montana, Keelen, Kyler, Indie, Brandon, Preston, and Michael.

Appointed by President Gerald Ford as chairman of the American Bicentennial, I visited the White House in 1975 with my family. (*L to r*) Michael, Mark, me, Leslie, Gloria, now Senator John Warner, and President Ford.

For my official film of the 1972 Munich Olympics I used nine great directors. With me and Stan Margulies are (*l to r*): Mai Zetterling, Sweden; Juri Ozerov, the Soviet Union; Ousmane Sembene, Senegal; Arthur Penn, the United States; Milos Forman, Czechoslovakia; Claude Lelouch, France; Kon Ichikawa, Japan; and Michael Pfleghar, Germany. Missing is John Schlesinger, Great Britain.

Visiting my office at the Munich Olympics is Jesse Owens, who had a confrontation with Hitler when he won the gold medal in the 1936 Munich Olympics (1972).

Gloria, inside the Olympic Village in Munich. Even with security so tight (even the dog had to have ID), the terrorists were still able to capture the Israeli athletes (1972).

Elizabeth Taylor did two films for me,
Victory at Entebbe! and *North and South*,
and performed at Liberty Weekend.

With Richard Chamberlain
and Rachel Ward on the set
of *The Thorn Birds* (1982).

Orson Welles hosted
The Man Who Saw Tomorrow,
my documentary about
Nostradamus (1981).

On the set of *Roots* with Maya
Angelou. She played Kunta Kinte's
grandmother (1976).

Gloria and I with the Bush family. Two presidents, a governor, and their wives aboard the Wolper yacht with Pat and John Mitchell when we visited Kennebunkport (1986).

With Jacqueline Onassis on *The Big G,* my yacht, anchored at Hyannisport (1977).

Warner Bros. co-chairman, Bob Daly; Warner Communications chairman, Steve Ross; and Warner Bros. co-chairman, Terry Semel prepare for their part in a giant Warner Bros. party I produced (1990).

Inside the model of the L.A. Coliseum preparing my production of the opening ceremonies of the 1984 Los Angeles Olympic Games with my staff.

With Cary Grant at a party after the opening ceremonies of the 1984 Los Angeles Olympic Games.

Peter and Ginny Ueberroth with the Wolpers celebrate the closing day of the 1984 Los Angeles Olympic Games.

Equipe Cousteau

Between Xmas 95 and New Year 96 —

Dear David —

I will never forget what you did to start my career. This short note is to wish everything to you, that will be part of a happy 1996 year.

I would love to see you again... but when?

JY Cousteau

i - Téléphone : (1) 40 53 63 00 - Télécopie : (1) 40 53 63 03 - Télex : 641 856 F Requins

A letter to me from Jacques Cousteau I will always cherish.

At a *Willy Wonka* recording session with Charlie (Peter Ostrum), director Mel Stuart, and Grandpa Joe (Jack Albertson).

Golfing with a couple of legends: the Yankee Clipper, Joe DiMaggio, and the first man on the moon, Neil Armstrong.

On the field filming *Visions of Eight* with directors John Schlesinger and Milos Forman (1972).

(*L to r*) Me, Wilt Chamberlain, Barry Diller, Berry Gordy, Marty Starger, and David Gerber. We formed a professional volleyball league in 1973, but it folded after two years.

Steven Spielberg and I worked on a big Warner Bros. event together.

My collection is housed at the David L. Wolper Center at the University of Southern California, where students use computers in the viewing section to access films, scripts, photographs, contracts, et cetera.

I owned an eighteen-hole golf course in the Napa Valley and named each hole after one of my golfing friends. Here are some of the name-of-the-hole gang—kneeling (*l to r*): Merv Adelson, James Woods, Robert Wagner, Ed Marinaro, John Argue, Irwin Russell; (*back, l to r*): Peter Ueberroth, Peter Barsoccini, Irving Karp, Tom Poston, Steve DiMarco, Dinah Shore, Bob Selleck, me, Mike Connors, and Richard Crenna.

Every year a group of American amateur golfers plays a tournament against a group of Canadian amateur golfers. Here is one year's American team (*l to r*): Dan Harberts, Bud Yorkin, Wayne Duband, Grant Tinker, Rowland Perkins, me, Jimmy Woods, and Rod Stone.

For sixteen years a group of us gathered New Year's week at Warner Bros. luxurious Acapulco estate. Seated (*l to r*): Jack Valenti and his wife, Mary Margaret Valenti; me; long-time friend Julian Ludwig; (*back, l to r*): Richard and Penny Crenna; Mary and Mike Wallace; Grant Tinker; and Margaretha Ludwig. My wife, Gloria, is taking the picture.

My son Mark, now a producer, with cinematographer John Alonzo on the set of *Roots: The Gift*, one of his first producing assignments (1987).

With sculptor Henry Moore at his studio in England when we bought our first major art piece (1981).

Jack Benny presents me with the Emmy for Program of the Year, *The Making of the President, 1960,* my first major award (1963).

Induction into the Television Hall of Fame with George Burns and David Brinkley (1989).

Gene Kelly presents me with my second Oscar—the Jean Hersholt Humanitarian Award (1985).

French Consul Gerard Coste presents me with the French Legion of Honor (May 2, 1990).

The old Wolper Gang reunion, March 17, 1999. (*Row 1, l to r*): Marylou Steinkraus, Wendy Winter, Christine Foster, Ted Strauss, Julian Ludwig, Auriel Sanderson, Bob Guenette, Jack Haley Jr., me, Mel Stuart, Alan Landsburg, David Vowell, Larry Neiman, Chuck Campbell, Bud Smith, David Blewitt; (*row 2*): Chris Kevin, Janet Di Bella, Ron Filecia, Gerald Fried, Janette Webb, Sascha Schneider, Nick Webster, David Saxon, Jackie Brady Baugh, Paul Mason, Linda Thornley, Dale Olson, Maxine Surks, Ben Bennett, Joan Koury Rhodes, Bob Larson, Jerry Johnson, Mark Wolper, Bob Leeburg, Diane Thompson, Roberta Edgar, Syd Field, Mary Hughes Thompson, Arnold Shapiro, Burt van Munster, Bruce Kerner, Mel Neiman, Paul Freeman, Nikki Lapenieks, Millie Want, Gladys Lumsden; (*row 3*): Charles Uy, Al Ramrus, Paul Hunter, James Schmerer, Stan Lazan, Freida Lee Mock, John Kaye, Tony Pinker, Bill Edgar, Irwin Russell, David Seltzer, Jerry Zeitman, Bill Cartwright, Malvin Wald, Arthur Swerdloff, Marilyn Lassen, Robert Abel, Jeri Sopanen, Lorin Salob, Rhonda Gradin Buha, Paul Boorstin, J. D. Feigelson, George Stephenson, Marshall Flaum, Marge Pinns Karney, Joan Owens, Tom Fuchs, Marilyn Ryan, David Ronne, Allan Folsom; (*row 4*): Doug Waterman, Terry Sanders, Jack Tillar, Chris Wiser, Bud Wiser, Mike Davis, Joe Sanford, Robert Fresco, Malcolm Leo, Nick Clapp, Andrew Solt, Bill Kronick, Mary Nelson Duerrstein, Frank Decot, Chris Friedgen, Irwin Rosten, Georg Stanford Brown, Phil Savenick, Glenn Farr, Hyman Kaufman, Peter Rosten, Bert Lovitt, Erica Flaum, Michael Manheim, David Oyster, John Orland.

stantly arguing about everything. Wally kept quitting, and when he wasn't quitting, I was firing him. But we just kept going.

We wanted the last scene to be a crumbling ghost town, devoid of human beings—with insects crawling over the ruins of civilization. There was such a town on the western side of Death Valley, California, called Darwin. It consisted of corrugated-iron buildings, which were falling down. I envisioned clouds of dust blowing through, so Sacha Schneider brought a big wind machine out there.

I arrived late, and by the time I did, half the town had been blown down. The buildings had collapsed into heaps of wreckage. I couldn't believe it. We had blown down an entire town. In Czechoslovakia I'd blown up a town, but I'd paid cash for it. Here, apparently, I'd blown down a town. Then an old man told me, "A dust devil like I've never seen before came right out of the sky and right through the town." Incredibly, a twister had touched down in exactly the same path as would have been created by the wind machine. So we never got blamed for knocking down the town of Darwin.

When the rough cut was assembled, I decided to screen it at my house. Wally Green was there, and Mel, Jack, Alan, John Soh, who had edited it, and writer David Seltzer. We were going to watch the film, then enjoy an elegant dinner that my wife, Gloria, had prepared. I watched the film in disbelief. It wasn't a movie; it was an assembly of interesting clips. Just insect after insect after insect. When it was over, I stood up and said, "This is an absolute disaster. A disaster." Then I started yelling. How did this happen? Didn't anybody know what was going on? I screamed. Even for me it was a great tantrum. People yelled right back at me. It was absolute mayhem, or more specifically, a typical creative meeting at the Wolper Organization.

Gloria heard the yelling and began wondering what we were going to do about dinner. She didn't believe it was possible we could actually have a friendly meal after my tirade. But, when she called us in, we came out of the room laughing, had a lovely dinner, at which we discussed everything but the movie, then went back to the viewing room and started screaming at each other again.

Nothing held the movie together. The entire picture seemed to consist of close-ups of insects. It needed something more. David Seltzer suggested we market the film as a vitally important environmental movie, but I disagreed, explaining, "I don't want environment. I want something to make money. This is a disaster film."

A lightbulb went on in Seltzer's fertile brain. "Then why don't we create the guy," he said. "Let's create a really controversial character that will claim that insects are taking over the earth." And so Dr. Nils Hellstrom was born. It was a brilliant idea, and we all agreed to it right away. What was missing was the human element, and Dr. Hellstrom gave it to us. His theory was that because insects reproduce so rapidly, in such large numbers, they can readily adapt to any change in the environment—and those that survive the changes are stronger than those that died. The natural habitat for insects is anywhere they live, he explained, which is everywhere. And Dr. Hellstrom, played by actor Lawrence Pressman, was trying to warn the world to beware, but no one was paying any attention to him. "The insects have the answer," he said seriously, "because they never asked the question . . . the true winner in the race for survival is the last to finish the race."

Dr. Hellstrom knitted together the whole film. He gave us a reason—and a warning—for each sequence. With him, it was a really frightening film. So good that, at times, even I believed it.

We also had a hauntingly beautiful musical score written by Lalo Schifrin, who used a variety of extremely unusual instruments—African thumb pianos and talking drums, water phones, Mexican clay shakers, dharma Indian bells, Japanese Kabuki drums—and combined it with David Seltzer's narration to create the perfect emotional mood.

I decided to enter the film in the Cannes Film Festival. We created a wonderfully scary logo—a close-up of the eyes of a butterfly against the butterfly wing that made it look like something from outer space, with the line "Shocking. Beautiful. Brilliant. Sensual. Deadly . . . and in the end, only they will survive." A great line. We were booked into the main theater of the festival—but at four o'clock in the afternoon. A terrible time. I didn't think anyone would be there to watch it. I had brochures printed really pushing the film, and for four straight days, Gloria and I and several other people slipped them under the doors of every hotel room in the city.

The theater was packed for the screening. I couldn't believe it. People were fighting to get in at four o'clock in the afternoon. And they were cheering at the end. As Wally and I walked out, I said to him, "Well, looks like we fooled 'em again!"

The Hellstrom Chronicle created a sensation in Cannes. Rather than allowing us to participate in the general competition for awards—a lot of studios had spent a lot of money in Cannes to promote major films—they practically created one for us. Before the committee voted on the major awards, we received the Grand Prix du Technique. For us that was perfect.

The day after the screening I made a substantial deal for European distribution with 20th Century Fox. But a great deal of doubt remained that Americans would pay to see a ninety-minute-long documentary about insects taking over the world. In the United States, *documentary* remained a negative word. The film opened in Los Angeles at the Crest in Westwood. After dinner, Gloria and I decided to drive over to see how the picture was doing. But, just as in a bad movie, as we approached the theater the streets were mobbed. I thought, oh, jeez, just what I need, an accident. But as we got closer, I discovered the crowds of people were waiting in long lines to get inside. The theater was sold out and people were still pushing to get in. It was exhilarating, astonishing. At the end of the week I discovered we were only $200 shy of breaking the house record—that's for all films. Joe Levine once told me a story that, when he was starting out as a distributor, a film of his was only a few dollars away from breaking the house record—so he took out the cash and paid it himself. I remembered that and bought $250 worth of tickets, then spent a lot of money advertising that we'd broken the house record in the first theater in which the picture played.

The reviews were spectacular. The *San Francisco Chronicle* called it "the film of the year!" *New York Times* critic Vincent Canby wrote that the inclusion of an actor as Dr. Hellstrom was unnecessary, that a documentary about just the insects would have worked very well. As I read that, I thought it was unfortunate that Vincent Canby hadn't seen the picture without the human element. It just didn't work. He did add though, "Anyone who has lived for more than a week in a New York apartment already knows that a détente with insects must be reached if the world is to survive."

One reviewer wrote that while the film was fascinating, it didn't really scare him, but "the ability of Henry Kissinger to multiply himself by the thousands every day would be truly frightening."

The film also did extremely well in the theaters and was nominated for the Academy Award for Best Documentary. It was our ninth nomination—although we'd never won. Unfortunately, the Oscars took place during the TV selling season and I had to be in New York. I wasn't going to miss a sale just to watch someone else pick up an Oscar. I was watching the ceremony with Gloria in our room at the Park Lane Hotel, and when they opened the envelope and announced that we had won, I got so excited I started jumping up and down on my bed and screaming. The people in the next room must have thought either I was the most extraordinary lover or I was insane. Well, I was insane; we'd just won an Academy Award! Wally Green accepted the Oscar, as was proper. And after the initial excitement wore off, I wanted to talk to everybody—but they were all at the ceremony.

The success of this movie proved that a market existed for theatrical documentaries, which led to the only X-rated film I ever made. Because we were producing films primarily for television, we rarely explored anything concerning sex, but when we began looking for ideas for our next feature-length documentaries, I met with Nick Noxon and Irwin Rosten to try to figure out what we wanted to do. What do people want, I asked, what subjects are they interested in?

"Sex and food," Rosten said.

Exactly. We discussed many different ways of approaching these subjects until finally someone mentioned animals. I responded to that immediately: "Right. Animal sex. That's what we'll do." This was followed by a long silence.

Finally Nick said, "What an incredible idea—animal sex."

It was a legitimate idea, reproductive biology. The only real surprise was that no one had done it before us. We knew exactly what we wanted to do—show animals doing it. But we couched it in documentary terms: "The mating of the breeding masses," we said, adding that the thesis of the film was that life started with natural selection, has evolved into planned selection, and will ultimately evolve into life created in the laboratory. We titled it *Birds Do It, Bees Do It*—the line from the Cole Porter song "Let's Do It," which was sung over the titles by Bobby Short. Then we went out and shot and bought footage of just about every species imaginable having sex . . . making love . . . procreating for the continuity of the species.

We began the film with a single cell dividing, then birds and bees and fleas, all the way to elephants and rhinos. We shot and collected more than one million feet of film while making this picture, with twenty wildlife cameramen shooting on five continents, following the mating rituals of animals and insects. Some of this footage was difficult to obtain; we knew from the beginning, for example, that we had to address the oft-asked question, how do porcupines do it? We sent a photographer to Wisconsin for four days. None of the porcupines mated. Someone in Michigan told us he had porcupines that would mate, so we sent a photographer to Michigan. Never mated. Porcupines do not mate on command. Finally, we got rare footage of porcupine sex.

I have to admit that few films we'd ever done had attracted the attention of staff members as this one did. Whenever new footage arrived, people would crowd into the cutting room to look at it on the Moviola. The bigger the . . . animal, the bigger the crowd. When other people heard about this project, they invariably asked me the same question: Which animal has the biggest penis?

The things one learns in this business. I can report with some expertise that the answer is . . . the water rhinoceros. It's about . . . it's about . . . it's very, very big. Maybe five feet long. We all laughed when we saw that rhino's penis.

When we did a sequence about horses mating, the film editor cut out the hard-core material. After watching several minutes of that footage, I said, "Turn on the lights," and then I told everyone, "Gentlemen, this film is about sex. I don't see the genitals. That's what the audience will be talking about and I want to see it." And so they put it back in.

At some point we decided we needed to show a human birth. The question was how to do it. Malcolm Leo had worked out a deal with an animator to use small, doll-like figures and a kind of stop-action animation. Who could complain about naked puppets? I asked Malcolm what it was going to cost—and he told me $50,000. Fifty thousand dollars! I picked up my cigar. "I got a better idea," I said. "We're going to use midgets. It'll cost us five cents and nobody will know the difference."

That sequence did not get into the movie.

When the film was completed, we submitted it to the Motion Picture Association of America to be rated. We were hoping for a G rating—we believed the film was a documentary about the reproduction of the species, not a sex film. But I would not have been surprised to receive a PG. Instead, this became my only film to be rated X. X! I was livid. An X rating would have guaranteed the film would fail and cost me a fortune. I complained bitterly to the ratings board. What are you going to do, I asked, put an X on every barnyard and zoo in America? Right out there in front, welcome to the X-rated Bronx Zoo? Because in the zoo, animals fornicate all the time. And they do it right in front of people. I said, "Every farm kid in America has seen animals mate, and you can walk by every zoo and see the penis of a baboon."

Apparently my argument made sense to them, because eventually we received a PG rating. We had to cut out only one shot—a close-up of an erect penis in the elephant mating sequence. The film was well received. The *San Francisco Chronicle* reviewer wrote, "It may just be the most amazing film I've ever seen. . . . It had the audience oohing, aahing, and applauding at the remarkable nature footage." It did acceptable business, but not nearly what we had originally believed possible, particularly for the amount of work that went into making it. But it remains an extraordinarily entertaining documentary.

By 1973, we had become a ministudio, providing as much programming for both television and the movies as several larger producers. But more than simply churning out product, we were making cutting-edge films that few other producers would risk. We didn't have a large bureaucracy; in fact, we didn't have any bureaucracy. We couldn't afford it. The final decision-making process could basically be defined as me. If I wanted to make a certain film and it made sense financially, we did it. *Wattstax*, the first black concert film, was an example of that.

I was approached by a man named Al Bell, who was producing a free, live seven-hour concert at the Los Angeles Coliseum featuring the top artists from his company, STAXX Records, performers like Isaac Hayes, Rufus Thomas, the Staple Singers, and Carla Thomas. The purpose of the concert was to commemorate the Watts riots, so it was to be called *Wattstax*. Al Bell wanted me to film it. I loved the idea. Eventually Columbia put up $500,000.

This is pretty much the casual way things happened at the company. A few days after meeting Al Bell, I walked into Mel Stuart's office and told him I'd agreed to film a black concert and I wanted him to produce and direct it. Mel worked closely with Forrest Hamilton, the son of legendary musician Chico Hamilton, and with a black producer assigned by STAXX named Larry Shaw. When they were finished, Mel realized they had done a fine job filming the concert, but it wasn't really a movie. There was no story, no connective tissue. Same problem as the insect film, *The Hellstrom Chronicle*. What was completely lacking was the meaning of this music to the African-American community. So Mel conducted many street interviews, which he interspersed with the performances.

The film still lacked cohesion. Then Forrest and Larry took Mel to a club in Watts. "I sat down to watch the show," Mel remembers, "and a young comedian named Richard Pryor came on. I realized I was watching a genius." After the show, Mel sat for hours with Pryor. Richard responded instantly and brilliantly to every question Mel asked. Mel came into the office next morning raving about this brilliant comedian he'd met. Pryor became the glue that held the whole film together.

I'd never met anyone like Richard Pryor. There were so many entrances to his mind, so many unique paths to follow. Richard was an extremely complex man. One day, for example, Mel set up a chessboard for a game and told him white makes the first move.

Not in Richard Pryor's world. "No way," Pryor said. "Black goes first."

I arranged with the head of the Cannes Film Festival to show *Wattstax* out of competition. I took Richard Pryor and the entire production team to France with us. While we were there, I hired a bus to take the group on a tour of the south of France, including a stop at the palace in Monaco. I savored the thought of a meeting between Princess Grace and Richard Pryor. Just thinking about it made me smile. Grace was not at the palace.

On the way back, we stopped at La Chaumière, one of my favorite restaurants. It is at the top of the Grande Corniche. As we sat there, I looked over at Richard and saw tears running down his face. "What's wrong?" I asked.

"Nothing," he said. "Spending this day in the south of France, I just never knew the world could be so beautiful."

That was the Richard Pryor few people ever got to meet. It was impossible not to like, even love, and certainly admire him. That was his first movie and, we like to believe, attracted the attention that led to his movie career.

Within the black community, *Wattstax* holds almost legendary status, but it never broke out into the mainstream. While profitable, it never received the attention it deserved. But for me, it marked the beginning of my relationship with the black community in film.

TWENTY-NINE

I'VE GOT A GOLDEN TICKET

With Howard Jeffrey rehearsing Gene Wilder (1970)

Of all the television programs and motion pictures I've produced—about all the fascinating subjects, in all the places around the world, with all the remarkable people and animals—only one has made me a hero for children. People often introduce me to their children by explaining, "This is David Wolper. He made *Roots* and the Jacques Cousteau specials and *The Thorn Birds* and *Willy Wonka*—"

And inevitably, their eyes open wide, and after a slight delay they say in wonder, "You did *Willy Wonka!*"

I made very little programming especially for children, although I always hoped kids would learn from and enjoy my documentaries. And I certainly never set out to make a classic children's movie. As with just about everything else we made, *Willy Wonka* was a good deal. It was based on the well-known children's book *Charlie and the Chocolate Factory*, written by Roald Dahl. The idea to turn that book into a movie came from Mel Stuart's daughter. Madeline, who was about ten years old, told

Mel, "Daddy, I love this book. Why don't you bring it to Uncle David to make it into a movie."

Mel pitched the concept to me, and I put it on the list. Several months later I met with Ken Mason of the Quaker Oats Company, which had sponsored several of my television projects. I was pitching several new projects to him when he mentioned that Quaker Oats was introducing a new candy bar.

A *chocolate* candy bar, perhaps?

It was a perfect match. *Charlie and the Chocolate Factory* immediately leaped to the top of my list. This is the story of an eccentric candy maker named Willy Wonka, I explained, who puts five golden tickets—each one a pass to visit his amazing candy factory—in his Wonka bars. Desperate people try almost everything imaginable to find those tickets, but poverty-stricken Charlie and four others finally win them. During the magical tour, Willy Wonka tests the honesty of all the winners—and only Charlie passes the test and wins the entire factory.

While it was highly unusual for a cereal company to finance a feature film, Quaker Oats decided to name their candy the Wonka bar and bought the rights to the name from the author. Their only condition was that the title of the movie be changed from *Charlie and the Chocolate Factory* to *Willy Wonka and the Chocolate Factory*.

"You're going to finance the entire picture," I said. "No problem."

The workers in Willy Wonka's chocolate factory were called the Oompa-Loompas, and in the book they were black. We knew it would be difficult to make a movie in which a supposedly beloved figure kept black slaves working in his candy factory, so we decided to make the Oompa-Loompas orange—our version of Oz's Munchkins. It worked; we did not receive a single complaint from an orange midget. In a later version of Dahl's book, he made the Oompa-Loompas short white hippies.

The first major decision was where to shoot the picture. In the film, the children sail down a chocolate river that runs through the factory. I had to find a soundstage large enough to hold our chocolate river. Because our budget was only $2.1 million, I needed to make a good deal with a studio. I traveled throughout Ireland, England, Spain, and Italy searching for the right location. Dino De Laurentiis wanted me to make the film at Cinecittà Studios in Rome, which he owned. So, when I was in Rome, he took me to dinner at an outdoor restaurant in a lovely piazza. Naturally he was accompanied by three or four beautiful Italian starlets. This restaurant, he told me, was the best-a steak-a place in the whole world. Naturally, I ordered steak, medium rare.

When I cut into it, I found that it was well done. "How you like the steak?" he asked.

"To tell you the truth, Dino," I said, "it's a little too well done."

He was furious. With that, he picked up my steak in his hands and heaved it into the street. As he was shouting at the waiter in Italian—Mr. Wolper, blah, blah, blah, big American producer, blah, blah, blah— everyone else at the table was laughing. I was in complete shock. Within seconds the waiter returned with another steak. I took one bite and De Laurentiis demanded, "Now how you like?"

Are you kidding me? After that outburst? "Dino," I said, "you're absolutely right. This is the best steak I've ever had."

I finally decided to film in Munich, Germany. The facilities were first-rate, the technical crew was as good as any other in the world, and Munich had a sort of fairy-tale look to it without being easily identifiable by the audience. And the Munich gasworks looked like an excellent Wonka candy factory exterior. Next, I naturally signed Mel to direct the film.

The success of the movie depended completely on the casting. To be believable, Willy Wonka had to have a magical quality about him, the joy of a child in a man's body. For a time, we seriously considered Joel Grey. But we also looked at a lot of other actors. Years later, I learned that Fred Astaire had wanted to play the role, but never approached me.

The powerful agent Sue Mengers represented both Anthony Newley and Barbra Streisand. One afternoon I got a call from her. She wanted Newley to play Willy Wonka and sing two songs. If I gave the role to Newley, she carefully suggested, or maybe I interpreted that, she would get me a date with Barbra Streisand.

The offer was entirely proper; I was separated from my second wife and dating many different women. But how could I respond to that? I certainly respected Barbra Streisand's talent, but I did not want to go out with her. I replied the only way I could: I told her I would think about it. So I hung up the phone and never thought about it again.

We were auditioning actors in a suite at the Plaza in New York when Gene Wilder back-flipped in. Wilder's career was just beginning; he had done *The Producers*, which later became a classic comedy and a hot Broadway show, but had not been that successful when it was originally released. When he walked into the room, both Mel and I knew instantly we had found our Wonka. Perfect does not begin to describe him; the role fit him tighter than one of Cousteau's wet suits. When he left the room, Mel said, "That's him, that's Willy Wonka. We've got to sign him."

I agreed, but warned Mel, "Don't tell anybody. I've got to make a deal and we can save a lot of money if they don't know how much we want him. Don't let anybody know."

With that, Mel ran out into the hall after Wilder. He caught him at the elevator and told him, "Gene, you got it. You're the guy." So much for subtlety.

I assigned Stan Margulies to produce *Wonka* with me and Mel to direct it. Dahl wrote the original screenplay. Anthony Newley and Leslie Bricusse wrote the music, including the classic "Candy Man." I remember the night they came over to my house and we all sat around the piano and Bricusse played the music while Newley sang. The first time I heard "Candy Man" I knew it was a great song. It just carried with it the most wonderful feeling. Of course, that was before the myth was created that it actually had to do with cocaine dealers—but it was a song about the joys of candy. It became a worldwide hit because of Sammy Davis Jr.'s platinum record.

We didn't get every actor we wanted. When we cast the parents of the children, we found the absolutely perfect actress to play the mother of Mike TeeVee. But, when we offered her the part, she hesitated, then admitted she had been offered a role in a TV series and couldn't decide which part to accept. We're going to Munich, Mel told her, this is going to be a major feature, and it's going to be a fantastic picture. Most TV series fail. . . .

The actress, Jean Stapleton, called the next day to turn down our offer, explaining she had decided to accept the role of Edith Bunker in a new sitcom entitled *All in the Family.*

A sixth-grader from Cleveland named Peter Ostrum was cast as Charlie.

We had a real problem with Dahl's script. It was completely faithful to the book, which made it almost unfilmmable, and he wouldn't change anything. Working with him was not a pleasant experience. Finally, we brought David Seltzer to Munich, locked him in a hotel room, and had him rewrite the script. When it was done, Seltzer flew to London to show it to Dahl, who made him sit downstairs waiting as Dahl read the revised material, a really terrible way for a famous author to treat a fine young writer. Dahl was very angry that we had dared rewrite his script, but finally, he came downstairs and bitterly admitted that it was acceptable. For a man capable of writing brilliant children's fantasies, Dahl was a difficult person.

We filmed the picture in only ninety days. In the final scene, as originally written by Dahl, Willy Wonka, Charlie, and his grandfather are in a glass elevator, floating up toward the roof, when Willy tells Charlie that he is giving him the chocolate factory. Dahl's script ended with Charlie's grandfather, the great Jack Albertson, yelling, "Yippee!"

Mel hated that line. He insisted we couldn't end the picture with Grandpa saying "Yippee!" Seltzer had left Munich and was holed up in a cabin somewhere in Maine, recuperating from his experience with Dahl, but Mel managed to get him on the phone. Gene Wilder and the rest of the cast and crew were just sitting around waiting for the last scene. "I can't end the picture with Grandpa saying 'Yippee,'" Mel said. "You've got to come up with something better than that and you have to do it right now. We're spending seventy-five thousand dollars to film this scene and we need an ending."

"All right," Seltzer said, "give me a few minutes." Five minutes later he got back on the phone: "Here it is. Willy Wonka looks at Charlie and asks, 'Charlie, do you know what happens to people who get everything they want in life?'

"Charlie looks at him and says fearfully, 'No, Mr. Wonka, what happens to somebody who gets everything he wants in life?'

"And Willy Wonka says, 'He lives happily ever after.' The end."

Maybe it wasn't "So power passes," but it was a pretty impressive display of talent under pressure. That's the way the picture ended. We tried hard and failed to get Seltzer the script credit he had earned for the movie, but *Willy Wonka and the Chocolate Factory* was written by both David Seltzer and Roald Dahl.

When it was completed, we cut only one scene, a great scene. While all the children in the world are buying Wonka bars hoping to find the golden tickets, an Englishman climbs to the top of a mountain to meet the great guru who is about to reveal the secret of life. "O great guru," the Englishman says, "I've been climbing for days. My party is lost. I'm hungry and freezing. Tell me, what is the meaning of life?"

To which the guru responds, "Do you have a Wonka bar?"

"I do," the explorer admits. "It's my last bit of food. You can have it, but please tell me, what's the meaning of life?"

The guru opens the Wonka bar, and when he sees that it does not contain a golden ticket, his shoulders droop and he reveals the secret: "Life is a disappointment."

Dahl pretty much hated the picture, as did his widow, who sold two of his other books, *James and the Giant Peach* and *Matilda,* to Disney. Neither of them succeeded. I can just imagine, whenever somebody meets Mrs. Dahl, they always tell her how much they loved *Willy Wonka and the Chocolate Factory*. It must drive her crazy. I hope so. I was never able to get the rights to do the sequel I proposed, but Warner Bros. did. *Wonka* opened June 30, 1971, during the same period as *Carnal Knowledge, Shaft, Klute, Escape from the Planet of the Apes,* and Warren Beatty and Julie Christie's *McCabe and Mrs. Miller*—and every one of those movies did better business than we did. *Willy Wonka* got mixed reviews, and certainly no one predicted it would become a cult classic.

The picture was also released simultaneously with the introduction of the Quaker Oats candy bar. However, they had a serious problem with the formula, and eventually it had to be removed from the market.

But kids of all ages loved the picture and continue to love it. Barbra Streisand would call my office every year during the Christmas holiday season—this was before the existence of VCRs—and request a print to show at home. Naturally, I sent it to her, although I still didn't go out with her.

Willy Wonka became a cult movie even among the young rock 'n' rollers. Shock rocker Marilyn Manson is a huge fan of the movie. The dialogue from the boat scene, "It's raining, it's snowing, it's a hurricane a-blowing," is on one of his albums. It was reported in the New York papers that he was going to play Willy Wonka as satan in a new version of the movie, but the report wasn't true.

This poem from *Wonka*, "There is no earthly way of knowing, / Which direction we are going," is at the start of all Marilyn Manson's concerts. His rock video is modeled after *Willy Wonka*, complete with Oompa-Loompas.

There is also a punk pop band out of L.A. billing itself as Vermicious K, taken from a line by Wonka in the film. One of the band members, Michael, had dubbed himself Mike TeeVee. They've just done an album and decided to call it *Scrumdidilyumptious*. And the modern rock band, Veruca Salt, got its name from the spoiled little rich girl in the movie.

Quaker Oats never realized what it owned. When I sold Wolper Productions to Warner Bros., I suggested Warner's buy Quaker Oats' 50 percent of the rights. The cereal company sold its share for about $500,000. It was an absolute steal. Warner's made a fortune on the videocassette. They've sold millions of copies and the picture continues to sell well. On the twenty-fifth anniversary of the film, Warner's rereleased it in theaters and sold another few million tapes. On the thirtieth anniversary, they released the film on DVD, adding interviews with all the kids. Very few children of all ages don't know about the Oompa-Loompas.

There are a few unusual incidents connected with *Willy Wonka*. The first is a horrible bit of *Wonka* trivia. In Guiana, before the Jim Jones cult followers committed suicide, they and the children watched *Willy Wonka and the Chocolate Factory* to keep the children's minds off what was about to happen.

The Utopian Socialist Party tried to use *Willy Wonka and the Chocolate Factory* as proof that socialism worked. They said the Oompa-Loompas lived in happiness in return for their fair labor. Wonka provided them with a place to live, peace, protection, and prosperity, just as in a socialist state. The government, represented by Wonka, provides for its citizens in return for a fair amount of labor.

In the late 1990s, *Entertainment Weekly* selected the top ten videos to watch "when you're stuck inside on a rainy day." *Jaws* was number four. *Lawrence of Arabia* was number three. The *Star Wars* trilogy was number two. And number one, "the video equivalent of an overstuffed comforter," was *Willy Wonka*.

Oddly enough, none of the kids in the movie had show business careers. Peter Ostrum, our Charlie, turned down a three-picture deal and became a successful veterinarian in upstate New York. Veruca Salt was an actress for a while and is now a physical therapist. Mike TeeVee went on a backpack trip around the world after he made the film and is now a stockbroker with Salomon Smith Barney in Los Angeles. Augustus Gloop is an engineer still living in Germany, and Violet Beauregarde is a hospital administrator in the Midwest.

I guess Willy Wonka is probably the most well-known film I've ever done in my lifetime. I've always said you have to see the film twice: once when you're a kid, then again when you're an adult, because there are two films. There are two stories in Willy Wonka.

Wonka fans throughout the world love to repeat quotes from the movie. Here are some of their favorites:

"Candy is Dandy, but liquor is quicker."
(originally from "Reflections on Ice-Breaking" by Ogden Nash)

"We have so much time and so little to do. Wait a minute, strike that. Reverse it."

"A little nonsense now and then is relished by the wisest men."

"The suspense is terrible, I hope it lasts."
(originally from *The Importance of Being Earnest* by Oscar Wilde)

"Oh, you should never, never doubt what nobody is sure about."

"We are the music-makers and we are the dreamers of dreams."
(originally from "Ode" by Arthur O'Shaughnessy)

"If she's a lady, I'm a vermicious knid."

"So shines a good deed in a weary world."
(originally from *The Merchant of Venice* by William Shakespeare)

THIRTY

TERRORISM

With Hitler's photographer, Leni Riefenstahl (1972)

Willy Wonka and the Chocolate Factory indirectly led to one of the most fascinating—and terrifying—experiences of my *life,* the making of *Visions of Eight.*

The 1972 Olympic games were held in Munich, the first time they had been in Germany since the 1936 Berlin Olympics, which had served as a stage for Adolf Hitler. While filming *Willy Wonka,* I had met many people at the Bavaria Studios in Munich, and they had invited me to make the official documentary film about the 1972 Olympics. Normally, a citizen of the host country makes the official Olympic film; this was the first time that an independent foreign producer had been asked to produce it. It was an exciting challenge.

Only then did I realize what a difficult job it would be. Prior to the Olympics being broadcast worldwide on television, the official film was the first, and often the only, opportunity for people to see the moments they'd been reading about. Once the games were covered on TV from beginning to end, the official film lost its value. If we just did it the old way, by the time we edited and released our film it would be very old news. So, I needed to find a new and exciting approach. Several years earlier I had discussed making a movie in which five great directors would each film their own sexual fantasies. After speaking with several directors, I realized it was a pretty sleazy idea and not the kind of movie I wanted to make. But I still loved the concept of seeing one particular subject through the eyes of the greatest movie directors in the world. This seemed like the perfect opportunity to do that.

My plan was to hire about ten great directors from different countries to cover the Olympics and let them choose their own subjects. This film wouldn't be reportage; instead, it would capture the feeling of the Olympics. I wanted to make poetry rather than prose. The German Olympic Committee loved the idea.

The first director I approached was the master Italian filmmaker Federico Fellini. I just loved the thought of seeing the Olympics through the mind of Fellini—and I knew that if he agreed to do it, every other respected director would follow. I spent three days meeting with him, and he seemed interested. But finally he said, "I tell you what I do, Blue Eyes," which is what he called me, "I can't do your Olympic film—but I'm going to do something just as good. I know why you came to see me. If Fellini will do this picture, all the other directors will also do it. Is that right?"

"That's right, Mr. Fellini."

"So I'm going to tell you what you can do. I'll be in the middle of filming during that time, but you can tell all those other directors that Fellini is going to do your picture. And when you have all the other directors, I will announce that I am dropping out because I have another picture to do, but you will have all the other directors signed and I will have accomplished my task."

I reached across the table and we shook hands. That afternoon I called Claude Lelouch in France. "Fellini's going to represent Italy," I said, "we'd like you to do it for France." After Lelouch agreed, I called Milos Forman, "Fellini is doing it for Italy, Lelouch will do it for France, and we'd like you to do it for Czechoslovakia."

Eventually ten directors agreed to participate, among them, Arthur Penn from the United States, John Schlesinger representing England, Juri Ozerov from the Soviet Union, Kon Ichikawa of Japan, Ousmane Sembene of Senegal, and Michael Pfleghar from Germany. I tried to get Ingmar Bergman from Sweden, but he wouldn't even meet with me, claiming he was busy making a picture. Instead, the great actress Mai

Zetterling represented Sweden. When Fellini dropped out, we replaced him with Franco Zeffirelli. It was, arguably, the greatest assembly of directors ever to work on a single project. Each director was to be paid $10,000 and would pick an event to film. My working title was *Visions of Ten.*

Just before the games began, a controversy erupted as several African nations threatened to withdraw if Rhodesia was allowed to participate. When they dropped out, I got a phone call from Zeffirelli, who was planning to do an operatic piece around the lighting of the Olympic torch. He said, "You tell the Olympic Committee that Zeffirelli will not do this picture if the African nations do not participate."

"Mr. Zeffirelli," I replied, "I don't want to insult you, but the International Olympic Committee doesn't give a crap if you or I make this film. They're operating on a different level." I pleaded with him to reconsider, but he was adamant and refused to participate.

And so the film became *Visions of Nine.*

As each director selected the subject he wanted to film, we listed the cameras he would need, the lenses, the technical assistance. It was well-organized chaos. Schlesinger selected the marathon and began shooting the practice runs in England. Kon Ichikawa decided to film the hundred-yard dash as it had never been filmed before: he used just about every camera we had, thirty-four cameras, to shoot the ten-second race. He wanted to capture on film every breath the runners took, he wanted to see their cheeks responding to wind pressure, he wanted their perspiration, their expressions, the sounds of their spikes cutting into the dirt—and that ten-second race lasted eleven minutes in the picture.

Arthur Penn initially began filming the dramatic story of a South Carolina convict, Bobby Lee Hunter, who was attempting to make the Olympic boxing team as a flyweight. It would have made a wonderful piece, but at the Olympic trials, he was beaten in the finals and didn't make the team. So, Penn ended up filming the pole vault. We thought Mai Zetterling would choose to film the women athletes, but she selected the weight lifters, "because they are very sensual. They're very obsessed and I'm fascinated by obsessions." I thought Claude Lelouch would want to film the women, but he was fascinated by the losers, the reaction of athletes who have been training for an event for a lifetime and have lost. "There are two hundred gold medal winners and seventy-five hundred losers," he explained. Finally, German director

Michael Pfleghar filmed the women, following them from their hair-dressers to the finish line.

Juri Ozerov also wanted to do the weight lifting, at which the Soviets excelled, but when he learned that Zetterling had already picked that sport, he did the moments before a race begins, how competitors prepare, how they deal with the pressure. "This is the moment of truth," he said. "I want to show the athletes' fears, anxieties, prayers." Ironically, Ozerov, the only Communist among the directors, was the only person to film inside a church, where he showed the athletes in prayer. Ousmane Sembene chose to document the Senegalese basketball team. The last person to make up his mind was Milos Forman.

"Milos," I told him every day, "if you don't make up your mind, you're not going to have any cameras to shoot with." I asked him to try to find some humor, as everyone else was being so serious. "Okay, I'll try to be funny," he said seriously.

Three days before the Olympics began, he decided to mix Munich nightlife, the social aspect of the Olympics, with the decathlon. He picked the decathlon, he told me, because "if we were lucky in the tenth event, five competitors would collapse from exhaustion.

"Most important," he continued, "is that for the last lap of the final distance run, I want to play this excerpt from Beethoven's Ninth Symphony, the 'Ode to Joy.'" He had it on a cassette and played it for me. "Just imagine these guys," he said, his eyes closed, seeing it, "after two grueling days of competition, they're in the final lap. When the winner hits the top of his stride, I'll cut to an opera singer hitting high C!"

When I agreed it was terrific, he told me, "The Munich Symphony is playing it tonight. I need several camera crews there to film it." For months Milos had not been able to make up his mind what he wanted to film, now he needed to shoot a symphony in a few hours.

Fortunately, we had a fabulous production manager, a woman I had used on a number of my European location films, Pia Arnold, who had been born and raised in Munich and knew everybody. Within two hours, she'd managed to get us permission and made arrangements to film the concert.

The directors shared a great feeling of camaraderie; they helped each other as much as possible. When Ichikawa shot the hundred-yard dash, for example, he needed extra cameramen, so Claude Lelouch volunteered to operate one of the thirty-five cameras for him.

Probably my favorite scene in the entire picture was shot by Zetterling. After this enormous Russian weight lifter has broken the world record, he drops the barbell on the stage. It sort of bounces once, but stays there—and then six soldiers come running out, struggle to pick it up and carry it off.

It was an incredibly complex production. To film the twenty-six-mile marathon through the streets of Munich, for example, Schlesinger used forty-five camera units operating sixty-five cameras, which we had to mount on electric trucks because Olympic officials did not want gas fumes to interfere with the runners.

But even with all the confusion, dealing with transportation and interpreters and bulky equipment and artistic temperaments and getting everybody fed and housed and making sure the cameras were where they were supposed to be, we were making a wonderful film—until the Black September terrorists destroyed the Olympics.

These Olympics were important to the Germans because of the association of the 1936 Berlin games with Hitler and Nazism. This time the Germans were determined to display the new democratic Germany, and to ensure this, they had the tightest security I had ever seen. It was impossible to move around the Olympic Village without carrying identification. In fact, many people were complaining that security was too tight.

Late one day, I was working in my Olympic Village office when someone ran in and said breathlessly that he had heard—this was not confirmed—that terrorists had gotten into the village and had taken members of the Israeli team hostage. Supposedly, two athletes had been murdered. It just didn't seem possible as this was the very thing the Germans had been working so zealously to prevent.

There was tremendous confusion. We turned on the radio and an interpreter told us that there was a "problem" in the Olympic Village, although the details were extremely sketchy. But the village was being shut down. No one was permitted in or out. German tanks and armored vehicles formed a ring around the village. No sooner had Mark Spitz won his seventh gold medal than a U.S. Army helicopter landed on the roof of his dormitory in the Olympic Village to whisk the Jewish swimming star away to safety.

Gloria and our friends Laraine and David Gerber had been visiting the town of Salzburg when they heard the report and raced back to Munich. As incredible as this sounds, Gloria discovered a secret passage into the village by going through the basements of several buildings. So, she led her two friends through this incredibly tight security right into our hotel.

My first thought was the enormity of the story. Even if we had wanted to film it, we could do nothing. Our directors were all busy working. We had no cameras in the office. While I was frustrated, I knew that thousands of people had brought cameras with them, and I would be able to buy whatever footage I might want. What I didn't know was that Claude Lelouch had headed for the Israeli dormitory with a camera and filmed Black September in action. "I'm filming the losers," Lelouch said, "while the real losers at the Olympics were the Arabs."

We heard that a helicopter summoned to transport the terrorists and their captives to the airport was going to land almost directly in front of my hotel window, which was inside the village, so we returned to my room. I met the film critic Rex Reed and an ABC radio reporter and cameraman in the lobby and invited them up to my suite. When we got up there and looked out, we saw a large helicopter land in the middle of the plaza. The reporter immediately picked up the phone and, seemingly within seconds, was on the air on the ABC network around the world. The entire situation was beyond surreal.

I still didn't believe reports that the terrorists had captured Israelis. I thought the Israelis were on the other side of the village and I assumed they were well protected.

German officials negotiated with the terrorists throughout the day. Hours passed. Only later did we learn that the German government wanted to let them fly to Egypt, but Egyptian president Sadat refused permission. The Israeli government stuck by its policy of never negotiating with terrorists.

Inside the village, Claude Lelouch got as close as safely possible to the Israeli dormitory to film the standoff. A New Zealand wrestler had taken still photos of the terrorists from less than fifty yards away and was trying to sell them to the media. A new rumor seemed to circulate every few seconds. It just didn't seem possible, terrorists invading the Olympics, yet when I looked out my window at the helicopter, I knew how real it was.

It was night when we finally saw people moving around. The courtyard was so well lit it was brighter than any sunlit morning. Suddenly, several buses drove up to the helicopter and stopped almost directly beneath my window. Then the hooded terrorists, carrying guns, led the Israelis—their hands tied behind their backs—from the bus into the helicopter. I felt as if I were watching this in a fog. When the terrorists and their hostages were in the helicopter, its blades came to life and it rose slowly. The ABC reporter was still on the air, live, to the world. We could look right into the helicopter, but there was nothing to be seen. Then, seconds later, the helicopter was gone.

Minutes later it landed at the airport, where German soldiers attacked. In the ensuing battle, five terrorists and eleven Israelis were killed and three terrorists were captured. The captured terrorists were later released when Arab hijackers took another airliner. However, over the next five years, all three of them were mysteriously killed at different places in the world by, it is suspected, the Israeli secret service.

I had spent my professional life documenting momentous events of history, but this was the first time I had been an eyewitness to one.

Nothing even remotely similar to this had ever happened before, so no one knew the proper way to respond. Many people wanted the remaining games to be canceled out of respect for the murdered Israelis, while others argued that a cancellation of the Olympics would give the terrorists a great victory. Finally, the Olympic Committee decided that the competition would be suspended for one day, and a memorial service would be held. Then the games would resume. That was a difficult decision, but it was understandable. Olympic athletes had trained their entire lives for this moment; in four years most of them would be too old to compete. If the games were canceled, the people who would be hurt most were the 7,830 young athletes, whose opportunity to compete on the world stage would be lost forever. So, after a touching memorial service, the Olympics continued.

And while at times it was possible to forget, briefly, what had happened, the horror hung over the games like an endless night.

I, personally, had not expected to play an active role in the Olympics. I was there to produce a film, not to defend the rights of my country. That changed when Gloria and I attended the men's basketball championship game between the United States and the Soviet Union with Gloria and David and Laraine Gerber. Although this was years before the formation of our "Dream Team," America had dominated Olympic basketball competition with college players, winning every game the team had played, sixty-three straight victories. However, the Soviets had become competitive and this was a tough game. It turned out to be one of the most controversial events in Olympic history.

With three seconds remaining, the United States took the lead for the first time, 50–49, on two free throws by Doug Collins. When play resumed, the Russians inbounded the ball and tried to call a time-out. In the confusion the Brazilian referee stopped the clock with two seconds to go. According to the international rules, the Soviets were not permitted to call a time-out in that situation. But, in direct conflict with those rules, the officials ruled that the Russians had called time out with one second remaining on the clock, and they gave the ball to the Russians. Again, the clock ran out and the Americans celebrated. Incredibly, the officials then gave the Russians a third chance, this time ruling that three full seconds were on the clock when the Russians had called a time-out. Given this third opportunity, the Russians threw a desperation pass the entire length of the court and scored the winning basket. This time the Russians celebrated.

The U.S. coach, Hank Iba, went berserk—as well he should have. Something had to be done. Someone had to protest this decision. Unfortunately, for some reason, no representatives of the U.S. Olympic Basketball Federation were around. So, no one was qualified to file an official protest.

In fact, the only American there with official credentials was me. I had complete access to all Olympic facilities. It was the highest official credential of the games. I raced down to courtside and started screaming, "I protest this game on behalf of the American team," and then I signed the official protest sheet. I scribbled my name because I didn't want anyone to know exactly which American had signed it. Three copies of the sheet were on the table, so I tore off one copy in the confusion to protect our interests. None of the Olympic officials at the game knew who I was; they just saw my credentials hanging from my jacket and assumed I was someone important.

The IOC representatives didn't really have a clue what to do. They were caught between American and Russian interests. Eight Russian officials were in one room, the Olympic officials were in another room, and David Gerber and I were in the hallway between them. Finally, the Russians were invited inside to make their case. When they finished, as the representative of the United States, I was asked to explain our protest. I didn't want to argue the case, I didn't feel equipped to do so, and so I just repeated that we protested the game, promising that we would make our case in front of the proper forum.

Ousmane Sembene, of Senegal, was filming the game for our movie. We developed his film that night and saw that, while the Americans were celebrating, the head of the international basketball association, William Jones, had come out of the stands and gone to the officials' table—which is about as illegal as it gets—to take charge and rule that the final three seconds should be replayed. We had all the evidence we needed. But, apparently, it was not enough.

When the Olympic basketball medals were handed out, members of the U.S. team refused to attend the ceremony or accept their silver medals. In fact, one of the players was so upset that he changed his will so that his family, in the future, could never accept the medal.

A protest was heard by a five-man international basketball federation jury of appeal. The jury ruled against the United States, three to two. Italy and Puerto Rico voted to disallow the Soviet basket while, during this Cold War, Hungary, Poland, and Cuba voted against the United States. And while it was clear that a wrong decision had been made, the committee allowed the final score to stand. The U.S. team never accepted its silver medals.

During the Olympics, we had screening rooms in operation all day to allow the directors to view their footage, but after the games ended, we sent each director all his film to be edited in his own country. Each piece had to run between ten and twelve minutes. When we received their initial cuts, including detailed notes telling us where they needed optical effects, fades, dissolves, and other technical changes, we began assembling the picture.

When we viewed these first cuts from the directors, we had two pieces that didn't work at all. Juri Ozerov's film wasn't up to our expectations, so I put Mel Stuart to work recutting it, and when it was completed, Ozerov, who is a terrific person, agreed it was much improved. And Ousmane Sembene never completed his piece about the Senegalese basketball team.

Which is how it finally came to be called *Visions of Eight*.

After it was assembled, Henry Mancini wrote a beautiful score that tied the picture together.

The film was controversial. I had decided not to include the terrorist attack because none of our directors had covered it—and I felt it would overshadow the film, as it had the Olympic games. But immediately, rumors began spreading that Ousmane Sembene had done a piece on the murders and I had dropped it because it was pro-Palestinian. I explained exactly what had happened, that Sembene had disappeared before completing his piece and we couldn't contact him. But then I went a little further: I admitted to an angry African journalist that if Sembene had done a pro-Palestinian piece about the terrorists, I would certainly have dropped it. That answer infuriated a lot of people, but it was absolutely true. As a responsible filmmaker, as a human being, I would never participate in the creation or distribution of a film sympathetic to terrorists.

I had financed the film myself but, before the games, I'd sold the television rights to ABC's Barry Diller, which helped me recoup some of my costs. *Visions of Eight* was chosen to be shown at the Cannes Film Festival, where it was honored with a special award. While I was satisfied with the final picture, the sum total was less than I had envisioned. I think my original concept remained valid; the film was a work of art rather than a sports documentary. However, after everything that had happened, it seemed anticlimactic. We received some nice reviews and parts of the film are still brilliant, but when the games ended, lives moved forward and we never found our audience.

Visions of Eight was not, however, to be the last time I was involved with the Olympics—nor with terrorism. On July 4, 1976, the entire world was electrified when an Israeli commando force rescued Israeli hostages being held captive by Palestinian terrorists at the Entebbe Airport in Uganda. The Israeli air force had landed, undetected, in Uganda, overwhelmed and killed the terrorists, and flown the hostages to safety. During this incredibly daring and heroic feat, only one Israeli soldier was killed, the leader of the raid, Yonathan Netanyahu, brother of a former Israeli prime minister.

The moment I heard the news, I decided to make a film about it—just as did at least a dozen other filmmakers. My friend Edgar Scherick began producing *Raid on Entebbe* starring Charles Bronson. Paramount bought the rights to an instant paperback, *90 Minutes at Entebbe,* and planned to turn it into a movie directed by Sidney Lumet from a screenplay by Paddy Chayefsky. Noah Films in Israel was making an independent film. Universal was planning to film the book *Rescue at Entebbe,* written by noted author William Stephenson, hiring George Roy Hill to direct. Warner Bros. reached an agreement with the Israeli government to make *Operation Yonathan,* in honor of Netanyahu, to be directed by Franklin Schaffner and supposedly starring Steve McQueen.

This story had completely captured the admiration of people all over the world, and they were eager for every detail. It seemed obvious to me that the most successful of all the films would be the first to be released. Less than a month after the raid, Brandon Stoddard at ABC gave me the go-ahead to make a three-hour movie for television. I hired the legendary writer Ernest Kinoy to write the script and Bob Guenette to produce it. I had made many good friends in Israel while making films like *Let My*

People Go, and some of them had been intimately involved in planning the raid, so Guenette went to Israel to meet with them and learn undisclosed details. After Kinoy's second draft, I convinced ABC that we should do the picture on videotape rather than film, which would enable me to shoot and edit it in much less time than it would normally require. But we had to keep the entire project secret or we would lose our advantage; in fact, part of the deal I made with ABC was contingent upon its remaining completely confidential. It was amazing how successful we were. Our director, Marvin Chomsky, signed to direct the picture without knowing completely what it was about; he knew only that it was a top secret project.

Meanwhile, Warner's film was running into endless roadblocks. Production was delayed for two months. Some of the problems were insurmountable: Warner's discovered an abandoned airfield, the perfect set, in the midst of cotton fields owned by a kibbutz. The company offered to pay twice the market value of the cotton to clear the field. Members of the kibbutz, still faithful to the original Zionist ideals, refused to sell. The military chief of staff disapproved of the entire project, which he believed overromanticized the operation, and refused to provide any information. Warner's had spent more than $1 million without being close to beginning production, and they finally dropped the project. I convinced them that the videotape could be transferred to film and shown in theaters. So we made a deal with Warner's to release my film theatrically throughout the rest of the world. In the United States it was shown on ABC. This was the first feature film ever shot on video, but I knew from the beginning that, technically, there was no reason it wouldn't work.

While making this film, I sold my company—for the third time—to Warner Bros. During the time my attorney, Irwin Russell, was negotiating with Frank Wells and Charles McGregor, Warner's executives, I never mentioned to anyone that I had gone to high school with their chairman, Steve Ross. I didn't want that relationship to affect the sale price. But, once the deal was pretty well set, I did call him, and he asked me, "Did you get the corporate jet?"

What corporate jet?

"Tell them you want to be able to fly in the corporate jet." So, when I finalized the deal, I included that demand. They responded that they had to get Steve Ross's okay.

"That's fair," I agreed. I used the Warner's plane for the rest of my career at Warner Bros. I've heard executives at other corporations complain about this expensive executive perk—but I can state, without hesitation, that the right to use that plane was one of the things that kept me at Warner's for over twenty-four years.

Victory at Entebbe! focused on the hostages rather than the military aspect of the raid, meaning a lot of our scenes were interiors, and video is perfect for shooting interiors. Shooting on video rather than film cut our production schedule from six weeks to three weeks and, more importantly, enabled me to hire major movie stars because I only had to pay them for a few days' work. We got the use of their names and star power without having to pay their million-dollar salaries. I was able to afford and assemble an extraordinary cast, including Kirk Douglas, Burt Lancaster, Richard Dreyfuss, Anthony Hopkins, Linda Blair, and Elizabeth Taylor. Just about the only big star I wanted but failed to convince was Ingrid Bergman—instead, the legendary Helen Hayes played the role of Dora Block, an older woman who had been taken from the airport to a hospital and died there.

We built the entire airport set on the largest soundstage on the Warner lot and began shooting on November 10, 1976. Almost immediately, we were faced with tragedy; the Israelis had brought with them on the raid a man resembling Uganda's president Idi Amin, knowing that the terrorists would see Amin leading the motorcade and believe he was coming to visit them. We hired Godfrey Cambridge to play Amin, but, as we began taping, he died of a heart attack right on the set. It was just awful. Later we learned he had been on a diet and had lost a significant amount of weight, perhaps too much too quickly, contributing to his heart failure. There was nothing we could do but replace him—which we did with a fine actor named Julius Harris—and continue taping in this tough situation.

The shoot went quickly. The actors loved working with video because it gave them the opportunity to really get into their parts. Unlike shooting on film, which requires endless starting and stopping—shoot two lines, cut; shoot two lines, cut—we used four cameras and shot scenes in their entirety. We looked at the results immediately.

I paid Elizabeth Taylor $100,000 for two days' work, one day of rehearsal, one day of shooting, with a $50,000 bonus for each additional day.

On the last day of shooting, she said to me, smiling broadly, "You know, David, after I finish a picture, every one of my producers gives me a gift. And I usually select the gift."

"I'd be happy to do that," I replied. "What would you like?"

"A Lincoln Continental," she said, still smiling.

I didn't even react, making me the finest acting producer on the set that day. Later, I actually did send her a Lincoln Continental—although it was a miniature car made by Matchbox.

We finished shooting in seventeen days, on December 3. Ten days later, five months after the actual event, it was broadcast on ABC. It was distributed around the world for theatrical release on December 18, 1976. Normally, the objective when making a film isn't speed, it's quality, but in this situation speed made a big difference. While I thought Ed Scherick's picture, *Raid on Entebbe,* was probably better than *Victory at Entebbe!,* that we were first allowed us to get all the attention.

In the movie business, time definitely equals money. The longer it takes to make a movie, the more expensive it will be. When producers were in charge of production, they could control the shooting schedule, but once directors gained that control, the role of the producer was diminished. Amazingly, with all the technical advances we've made, it takes considerably longer today to shoot an average movie, without special effects, than it did in the old days. I do not advocate shooting films in seventeen days because it puts enormous stress on everyone involved and makes it difficult to achieve the best quality. But the lesson I learned from *Victory at Entebbe!* is that a group of dedicated professionals working together, with respect for the abilities of their coworkers, do not need to take months or spend tens of millions of dollars to make a movie.

Because we made this film for less than $4 million, it was a financial success. It played in movie theaters around the world; in some countries it was considered quite controversial. In Rome and Palermo, for example, theaters showing the picture were firebombed and pelted with stink bombs by Arab sympathizers. About the only complaint we received in the United States came from an Arab organization, which wanted ABC to do another film telling the story in a manner more sympathetic to the Palestinian cause. The network politely declined.

THIRTY-ONE

MR. IMAGINE
AND BLUE SUEDE SHOES

With Yoko Ono (1988)

Many of the young filmmakers who began their careers at my company eventually graduated from Wolper University to make their own movies, and on occasion, they would ask me to get involved. I hired Malcolm Leo and Andrew Solt when they were kids. "It was like getting paid to learn how to make films," Malcolm Leo said. "There was an incredible talent pool, and if you couldn't cut it, you dropped out, and that competition introduced you to the reality of the film community at large."

Eventually, they left to make a series of documentaries about the heroes of rock 'n' roll. But what they really wanted to do was to make a feature documentary about Elvis Presley. They obtained the rights they needed, but couldn't sell it. Bob Guenette suggested they contact me. But they did better than me; they called Auriel Sanderson, who was my assistant, my chief problem solver, for almost thirty years. I was in London, but Auriel was a big Elvis fan and made sure I returned the call the day I returned.

I took them to their first power lunch at the famed Warner's commissary. The truth was that I didn't like Elvis Presley much; I was from
the generation of Sinatra fans. But Gloria loved Elvis, and she practically insisted I make the film. I made a deal with Warner's to do a full-
length theatrical documentary entitled *This Is Elvis*.

Despite the tremendous amount of film footage about Presley's life
from the moment he became a star, almost nothing existed from his
childhood or the early days of his career. So, after long arguments, we
decided to re-create those times of his life, just as we had done in the
Appointment with Destiny series. There are perhaps two thousand professional Elvis impersonators, and we needed three to portray him at a
variety of ages. It seemed as if we auditioned most of them, but one of
the impersonators we used may actually have been Elvis's son.

We'll probably never know the truth, but the story is sad. An actor
named David Scott was cast to play Elvis as a teenager. Supposedly,
when Elvis was in the army, stationed in Germany, he got sick and was
sent to a hospital, where he met a beautiful Canadian nurse named Carmen. They spent one night together, and so the story is told, she
became pregnant and returned quietly to Toronto, vowing to Elvis
never to tell anyone that this was his child. On December 1, 1960, she
gave birth to a boy she named Scott. His birth certificate read father
unknown. Carmen then became a stripper in Montreal nightclubs.
When Scott was twelve, Carmen told him his father was a famous
singer—but she didn't tell him who it was. Elvis wrote one letter to
Carmen, enclosing some money. The day Elvis died, Carmen told Scott
that Elvis was his father.

In 1977, Scott entered an Elvis look-alike contest in Montreal—and
won. The prize in a second look-alike contest was a trip to Elvis's hometown, Memphis, Tennessee. There Scott met Elvis's uncle and several of
Elvis's friends, all of whom were shocked at the boy's resemblance to
Elvis. Eventually, he auditioned for our movie and, while we knew
nothing about this story, won the role of the teenage Elvis.

Supposedly, while making the movie, he had an affair with the actress
playing Priscilla, then began using cocaine. After finishing the movie, he
went to Las Vegas to play Elvis in a lounge show, but his drug problem
and bad attitude cost him that job. Finally, to support his cocaine habit,
he began smuggling drugs into the country. In 1991, his girlfriend gave
birth to a baby girl, which would be Elvis's granddaughter. Two years
later, unable to beat the problem, he sent his girlfriend to the store and
committed suicide.

Was he Elvis's son? I believe that he believed he was, and that was the root of this tragedy.

We filmed the movie where the actual events of Elvis's life took place, from the studio in which he recorded his first song in Tupelo, Mississippi, to Graceland in Memphis, Tennessee, where he died. We were the first people permitted to film inside Graceland. We spent three days working in his bedroom, which had basically been untouched since his death. They even let us shoot in the bathroom in which he died—it hadn't been changed at all; the same rug was still on the floor.

It was at this time I was offered the opportunity to buy Graceland—and turned it down. In the past I had been successful in real estate, but not buying Graceland was one of the really big mistakes I've made. I tried, but Steve Ross told me Warner's wasn't interested, and I certainly couldn't have afforded to buy it myself.

While making this movie, I finally began to appreciate Elvis's magnetism. By the time we were done, I had come to truly enjoy his music. Elvis was handsome and cool—every boy wanted to be him, and every girl wanted to mother him. His life was a tragedy of operatic proportions.

I've often wondered about the different paths followed by Presley and Frank Sinatra, both of whom became superstars very young. While Sinatra evolved, Presley never outgrew the confines of his childhood. His life was a sad cocoon.

It was the material for a fascinating movie. The first cut of the picture ran about five hours and included thirty-six songs. Then we began cutting and slicing. Too often, when making a film like this, particularly if you become infatuated with your subject, cutting is very, very difficult. I had my share of screaming arguments with Malcolm Leo and Andy Solt. We disagreed loudly over whether to do the dramatic re-creations of his early life. I was adamant that we do them; Malcolm and Andy felt just as strongly that they would destroy the picture. Just like them, I was fighting for my vision of what this movie should be.

Eventually, we all went up to a hotel in Santa Barbara and locked ourselves in a room for five days to cut the film down to two hours. At times the argument about re-creations got pretty intense. By this time in my life I had had two serious heart operations and stress was not the best thing for me. So, at one point during this debate I popped some heart pills, then decided we should stop for the rest of the day.

After I'd left, Solt told Leo, "You know what, we're not going to win this argument, and we really don't want to be known as the guys who killed David Wolper. Let's give him what he wants."

When we came out of that Santa Barbara hotel room, we had our movie, we were still speaking to each other, and I had become an Elvis fan.

This Is Elvis included forty songs and a voice-over narration done by an actor imitating Presley's voice. The premiere was held in Memphis. It remains a fine film, and certainly the most complete story of the King's life—and death—ever done.

I wasn't much of a Beatles fan either, but while in New York in 1986 producing Liberty Weekend, the gala event staged to celebrate the Statue of Liberty's one hundredth anniversary, I received a phone call from John Lennon's widow, Yoko Ono. She told me that she had more than two hundred hours of film of Lennon, most of which had never been seen by the public, and wanted me to make the definitive documentary about his life.

I told her I knew little about John Lennon; "I'm a big Sinatra fan," I explained.

"That doesn't matter," she responded. "I asked you because you know how to make documentaries. That's what interests me.

"I want you to do this film," Yoko continued, "because I want somebody tough, somebody big, somebody I can't push around."

Little excites a documentarian more than the thought of rare and unseen footage, particularly personal films about a cultural icon like John Lennon. And almost every aspect of his life had been filmed, from the Beatles concerts to John and Yoko having sex. But I wasn't sure I wanted to get involved. It wasn't because I didn't really know his music—I'd found that, more often than not, coming to a subject without any preconceived notions is beneficial. I just wanted to be sure that we could assemble the material in such a way that we would reveal not just Lennon's music, but the real man behind the myth.

I told Yoko if I agreed to do this project, I would need control. She could make as many suggestions as she wanted. Yoko is an impressive, smart woman. She agreed with absolutely no conditions, later telling me, "My influence would be subjective when it is very important that it be made by someone who is objective."

Once again, Gloria urged me to do the film. After my meeting with Yoko, I called Andrew Solt and asked him, "Do you think this is worth doing?"

I could almost hear him fainting on the other end of the phone. "Are you kidding?" he asked. We agreed to do the project together.

It took our production team, headed by supervising editor Bud Friedgen, eighteen months to go through all the material. The problem was just the opposite of what we had experienced with Elvis Presley—there was too much footage of John Lennon. Lennon's life is arguably the most documented of the century; few other public figures dared open up so much in front of the camera and tape recorder. The real challenge was reducing the material to only two hours, while managing to capture the essence of the man.

I began listening to Lennon's music in my car driving to and from the studio. I read everything I could about him. Lennon was always evolving, always experimenting, and continually changing. He was much more than a talented songwriter, he was a philosopher and a poet and someone who cared deeply about the important issues that affected millions of lives. Like Picasso, he was an innovator hungering for new ways to express himself. Boundaries were for destroying, limits were for redefining.

Capturing that was an awesome challenge.

The footage was amazing. There is a dynamic debate between John and Yoko and cartoonist Al Capp, who cynically attacked the Lennons' peace efforts, which took place during the Montreal bed-in. When John and Yoko made the *Imagine* music video, they chose to show little of John singing on camera. In our film we have five songs from what's considered his creative high point, and they were shot during the recording session in the studio of their home in Ascot. In addition to the two hundred hours of his personal film, many other people contributed their footage and memories. His first wife, Cynthia Lennon, gave us as much time and cooperation as we needed. His aunt Mimi gave Andrew Solt an extraordinary seven-hour interview. And the surviving Beatles, while not directly involved in the film, helped us obtain footage and made suggestions after viewing an early screening. When Ringo Starr saw the film, he became quite emotional; George Harrison said it was strong but wondered if it was too much about the Beatles rather than John. And Paul McCartney sat in the screening room singing along with all the songs, even Lennon's solos.

Because Lennon had been interviewed so many times, we were able to use his own voice to tell his story. At times it became difficult to match the visuals with the audio, but hearing Lennon's life story in his own words made the picture far more personal—and emotionally powerful.

The core of the film is a 1971 recording session at Lennon's estate in

England during which he recorded the album *Imagine.* At one point he is sitting at his piano playing the song "Imagine" softly and says quietly, "That's the one I like best."

One of our most difficult decisions was how to deal with his murder. We did not want to give any more notoriety to the crazed individual who killed him. So, in the film, the killer's name is never mentioned, and rather than a stark image or footage from that night, we show the huge crowds paying silent homage to him by standing vigil outside the Dakota. It is a solemn, tasteful conclusion.

Both Yoko Ono and Lennon's first wife, Cynthia, attended the world premiere in Hollywood, their presence helping to promote the picture.

Imagine did respectably in the theaters, in documentary terms, but more than earned a profit on video and DVD. As Lennon's legend grows, the film continues to find new audiences. Something, I suspect, that will go on and on for many years to come.

THIRTY-TWO

PABLO AND THE L.A. POLICE

With Kevin Spacey and Danny DeVito (1997)

In 1996, I did get to make a film about one of the people whose work I most admired, Pablo Picasso.

Through the years, I have bought eighteen major Picasso sculptures, becoming the largest private owner outside the Picasso family. A psychiatrist once speculated that my passion for sculpture was born of the fact that I could touch it, in contrast to the films I made, which I could only see. I could never touch my creation. Gloria and I never bought a piece unless we both loved it, and we never bought a piece as an investment. We have similar tastes so we rarely disagreed. We spent millions of dollars on art, which eventually earned a huge profit. In fact, and this is shocking to most, I think I've earned more money in the art world than in my fifty-year career in show business.

I just seemed able to relate to Picasso's work. I read every book I could find about him. I spoke to experts, and eventually, I became one. He was certainly one of the true creative geniuses of the twentieth century.

In 1986, I optioned a book about Picasso, being written by Arianna Stassinopoulos, to develop into a feature film. It was a tough book, which depicted Picasso as brutal, a moral coward, and a sexual sadist. Picasso saw women either as "goddesses or doormats." Unless readers were knowledgeable about his art, there seemed to be nothing attractive about him. The reviews of that book were stinging.

It occurred to me that the producing team that would be most comfortable with a complicated, controversial subject like Picasso was Ismail Merchant and James Ivory, who had successfully made a series of brilliant period feature films, such as *Howards End.* I called Ismail in London and explained that I wanted to tell the story of the women in Picasso's life. "My God," he said, "that's exactly what we're working on."

It was an extraordinary and fortuitous coincidence, and we agreed to work together on the film that was eventually titled *Surviving Picasso.* There were endless problems: Picasso's family, particularly his son Claude, did not want us to make this picture and threatened to take legal action if we filmed in France, where the laws concerning the rights of public figures are considerably stricter than in America. He claimed to be concerned that the film would be a historical distortion of his father's life, but I think he was just pissed off someone beat him to it. Pablo Picasso's longtime mistress, Françoise Gilot, had written her own book and refused to sell us the film rights, threatening to take legal action if we used anything from that book. Incredibly, because of the dispute with his family, we could not get permission to show any of Picasso's art, so we had to have other artists create work in the style of Picasso. It was an extraordinary irony: we were doing a motion picture about a man who was, arguably, the best-known artist in the world, whose work was so original as to be instantly identifiable, yet we were unable to use his work—and almost no one in the audience noticed it.

The screenplay was written by Academy Award winner Ruth Prawer Jhabvala. Anthony Quinn, who quite resembled Picasso in his later years, wanted to play him and coproduce the picture, but we felt he was too old for the film. So Anthony Hopkins, with whom I had worked years earlier on *Victory at Entebbe!,* and who had subsequently become an Academy Award winner and one of the most respected actors in the world, played Picasso. He lost twenty-five pounds to play the role and gave, I believe, one of the most fabulous performances of his magnificent career.

I was actively involved in the shaping of the screenplay, and Merchant and Ivory were there for the production of the picture, making this a Merchant Ivory/Wolper Production. Ismail and I were coproducers, while James Ivory directed.

I thought it was an absolutely wonderful movie. Critics raved over Hopkins's performance, but it did absolutely no business. Fortunately, because we made it on a reasonable budget, nobody took a financial loss. For a producer like me, who is constantly involved in numerous projects, no one project can make all the difference. In fact, because pictures take so long to finish, by the time a movie was released or televised, I was usually so focused on other projects that I didn't even have time either to enjoy its success or regret its failure.

I did want to make big, hugely successful commercial films. Every producer does. And while I had made many profitable movies that had won many TV Emmy awards and even an Oscar, I still hadn't had that big Academy Award–winning hit. I had the ability to get pictures done and I was offered a lot of scripts, a lot of projects, but I only wanted to make movies that interested me. I wanted to make the kind of pictures I would have loved to see if someone else had made them. Making a feature film is a long and often arduous process; you have to live with it every day for a long time. The job begins long before the start of production and doesn't end until long after the film is in the can. At that stage of my life, if the subject didn't intrigue me, if the possibilities didn't excite me, I just couldn't do it.

One film in my career that I very much wanted to make that never got made was of the classic Pulitzer Prize–winning novel by William Styron *The Confessions of Nat Turner.* I purchased the rights to the book in 1967 for $600,000, $50,000 more than Fox had bid. I knew when I made my bid that I could go back to Fox and make a deal with them, as they could pay me $50,000 less than my normal producer fee and still come out even. That's exactly what happened.

The Confessions of Nat Turner is a novel based on a then little known historic event. In 1831, a band of approximately seventy slaves, led by thirty-year-old Nat Turner, revolted in rural Virginia and, during their three-day rampage, killed sixty white people and plundered and destroyed numerous homes. After the uprising was put down, more than two hundred slaves and black freemen were killed. Nat Turner and seventeen of his followers were hanged. It was a novel of extraordinary power; its publication was greeted by magnificent reviews.

As powerful as it was on the printed page, I believed it would be even more dramatic on the screen. I reached an agreement with Norman Jewison, the respected director, and we set out to develop it together. We hired a black writer, Lou Peterson, to write the screenplay. America was still in the midst of the civil rights revolution, and we were optimistic that we would be able to make an important motion picture.

What we did not realize and could not anticipate was the anger from some members of the black community toward this book. Very little accurate historical information is available about Nat Turner. The character created by Styron was a celibate who fantasized a love affair with a young white girl, the only person he killed in the uprising. The book was called a literary masterpiece and was awarded the Pulitzer Prize. But many blacks believed it to be a dangerous fraud. I first became aware of the depth of that vitriol when an ad sponsored by the great actor and my friend Ossie Davis appeared in *Variety*. "I find this book to be false to black history, an insult by implication to black womanhood," it began. "The book is dangerous. . . . Styron's implication about black men and black rebellion is what aggravates the black man. He is not in search of freedom but a search for white women. To magnify this inflammatory lie on a mass scale as only a motion picture can magnify it, is the height of social irrelevance. For a black actor, a black man to lend his craft, his body, and his soul to such a flagrant libel against one of our great heroes, would be to have one of us become an agent for the enemy. . . . It is quite possible I would despise such a man who would do such a thing."

That was the beginning of a rebellion against the book. Almost immediately, numerous black organizations announced support for Ossie Davis's position. Some people were even more harsh than he was, accusing us of "murdering the spirit of Nat Turner . . . distorting black history . . . defaming the entire black race." The author, William Styron, was lambasted, and as the people attempting to turn it into a film, we were vilified.

Stunned would be an accurate appraisal of my feelings. I couldn't believe this was happening. I finally asked Ossie Davis to arrange a meeting between my director, Norman Jewison, screenwriter Lou Peterson, and myself with as many black activists as he wanted to invite. I felt certain I could allay their fears. The meeting was attended by representatives of the NAACP, the Black Panther Party, the Black Congress, the Black Student Union, CORE, and several other organizations.

While the meeting began calmly enough, tempers soon got hot. At one point, someone from the Black Student Union told us, "You people have no idea what it is to be black, so how can you even do this picture?"

Hearing that, Lou Peterson, who had written the script, replied angrily, "What do you think I am? Look at my skin. I'm as black as you are and I know what it means to be black, so don't give me any of that shit!"

I'm a good listener and I was trying to listen and understand the basis of these fears. One man stood up and explained, "Look, Nat Turner wasn't perfect, we admit that. But, when you're building a black hero, you gotta forget about some of his faults and remember the good. You can have all the revisionist history you want about George Washington; he is already a hero; you don't tell schoolchildren all the stories that came out about him later. You build him up. That's all we're asking about Nat Turner. Let Nat Turner be a hero, don't tear him down yet, don't show the scars right away."

As I listened more, I realized that their primary fear was that, no matter how we portrayed Nat Turner in the picture, it would help sell more books, which is exactly what this group wanted to prevent. Styron's inner monologue of Turner's desire for the white women was probably the one thing generating all this fury. I told them that I was committed to making a great film. Finally, after a lot of negotiating, we reached an agreement. The movie would not have the same title as the book; it would be called just *Nat Turner*. And we would specifically exclude Styron's inner monologue of Nat Turner lusting for white women.

Because so much time had passed, Norman Jewison had to bow out. He was committed to direct another picture, so I signed Sidney Lumet to direct. Lumet was married to a black woman, Lena Horne's daughter, so I felt he would certainly be acceptable to the black community. Lou Peterson completed the script and we got a go-ahead from Fox to produce the film. Lumet and I toured the actual area in Virginia where the rebellion had taken place, and we started to scout other locations.

But then Fox announced it was in disastrous financial shape and was suspending all production and closing the studio for at least six months. The story of Nat Turner got caught in that chaos and never got made. I was sorry to lose the film. We had the right director, a fine screenplay, and an amazing story.

Probably the best-known motion picture that not many people know I was responsible for is *L.A. Confidential.* In 1990, Gloria and I were on a boat trip through the San Juan Islands when she gave me a copy of a gritty detective novel by James Ellroy and said, "You ought to read this, David, it's really a wonderful book. It's really juicy and complicated."

Gloria was right. It was a terrific book. It was a complex story, set in

Los Angeles in the early 1950s, about a group of crooked cops busily betraying each other. It was an intellectual maze, with another turn always just beyond the next corner. Nothing was as it seemed to be. I loved it.

I thought I could make a television miniseries out of it. So, in August, I met with James Ellroy's agent, Irv Schwartz, and took an option on all film rights for *L.A. Confidential.* I pitched it to the three major networks, HBO, Showtime, and Turner as a four-hour miniseries and no one was interested. It sort of languished on the shelf for a while as I tried to figure out what to do with it.

After a year passed, Jack Gilardi, an agent from ICM, informed me that the great Italian director Bernardo Bertolucci had read the book and wanted to make it as a feature film. Jack suggested we work together to develop it.

I brought the project to Billy Gerber, the head of features at Warner's, who had been my executive contact with the studio on several projects, and told him that Bertolucci wanted to make this picture. Gerber read the book and liked it, but not with Bertolucci directing, and suggested, "Why don't you develop it yourself."

I informed Bertolucci's agent that we were not going to proceed with him and began developing the project between December 1991 and January 1992, talking with many writers and their agents. Then, in March, the *L.A. Confidential* option ran out, but we renewed it. A young writer-director named Curtis Hanson fell in love with the book and tried to buy the rights. When he discovered I held those rights, he contacted me in July 1992 and told me he wanted to direct it. He was passionate about this project. The first day he walked into my office, he knew what he wanted to do. I liked him immediately, and as I got to know him and his work, I liked him even more. I tried to make a deal with Warner's for Curtis to write and direct it, but the studio would not agree to his terms, so we shook hands, parted, and in July 1993 he went to make *The River Wild.*

Months passed. A year passed. Finally, in late 1993, after interviewing more than fifteen writers, the studio and I agreed that Brian Helgeland should write the first draft of the screenplay. Brian and I worked together to get the material in shape. In August 1994, he delivered his outline. Later that month, we came to an agreement with Curtis Hanson to direct and cowrite the script.

Four years had passed since I'd first optioned the book and we still didn't have a screenplay. Filmmaking is not rapid.

In June 1995, we delivered a screenplay to Warner's. They weren't ecstatic about it. Truthfully, they didn't like it much at all, but they told me if I could get Sylvester Stallone, Michael Keaton, and Alec Baldwin to star, Warner's would do it.

Brian was working on a film with Stallone and gave him the script. Stallone turned it down.

As more months passed, Brian and Curtis did another draft of the screenplay. I, and most of Warner's production staff, liked it a lot, but we needed a green light from the top executives, Terry Semel and Bob Daly. After waiting a long time for a response, I set up a meeting with Terry, who told me, "This is every bit as good a script as *Chinatown*. But *Chinatown* didn't make a nickel. It's a film noir and they don't make any money. As good a script as this is, I don't think it's going to make a penny and I don't want to do it here at Warner Bros."

I tried to talk him into it. No, he said. Curtis Hanson had story-boarded the entire picture; he had laid out scene by scene what it was going to look like. It was impressive. No, Semel repeated. Finally, I realized that this no was a real no.

Arnon Milchan, head of Regency Pictures, wanted Hanson to direct another movie for him, but Curtis told him that *L.A. Confidential* was the film he really wanted to do. Milchan liked the script and agreed to do it.

Casting began in late 1995. Curtis hired relatively unknown but talented actors, such as Kevin Spacey, Guy Pearce, and Russell Crowe. Only two major stars were cast in the picture: Kim Basinger, to play a prostitute, and Danny DeVito, to play a sleazy newspaper reporter.

When we screened the rough cut for an audience, I thought the beginning was much too confusing, and I noted that two of our actors looked very much alike, which made it even more difficult to understand the plot. Also, a pivotal scene needed clarification. So, we changed the beginning, we moved some scenes around. It didn't completely eliminate the confusion, but it helped considerably, and Brian took my suggestion and fixed the other sequence. At the next screening, we knew the picture worked. It enveloped the audience. It passed the popcorn test—during the screenings, no one got up to get some popcorn. No one. Incredibly, it was precisely the picture that Curtis Hanson had envisioned in my office so many years earlier. He had brought his vision to life and I told him so.

The critics loved it. It was a smash hit, an intelligent, commercial movie; it was the kind of film I'd dreamed of one day making. *L.A. Con-*

fidential was first on every major critic's top ten list. The New York Film Critics, the Los Angeles Film Critics, the Boston Society of Film Critics, the National Society of Film Critics, all voted it the best picture, named Curtis Hanson the best director, and honored Brian Helgeland and Hanson for writing the best screenplay. Fifteen different major critics organizations named it the best picture of the year, the first time in history these groups had unanimously named the same picture. The Academy of Motion Picture Arts and Sciences nominated it for nine Oscars, including Best Picture. Kim Basinger was nominated for Best Supporting Actress.

I was looking forward to attending the Oscars. Gloria and I were both dressed and ready to go. And our limousine never showed up. Curtis Hanson's limousine didn't show up either. I waited. He waited. It was an hour before the ceremony was to start, and I knew, with traffic, it would take us at least forty minutes to get to the auditorium. I called the company. Oh, they were so sorry, and they were going to send another limousine immediately.

Curtis hitched a ride with his neighbor. Our car never showed up. Gloria and I took off our formal clothes and watched the ceremony on television. We were swamped by *Titanic,* winning awards only for Brian and Curtis's screenplay and Kim Basinger's performance.

Later, I received a nice letter from Brian Helgeland. In part, it read, "On the bulletin board in my office hangs a sheet of paper with the number 121 on it. This was the page in *L.A. Confidential* you kept pounding on. . . . You were absolutely right in your concern and I keep that number up there to remind myself to listen. The subsequent clarification and simplification of that scene helped make *L.A. Confidential* the movie that it is. There, that's the first time I've ever thanked a producer for a note. . . . David, this ball never would have gotten rolling if you hadn't pushed it up the mountain."

I had one disappointment. I am a big fan of James Ellroy's. But, he never called, congratulated, or thanked me for taking his book and working eight years to bring it to the screen.

L.A. Confidential was my last theatrical motion picture. The project had started when Gloria handed me a book and told me to read it. It ended eight years later at the Academy Awards. I had done my job as a producer. And I had my hit movie.

PART V

The Miniseries

With Marlon Brando playing American Nazi leader
George Lincoln Rockwell (1977)

THIRTY-THREE

SANDBURG'S LINCOLN

With Hal Holbrook as Abe Lincoln (1974)

I may not actually be the father of the miniseries, but I can certainly claim to be a close relative. The formats of most television programming were simply borrowed from radio or the motion pictures. But the miniseries—the telling of a story over several nights or weeks—was unique to TV and one of its finest creations. While ABC claims credit for inventing the miniseries in 1974, with Leon Uris's powerful *QBVII*, the fact is, in March 1966, that network ran my adaptation of William Shirer's Pulitzer Prize–winning book *The Rise and Fall of the Third Reich* over three consecutive nights. That was the first time in TV history that a single program had been run on consecutive nights, and with these three hour-long segments, we proved that, if a program was compelling, the audience would return night after night.

But no one noticed that we invented "the miniseries." That term did not even exist. Instead it was called "running three one-hour segments on three nights." And admittedly, *Rise and Fall* was a documentary. But until the success of *QBVII*, Brandon Stoddard, the legendary television executive, once admitted, "Everyone was doubtful and skeptical about the form."

I had always been intrigued by the concept. For a long time I had thought it was ridiculous to try to fit a broad variety of stories into a prescribed length. All stories are not created equal, and some simply require more time. Once a miniseries allows that time, the entire, magnificent sweep of history becomes a viable subject.

One of the first network miniseries, *Rich Man, Poor Man,* was shown in 1976 on Sunday night for eight consecutive weeks. Using that as a standard, it's certainly possible that my six-part program *Sandburg's Lincoln* was the first miniseries. It certainly took the longest to broadcast—nearly two years to tell the story of Abraham Lincoln's life as reported by the Pulitzer Prize–winning poet and historian Carl Sandburg. The first hour program of the six hours was shown on September 6, 1974, while the final show was broadcast on April 4, 1976. Does that constitute a major miniseries?

My real interest in history began when I was just a kid. One afternoon I was walking down Fifth Avenue and saw a small sign in the window of Walter Benjamin and Company advertising the sale of George Washington's autograph. The thought of owning something that had actually been signed by George Washington excited me. The price, I believe, was $20. I bought it—and that marked the beginning of what was to become my large and valuable autograph collection and my special interest in American history.

Collecting autographs became my portal to the past. When I held an autograph in my hand, I could almost feel the person signing his or her name. I could visualize the scene—and I could feel the connection through time. I had Washington's, I had Thomas Jefferson, Carl Sandburg, Clarence Darrow, I had canceled checks signed by most of the presidents of the United States.

Eventually, I began concentrating on collecting Abraham Lincoln. As I learned more about him, I came to admire him greatly. I became a real Lincoln buff and collected some fascinating Lincoln memorabilia, ranging from an original edition of the *New York Herald* reporting the issuing of the Emancipation Proclamation to a pencil sketch of Lincoln in his coffin done by a noted artist who bribed a guard in the middle of the night to be allowed to make the sketch. The most I ever spent for an autograph was $20,000. On March 22, 1966, I purchased a letter at auction from Lincoln responding to a letter written by a little girl named Grace

Bidell suggesting he grow a beard. In his letter Lincoln explained, "I have never worn any. Do you not think people would call it a silly piece of affection if I were to begin now?" And soon after he grew his quite famous beard. When I became interested in sculptures, I sold my entire autograph collection; for a tidy profit, I might add.

My interest and fascination in Lincoln has lasted my entire life. From the very beginning of my producing career, I wanted to put on film Carl Sandburg's magnificent biography of Lincoln, but Sandburg's estate did not want to sell the rights to me. They just didn't trust a television producer to do justice to the material. But as the 1976 U.S. bicentennial approached, I thought there could not possibly be a more appropriate time to honor Lincoln, and I approached Sandburg's longtime agent, Lucy Kroll. By this time I had established a reputation as a serious documentarian and was able to obtain the rights.

To produce and direct *Sandburg's Lincoln,* I signed George Schaefer, who had won six Emmys and countless Directors Guild Awards and had directed fifty-six programs for the *Hallmark Hall of Fame.* His credits included "Abe Lincoln in Illinois," starring Jason Robards, for *Hallmark* and the Broadway play *The Last of Mrs. Lincoln,* for which Julie Harris had won a Tony Award.

George and I began by discussing how best to approach the material. Sandburg's books covered Lincoln's life from the prairie days through his assassination. We decided to do six one-hour-long shows, each one focusing on a specific part of Lincoln's life or character. *Mrs. Lincoln's Husband,* for example, in which Sada Thompson played Mary Lincoln, focused on his family life, while *Sad Figure Laughing* was about his very human wit, the pressures he had to contend with during the Civil War, and his personal ambitions. Because the six shows were scheduled to be broadcast over two years, we either needed an audience with the longest attention span in history or there could be no continuity. Each show would have to stand on its own.

We cast Hal Holbrook, who had attained fame portraying Mark Twain in a one-man show, as Lincoln. With makeup, which took about three hours every day, Holbrook was difficult to tell apart from Lincoln. Holbrook is a fine actor, and he created perhaps the most believable Lincoln ever put on film.

Usually, I tell people I'm not an expert in any subject except the making of documentaries, the American Revolution, and Picasso sculptures, but I do know quite a bit about Abraham Lincoln, and I was able to put that knowledge to good use. As a good producer, I got out of the way while George Schaefer was making the shows; I was most helpful to him in their editing.

In our only significant disagreement, I insisted we shoot in 16mm while George wanted to do it in 35mm. This really was my decision, and I had no choice because I was having terrible problems with the budget. If I'd had videotape, I would have done it on tape. The difference between 16mm and 35mm film was about $10,000 an hour—and in 1976 that was a considerable sum—including all the expenses from the cost of the stock to developing it. Projection in theaters requires 35 mm, and I did not intend to show these films in theaters. George Schaefer wanted to shoot on 35mm because he believed we'd use the footage for a feature film. I don't think he was wrong, but I just couldn't afford it.

These shows were important to me. After more than a decade in the business, I now had the luxury of making programs that actually meant something to me. It wasn't simply creating entertainment. *Sandburg's Lincoln* tells the story of this great man in a way that has never before or since been done. For anyone who wants to understand Lincoln, on both a personal and political level, these six hours are an absolute necessity.

The premiere was held at Ford's Theatre in Washington, D.C., where John Wilkes Booth killed Lincoln. In my welcoming speech I said, "Lincoln once said, 'It is better to be thought a fool than to open your mouth and dispel all doubts.' Keeping that in mind, my remarks will be brief." The reviews were superb, we received five Emmy nominations, among many other rewards—and Hal Holbrook won an Emmy for his portrayal of Lincoln.

So, while *Sandburg's Lincoln* was probably not a miniseries in the sense that it was not a continuous program shown over a brief time, it was in fact a dramatic series about a single subject shown over a long period.

THIRTY-FOUR

ALEX HALEY
AND THE *ROOTS* PHENOMENON

With one of my favorite people, Alex Haley (1977)

Roots was the first true miniseries I produced. It not only changed the format, it challenged all the traditionally accepted beliefs about television viewers. Although it was one of the first miniseries ever produced, it remains the best-known, highest-rated, and most popular ever made. The last episode is the third most watched program in TV history. And with the addition of so many new channels, it is extremely likely it will remain the most watched miniseries in history.

In 1969, actress Ruby Dee first told me, at the Moscow Film Festival, about a book then being researched by a black writer, who was tracing his family origins back to Africa. I was fascinated and never forgot it. At a dinner at my home three years later, Ruby once again began talking about Alex Haley, who was still working on his book tracing seven generations of his family from Africa to the United States. From the moment I heard that simple description, I knew I wanted to turn that story into a film.

Somebody once told me that the best programs are those that can be described in one or two sentences in *TV Guide:* seven generations of a black family from Africa to today. One sentence. Instantly you can imagine it: slavery, freedom, reconstruction, life in the South and the Ku Klux Klan, Martin Luther King and the freedom marchers, freedom. It was all contained in that one sentence. I didn't even know the story. I didn't have to. The concept was there from that first night.

When I tried to get the rights to the project, I learned that Columbia had already taken an option on the book for a feature film. I also learned that Haley had been working on the book for six years and was still a long way from finishing it. Well, nice try, nothing lost, on to the next project. I forgot about it completely.

Amazing things do happen to me, things like bumping into a man on the street selling Russian footage to put me in business, or bumping into the man against whom I was bidding for a film library, which saved me hundreds of thousands of dollars. In fact, Alex Haley often quoted his grandmother, who said, "The Lord may not be there when you want him, but he will always be on time."

Perhaps. But until this time, I had never known the Lord to work through the William Morris Agency, who represented me. One day, I had a quick meal at the restaurant just across the street from the agency. The place was really crowded and people were waiting for tables. As I was finishing, I noticed Cynthia Robinson, a William Morris agent, waiting for a table with another woman. I motioned them over, telling them to sit down with me and order so they wouldn't have to wait for another table. The second woman, I learned, was Pat Alexander, the assistant and secretary to a writer named Alex Haley.

"Alex Haley?" I said. "Isn't he writing that book about several generations of his family?" I smiled, then admitted, "You know, I wanted to make a film out of that book, but Columbia has the option on it."

Then Pat said the words that changed my life: "Well, I don't think they have an option anymore; I think their option is over."

Alex Haley, I learned, was represented by an attorney I knew named Lou Blau, who also represented my friend from childhood Jimmy Harris and his partner, Stanley Kubrick. Within hours, I was on the phone with him, convincing him that Haley's story was too big for the big screen; two hours wasn't long enough, I said, a story of this magnitude really needed to be done as a miniseries.

The first miniseries had done well, so all the networks were looking for long-form projects. And because networks paid by the hour, a miniseries could generate a substantial up-front payment to Haley. Blau agreed and we began negotiating terms.

Haley had still not completed his book, although a long excerpt had appeared in *Reader's Digest*. I was so excited about this project that I began selling it to the network even before I owned the rights. I met first with Barry Diller, then head of ABC's television movies, and gave him a copy of the *Digest* article. Diller, his assistant Lou Rudolph, and Brandon Stoddard liked the concept, but it was not an easy sell to the top executives. There had never been a successful black dramatic series on television, and there was substantial doubt advertisers would support a miniseries about black history.

Several days after making my pitch to Diller, I flew to Hawaii, and after being with Gloria for five years, on July 11, 1974, I married that fabulous woman.

After three months of negotiating with Blau, we finally reached an agreement. At the last minute, legendary Broadway producer David Merrick made a substantial offer for the book, but Lou Blau honored our relationship and concluded the deal with me. I optioned the still unfinished book from Alex Haley for $50,000 against a $250,000 purchase price and 15 percent of the profits. On August 15, I met with Barry Diller and we reached an agreement. A month later Diller left ABC to become president of Paramount Pictures.

I met Alex Haley for the first time the following week. When I came home that night, I told Gloria, "I've just met the most dynamic, fabulous, unbelievable person." Alex Haley and I remained close friends and coworkers from that day until his death in 1992, almost twenty years later. I've always felt privileged to have been his friend. Alex Haley and Teddy White were the two most fascinating men I've ever known. Each of them had a reservoir of talent to which there seemed to be no bottom. But, in addition to their intelligence and ability to communicate, their beliefs were grounded in extraordinary compassion for other people.

Soon afterward, I hosted a lunch for ABC's executives with Alex Haley at the Beverly Hills Tennis Club, during which he told the story of his search for his family's roots—and by extension, the foundations of the black experience in America. There has been no better storyteller in my lifetime than Alex Haley. As Lou Rudolph later recalled, "The lunch lasted four hours. I cried a great deal . . . the eyes of other executives at that table were moist also."

ABC advanced me $50,000 to figure out how to turn Haley's book into a miniseries. I used that option payment to make my option payment to Alex Haley.

I believed Stan Margulies was the perfect producer for this project, but initially ABC, which had the right of approval, turned him down. However, I persisted. I knew that Stan had the intelligence and compassion for this project. ABC just didn't know how good he was—yet. Stan Margulies was the finest producer with whom I ever worked. And finally, ABC agreed.

The story, as Alex told it, was simple enough. When he was a boy growing up in the small town of Henning, Tennessee, he used to sit on the front porch and listen as his aunt and grandmother talked about the family. After leaving Henning, Haley spent twenty years in the Coast Guard as a steward, a glorified waiter. His most important promotion was to be a waiter to an admiral. During his Coast Guard career he earned extra money writing love letters for his shipmates—fifty cents a love letter. He taught himself to write while in the Coast Guard. One day the admiral said to Haley, "Ensign Haley, I know you are a writer. You would enjoy a story in the current issue of *Liberty* magazine." To which Haley replied, "I wrote that story. Sir." The admiral said, "If you can write like that, Mr. Haley, you're not going to be my waiter anymore. I'm sending you to the public relations office of the Coast Guard in New York." And that's where he went and spent the last years of his career in the service.

After the Coast Guard, Alex went to work for *Playboy* magazine, where he was assigned to interview the great jazz musician Miles Davis. When he delivered the piece, Alex suggested, "Why not run the interview with questions and answers? It works so well." They did, and that became the first question-and-answer story in *Playboy*. Subsequently, Alex Haley became one of those who conducted the famous *Playboy* interviews. He then collaborated with black radical Malcolm X, whom he had earlier interviewed for *Playboy*, on *The Autobiography of Malcolm X*, considered one of the most important books in the history of black literature. But after telling the story of Malcolm X, Haley began wondering about his own roots.

He remembered only two pieces of information from those tales told by his Henning relatives, the name of a person, Kunta Kinte, and something called Kamby Bolongo. After speaking at Hamilton College of his personal search, someone in the audience approached him and said, "Mr. Haley, I'm Ebou Manga and I know the Kamby Bolongo. It is a river." As Haley learned, the Kamby Bolongo is a small river in the

African nation of Gambia. He had the first link in what grew to become a very long chain.

With Ebou, Haley went to Gambia and began visiting the villages along the river. In each of the villages he spoke with the griot, the storyteller responsible for passing down an oral history of the village from generation to generation. Haley would listen for hours to the griot's story, to the history of the village, but nothing in any of these stories struck him or connected to him at all. Finally, in the village of Juffure, a griot named Kebba Kanji Fufana was reciting local history. All of a sudden, out of his mouth comes, "One day a young villager went out to make a drum for his father and he never return. His name was Kunta Kinte and he disappeared forever." As Alex heard the words *Kunta Kinte,* his entire body started shaking uncontrollably; he started to cry. After two hundred years, a relative of Kunta Kinte's had come home. May 17, 1967, was the defining moment in the life of Alex Haley.

From the stories told by the griot, Haley determined the year that Kunta Kinte had disappeared, enabling him to identify the slave ship, the *Lord Ligonier,* on which Kunta Kinte had been brought in chains to America, landing in Annapolis, where Alex found his sale slave papers. From this Haley traced the entire history of his family.

In 1970, before *Roots* was completed, Alex was lecturing at Simpson College in Indianola, Iowa, telling the story of his research. After the lecture, a man of medium size, with blond hair and blue eyes, approached him and said, "I don't quite know how to tell you what I have to." During his lecture, Alex had related his family's story, even naming the plantations on which they had worked as slaves. Dr. Waller Wiser explained that those plantations had belonged to his ancestors—the people who had bought Kunta Kinte when he'd arrived in America. Alex and Dr. Waller were the seventh-generation descendants of the "massa" and his African-born slave. Eventually, Alex and the Waller family developed a warm friendship

Alex Haley's *Roots* was a magnificent story. Not a magnificent *black* story, but the kind of universal story that I believed would appeal to people of all races. I certainly did not set out to make a racial statement.

My object in dramatizing Alex Haley's search for his roots was to make an emotional television program about seven generations of a family that would both inform and entertain the audience.

A fine writer named William Blinn did a long outline of the story. Originally, *Roots* was to begin in the present day, with Alex Haley in search of his identity. Through flashbacks, the story of Kunta Kinte would be interspersed with Haley's relentless detective work. But after several months, we realized the story just didn't work that way. Stan Margulies suggested we drop Haley's character and tell the journey of Kunta Kinte's family chronologically. When we did that, the story seemed to soar.

Originally, *Roots* was intended to be six hours long, telling only half the story of Kunta Kinte's family. But when Fred Silverman, the programming genius, stunned the television world by moving from CBS to ABC, he, along with Brandon Stoddard, okayed increasing the length of our show to twelve hours with a budget of $6 million. It was a courageous decision, but I was absolutely thrilled. I believed we needed every minute of those twelve hours. The more I got to know Alex, the more extraordinary the story became to me; Alex Haley was the living embodiment of a history that had begun more than two centuries earlier. Every event that had taken place during that time had honed him. I had spent much of my adult life recording history, but never before had it been so personalized.

Alex sent us pages from his still incomplete book. As powerful as the drama is on the printed page, certain changes had to be made. Sometimes we had to combine several different characters into a composite, and on occasion, we had to create characters to bring to life on the screen what were described as thoughts in the book. Alex Haley never objected, never complained. He understood that a book and a movie differed and he trusted us.

Blinn was writing the outlines at the same time Alex was completing his book. We were working from Alex's original drafts rather than the completed work, so some of the characters that appeared on the screen had originally appeared in the book, but had been deleted by the time it was published. But, in every way, this was Alex's story.

Alex never ceased to surprise me. After William Blinn had completed the "bible," the story outline, we began looking for writers for each segment. My intention was to hire as many black technical people as possible when we actually started filming, but I just didn't know many black TV writers who had the experience we needed. When I asked Alex if he could recommend any black writers, he said, "Let me tell you something, David. I don't want you hiring writers because of their color, race, or religion. I want you to hire the best writers you can find. It's more important that this be made into a great show to be seen by millions than for two black writers to get a job."

We didn't have a single African-American in the first group of writers—and Alex approved all of them. As far as we could determine, though, we did have the largest black film crew in the history of movie-making.

The word was beginning to spread in the black community that something very special was taking place over at Wolper's, and when we began casting, just about every black actor in America wanted to participate. But we were working within a television budget and just couldn't afford everyone we wanted. It was important, I decided, that we use black actors known and liked by white audiences. The first people we signed were Richard Roundtree, Leslie Uggams, Lou Gossett, and John Amos. Poet Maya Angelou, Scatman Crothers, George Stanford Brown, and Lawrence Hilton-Jacobs from *Kotter* enthusiastically accepted roles. For some actors the salary made no difference. Cicely Tyson still felt she owed me a favor for releasing her from her *Get Christie Love* contract two days before we began filming, and she accepted the small role of Kunta Kinte's mother. A 1976 poll named O. J. Simpson the most popular personality in the country, yet he called me and offered to play a role for scale, and he flew to Savannah for one day to do his part. When O.J. arrived, he was greeted like a hero by the press and the *Roots* gang. Later that kind of reception for Simpson would obviously change.

Career conflicts prevented some black actors from accepting roles. Alex Haley's friend James Earl Jones was originally cast to play the pivotal role of Chicken George—Haley's great-great-grandfather—but Jones was committed to another film. Ben Vereen was then cast in that memorable role. Billy Dee Williams was starring in a play about the life of Martin Luther King and couldn't be in the film. I wanted Sidney Poitier to play Kunta Kinte's father, but he was embroiled in a dispute with ABC that could not be resolved.

In what I considered a perfect piece of casting, we wanted gritty comedian Redd Foxx to play an old slave who goes to auction—the buyers examine him carefully, they look at his teeth, his body—and nobody bids on him. Redd Foxx could have turned that small part into a little bit of magic, but he did not want to do it. It wasn't the money; Redd Foxx just didn't want to play a slave. But that scene—which we never filmed—remains firmly entrenched in my mind.

The most difficult role to cast was young Kunta Kinte. He would dominate the first several hours of the miniseries, and if he didn't make an emotional connection with the audience, the rest of the story wouldn't matter. The only suggestion Alex Haley made was that the actor cast in the role had to be very dark-skinned; then, as we progressed into the

American part of the story and began to get mixed blood, the actors could be lighter-skinned.

Casting director Lynn Stalmaster looked at hundreds of young black actors before settling on three candidates, and we gave each of them a screen test. LeVar Burton, a USC student from Sacramento, California, had almost no experience. The day of his screen test was the first time he had ever been on a movie set. Until then, he'd never even seen a motion picture camera. Entrusting the pivotal role in a multimillion-dollar miniseries to an inexperienced actor was a great risk, but independently Stan Margulies, Lynn Stalmaster, director David Greene, and I agreed he was right for the part. He looked African, as an actor he had tremendous emotional range, and as a person he exuded self-confidence—and most importantly he had charisma. He made the screen come alive. A few network executives fought us briefly about him, believing he was too dark-skinned to be acceptable to white audiences—but we refused to back down. We knew he had the talent to bring Kunta Kinte to life.

For the white roles we cast faces familiar to television viewers, popular series stars like Ed Asner, Ralph Waite, Vic Morrow, Lynda Day George, Lorne Greene, Doug McClure, Lloyd Bridges, Chuck Connors, Robert Reed, and Sandy Duncan.

After a long search, we decided to shoot in Savannah, Georgia, the only location we could find in America that could serve as everything from the village of Juffure in Africa to the cotton plantations of the Old South. While the scripts were being written, several significant decisions had to be made. To be historically accurate, we wanted to show the women of Juffure bare-breasted. Bare breasts on television? This created a real problem for ABC's Standards and Practices. We had a lot of meetings about it with Standards and Practices head Al Schneider, but finally, they allowed us to film the women bare-breasted, although only in long shots that were in no way sexually suggestive. This was the first time that the network permitted any nudity in a dramatic program.

We were aware that our decision might cause a controversy: Why was a network allowing black women to be shown naked when it had never permitted white women to be shown bare-breasted? I explained that we were simply being historically accurate—and if we were doing a period program in which white women were bare-breasted, we'd ask to show that too.

Unfortunately, we found out, after completing filming, that one of the actresses who had volunteered for a nude role had been underage.

We had to identify her on every frame of film and make sure she could not be seen.

The second problem was the language. In his book, Haley had the slaves speaking a sort of pidgin English—a mixture of English and their native tongue—but on the screen it was going to sound denigrating. Some members of the crew tried hard to convince me to change the dialogue. "You're gonna get killed with this," they told me.

"That's the way they talked," I explained, "we're going to go with it." And while some critics found fault with it, once viewers got used to the dialect, they accepted it completely.

As I've often joked in similar situations, "Don't worry about it. When they show this in Japan, they're going to be speaking Japanese. In Germany, they'll be speaking German . . ."

I've made more than five hundred films of every conceivable type, covering just about every period in human, animal, and insect history; I've made documentaries, biographies, dramas, and comedies. I've worked in every form from animation to videotape. I've produced live events telecast around the world featuring thousands of performers. But I've never seen a cast or crew more committed to a project than *Roots*. Without question, making this miniseries had an effect on every person involved with it.

Of all the sets I've been on in my career, nothing has ever come close to being on the slave ship. Slavery has always seemed a distant and dark part of American history, pages in history books. This "ship" brought it to life. Standing in this dark, cramped hold, it was possible to imagine the horror of men and women chained inside these boxes barely large enough for a human being. It was one of the most oppressive environments I've ever experienced. The first day we shot on the set, all our actors wore breechcloths and were chained hand and foot. When we finished shooting that day, an assistant director asked the extras to return the next day. Eighty percent of them refused. They just didn't want to go through that experience again.

For many of the actors this was the most difficult performance of their life. Richard Roundtree, for instance, who had gained fame as the ultra-cool private eye in *Shaft*, was cast as a buggy-driving slave named Sam who belonged to Stephen Bennett, played by George Hamilton. It was a rather good position for a slave. In the story, Sam was in love with Kizzy, played by Leslie Uggams and, one day, asked and received permission from Bennett to drive Kizzy to her former plantation so she could visit the graves of her family. Dressed in his best clothes, feeling proud, Sam took his girlfriend for a buggy ride. It was a wonderful day for him, but, unfortunately, he returned late, and to punish him, Bennett threatened to return him to the fields to pick cotton. Desperate to keep his job, the slave got down on his knees and began begging his "massa" to be forgiven, promising never to do anything like that again. It was a tough scene.

Long before Roundtree got the part, I warned Stan Margulies how difficult that scene was going to be, and he said he'd talk to Roundtree. "Let's talk about it now," Stan said to Roundtree, "because, when the time comes to do it, I don't want to find out you're not willing to get down on your knees." To prove that he understood exactly what was required of him, Richard Roundtree read the scene in the office, literally getting down on his knees and proving he could do it.

We shot the scene at night. As Stan remembered, he had just left the set to do some paperwork when he heard tremendous shouting. He ran back over there and Richard Roundtree told him bluntly, "I cannot, I will not, get down on my knees in front of a white man." "He was adamant," Stan told me, "he just wasn't going to do that scene. I asked him to take a walk with me, and as we did, he said, 'It just got into me. I know this is what my grandfather or great-grandfather had to do. But this is now, and I just can't do it.'"

Stan said, "Richard, that's not fair. Believe me, I understand your feelings. But you read the script. We've got to shoot this scene tonight, you know, it's called acting. It's not you, Richard Roundtree, getting down on your knees. It's not you who's being humiliated; it's this man who was a slave. Talk to Alex, he'll tell you; this is what people had to do to survive.

"Think of it this way, if I asked you to play Hamlet, you're not Danish, but you'd somehow work your way into it." And after a long walk, Richard had calmed down and went back to the set and did the scene.

Embodied in that scene are all the pent-up emotions of a century of slavery. Anyone who has seen it has felt it through Richard Roundtree's performance.

The budget for *Roots* was originally $385,000 per hour, but as we proceeded, we knew we were in the midst of an experience, and I decided to spend whatever was necessary to get it absolutely right. By the time we had finished, I had gone overbudget $1,386,000. That was money out of my pocket, but money, I felt, well spent.

Alex Haley actually finished writing the book about two months after we'd finished shooting. I didn't doubt that his book was going to be an enormous best-seller, but in publishing history this situation was unprecedented. Normally, the hardcover book precedes the movie or miniseries, then the paperback or mass-market edition is published to take advantage of the TV exposure. When *Rich Man, Poor Man* was broadcast, for example, the softcover version became a major best-seller. In this case, the miniseries was going to be broadcast while the hardcover edition was on sale.

One day, ABC's Brandon Stoddard and I met with Haley's editor at Doubleday, Lisa Drew, to discuss the tie-in. Lisa noted that the first printing would be fifty thousand copies, a huge number for a book that might appeal only to a small segment of the reading public. "Fifty thousand?" Brandon said. "That's what I'm going to buy. How many are you going to print for everybody else?"

The book exceeded everybody's wildest expectations. It was such a huge hit that Doubleday could not initially fulfill the demand. Originally, the book had been printed in a large trim size on relatively slow presses; the publisher reset the book to fit much faster presses to keep up with orders. Alex Haley had not just touched a nerve—he'd hit it with a sledgehammer. *Roots* gave a proud history to black Americans; it allowed them to understand their heritage. People were buying multiple copies for all the members of their family and their friends.

While the success of the book was exciting, it really had no impact on Fred Silverman's decision when to broadcast the miniseries. The network had invested $6 million, and if it did not attract a wider audience than black America, it would be a costly failure. A program in which the whites are the villains and the blacks are the heroes, in a country that's 90 percent white and 10 percent black, has a huge barrier to overcome. ABC executives were nervous about it.

Initially the network had a tough time selling advertising for the show, even at a substantial discount. Advertisers were afraid of the possible audience reaction. The first commercial shown during the broadcast was for Preparation H, which provides relief from hemorrhoids. But after the ratings were reported for the first night, every remaining spot was sold immediately. The original sponsors, those people with courage, got the greatest deal in television history.

Roots was originally scheduled to be broadcast one night a week for eight weeks. The decision on when to run it was completely Fred Silverman's. Circumstances practically forced him into a historic decision: he would broadcast *Roots* over eight consecutive nights. No program in TV history had ever been aired that way. Silverman later gave several explanations for this decision, but it made perfect sense. February was a sweeps month, meaning the network ratings that month would be used to determine the price of advertising spots for the next several months. No one, not Silverman, not even me, knew if the program was going to be successful. If it ran once a week during sweeps and failed, it could cost the network's affiliated stations a fortune. To prevent that from happening, Silverman decided to run it on consecutive nights the entire week before sweeps began. If it died, it would impact only one week rather than the entire network schedule.

Once he decided to run it on consecutive nights, he did something else smart. Each night he ran it in the time period normally occupied by his weakest show. He replaced shows that were coming in last in the ratings so, if *Roots* finished last, the network wouldn't really be hurt.

Fitting ABC's schedule required that we recut the show. Some nights it ran for one hour, other nights it was two hours long. The first show was broadcast January 23. We were in the editing room until Wednesday, the twenty-sixth, recutting the miniseries to fit the schedule.

We knew we had told a wonderful story, but there is just no way of accurately predicting how an audience will respond. We were hoping to get a 40 share, which was about what *Rich Man, Poor Man* had received. That would have been considered a major success. ABC had done its part to promote the show. There had been a lot of advertising and educational tie-ins. *TV Guide* had done a cover story. The first review had appeared prior to broadcast in *Time*; it was less than a rave. Critic Richard Schickel called it "a middlebrow *Mandingo*." *Mandingo* was a movie about slavery that had been only mildly successful. Twenty years later in a letter to me, Richard Schickel wrote, "I am so pleased that the statute of limitations ran out on my critical indiscretions. I was fairly young and dumb back then." The first time I have ever received—I think anybody has ever received—a retraction from a critic, which, I must say, shows what a gentleman Richard Schickel is.

On Sunday, January 23, 1977, the first episode of *Roots* was broadcast. First thing Monday morning, I got a call from Fred Silverman. "We got a forty," he said happily.

We had gotten a 40 share. I was thrilled: "That's just great, a forty share is terrific."

"No, not a forty share." He'd been setting me up. "We got a sixty-one share. Our rating was forty point five. Even Nielsen can't believe it. It's so high they think maybe something is wrong with the system. So, Nielsen will need to confirm it in an hour or so."

The first night was the sixth most watched program in television his-
tory. The first night! And the ratings got better every night. The final
night we had a 51.1 rating, a 71 share. By the time the series concluded, it had become part of America's cultural history. More than 130
million Americans had seen at least part of the show—making it the most
watched program in television history. Of the thirteen most watched individual programs in TV history, *Roots* captured eight spots. It became a
cultural phenomenon: for one week in January it captured, completely,
the attention of the nation. Everybody was talking about it. When it was
on at night, restaurants and movie theaters were empty. In bars they
watched *Roots* rather than basketball games. In Las Vegas the nightclubs
rescheduled the times of their shows so they would not conflict with
Roots. More people watched *Roots* that week than have seen Shakespeare's plays performed since the day he wrote them. For me, that was
the most thrilling week of my career. Every day it just got better and better. After I got the numbers each morning, I would call Alex and we
would just scream in excitement at each other on the phone. We had
made a program of which we were extremely proud, in many ways, the
ultimate docudrama; we had told an intelligent, educationally important
story—and the nation had responded.

We had filled in a historical blank, and no one would ever forget it.
Roots became the most honored miniseries in history, receiving thirty-
three Emmy nominations and winning nine Emmy Awards. The reason we won only nine out of thirty-three is that in most categories all
the nominees were from *Roots.*

More than two hundred and fifty colleges and universities proposed
to offer courses based on the film and book. Thirty mayors proclaimed
the week of the broadcast, *Roots* Week. In the cities where there was civil
rights turmoil in the 1960s, no crosses were burned on TV station lawns
and disturbances were negligible.

Two weeks after the program had been broadcast, ABC's founder and
chairman, Leonard Goldenson, said he had learned from Brandon Stoddard that we had spent more than a million dollars of our own money to
complete the show—and when we finalized the budget for the sequel,
Goldenson added approximately a million dollars. The network was giving us more than $1 million—now *that* was history. *Roots* had so dom-
inated television that it had enabled ABC to finish first in the ratings for
the first time.

Not every American was pleased with the success of the miniseries.

The network did receive a demand from the Ku Klux Klan, asking that their side of the story be told. And some critics did find minor faults with it.

Actually, *Roots* was probably as great a financial success for us as it was for the network. They had guaranteed advertisers a much lower rating than it received, so advertisers received far more than they paid for it. ABC had bought two runs—we owned everything else: European rights, world rights, and most importantly, as it turned out, the rights to the sequel.

I had learned an important lesson while filming the original program. While I had done a twelve-hour show, I really had more than enough material for several more hours. This time, I told Brandon Stoddard I wanted fourteen hours of airtime, which he was more than happy to give us, but I knew if I shot on a twelve-hour budget I'd still have enough footage to create a longer show—and be able to make an additional million dollars an hour profit on those two additional hours.

While *Roots* told the story of Alex Haley's family, it did not tell how Alex had traced those roots. So, while working on the sequel, we also made a documentary, entitled *Roots: One Year Later,* in which we told that story. For this special, director Bob Guenette and his camera crew went with Alex back to Juffure, where he met a seventh-generation descendant of Kunta Kinte who had remained in the village. They filmed Alex on the dock in Annapolis, where the ship carrying Kunta Kinte into slavery in the Old South had landed. But the most amazing aspect was how Alex Haley's family had been assimilated into America.

During his research, Haley had gone to visit the graves of the people central to this story. In Spotsylvania, Virginia, he had found the burial site of both Kunta Kinte and John M. Waller, who'd owned Kunta Kinte. Gloria and I went to a dinner at Alex's house with members of the Waller family. At the end of the meal, John Waller raised his glass and proposed, "I drink a toast to my relative, my friend forever, Alex Haley." It was an essential American moment, the descendant of the slave owner and the descendant of his slave, together as equals. And friends.

Alex also visited the grave of another slave owner, the last owner of Kunta Kinte's descendants before Lincoln freed them. The Murray family had bought Kunta Kinte's daughter, Kizzy, Alex's great-great-great-grandmother, and one of the men had raped her, producing the child who grew up to become Chicken George. Coincidentally, visiting the grave that day were members of the Murray family. When one of them asked what Alex was doing there, he explained, "This is my ancestor."

"I'm sorry," this man replied, "but you must be in the wrong place. Mr. Murray was white."

Alex told the whole story to these somewhat stunned distant cousins. As the Murray family learned about this, some of them refused to speak with him, fearful that people might think they had black blood. But, as they got to know Alex, the Haleys and the Murrays also became friends. It was almost impossible to meet Alex and not become his friend. Eventually, both families held a big reunion together.

Roots II, as it became known, started where the first series ended and concluded with Alex Haley returning to the village of Juffure, meeting the village griot—who recites the oral history of the village—and meeting his cousin. The circle of family life was completed.

Because many of the significant characters had "died" in the original production; we now had new characters and we had to start the casting all over again. This time, James Earl Jones was available, and we cast him as Alex Haley. But I was surprised and, admittedly, extremely disturbed when LeVar Burton's agent turned down a cameo role because we did not offer enough money. His agent insisted we pay LeVar the same daily rate as we were paying major stars such as Olivia de Havilland and Henry Fonda. His agent admitted that the offer we made for one day of work would have been generous had it been made by any other producer, but "coming from David Wolper and Alex Haley, who were going to get rich from *Roots,* it was not sufficient." We got rich, he got famous.

I was absolutely not going to pay LeVar Burton the same fee after performing in one program that I was willing to pay great stars. LeVar is very nice and I love him dearly—and he went on to a fine career—but his agent was a pain in the ass.

Ben Vereen also decided not to reprise his role as Chicken George. We wanted him to return, but for some reason, he decided the sequel was a rip-off—which shocked me. He spent eight weeks working on *Roots,* then had the audacity to tell a man who had spent twelve years researching his family's story that he is ripping off his own life? I was terribly disappointed in Ben Vereen. I felt he owed something to the project. But, with the exception of these two actors, our cast was reunited.

To replace Ben Vereen we hired Avon Long, a veteran of fifty-five years in show business. He played Chicken George as a seventy-nine-year-old.

One actor who appreciated the importance of *Roots* and wanted to play a role in it—to my surprise—was Marlon Brando.

Obviously I was thrilled. We were facing a monumental task in trying to meet the expectations raised by the original *Roots*. Since his youth Marlon Brando had never acted in a television program. Having him appear in the sequel would certainly help. "It would be an honor to have you," I told him.

"One thing though," he replied, "I want to play a villain. You have a good villain in this one?"

Did I have a villain for him? I said, "Yes, I do. George Lincoln Rockwell." Rockwell was the head of the American Nazi Party, whom Alex Haley had interviewed for *Playboy*. I knew it would be a chilling scene. "It can't get any more villainous than that."

Brando wanted to be costumed at home because he was so heavy, and he wanted time to rehearse with James Earl Jones, so we had to shut down the entire production for one day. I was on the set early the next morning to greet Brando. When we began shooting, I was stunned— Brando had not bothered to learn his lines. Instead, he had cue cards made and hidden everywhere on the set. His lines were taped to a picture frame on his desk. His lines were taped to the walls, the floor, everywhere on the set that he might look. Finally, he wanted to tape his lines to James Earl Jones's chest so he could look directly at Jones as he spoke. James Earl Jones refused. This is how Brando worked for years.

When I asked Brando why he did this, he explained that it enabled him to give a much more realistic performance. It's fresher, he said. I nodded. What I wanted to say to him, but didn't, was that Laurence Olivier was a pretty good actor—and he always knew his lines. My responsibility was to get a performance out of Brando any way I could, so I smiled broadly and agreed with him.

After he shot his first scene, he said to me, "David, I know that you don't usually sit on the set all day. You've got a lot of shows going on. You're just afraid that I'm not going to finish today, is that right?"

"Well," I said, "to tell you the truth, yes. Because if you don't, I've got to pay you for another day."

"Here's what you do," he replied. "Go back to your office and I'll give you a call when we finish, about six-thirty. You come and say goodbye to me then." And sure enough, just before seven P.M. Brando called to tell me he had completed his work.

It was a great pleasure watching the footage of the scenes between Brando and Jones, two great actors in their prime. They each brought out the best in the other, and the undercurrent of curiosity, respect, and intellectual testing that flowed between the actors—as well as the characters they played—just electrified the screen.

As always, we did encounter some difficulties. Stan Margulies received a demand from the chairman of labor and industry for the Beverly Hills/Hollywood branch of the NAACP that we employ blacks in all technical jobs: "*Roots II* is about black heritage and the atrocities perpetrated by the vicious and inhuman white America. Therefore, it is only obvious, blacks must be the recipients of the monetary benefits from such a program." He also pointed out that as we would not expect blacks to write, produce, and direct a program about the "six million Jews who supposedly died in the gas chambers," we certainly could not expect . . . well, the idea was pretty clear.

This letter infuriated me and I responded to NAACP chairman Benjamin Hooks explaining that we had used more blacks in the production of *Roots* than any other production in Hollywood history. Then I added, "Why shouldn't blacks write about Jews, whites, Italians, or anything else they want to write about? Shakespeare, an Englishman, wrote a fine play about Julius Caesar, an Italian. And, finally, that sentence, 'Jews who supposedly died in the gas chambers,' really pissed me off." I recommended the author of that letter be removed from his position. That didn't happen, but we never heard from him again—and that was the only objection we ever received from a black organization.

Roots: The Next Generations was broadcast in February 1979—this time during sweeps week. The other networks did everything possible to prevent *Roots II* from repeating the success of the original miniseries, competing with blockbuster movies such as *American Graffiti*, *The Sound of Music*, and *Marathon Man*. And to some degree it worked: *The Next Generations* was only the second highest rated week in TV history—finishing behind *Roots*. However, it did receive the best ratings in history for any sweeps week programming. Critically, most reviewers found the sequel to be superior to the original. Perhaps because the material was more accessible to viewers—they'd lived through much of it—or maybe just because of the emotional connection to the family of Kunta Kinte, *The Next Generations* received lavish praise. As Tom Shales, in the *Washington Post*, wrote, "There has never been anything quite like the conclusion of *Roots II*. . . . *The Next Generations* builds to one of the greatest emotional crescendos in the history of television."

What made *Roots* a phenomenon? I've always believed it was a combination of many factors; certainly the timing was perfect, the civil rights movement had matured and the country was changing. Segregation was outlawed. But, more importantly, I think, *Roots* was simply a family story. Because we are a nation of immigrants, most Americans have moved farther away from their family roots than any other people in history. Few people even know the names of the immigrants in their family who risked their lives to come here. *Roots* made people want to know more about their own backgrounds; it started a genealogy craze. And finally, it was a wonderful story. From Kunta Kinte to Alex Haley, these were people we cared about as human beings. We Americans of all colors and backgrounds invested our emotions in their fate.

Roots II: The Next Generations was the end of the saga. Alex Haley's family had become an American treasure. But, as it turned out, the amazing success of *Roots* did not propel many of its actors to stardom. Those actors who were well known before appearing in the miniseries continued to work, but few of the newcomers, except LeVar Burton, were able to take advantage of the momentum to build a career.

Writing did not come easily to Alex Haley. Although he won the Pulitzer Prize for *Roots,* and *The Autobiography of Malcolm X* has become a classic, for him, it was always hard work. He was a meticulous researcher; his home was filled with boxes and boxes of materials, but it was difficult for him to commit words to paper. In the early 1990s, he had been working on a book about his paternal grandmother, Queen Haley, for quite a few years without having written more than a few pages. Queen Haley was a mulatto, the almost all-white daughter of a plantation owner's son and his slave. In her lifetime, she lived as both a white and a black but, finally, married widowed black ferryman Alec Haley, great-grandfather of Alex Haley. The story of her amazing life was set during and after the Civil War, from Reconstruction to the dawn of the twentieth century.

I wanted to do the story of *Queen* as a miniseries from the first moment Alex told it to me. I knew it would be controversial; no matter how much social progress we'd made, racially mixed love stories were still difficult to sell—particularly to a television audience. By the late 1980s, the climate for miniseries had changed considerably. The stories had become bigger, more commercial—and much more expensive. The advent of easily available cable TV had splintered the audience—suddenly, in addition to the three networks, there were dozens of smaller channels with a narrow focus, from science to sports, changing both the demographics and the economics of network television. ABC decided that no miniseries would run more than four hours. Four hours, it was decreed, period. Alex and I agreed that *Queen* needed six hours, period.

We had reached a stalemate with ABC. One January when my friend Mike Wallace and I were vacationing in Acapulco, I was negotiating with ABC, by phone, trying to get the six hours. Mike was listening in on my negotiations, and unbeknownst to me, he called Howard Stringer, the head of CBS, who told him, "Tell Wolper we'll give him six hours." I called ABC back and told them Alex wanted six hours and I wasn't going to change. It was six hours or nothing. They decided nothing. I respected their decision. I didn't understand or agree with it, but I respected it. They had owned the Alex Haley franchise and they were willing to let it go. CBS, enthusiastically, bought the entire six hours.

Because there was no book from which to work, screenwriter David Stevens spent considerable time over eighteen months with Alex at his farm in Henning, Tennessee, and aboard a cargo ship where Alex did a lot of his writing. "It was like Aladdin walking into a treasure trove," David Stevens remembered. "There were boxes and boxes of material, but above everything else, there was Alex. I quickly discovered there were bits and pieces of the novel written down everywhere. I realized I was never going to have a manuscript, but it was there in his head and mine. I came to extract it from his head."

When Alex read the completed screenplay, he told me that emotionally it was the equal of *Roots*. On February 10, 1992, he had lunch at the Bel Air Hotel with John Erman, who would direct it, and Mark Wolper, my son, who was to produce it. Stan Margulies had moved on to form his own production company. I don't remember exactly what I was doing, but I had another appointment and was unable to join them. I never saw Alex again. Later that day in Seattle, he died of a massive heart attack. I was born with a defective heart. I've had four major heart operations in my life. I've lived a full life with a not so great heart. But Alex? As far as I knew, he had no history of heart problems. He was an active, alive, wonderful man who lived with joy every day. Alex? He still had so many stories to tell. I met Alex Haley just before *Roots* was published, before he became famous. The incredible thing about him was that he never changed in the slightest from the person he had been the day we met. Although he was world famous and, in some places, people would mob him, he remained generous and warm and kind to everybody. He truly believed in the family of man.

I missed him the moment I was told about his death, and I will continue to miss him for the rest of my life. The only tribute I could pay to him was to continue making *Queen* just as he would have wanted it done.

Casting the role of Queen Haley was tough. It required an actress with the range to play both black and white, and to age from fifteen to sixty-five. While we could probably have cast a white actress, there was never a chance that that would happen. Queen Haley was a proud black woman, and had we not cast a black actress in that role, we would have started a controversy that might still be raging. We looked at a lot of actresses. We had to cast a light-skinned black actress. For a long time we considered Jasmine Guy, a truly talented actress who was eventually cast in the miniseries but not as the lead. We also seriously considered Lonette McKee. Finally, we met Halle Berry.

Halle Berry was born to play this role. She is an absolutely beautiful young woman, and she is also the product of a mixed marriage, the daughter of a white mother and a black father. When she was a young girl and wanted to know why she was different, her mother, Judy, put her in front of a mirror and asked her what she saw. "You're white, I'm brown," Halle replied. "You're grown-up, I'm little."

"That's the reality," her mother told her. "You are black. We are different colors but I'm still your mom." Knowing that, Halle said years later, "made it easy to accept who I am and to be proud of my heritage."

The network didn't want her at first because she was not that well known. She'd played the pretty-girl role in several movies, but the networks questioned whether she would draw an audience. But we fought for her. She is a spectacularly beautiful woman and, in show business, that counts and she could definitely act. Finally, the network relented.

To prepare for the role, Halle Berry read the diaries of slaves and haunted the streets, houses, and plantations of the South to soak up the atmosphere. But still, the experience of playing a slave affected her the way it affected most of our black actors. Sometimes, during filming, she got angry and, even after the cameras stopped, had trouble letting loose the emotions. But director John Erman found the right things to say, and several times her husband at the time, baseball star David Justice, flew to the set to be with her, which helped tremendously.

Playing Queen Haley required Berry to sit through hours of makeup each day—her skin had to be lightened to give her a more Caucasian appearance, her teeth had to be stained, she wore a wig throughout the entire film, and prosthetic devices enabled her to age. That was difficult enough, but added to that, during filming she fell from a horse and badly hurt her back. We had to shut down production for ten days, but to delay any longer would have meant losing Danny Glover, who was playing her husband, as he had other movie commitments.

Halle took pain medication and we did everything we could to help her get through it. She was transported to the plantation set in an ambulance. We brought in a reclining dentist's chair for her makeup trailer. She was in pain pretty much throughout the entire production—she was a real trouper. But that certainly is not evident to anyone watching *Queen*.

Later, Halle Berry was to win the Academy Award for Best Actress for her brilliant performance in *Monster's Ball*.

Queen also starred Ann-Margret, Tim Daly, Ossie Davis, Paul Winfield, and Martin Sheen. Although it did not approach the ratings achieved by *Roots*, considering how TV had changed, it did well for CBS, getting a 37 share in sweeps month.

CBS's Howard Stringer was so pleased with the response that he called me with a complaint: "What's wrong with you, Wolper? Why didn't you sell me eight hours!"

The book Alex never completed, *Queen*, was finished by David Stevens. Had Alex lived, we would have told two more stories together. I remember he said once, "You know, David, I'm not African-American. I'm Afro-Irish-American." He wanted to remind Americans who had come from Africa and were not pure black that they had more than one heritage and that they should recognize every part of themselves with pride. He knew how controversial that was going to be, but Alex was not a man to back away from controversy. I can just imagine what might have happened when Alex Haley, who gave black America its heritage, announced he was also Irish.

Ironically, Alex, who was so completely identified with his family, had a terrible personal life. He was married several times; he had distant relationships with his own children and a difficult relationship with one of his brothers. When Alex died, several universities and many of his friends seriously considered establishing a museum in which all his materials could be displayed. But before we could do anything, most of his estate was sold at auction—his Pulitzer Prize, his Emmys, the original manuscripts of his published books, virtually everything he owned in the world. His brother George will contend that Alex died in debt and his belongings had to be sold to settle those obligations. All that remains is Alex's boyhood home in Henning, Tennessee, which has been designated by the state as a historic landmark, and a small museum at the University of Tennessee.

There was one last story of Alex's we wanted to turn into a miniseries, that of Madam C. J. Walker, the wealthiest black woman entrepreneur in America, who was worth the modern equivalent of more than $7 million in the 1910s. It was a wonderful story about a woman who turned a hair preparation into a fortune. But, after his death, both Alex's widow and his brother claimed they owned the rights to this story, and we could never get them to agree to a deal.

In the year 2002, I was involved with filmmaker Judy Leonard in an hour-long documentary celebrating the twenty-fifth anniversary of *Roots* and its impact on America. We brought it to ABC, fully sponsored, and believe it or not, they rejected it. A one-hour documentary, fully sponsored, on the twenty-fifth anniversary of *Roots* and the network rejected it because they thought maybe it wouldn't get ratings. So what? *Roots* was a part of the history of ABC and it should have honored its own past, regardless of ratings. None of the original ABC network executives who worked on *Roots* were still there, and I thought it was a disgrace that the show was turned down. It eventually played on NBC.

When I think about Alex, when I think about the adventures we had together, the success we had, it sometimes seems less than real. Some people claim that *Roots* changed the fabric of American culture. But America was already changing when we did those programs, and while they were certainly a big step, the nation was already moving well in that direction.

We certainly did make history though; we proved the power of television to educate and enlighten while entertaining a mass audience.

I miss Alex Haley. I think of him often. This was a man I truly loved.

I wrote this poem about my experience.

After Roots

Roots-a flash across the sky
A meteorite lighting the earth
Maybe for a moment
Maybe for a century
Maybe a change
Maybe not
A lite in the sky that's for sure

Masses, masses, masses watching
Hardhat, baseball hat, derby, no hat
Children, children, people, people

Millions, millions,
White face, black face lit in a
        dark room of flashing images
Of life and death
Of family and courage and mercy and
        honor

My skin is white
I felt no shame, no guilt
Many feelings came
Proud, jealous, joy, sorrow
Proud that some of my species can strive
        and grow
From hell and beyond
Jealous of their courage
Joyful of their love
Sad of the lies told me in my life

I knew the man in the white hat
With the white suit
On the white horse
Had family, courage, mercy, honor

Nobody told me the man in the black hat
With the black suit
On the black horse
With the black face
Had family, courage, mercy, honor
I was lied to, Cheated, Fooled

Now I know better
Much better
Much More

THIRTY-FIVE

FORBIDDEN LOVE

With Richard Chamberlain (1982)

In the world of television, few people are willing to take the risks necessary to be first, but they are forceful followers. *Rich Man, Poor Man* and *Roots* established the miniseries format and proved that if the audience was sufficiently engaged, it would come back to a program night after night. It was the oldest trick in the motion picture book: in the days of silent movies, each weekly episode of a serial had ended with someone in jeopardy. The secret to the success of many miniseries was to imitate that same plot device, so viewers couldn't wait for the next episode.

For a time, it seemed as if everyone in television wanted to do miniseries, but no one really knew what type of story worked best. Because the first successes were based on popular books, the networks decided that best-sellers made the best miniseries. NBC began to do best-sellers as weekly series. That concept died quickly.

Romance worked briefly—the sexier the better—and books like *Lace, 79 Park Avenue,* and *Bare Essence* appeared until, as with many romantic relationships, viewers got bored with it.

As network executives learned, the extended format has several inherent problems. Because miniseries cost so much to do, networks usually ran them during sweeps—against the other networks' best programming, which included miniseries. That made it difficult to sustain strong ratings. Many viewers missed the first part of the miniseries *Kennedy,* for example, because they were watching the highly promoted three-hour apocalyptic movie *The Day After.* There was just too much of too many good things.

And the networks discovered that without extensive promotion, miniseries did not usually perform well in reruns. With exceptions like *Roots, The Thorn Birds,* and *Lonesome Dove,* the audience didn't make the same commitment to the second or third run of a miniseries, and with production costs so high, often the only profit could come from the second run.

The networks responded to these problems by deciding the form didn't work, and by the middle 1980s, basically the party was over. The long-form miniseries had been replaced by the two-part, four- or five-hour movie. After the failure of *War and Remembrance,* a twenty-nine-hour sequel to *The Winds of War* that cost $110 million and included a cast of forty-four thousand actors and extras, ABC refused to make anything longer than four hours, which was why I did *Queen* for CBS.

None of these arguments made sense to me. When a series failed on one of the networks, it would be canceled and replaced by another series. No one argued that the format didn't work. But when expensive miniseries received less than blockbuster ratings, television executives decided the problem was length rather than content.

To many executives, a miniseries was defined only by length. I felt that the networks were seduced by the tremendous success of the early miniseries and believed almost any story could be turned into a miniseries. That was a terrible mistake. To be successful, a miniseries had to be a special moment in television, an event, something to make viewers take notice. When I did a miniseries, I hired as many major movie stars for cameo appearances as possible, knowing those actors would attract people to television who did not normally watch it. I paid Elizabeth Taylor $250,000 for one day's work in my miniseries *North and South*—on the condition that she do twelve interviews that one day. Every magazine and television program begged me for an interview; I had my choice of the best media outlets in America.

Promotion was always key.

But most important of all was the story. I loved telling epic stories, stories set in a fascinating time involved intriguing characters. I believed that realism—historical accuracy—made a huge difference to viewers. I believed if we could transport viewers into a time and place that captured their imagination, a place they wanted to spend time in, they would come back night after night.

Some miniseries failed because they were simply extended television programs. You really don't need another police or hospital story or subjects that could be told on *N.Y.P.D. Blue* or *ER.* For that reason, war stories, epic romances, and costume dramas seemed to be the best subjects for miniseries. For me, the perfect story for a miniseries was *The Thorn Birds.* Set in Australia, it told of a lifelong love between a woman and a priest, an unrequited love that dominated both their lives. It was the story of a man torn between his love for a woman and his love for the church, from the book by Colleen McCullough, which had been at the top of best-seller lists for months. It was one of the most popular and successful love stories since *Gone With the Wind.* Warner Bros. had tried to develop the movie with directors Peter Weir, Arthur Hill, and Herb Ross. Despite Robert Redford's interest in playing the part, it failed to come up with a script that worked. After I took over the rights, it took one phone call to Brandon Stoddard to sell it to ABC. My second phone call was to Stan Margulies, whom I wanted to produce it.

Stan and I hired a wonderful writer named Carmen Culver, and we spent ten days outlining an eight-hour miniseries. We ripped the book apart. The core of the story is the priest's—Ralph's—refusal to consummate his love with Meggie. They met and fell in love when they were both young, and Meggie was shattered when Ralph chose to be faithful to the church. While she suffered through an unhappy marriage, Ralph never stopped thinking about her. Finally, many years later, they meet again—and finally, after everything that has happened to them, so many years later, having been through a lifetime of experiences, this time they do make love.

I realized why the movie scripts didn't and really couldn't work. At most, a theatrical motion picture was two and a half hours long. In the movie time span, Ralph would have to give in to Meggie's desires in an hour and a half. It was actually kind of sleazy: you meet a priest, and an hour later he's in bed with Meggie. What made the miniseries work so well was that it took almost eight hours, four nights, for Ralph to make his decision. We had time to really stretch it out—no, no, when is he . . . now's the time . . . please get them together . . . not another night—we had our audience practically begging us to get them together. And just when they thought it was *the* night . . . wait until the next episode.

Carmen Culver's first draft was perhaps the finest first-draft script I've ever read. We could have filmed it without alterations. We brought the script to ABC and began casting it. At just about that time, Gloria and I attended a conference on docudramas and ended up sitting with an ABC executive. He was as enthusiastic about *The Thorn Birds* as I was. "David," he said excitedly, "I've got this wonderful idea for who should play the priest."

It was obvious from the beginning that casting was going to be the key to the success of *The Thorn Birds*. The advantage of turning a best-seller into a motion picture is that you have a high recognition factor; the bad news is, just about every person who has read the book has images of the leading characters. We had to fulfill those expectations. If we failed, no matter how good the script was, the miniseries would fail. Ralph was a complex role, and it required an actor with real emotional range—who would also be desirable to women. So, naturally, I wanted to hear this executive's suggestion. "Who?"

"Chevy Chase," he said.

He was serious. Chevy Chase as the romantic lead in a great love story.

Chevy Chase.

It was Gloria who suggested Richard Chamberlain. We also considered Christopher Reeve and Peter Strauss. Richard Chamberlain had played the lead in several miniseries. He was certainly handsome enough, and talented. I spoke to several producers who had worked with him, and without exception they reported that he was professional, always cooperative, and responsive to direction. He loved *The Thorn Birds* because it fit perfectly into his career: it had everything he wanted to portray—romance, conflict, glamour, and the chance to age his character forty-two years. Chamberlain was considered a brilliant technical actor who could move across the stage with grace, who understood his craft, who had a resonant voice, but sometimes lacked passion. The role of Father Ralph dripped passion. Passions followed, passions rejected, ruled his life. It was his chance to break free of his image. "This is a great challenge," he said. "This is a man whose heart is torn in half in a lifelong struggle. I realized there were amazing parallels in my life and this character's. Ralph's big problem is his image; like me, trying to live up to an image. Ralph strives for this image of perfection and he keeps failing and it drives him crazy. Finally, he gets chopped down and he realizes he is a flawed human being, and then he is free."

To prepare for the role, Chamberlain spent considerable time questioning our technical adviser, a Jesuit priest named Father Terence Sweeney, reading Catholic theology, and finally, living for three days in a Jesuit novitiate.

Casting the role of the beautiful temptress, Meggie, was not quite so easy. We auditioned a lot of actresses: Olivia Newton-John, Michelle Pfeiffer, Kim Basinger, Kate Capshaw, Jessica Lange, Susie Blakely, and Jane Seymour. We insisted that every actress audition for the part. Jane Seymour, who had established herself as the leading lady of mini-series, was reluctant to read for us, but she really wanted the role and finally agreed.

The first person to suggest Rachel Ward for the role was the legendary agent Irving "Swifty" Lazar, who had represented the book. The moment she walked into the office, it was obvious Lazar was right; she was spectacularly beautiful. She was the kind of woman who could make a priest question his vows.

We screen-tested two women. Rachel Ward was as nervous as hell in her first reading, so we asked her to test again, and she improved tremendously. When Stan and I looked at the tests, we both felt that Jane Seymour was a little strong for the role, too strong for anyone to believe that she would spend her whole life mourning her relationship with the priest. We needed an actress who looked so vulnerable that she'd fall to pieces if you said the wrong thing to her. Rachel Ward was so fragile, so delicate, we knew we had our Meggie.

Rachel was extremely shy, but also very determined. She was in the midst of becoming famous for her looks rather than her talent, and she was determined to prove she could act. The combination of shyness, drive, and insecurity took many forms on the set. Gossip columnist Liz Smith wrote, "Rachel simply made herself thoroughly detested by her high-handed attitude," but that wasn't quite accurate. At times, she was difficult, but no more difficult than numerous other actresses with whom I've worked. But she gave a wonderful performance, and that's all the audience should care about.

Much of The Thorn Birds is set on a lush Australian sheep ranch known as Drogheda. For the role of the grande dame of Drogheda, a strong-willed woman named Mary Carson, who is also in love with Ralph, I asked Barbara Stanwyck to come out of retirement. No one in Hollywood was more loved and adored by everyone with whom she worked. She was seventy-five years old, but because she looked so young, we had to use makeup to make her appear that age.

Although Mary Carson appeared only in the first three hours, we sent the entire first draft of the script to Stanwyck. She loved it. But because the first episode was so long, we had to cut it considerably. "I sent the amended pages to her," Stan remembers, "and the next thing I know I got a phone call from her and she was livid. I could feel the ice coming out of the phone. She said, 'What have you dumb bastards done to this script?'

"Missy," Stan replied—that was the name by which she was known on every set—"the script was long and we had to make some cuts. You've done TV before, you know sometimes we've got to cut material, even when it's terrific."

The conversation continued for some time, until she finally said, "Stan, I never hang up on anyone, but I'm doing it now." Pow!

We wondered if she was going to show up for the first reading, but she was on time and fully prepared. In fact, while all the other actors were fumbling with their lines, she just sat there. That's when we realized what had provoked her: she had memorized her entire role and had to learn all the new cues for her lines. She didn't speak to us for more than a week.

Almost as important as the cast of *The Thorn Birds* was the Australian setting. Originally, we intended to shoot the entire miniseries in Australia, but when Stan went to Australia to scout locations, he discovered it wasn't really right. At that time, there were two levels of Australian crews: very good and much, much less good. All the very good crews were already working for Australian directors; those people who weren't working weren't working for a reason. Second, the sheep ranches of Australia were, generally, miles from any kind of town, so if we were going to film on a sheep ranch, we would have to build our own production facilities and housing for the crew. And finally, the Australian Actors Union would only give us permission to use two American actors. Basically, all of this meant that the cast and crew were going to have to live for four or five months in a small town, drive at least fifty miles to the set each morning, and return each night, to work with a second-rate crew.

It's amazing how much Simi Valley in southern California looks like Australia—particularly given our budget. We found a perfect location forty miles from Warner's Burbank studios. Production designer Robert MacKichan, who'd built Alex Haley's hometown of Henning, Tennessee, for *Roots: The Next Generations*, created an Australian sheep station—complete with an outback mansion, barn, and outbuildings. To show the passage of time, we simply replaced the trees surrounding the house with larger and larger trees. We decorated the set with eucalyptus trees and silk roses—which would not wilt in the California heat. Scenes that took place in the book on Australia's Great Barrier Reef, we shot in Hawaii. Most viewers never realized that the lush backgrounds were California rather than the Australian outback. The biggest difference was that instead of thousands of sheep and kangaroos, we had about 150 sheep—and one kangaroo.

The kangaroo didn't have much of a part. To make sure the audience knew this story was taking place in Australia, as Richard Chamberlain drove up to the front gate of Drogheda in the opening scene, in practically the first shot this kangaroo went hip-hopping across the entrance. We had rented the kangaroo for the day. The temperature that day was 105 degrees—and as the kangaroo hip-hopped across the lawn, it fainted. It just keeled over. The first thought was, oh, no, we've killed the kangaroo. But they sprayed it with water and it recovered to hip-hop again.

We were not so fortunate with the sheep. Just as we had done in *Roots,* we changed many scenes from the book, adding and eliminating characters and events. One scene we did add was a sheepshearing contest—hours of the miniseries took place at a sheep station in Australia. As we learned, sheepshearing is an art. We hired a former Australian national sheepshearing champion to teach the proper technique to our actors, among them, Australian Bryan Brown.

Unfortunately, during rehearsals, one of our actors accidentally killed a sheep by gouging its esophagus, and another sheared off a sheep's nipple. Two investigators from a California state commission on cruelty to animals visited the set and threatened to arrest director Daryl Duke if he again allowed actors to shear sheep. We had to hire professional shearers for the film.

The Australians objected to various things about the miniseries, but they were especially upset that we used American sheep, which are apparently smaller and much thinner than Australian sheep; in essence, we were pulling the wool over viewers' eyes. Some felt that we were besmirching the entire Australian sheep industry.

Chamberlain had been unhappy with the way his relationship with Meggie was written. In a moment of frustration he broke his hand by slamming his fist into a chair. He met with Carmen Culver and director Daryl Duke and they argued for hours. He made his points, they made theirs. They compromised, and the outburst of emotion gave Chamberlain more passion than he had originally brought to the part.

While Stan was on the set, I was looking at the rushes, working with the writer, meeting with the network to go over ABC's concerns—the network always had concerns: the women's gowns are too low, the kiss lasted too long—and busily trying to develop and sell new projects. An advantage we had while making *The Thorn Birds* was Brandon Stoddard, one of the finest network executives with whom I ever worked. If the network made a suggestion that we thought was stupid, Brandon would solve the problem.

One problem with which I did get involved was the love scene. From the film's opening, this entire story moved toward the climactic love scene between Richard Chamberlain and Rachel Ward. Finally, after decades of restraint, they made love. We'd been making the audience wait a lifetime for this—the expectations were enormous—so it had to be an explosion of released passion.

It wasn't. As Richard Chamberlain explained, love scenes are difficult: "There's a microphone hidden in the armpit, another in the sheets. There's a wig to worry about, a shadow, an angle. Your arm is giving out because you've been sitting above her for three hours on the same elbow, and you're trying not to smear her lipstick or make slippery sounds when you're kissing."

When I saw the rushes of the love scene, I didn't think it worked at all. It lacked intensity and passion. It had to be reshot. Someone had to tell Richard Chamberlain, and I thought it was my job to do that; I didn't know how he would react, and as we still had a considerable filming to do, I didn't want to risk affecting his relationship with the director.

Richard Chamberlain remains one of the nicest people I've ever worked with. "It's a wonderful scene, Richard," I told him, "but we have to do it again. It just wasn't passionate enough. . . . The audience is panting for this. I mean, it has to be wild, you have to be grabbing each other, you've just got to devour her. . . . Remember, this is a priest finally bursting completely free of all restraints. We need to see that."

It was a pleasant conversation, just two men discussing how best to create a wildly passionate sex scene—without sex, of course. This is television. But Chamberlain got it. And the next day, he did it. In front of the microphones and lights and a hundred people or more standing around, he let loose his passions. The scene was so good, in fact, that *TV Guide* eventually rated it "the most romantic moment in the history of television," deciding, "love doesn't get any more forbidden than this. . . . Ralph DeBricassart, a Roman Catholic archbishop, casts aside God and ambition for a few stolen days in a remote beach with Meggie, the woman he had loved since she was a child and desperately wanted since she was a teen. . . . Each knew well this would be their only time together."

But not only on the set for the film were great romantic scenes taking place. Movie-set romances are pretty common; they are almost unavoidable. Intense, creative people are thrown together in a high-pressure situation—usually far from home and family—for several months. The work consists of a few moments of actual filming, a substantial amount of time spent in preparation for those few moments, and an enormous amount of free time. Usually, these romances end when the production ends. Sometimes, though, they persist and cause marriages to break up.

While we were filming scenes in Hawaii, Rachel Ward and Australian Bryan Brown fell passionately in love and were eventually married. Everyone on the set knew what was going on in private. But one of my favorite scenes in the entire nine-hour production had Bryan Brown taking Rachel Ward home after a dance. At her door, he expresses in a tender way his feelings for her without really touching her. As I watched the film, I thought that was a remarkable performance considering the torrid romance taking place between scenes.

Interestingly, our technical adviser, Father Sweeney, eventually married one of his parishioners. In words that might have come directly out of the script, he said, "Priests are men. They are human beings. They fall in love. The only thing that is unnatural about that is the laws of the church that say we can't. I know in my heart there is no contradiction between being a priest and being married."

Part of the success of *The Thorn Birds* was due to Henry Mancini's score. Rather than waiting until we were done filming as many composers do, he would come to the set on occasion to get a real feel for the story. We knew we needed a big, sweeping theme to reinforce that this was taking place in Australia, where the land seems to go on forever, and a fabulous love song. A producer never knows what to expect when he or she hears the music for the first time. Both Stan and I had lived with this project for so long that, somewhere in our heads, we had a "vision" of what the music should be. The job of the composer is to give to the producers what they think they already hear. Henry Mancini, who has been a close friend for many years, came in with a tape recorder and said, "It's taken me a week to find a dulcimer player and here's what I've got."

A dulcimer player? Rather than a large orchestra playing a grand theme, he had a single dulcimer playing a clear, seemingly simple song. But it was anything but simple. Within a few notes he had successfully captured precisely the mood we were trying to create. Listening to it, you couldn't help but feel space and air and the freedom offered by vistas that seemed to go on forever, and the love theme was beautiful.

The Thorn Birds was nominated for fifteen Emmys, winning six, as well as four Golden Globe Awards. It is the second most successful miniseries of all time, ranking only behind *Roots,* and one of the ten most watched television programs in history. It was successful throughout the world, even in Australia, where people only objected to the sheep and that it was filmed in the United States.

Among the complaints we did get, however, were from the Catholic Church and the author, Colleen McCullough. Obviously, the church was not going to like a story in which a priest, who was sworn to celibacy, made love with a married woman. In fact, that scene was so controversial that it was even debated on the ABC news show *Nightline.* We understood how sensitive this subject was to the church and did not actively try to defend it—we simply explained that we were making a best-selling book into a movie. But, in its advertising, ABC did empha-size that this was the story of "a priest torn between the desires of the flesh and the duty to God, a woman tormented by the man she could never have . . ."

Colleen McCullough absolutely hated *The Thorn Birds.* It was a sit-uation I'd never encountered before. Alex Haley, Betty Ford, Teddy White, and John Jakes loved our interpretations of their work and became close friends. But Colleen McCullough just hated it. I never met her and I don't remember why she disliked it so much. But she was not reticent about telling newspaper reporters or pretty much anyone else how dissatisfied she was. It reminds me of the story that Ingrid Bergman did not like *Casablanca,* and she had to spend her whole life listening to people tell her how wonderful it was. I'm sure endless people told Colleen McCullough how much they enjoyed the miniseries, which must make her furious. And, of course, the widowed Mrs. Roald Dahl suffers every time someone tells her *Willy Wonka* is their favorite movie. Stan Margulies did meet Colleen McCullough once, and her only contribu-tion was to tell him the Australian pronunciation of Drogheda.

If she didn't like the original miniseries, she absolutely detested the sequel, *The Thorn Birds: The Missing Years.* More than a decade after completing the original miniseries, we were looking for new projects and someone suggested a sequel to *The Thorn Birds.* The original miniseries had been run five times, three times on the network, and the ratings were excellent each time. People loved it, and we decided to listen to the audi-ence. McCullough once said that she had intentionally killed her characters to prevent any possibility of a sequel, but we fooled her. When we did the original film, we'd left out, completely, the middle of the book, fourteen years in which Ralph leaves Drogheda, not knowing that Meggie gives birth to their son. We had to make up a substantial amount of new material—which we had the contractual right to do—but the basic story and the characters were all there. But not the actors: Rachel Ward, Bryan Brown, and Richard Chamberlain all said, firmly, that they were not interested in doing the sequel. Chamberlain said, "Don't even send me the script. I'm not interested." I tried hard to convince him to consider it, but he was adamant. So, I proceeded without the original stars. I sold the concept for a six-hour miniseries to ABC and tried to cast it. Tom Selleck, Kurt Russell, Christopher Reeve, and Tom Berenger all turned us down. And finally, ABC passed. Without Chamberlain they didn't want to do it.

We made a deal with CBS for four hours. But we still didn't have our star. Finally, Richard Chamberlain's agent, Billy Haber, called and told me that Chamberlain would read the script. His response to it was not exactly what I had hoped: "I have serious doubts about the wisdom of a sequel," he wrote. ". . . The draft I've seen has not dispelled my fears. There is nothing here to play, and nothing in the story for an audience to root for. . . . The story was told brilliantly and completely in *Thorn Birds I*. There is nothing left to dramatize."

We continued to search for another actor to play the role. Peter Horton passed. Scott Bakula passed. We refused to give up on Chamberlain. He wrote to Haber, "One, even a good rewrite along the lines I suggested, could not possibly measure up to the original . . . [which] was absolutely the high point of my career." He concluded, "Consequently, even with a good rewrite, my price for *Thorn Birds II* would be $4 million."

Four million dollars was the projected budget for the entire miniseries. No actor in the history of television had ever been paid that kind of money. But I was thrilled with his response: finally, we were negotiating. Fortunately, at just about that time, Les Moonves became head of programming at CBS and told us, bluntly, that if we could get Chamberlain for the sequel, "money would not be an issue."

I love to hear network executives speak that way. After considerable rewriting, Richard Chamberlain agreed to reprise his role for the sequel—for which he was paid $4 million. I tried almost as hard to convince Rachel Ward to return, but she was happily married to Bryan Brown and living in Australia. She just wasn't interested. To replace Ward we hired Amanda Donohoe, familiar to TV viewers from *L.A. Law.* I liked her performance, but like Jane Seymour, she lacked a sense of vulnerability and was too strong for the role.

This time we filmed in Australia. "Finally," read our advertising slogan, "the never-before-seen struggle that reignited an everlasting love." Although the critics didn't love it, the ratings were acceptable, and it proved profitable for my company, the network, and Richard Chamberlain.

Colleen McCullough was not pleased, issuing a statement that read in part, "The projected sequel has absolutely nothing to do with me. . . . As the original miniseries did not do my characters justice, I do not expect that the sequel, based on it . . . will fare any better. I imagine if I watched it, which I do not intend to, it would have had the same effect on me as an emetic. . . .

"I will benefit to the tune of $40,000 total. . . . This princely payment should enable me to undergo proctologic surgery for an insult. I need it." I wonder what she would have written if she had read the script.

THIRTY-SIX

CIRCLE THE WAGONS

On the set of *The Mystic Warrior*
with Will Sampson (1981)

I had long ceased being upset by people trying to stop me from completing my projects. Not after the struggles I'd been through. Colleen McCullough's comments mattered little to me after the fight I'd been through to make Ruth Beebe Hill's epic Indian novel *Hanta Yo* into a five-hour miniseries entitled *The Mystic Warrior.*

With all the projects I developed from books, only two authors ever objected to our translation of their printed work to the screen. In 1978, I purchased the rights to a huge book, 834 pages, that had been touted as the Indian version of *Roots.* Ruth Hill, working with an Indian named Chunksa Yuha, had spent twenty-five years researching and writing this book about the Lakota Sioux in the late eighteenth and early nineteenth centuries. She had even written one draft entirely in the Sioux language. At her house, she had the furs of every animal mentioned in the book. She had gathered feathers from the forty-four different birds mentioned. It was very different from just about anything else that had been done about Native Americans—even my own television movie, *I Will Fight No More, Forever.* This book was about Indian families and the Lakota Sioux society rather than Indians fighting the cavalry or settlers. It was an insightful look inside a fascinating culture.

Many Lakota Indians questioned its accuracy, specifically passages referring to various sexual and religious practices. There were many other complaints—including the translation of the book's title: Hill stated that her title, *Hanta Yo,* meant "clear the way," which is both a war cry and a metaphysical statement of Lakota spiritualism, while contemporary Sioux claimed her title was simply a throwaway phrase meaning "scram, get lost, get out of here." We did considerable checking and found a book, written in 1918, that confirmed Hill's contention that it was a spiritual term.

The Lakota Sioux objected actively to the book; several times, when Hill was scheduled to speak about the book, members of the Sioux tribe showed up and picketed her. Stations on which she was supposed to appear received bomb threats. Seven Sioux reservation councils passed resolutions condemning the book. Had I been aware of all this when I bought the rights, maybe I would have hesitated. But I don't think so. Like *Roots, Hanta Yo* is a compelling story of a unique and fascinating culture, told through the normal lives of a family. It just seemed like a natural thing for me to do after *Roots.*

Almost immediately after it was announced that we had obtained the rights, I started receiving letters criticizing the book, claiming that both some facts and the overall impression of the book were inaccurate, and that, as a white woman, Hill could not possibly understand Indian society. That criticism reminded me of so many battles I'd previously fought, unsuccessfully for *Nat Turner,* and successfully for *Roots,* and even for *Say Goodbye.*

I've never claimed to be altruistic; in fact, exactly the opposite is true. But my entire career stands as evidence that I don't take shortcuts around the truth simply to get programming done. My objective here was to accurately recount the story of Indian life as it had never previously been done. I was not looking for sensationalism, I wanted the truth.

But even before I started, the Lakota Sioux tried to prevent me from making this miniseries. They wrote letters to the networks, they picketed the studio. On March 3, 1980, a reporter from KTTV in Los Angeles told me that threats had been made to burn down the studio and even take lives to prevent this book from being made into a picture. What I didn't really understand was why. The first thing I did was try to contact the

Indians who were objecting to find out precisely what they were objecting to; once I understood that, I felt I could deal with their objections.
But because there were several competing groups, it was difficult to get
a clear answer.

Ruth Hill was devastated by the criticism. She'd spent much of her
adult life working on this book, and while it had become an enormously
popular best-seller, she had never anticipated the vitriol the Indian
community would direct toward her.

In addition to physical threats, several tribal councils threatened
lawsuits. In fact, a lawsuit was filed against me, Stan Margulies, Fred
Pierce of ABC, and the ABC network in the Oglala Sioux Tribal Court,
on the Pine Ridge Reservation, claiming the book defamed the Sioux
nation because it depicted them as participating in sexual activities as
part of their religious life. When our attorneys responded by claiming the
Indian court had no jurisdiction, their attorney responded, "The presence of television waves on the reservation is tantamount to them being
present," meaning that, since our show could be seen on the reservation,
they should have jurisdiction. The whole suit was ridiculous. The only
instance in which the tribal court may have had some power was when
we were physically on reservation land. We decided not to become
involved in this lawsuit, so we were found guilty.

The fighting was causing major problems, and I began to wonder if it
was really worth it. The money we would earn would make absolutely
no difference in my life or for most of the people with whom I was
working. The network would fill the time slot. But the concept of letting
these people win simply because they spoke loudest was repugnant to
everything I believed in. So I became more determined than ever. I
fought back, telling reporters, "A bush may have many thorns and yet
produce a beautiful flower. The television show will be the flower that
will emerge from this book." But, admittedly, at times I wondered why
I was bothering. "I think this will be great for the Sioux when they see
it," I said, "but I may surrender."

I did everything possible to placate the Indians. Finally, I read about
a Lakota newspaper editor winning a major journalism award. He was
the editor of the reservation newspaper *Lakota Times*, Tim Giago. I asked
him to serve as our contact with the tribal leaders, as well as a technical
adviser on the film. Tim Giago was as good a diplomat as I have ever
encountered, as well as being a fine person.

Eventually, Giago arranged for three representatives of Lakota Sioux
to come to Los Angeles to discuss the problem. Louis Badwound,

George Amiotte, and Larry Redshirt were interesting, serious men. They made no threats, they didn't bluster, and they understood the problems and worked with me to solve them.

I explained to them, at a dinner in my house, that the sexual aspects of the book to which they objected weren't going to be part of my film. The elders suggested that we could resolve all the issues by changing the name of the miniseries to make sure the book—which was really what they were objecting to—got no additional publicity or recognition, by giving them script approval for accuracy only, and by allowing an Indian to be on the set as technical adviser while we were shooting.

The three elders decided to hold a meeting with the nonreservation Indians who were complaining loudest about the miniseries. Most of these people lived in Los Angeles; "urban Indians," they were called. The meeting was in English. Few of the urban Indians spoke the Lakota language, and it quickly became hostile. I tried to defend my position. These people were obviously responding to their passions, not the facts. I reminded them that they hadn't read the script; in fact the script hadn't even been written. Their argument was that the script would be based on the book, and I reminded them that I had only five hours, I couldn't do the entire book. The thrust of their argument was that, as a white man, I couldn't possibly understand or appreciate their position. It got really ugly when someone threw the word *Jewish* in there.

Suddenly, from beneath the table, one of the elders, Larry Redshirt, picked up a pipe about a foot and a half long and gently placed it in front of him on the table.

One of the urban Indians continued screaming, and when he paused to take a breath, Larry Redshirt said quietly, "You may leave the room now. I put the pipe down and you obviously did not understand its meaning, so you may leave."

As they explained to me, this was the chief's pipe. In Lakota tradition the chief would listen to all the arguments, but when he put the pipe down in front of him, all conversation was finished and he was going to make his decision. And that decision was firm and final. Apparently, these urban Indians, fighting so hard to protect their heritage, didn't know the meaning of the chief's pipe.

Larry Redshirt decided to accept the compromise we had worked out. We would change the title so the miniseries did not give additional publicity to the book. We would submit the script to the tribe only to ensure that everything in the script was faithful to Sioux religious traditions. Specifically, we would send the script to Tim Giago, who would read it to the tribal fathers for approval. If they approved, the Lakota Sioux would support the miniseries; if they suggested a change that we refused to make, they would call a strike.

Ruth Hill was furious when she learned we were changing the title, but I felt we had no options. She insisted the Indians had no right to touch her material and certainly did not have the right to force me to change the title. Personally, after consulting several experts, I felt her telling of the story was probably accurate, but I took the straightest path to the end. After considering many different titles, including *High Plains Warrior, Cry of the Warrior, Dream Warriors*, and *Majestic Warriors,* we settled on *The Mystic Warrior,* which I believed accurately described the Lakota Sioux of our film.

Although neither ABC nor I had ever given script approval to anyone for any purpose, in this specific case it made sense to me. These were the experts on their religion in my film; they wanted it to be as accurate as I did. As I knew that the scenes to which they most objected, depicting homosexual activities, were not going to be in the film anyway, I didn't think we would have much of a problem getting their approval. The film contained several religious scenes, which would be sensitive to every group, and I wanted them to be absolutely correct. As long as they did not get involved in artistic decisions, I was willing to give them that approval. Additionally, ABC hired a Lakota Sioux expert to examine the script.

As a direct result of this controversy, the networks decided not to proceed with six other projects about Native Americans. Among them, NBC dropped its plans to do *The Saga of an American Indian* and ABC did not proceed with my close friend David Gerber's *Creek Mary's Blood.*

We cast as many Native Americans as possible. We sent casting people to several Indian colleges and reservations. Twenty-three of the major roles, including the four lead actors, were Native Americans. Just as actors had claimed to be African-American to try to get a part in one of the *Roots* productions, suddenly actors were discovering their own long-lost Indian heritage. To cast the picture, we had to decide exactly what constituted a Native American. The answer was that an Indian was a person with at least one-quarter Indian ancestry, of a tribe recognized by the federal government, whose rolls have been closed by an act of Congress. We actually checked the lineage of our actors to find out precisely which tribes were represented.

As promised, we sent the script to Tim Giago for approval and, in return, received quite a long list of suggestions. "Hopi is not all naked," he wrote. "He should use a breechcloth. . . . Before any war party goes out on a raid, or engages in any warlike activities, the military council must plan and decide upon a plan of action . . ."

These were all great ideas. I would have been thrilled to receive these suggestions from anybody, and we incorporated all of them in the production.

Perhaps the best-known fighter for Indian rights, at that time, was Russell Means, who tried to get involved with our production. Among Means's suggestions was that, for safety reasons, we should not shoot the movie at the Pine Ridge Reservation, that, in fact, the company should stay out of the entire state of South Dakota. It was good advice, but we had already decided that it would be too dangerous to make our movie where many of the events actually took place, so instead, we shot in California, where generations of faux Indians had died for the camera.

The battles didn't end when the film shooting started. We had sent Ruth Hill a copy of the script, which she returned marked up with venomous comments. On just about every page, she'd written "stupid," or some other caustic comment. For example, where the writer had described "beautiful white buffalo," she'd written, "They are not beautiful. I saw white buffalo and they're ugly." Her comments seemed particularly bitter, but where it made sense, we incorporated her suggestions. Ruth Beebe Hill was on the set several times, but because she continued to object so loudly to changes we had made to satisfy the tribe, eventually we had to ban her. She was not necessarily wrong in her objections, but we didn't want to arouse the ire of our technical advisers. Eventually, a friend of Chunksa Yuha's wrote a long letter to Tim Giago, for his newspaper, complaining that Ruth Hill was angry that she had been replaced as the technical adviser. In the letter, he referred to me as Money Makes Me Tick, although I suspect that is not a precise translation of Wolper into Lakota Sioux.

The budget was slightly more than $10 million. As always, I tried hard to make *The Mystic Warrior* as authentic as possible. We used an enormous number of real items, which we obtained from the reservation, including medicine pipes, horse-dance sticks, bone knives, quilted knife sheaths, buffalo robes, love flutes, bows, and arrows. When we finished filming, we donated those items, as well as thousands of props, to the Oglala Lakota College. Warner's made a sizable donation to the reservation school system, we made a small donation to the old folks home on the reservation, we circulated educational materials to schools before the show was broadcast, and we included a bibliography of other books about Indians at the end of the show. Later, we also helped an Indian runner living in Los Angeles get training at UCLA and got him some financial support to prepare for the Olympics.

The Mystic Warrior got mixed reviews from the critics, but it was well received by the Oglala Lakota Sioux. At a screening in a theater in South Dakota, it got a big ovation. After viewing the completed miniseries, Tim Giago said, "The movie will give many white viewers their first true look at a people depicted in many previous films as silent, sullen, and monosyllabic."

But, as a direct result of the problems we had, to my knowledge this was the last major TV film project about Native Americans. I don't blame only the Indians. Over and over I've seen that each ethnic group believes it owns the rights to the story of its culture and history—and that their story must be told the way they want it told. Within each larger ethnic group there have always been activists, some of them with a personal agenda, others simply being opportunistic, and still others who genuinely care about their heritage. Trying to deal with these diverse groups has made it difficult for producers to successfully complete projects about the different races and cultures that comprise this country, to the detriment of us all.

THIRTY-SEVEN

NORTH AND SOUTH
AND HOLLYWOOD BOULEVARD

With Patrick Swayze (1984)

Based on my experiences with various groups trying to protect their image, I suspect that if a single soldier who had fought on either side in the Civil War were still alive, no one would ever be able to make a film with a Civil War background. The length of the first several miniseries was a little more or less than ten hours. When I was approached to do a twenty-four-hour-long miniseries, I was quite surprised. Once I'd fought to get a few minutes on television; now I was being asked to produce the longest motion picture in television history. Certainly I was thrilled, but still, astonished. The word *miniseries* may not accurately describe a story that lasts twenty-four hours. Perhaps it might better be called a limited series, but the Civil War story *North and South* was unique—and it seemed quite appropriate to tell the epic story of the war that almost ended this nation over that length of time.

The project began when ABC executive vice president Martin Starger, with whom I'd done several shows, told me that the network was interested in adapting into a miniseries John Jakes's best-selling books about two young soldiers who meet while studying at West Point, one from a Northern industrial family, the other from a Southern plantation family, following their lives through the Civil War and beyond. These books accomplished the often difficult task of personalizing history. Actual events were seen through the eyes of fictional characters readers cared about.

I did not know that the network was planning to change the rules of miniseries until I met with Brandon Stoddard. I figured he was thinking about a ten- or twelve-hour program. In previous meetings, we had both decried that the network would spend a fortune in dollars and TV time promoting a miniseries, and after it was broadcast—no matter how successful it was—all that promotion had no value. No network was willing to risk filming an expensive sequel until the original miniseries proved successful. That meant it took several years to produce a sequel, which required an entirely new campaign. We'd wondered what would happen if you mounted a campaign for a miniseries—then followed it up with the sequel a couple of months later. Brandon decided that we would do exactly that for the John Jakes Civil War series.

It was enormously risky. If the first part failed to build an audience, the network was stuck with an expensive film in the middle of a ratings month. No network had ever spent millions making the sequel to a miniseries *before it had run!* But Stoddard was never averse to taking risks. We didn't immediately determine the length. Instead, I hired writers to do a complete outline—which came to a legitimate twenty-four hours. If Brandon believed there was fat in the story, he would have cut it out, but he didn't. ABC gave me a firm order for twenty-four hours, at $2 million an hour. Naturally, I reported to my staff that we'd made a deal for twenty-two hours, knowing from decades of experience that we were going to have plenty of footage left over to fill the remaining two hours. But, from a budget standpoint we were shooting twenty-two hours. Everything was planned for twenty-two hours.

When we finished shooting, we had enough film for a twenty-four-hour show. I paid everyone additional money. They were thrilled; they didn't have to do any more work and got additional pay. But if we had planned to do twenty-four hours initially, we would have ended up shooting twenty-six hours. Those four additional hours, all of which would have had to have been cut, would have required about twelve days of shooting. So, even after paying extra to the cast and crew, I'd saved considerable money.

The two parts of the miniseries were entitled *North and South,* which ran in the November sweeps period, and *Love and War,* which was broadcast in the February sweeps. The thing that made this project so different from anything that had been done before was its size and scope. It was an enormous production. Sometimes, it felt as if we were casting the original Civil War. It took almost two years of development, five months of principal photography, and four months of postproduction between the meetings with the network and the first day it was broadcast. Initially we announced the project as a twelve-hour miniseries. But, during a press tour to promote *North and South,* we told reporters we were going to do an instant sequel ten hours long.

We filmed in Charleston, South Carolina, which was pretty much the closest we could come to capturing the urban charm and grace of the mid-1800s. Charleston is really a gem. At one time, it was the hub of American commerce, shipping, culture, and wealth, but for us, the most important thing was that Charleston had successfully managed to hold tight to its history. Part of the reason it has never been overrun by tall buildings is an ordinance prohibiting buildings within a certain area from being any taller than the steeple of St. Michael's Church.

Charleston opened its history to our production. We were permitted to film inside historic mansions—which served as both Southern and Northern homes—and public buildings. To make the streets look as they might have during the Civil War, we hid poles and telephone lines, air conditioners, cars, mailboxes, street signs, parking meters, wires and cables, even doorbells. We used every type of effect to hide modern technology, hiding poles inside phony tree shells, and candles inside light poles to make them appear to be gas lanterns. The most difficult thing we had to do was "unpave" the streets, spreading five hundred tons of dirt to hide the paved roads. One woman, I remember, complained that our dirt would ruin her stately mansion, a house that had been built about 1700. I reminded her that for two hundred years that house had actually been sitting on a dirt road, so it was difficult to understand how it might be ruined.

With so many speaking roles, this was a perfect opportunity for me to fill my cast with major stars, few of whom worked more than a day or two. Just imagine what it might have cost only a few years earlier to cast a picture with Elizabeth Taylor, James Stewart, Robert Mitchum, Olivia de Havilland, Gene Kelly, Robert Wagner, Johnny Cash, Lloyd Bridges, Jean Simmons, and of course, Hal Holbrook, who played Abraham Lincoln—as he had done for me a decade earlier in *Sandburg's Lincoln.* But, as these people made mostly brief appearances, I could afford them, and in addition to the talent they brought to their roles, I received the promotional value of their names.

Casting the leads was a little more difficult than might be expected. While these roles were potentially star-making vehicles, we needed actors already well known enough to attract an audience, yet not so big that they would refuse to spend many months on location for a television salary. We cast a handsome young actor named Patrick Swayze, who had done several minor movies and TV films, as our Confederate lead. Swayze was capable of roping a calf or dancing ballet; in fact he had been a principal dancer with the world-renowned Elliot Feld dance company.

The female lead, a New Orleans Creole who falls in love with Patrick Swayze, was British-born beauty Lesley-Anne Down. Once selected as Great Britain's most beautiful teenager, she'd starred in several major motion pictures, as well as my film for television *Agatha Christie's Murder Is Easy.* The first meeting of two actors about to spend the next several months as lovers is always interesting. When we had the initial reading of the completed script, Patrick Swayze arrived early and I told him, "Patrick, you're really going to freak out when you see how beautiful Lesley-Anne Down is."

She walked in a few minutes later wearing old clothes, no makeup, her hair disheveled, looking like a mess. It was hard to believe that this was the same woman who had dazzled everyone she had met with her beauty. Swayze said to me, "That's what you call beautiful, Wolper? You got to be kidding me."

"Wait," I said as confidently as possible, "wait until you see her made up."

On the first day of shooting, I was sitting with Swayze when Lesley-Anne Down walked out of her dressing room, her makeup in place, her hair perfect, wearing this long dress with a low bodice—she looked . . . legendary. "Wolper," Swayze said, "I apologize."

In the tradition established by *Gone With the Wind, North and South* was, essentially, several love stories with the Civil War as the background. It included many love scenes, which caused some problems with Standards and Practices, the network censors. After reviewing the screenplay, they sent us about forty pages of notes. This included warnings like "Caution on the staging of—they sink to the floor fumbling with each other's clothing, dress almost unbuttoned"; "Comment: Please avoid having Billy stare at Ashton's breasts as she pushes her pretty bosom forward"; "In the staging of Grady undressing Virginia, please tone down the level of titillation—avoiding directions like, he slowly begins to unbutton her dress—the loosened material of the dress falling"; and "Ensure that Ashton is adequately covered at all times during her love scene, and limit the extent of moaning and screams."

The cast consisted of thirty principal roles, one hundred smaller speaking roles, and fifty-two hundred extras. We had a lot of small parts to cast, and in several instances, we used them to advantage. Jack Valenti, president and CEO of the Motion Picture Association of America, and a good friend, called to ask me to find small roles in the production for the two young daughters of South Carolina's senator Strom Thurmond, who had long been supportive of the film industry. This made me quite a hero to Senator Thurmond. In fact, in honor of my contribution to the great state of South Carolina—we did spend millions of dollars in that state, in addition to casting his daughters—I received the Palmetto Award, the highest honor that is bestowed by that state.

Thurmond was not the only politician involved in our production. We gave Congressman Bill Blackwell one easy line of dialogue to remember: "No." Elvita King Beal, an actress who served four years in the Georgia state legislature—and was Martin Luther King's niece—portrayed a slave. The head of South Carolina's State Film Office, Deborah Rosen, who worked incredibly hard for us, put on a long red wig and period lingerie to play a prostitute in a bordello. Kirk Douglas called and asked us to find a small role for his son Eric Douglas, whom we cast as a soldier. Even John Jakes's wife made a brief appearance as Mrs. Lincoln.

I tried hard, but without success, to sign one particular young man. I had a great role for John F. Kennedy Jr. I spoke with Senator Edward Kennedy, to ask his help, and followed up with a detailed letter outlining the role and promising to hire a coach who would work with JFK Jr. throughout the production. Eventually, I learned that Jackie Kennedy had objected strenuously—and that John would not be appearing in my film.

The cost of staging the battles would have been substantial, but we were able to find troops of Civil War buffs who would re-create famous battles in their spare time. These are true weekend warriors who have their own uniforms and equipment and insist on historical accuracy. They've got their own horses and cannons and dummy ammunition. They follow the line of battle as it actually happened. We hired them for a flat fee and pretty much got out of their way. They pitched their tents and lived on the set. These people don't do it for money or fame, they do it for a love of history. Working with these units was a great pleasure.

As much as we tried, we still made historical errors. We received a letter from a viewer pointing out that we had a chair in the background that hadn't been designed in the year the scene supposedly took place. As I read that letter, I thought, we're spending $50 million, we have a cast of thousands, including some of the biggest movie stars in history, we worked two years, we turned parts of South Carolina back in time more than a century—and this person noticed a chair!

The media campaign that we put together for *North and South* would probably rank among the most extensive in television history, and it was an important aspect of our original strategy. While the miniseries was being shot in Charleston, I spent most of my time in Los Angeles helping coordinate the promotion. Among the highlights of this campaign—in addition to the interviews that we paid Elizabeth Taylor to do—were a half-hour program entitled "A War in the Family" on ABC, and extensive educational materials distributed to schools all over the country. *TV Guide* did five stories as well as giving us the cover, we were on the covers of seventy-eight Sunday newspaper supplements, and just about every entertainment magazine did long pieces on our stars or the making of the miniseries. *Good Morning America* ran a weekly segment on the miniseries for almost a year before it ran, and we had major press junkets in which we brought dozens of newspaper and magazine writers to Charleston, Los Angeles, and New York. *20/20* did a story about me, *Entertainment Tonight* did several pieces, and just about every major newspaper ran articles. *USA Today*, for example, ran fourteen stories. It would be impossible to estimate the total number of stories either broadcast or printed, but certainly it was many, many thousands. We even set up a 900 number for people to call if they missed an episode, to find out what had happened.

I did countless interviews by satellite and by telephone. I was so exhausted that, during a telephone interview, I literally fell asleep when the radio show broke for a commercial. When the show went back on the air, it seemed as if I had disappeared. Finally Gloria came running into my office to tell me I had been disconnected—and found me head down, fast asleep on my desk.

The media campaign was as well planned as the actual filming. It began more than a year before the program ran and extended beyond the first of the twelve hours right to the concluding night. While we did a "Making of . . ." show, perhaps someone should have done "The Making of the Making of . . ." because this was a classic promotional campaign.

The object of the campaign was to transform *North and South* from a television miniseries to an event. We wanted people to feel that they would be missing something everyone else was watching if they didn't tune in. In that, we succeeded.

ABC received higher ratings in almost every single time period than it had with the programming it replaced. And considering this was sweeps month and it was running against the strongest programming the other networks had, it did well. It built and held a substantial audience share, at times approaching 50 percent.

The real test of the concept came several months later, when part two, *Love and War*, began. Once again our ratings were substantially higher than those for ABC's regular programming. The network was pleased with the results.

North and South was a major hit in the international market. For some reason—perhaps the *Gone With the Wind* factor—the American Civil War is of great interest throughout the world. Financially, this miniseries was incredibly profitable for us. While the network owned the rights to the first two complete showings, Warner Bros. and I owned everything else. And there was a lot of everything else. Over several years, the show made more than a $25 million profit.

Our crew was together for more than a year. Many relationships were formed during this time resulting in three marriages: actress Genie Francis married actor Jonathan Frakes, actor James Read married actress Wendy Kilbourne, and Lesley-Anne Down got a very public and bitter divorce from her husband, director Billy Friedkin, and married cameraman Don Fauntleroy.

To our surprise and delight, as a result of the success of the miniseries, ABC asked us to create a sequel: part three, based on another book in the Jakes series. We'd left the two families sort of hanging after Reconstruction. After the original miniseries, Patrick Swayze had become a major movie star and had little interest in reprising his role. Although, obviously, I was disappointed because, in addition to being a fine actor, he was a pleasure to work with, I understood it completely. Unlike John Travolta, who had become famous while still under contract for *Welcome Back, Kotter*, we had no such arrangement with Swayze.

Our only option was to kill him, in character, which we did in the opening scenes.

Heaven and Hell, as it was named, was better received by the critics than the previous film, and most of the audience came back seven years later to see the conclusion. So, in essence, it took us longer to tell this story, more than seven years, than it did to fight the Civil War.

Only one of my miniseries was really not a success. For the first—and only—time, we tried a variation on the basic concept. Instead of telling one story over several episodes, I thought we could tell some of the greatest stories of motion picture history in a series of self-contained movies.

In most cases, when a miniseries is based on a book, the book has been a best-seller long before the movie is made. And when the miniseries is run, the publisher usually brings out a special softcover edition, a miniseries tie-in. The exception was *Roots,* which had just been published in hardcover when the series went on the air. That wasn't the plan, it was simply that Alex Haley took so much longer than anticipated to write the book. But it turned out to be fortuitous for Alex and Doubleday, as they sold 2 million copies of the more expensive hardcover edition.

It occurred to me that, with a little planning, we could make that happen again. One evening, Gloria and I were with best-selling author Garson Kanin, who told some wonderful stories about Hollywood. As I listened to him, the proverbial lightbulb suddenly shone brightly in my head. I suggested Garson write a book about Hollywood, which I would buy for a miniseries. "I'll be able to sell it to a network before you write it," I told him confidently. "You'll be able to sell the book for a fortune and you can publish the book when the miniseries goes on the air."

The basic idea was that we would tell the history of the movie industry through this miniseries. Garson Kanin agreed, and as I had promised, Brandon Tartikoff, at NBC, bought it for a six-hour miniseries. *Moviola,* as it was called, didn't work out quite as well as we had hoped. When Garson wrote the book, he included some stories we hadn't discussed, but the miniseries consisted of three two-hour movies: *The Scarlett O'Hara Wars,* the entertaining story of the nationwide search for the actress to play the leading role in *Gone With the Wind; This Year's Blonde,* the story of the discovery of Marilyn Monroe by William Morris agent Johnny Hyde; and *The Silent Lovers,* the story of Greta Garbo's rise to stardom and her love affair with leading man John Gilbert.

In casting this miniseries we found a young woman who gave one of the greatest performances I've ever seen—in real life. Greta Garbo had come to the United States from Sweden and become the greatest femme fatale of the silent and early sound movies. When her career ended, she became, basically, a recluse. She rarely appeared in public and never gave an interview. To play Garbo we needed a beautiful woman with an enigmatic quality.

One day, an absolutely gorgeous Swedish actress named Kristina Wayborn came in for an interview. She brought with her a letter from the great director Ingmar Bergman, explaining that he had worked with her and was pleased to be able to recommend her. She seemed perfect for the role; even her accent was similar to Garbo's.

She gave an excellent performance in the movie. But on the set, she was as mysterious as the real Garbo. Each morning she would arrive at the studio in a limousine, and at the end of the day the same limousine would whisk her away. She kept to herself on the set, she didn't socialize with anyone at all. She never said a word to anyone about her personal life.

At the wrap party after we'd completed the film, she came up to me and said, in perfect English, "I want to thank you very much for this opportunity, Mr. Wolper."

In perfect English. Without any accent at all. I was stunned. I didn't know what to say. Then she admitted she had created her whole persona. Not only was the note from Bergman a forgery, she'd never even met him. We had all been fooled by her performance—off the set.

Kristina Wayborn had enjoyed a moderately successful career as a model in America. But, after returning to Sweden, she'd read that we were searching for an actress to play Garbo and decided to try to win that role. She screened every Garbo film, read every book about her, and then returned to America with her phony letter. She'd bluffed her way into the part. For someone with that kind of determination, playing shy must have been the most difficult portrayal of her career.

I was certain that her combination of beauty, chutzpah, and talent would enable her to become a major movie star, but it just never happened for her. I believe she appeared in one of the James Bond films, and I saw her name once in a while, but basically, she disappeared. I never knew what happened to her.

Moviola just didn't work. Because we did it as three separate two-hour movies, the audience had no compelling reason to come back for the next episode. In fact, after the miniseries completed its contractual runs, we broke it up into three separate movies and sold each of them independently.

Most critics didn't like it. Tom Shales was particularly vitriolic, blasting every aspect of the production in a scathing review. It was such a terrible review I decided to respond. "Dear Mr. Shales," I wrote, "I read your review in yesterday's *Washington Post*. A simple 'lousy' would have sufficed . . ."

The book proved more successful than the miniseries. Garson Kanin eventually included some stories we hadn't discussed and wrote a big best-seller. But my original idea, my plan to create a synergy between the book and the movie, just never worked.

When we began doing miniseries, there were three major networks. The growth of cable as well as new networks such as Fox, UPN, and WB segmented the audience, making it difficult to justify the investment necessary for a major miniseries. So, with occasional exceptions, the format has disappeared, which is truly a shame. Of all the types of programs I've done, miniseries were my favorite. I loved everything about them, the size, the scope, and the final product. The most amazing time of my life was that week in January 1977 when *Roots* was running for the first time. And to some small degree, each time I had a miniseries running, I relived that initial excitement.

But only one other time in my career did I experience a thrill equal to that week. It lasted only a day, but that day will long be remembered.

PART VI

The Spectaculars

Gloria and I with the Bushes in Kennebunkport (1986)

THIRTY-EIGHT

A TWENTY-GOOSE-BUMP EVENT

Peter Ueberroth and I on the final night
of the 1984 Olympic Games

The greatest challenge to any producer is an impossible challenge. For a successful producer, the word *no* is more often the beginning than an end. Being told something can't be done or is difficult seems to get all the competitive juices flowing. So, when I was offered the opportunity to produce a live show of truly Olympic proportions, I was thrilled.

In 1932, the Olympic Games were held in Los Angeles. Although people around the world predicted the games were doomed to failure, they were a great success. One of the results of that event was the formation in 1939 of the Southern California Committee for the Olympic Games, which had been trying to bring the Olympics back to Los Angeles since just about the day it was formed.

I'd become involved in the Olympics in 1972, when I produced

Visions of Eight in Munich. When the city of Los Angeles decided to bid
for the 1984 games, Mayor Bradley asked me to go to Athens and help,
as I knew the members of the International Olympic Committee. The
concept of bringing the world to Los Angeles appealed to me; I thought
it would be wonderful for the city. I also knew we had a good chance of
succeeding: the 1972 summer Olympic Games in Montreal had been a
financial disaster, costing the city over a billion dollars. To many cities,
the entire Olympic movement had lost its appeal. But we were eager to
play host, so in May 1978, I went with the mayor and the committee to
Athens to make our pitch. Another member of the team was John
Argue, a Los Angeles lawyer who was head of the Southern California
Committee for the Olympic Games and who, more than anyone else,
was responsible for this effort.

In subsequent years, there has been considerable controversy about
bribes offered to members of the IOC by cities bidding for the Olympics.
But we didn't offer them a thing. Our only competition for the right to
host the '84 summer Olympics was Tehran, Iran. No other cities were
willing to take the financial risk. Although the shah of Iran still ruled that
country, we were already hearing rumors about political unrest, and Iran
still lacked the infrastructure necessary to host thousands of athletes and
journalists. So, for the Olympic committee, we were pretty much the
only city in the world. The Olympic movement was in trouble.

While Mayor Bradley was a strong supporter of bringing the games to
Los Angeles, there was tremendous opposition. The criticism was so
strong, and the potential for financial loss so great, that Bradley knew the
city couldn't officially sponsor the offer. Mayor Bradley's presentation was
impressive, and after it, we were provisionally awarded the games. As
part of the deal, the IOC wanted us to provide insurance that the games
would actually take place and all bills would be paid. We agreed to do
that, although privately, John Argue and I knew that it would be impossible. When we returned to L.A., Hank Rieger, a publicist; Rodney
Rood, an Atlantic Richfield vice president; and I suggested, in a letter to
the mayor, that we turn over the games to a private committee. Bradley
accepted the suggestion and quickly named a seven-person negotiating
panel on which John Argue, others, and I were members.

Eventually, the IOC, to save face, let the U.S. Olympic Committee
(USOC) guarantee our bid, although it had even less money than we
did. The whole U.S. Olympic Committee probably had less than $5 mil-
lion, hardly enough to cover hundred-million-dollar losses. For their
backing, we agreed to give the USOC 60 percent of the profits, while

our committee—not the city of Los Angeles—would get 40 percent. But at that time few people believed there would be much of a profit to split up. I thought we had a chance to make a lot of money. I knew that anyone can spend money, the key is to spend it in the right places. I looked carefully at the financial reports from the last three summer Olympics, and in each case, one thing had stood out: the difference between financial success and disaster had been the cost of capital construction. The games actually produced a profit—but the cost of building stadiums and arenas for the events had produced a deficit. Montreal had spent more than a billion dollars preparing for the games. In Los Angeles, we already had most of the sites we would need—including the Los Angeles Coliseum. In 1978, I predicted we would make a $135 million profit. Nice people thought I was simply wildly optimistic; less nice people thought I was nuts.

With the backing of the USOC, the International Olympic Committee happily announced that the 1984 games would be held in Los Angeles, California. I think, privately, they were thrilled that any major city would host the games after the debacle in Montreal.

The first thing we had to do was select a president to run the games. Many prominent people were suggested, among them, broadcaster Curt Gowdy, pro football commissioner Pete Rozelle, Chrysler chairman Lee Iacocca, General Alexander Haig, and several successful businessmen. Finally, the executive committee had to select between two of those businessmen, the president of the May Company, Ed Steidle, or the president of a major travel agency, Ask Mr. Foster, Peter Ueberroth.

I had met Ueberroth only once before. In 1973, with several other people, including Barry Diller, Berry Gordy Jr., my close friend David Gerber, and Wilt Chamberlain, I had helped form the International Volleyball Association, a six-team, six-city league that included both male and female players. I was elected commissioner of the league.

At one point, Peter Ueberroth had expressed interest in buying a franchise. He'd come to a league meeting and asked a lot of detailed questions about how the league was being run. After hearing our answers, he told us, in detail, everything we were doing wrong. By the time the meeting was over, rather than selling him a team, I practically threw him out of the meeting.

The league went bankrupt in two years—although the team Dave Gerber and I owned, the Los Angeles Stars, did win the championship. As it turned out, Ueberroth had been right on just about every point.

Five years later, Ueberroth walked into my office to be interviewed for the position of president of the Los Angeles Olympic Committee. Later, he told me that while he was waiting for the meeting to begin, he had started thinking about the last time we'd met and said to my assistant, Auriel Sanderson, "I guess this is one job I'm not going to get."

But I also remembered that first meeting, and I remember thinking that, if we'd listened to his ideas, the league would have survived. I thought he was a bright guy. This time we had a good meeting. He impressed me, once again, with his ability to isolate the most serious potential problems and move to solve them.

When we voted in the executive committee meeting, Justin Dart and I made an impassioned speech on Peter's behalf. Ed Steidle, I pointed out, had spent his entire career inside big corporations, moving from one major retail chain to another. He'd never had to organize or establish a business. Ueberroth was a self-starter, he'd built a successful chain of travel agencies. He'd been confronted with serious problems with his own money on the line and had successfully resolved them. We needed someone who could start with a single secretary and build an organization of fifty thousand people. Eventually, Peter was selected to run the games.

One thing had become clear to me from all the research I'd done: the key to the financial success of the Olympics is the television rights. That's the single largest revenue source. Because of my experience in television, I was asked to head the television committee. I was glad to do it; I felt I'd worked hard to bring the Olympics to Los Angeles and I wanted them to be the most memorable Olympics in history.

In early September 1979, at my home in Los Angeles, bidding took place for the television rights to the 1984 Olympic Games. I was chairman of the committee and Ueberroth, Argue, and a number of others were present. Each of the networks was coming to make its presentation. CBS bid $150 million; NBC went to $200 million; Jerry Perenchio, an independently wealthy financier and television executive, bid $175 million; and ABC won the bid with $225 million plus providing host broadcasting arrangements, which means the total package came to $300 million. Most importantly, we got a $40 million down payment at a time when interest rates were close to 20 percent. Those moneys carried the Los Angeles Olympic Committee's first couple of years of operation. The European Broadcasting Union offered $12 million for the television rights for all of Europe. As head of the television committee, I was furious at the offer—it was ridiculously low. I flew to Italy to meet with Silvio Berlusconi, owner of the largest media corporation. (Later, he was elected prime minister of Italy.) He offered me $12 million for Italy alone. I also found out that London had paid $6 million for the television rights to just a single movie, *Chariots of Fire.* I returned to Los Angeles and reported this to Peter Ueberroth and suggested that we sell the rights for Italy immediately to Berlusconi. Ueberroth did not want to get in a big battle with the International Olympic Committee and said he would try to up the price of the European Broadcasting Union's offer. I got pissed off and said, "Peter, I am so busy anyway with the opening and closing ceremonies that, why don't you put someone on the foreign television rights. I am just so frustrated I am sure I'm going to say something I am going to regret." So, I resigned from that committee. Eventually we got $25 million, which I think was outrageous. The Europeans always claim their television networks are run by governments, as compared to our commercial networks. True, but they have just as many viewers, and I think they should pay the same as the United States pays for the games. There has been a cozy relationship between the IOC and the European Broadcasting Union; both are headquartered in Geneva.

Because of the Soviet invasion of Afghanistan, President Carter ordered a boycott by the United States of the 1980 Olympic Games in Moscow. The Los Angeles Olympic Committee's board of directors had a vigorous debate over the issue and voted to support and stand behind Carter in the boycott. I was the only dissenting vote. Peter Ueberroth and I were invited to the White House for a meeting in the war room to discuss an alternative event, a ten-country conference. Presidential assistant Lloyd Cutler, national security adviser Zbigniew Brzezinski, CIA director Admiral Stansfield Turner, and Secretary of State Cyrus Vance were among those attending the meeting. They hoped that I would organize the alternative games. I felt, if the athletes missed the Moscow games, they would probably be too old or too discouraged to compete in the 1984 games. I accompanied Lloyd Cutler to Geneva to drum up support. But our efforts were futile. So, the American athletes who had prepared for the 1980 games were, basically, all screwed. Of course, in retaliation the Soviet Union announced their boycott of the Los Angeles games on May 5, 1984.

From the beginning, Peter began negotiating with the Disney organization, which had done many large outdoor events, to stage the opening and closing ceremonies of the games. The opening ceremonies set the tone for the entire Olympics. If we got off the ground fast, the newspaper and television reports would turn the Olympics into a "must-see" event.

Several months later, Disney made its initial presentation to the ceremonies committee. It was grand and colorful, but it had all the originality of the daily parade at Disneyland. It had no heart. It had no sense of originality. I felt that I'd seen it all before. Most of the committee agreed, and Peter asked Disney to redo it. Before making a second presentation, they asked for funds to build a model of the Los Angeles Coliseum. The problems began when Peter got their bill—it was for double what they had originally requested. Peter Ueberroth is a tough businessman. If you tell him you're going to do something for a certain price, that does not mean double that price. Peter knew that, to prevent the games from going bankrupt, he had to be extremely strict about sticking to the budget.

If I remember correctly, Disney's proposal was budgeted at about $20 million, which was far more than Peter intended to spend. They went back and forth a lot, and at one point he admitted to me, "I was never totally confident Disney would capture the imagination of two and a half billion people." At a breakfast meeting at the Bel Air Country Club in May 1983, Peter told the Disney representatives that he would prefer to have the committee, rather than Disney, produce the opening and closing ceremonies.

It was a gutsy move. We were just about a year away from the Olympics and we had no one to produce these shows. In August of 1983, Peter invited me to lunch to discuss the problem. I thought he'd bring with him a list and we would narrow down the candidates. Instead he said, "David, I'd like you to produce the opening and closing ceremonies. It's really difficult and it's going to drive you crazy, but would you do it?"

Gloria and I discussed it that night. "Do you know how to do something like that?" she asked.

Actually, I didn't. But I wasn't about to admit that to anyone. I had been to three previous Olympics, so I knew what was expected. It's just a live show, I convinced myself. So what if it has to be the biggest, most original, most tasteful, most emotionally evocative show ever done? I spent the night convincing myself, and the next day I accepted the job with three provisions: I wanted my own office far away from the Olympic offices, I wanted to have direct and instant access to Peter, and I needed complete control of the ceremonies. I didn't want anyone second-guessing me; if I was going to take the responsibility, I wanted the control. Peter agreed immediately to all of my requests. I now had the job I had never asked for and didn't particularly want.

It was some job. It would last a year and pay nothing. But Peter had convinced me it was a great honor.

I began by reading the Olympic rule book to learn the parameters of the task, then looked at film or tape of every opening and closing ceremony I could find. I didn't know exactly what I wanted to do, I just knew I wanted to do it differently from how it had ever been done before. I wanted it to be big and exciting, I wanted it to exceed imagination. One of the first people I hired was Tommy Walker, who was one of the great producers of outdoor live events, and who proved invaluable throughout the entire process.

The Olympic rule book says that the opening ceremonies must, in some way, display the culture of the host country. What about our culture is universal? I thought. Music, obviously, the music of America is played throughout the world. The theme of the opening would be the music of America. What about the culture of the host city? Cars, certainly.

Imagine this—you have to imagine it because it never got done. My first idea for the opening number was to drive three hundred white convertibles onto the field. The cars would do a series of maneuvers, stopping to form our Olympic logo and the word *Welcome*. Then the tops would open to release thousands of balloons and reveal beautiful women and handsome men. It would be a celebration of the automobile.

In my mind, I could see it clearly. But when I explained it to Peter, he asked me, "What happens if one of the cars doesn't work and it gets stuck on the field?"

"That's easy. We'll just send out a tow truck, and on the side of the tow truck, we'll hang a sign reading, 'Nobody's perfect!'"

We considered, then eliminated, a lot of other potentially dazzling concepts before settling on the show. For example, I wanted to create a waterfall, I wanted to have water flowing down into the coliseum. But as we looked at the sketches we had done, we realized that this waterfall might make people want to go to the bathroom. We joked that it could cost us half our television audience, which of course wasn't funny. So we eliminated the waterfall.

I definitely wanted balloons. Every outdoor event has to have fireworks and balloons. We wanted to do a giant, helium-filled balloon replica of the world, which we would eventually release, assuming the winds were blowing favorably. Unfortunately, it would have taken about fourteen days to inflate and have cost $3.6 million. At that price, we couldn't find a corporation to sponsor the world.

One of my great ideas turned out to be a public relations disaster. Wouldn't it be magnificent, I thought, to have a bald eagle, the symbol of America, fly across the stadium and land on a platform next to the flag stand, while everyone was singing "The Star-Spangled Banner"? We found an eagle trainer, Steve Hody, who brought an eagle to my office for a demonstration. We went up to the roof and he released the bird, which did several circles in the air and returned to Hody. He repeated it several times; it was quite impressive. The problem was, this was a golden eagle, not a bald eagle.

When I explained that to Steve Hody, he said, "That's okay, we can paint the head."

I didn't think that was a particularly good idea. I could just envision the criticism we would have received if it became known that our eagle was an impostor. Instead, we contacted the Fish and Wildlife Service— the bald eagle is a protected species—and got a permit to train a bald eagle for this stunt. We found an eagle in Alaska named Baba and had it flown to Los Angeles, where Steve Hody began training it. Apparently, the training sessions were going well; right up until the day the eagle dropped dead. Boom, dead. This death was reported by a lot of newspapers; the general impression given by the stories was that I had killed a member of an endangered species. It was awful, the phone didn't stop ringing for several days. But, finally, people forgot about it.

But the things we were not able to do were eventually overwhelmed and forgotten due to the things we were able to do. I have always believed that my greatest strengths as a producer are my creativity, my ability to organize, and my attention to detail. I can also be as tough as I need to be. I'm a planner, a careful planner. Whether it's going out for the evening or creating both the opening and closing ceremonies of the 1984 Olympic Games, I plan every step carefully. Laying something out before it happens, considering all the possible problems and solutions, ensures that the result will be what you want it to be.

We put on two shows that will never be forgotten by anyone who saw them. The opening ceremonies included eight thousand volunteer participants—not including the one hundred thousand people who participated in the card stunt—and nine thousand athletes.

The show began with every church ringing its bells to welcome the world to Los Angeles.

One hundred and ten trumpets and twenty timpani played the Olympic fanfare especially written for the games by John Williams.

After a countdown inside the coliseum, a man flew with a rocket pack on his back, circling the entire stadium and landing in midfield. It was the signal for two thousand cast members to release 1,262 five-foot-high Mylar balloons with banners attached to them reading WELCOME in the languages of the world, as the cast members sang an original song, "Welcome," written by Marvin Hamlisch and Dean Pitchford.

This four-hour musical extravaganza included singing, dancing, marching, and acrobatics. We had an eight-hundred-member marching band directed by Dr. Art Bartner, head of the USC marching band. The band's members had been recruited from the best college musicians in the country. We had a thousand-member choir. We had assembled a two-thousand-member drill team coached by the legendary Kay Crawford, the lady who had invented the drill team. At one point, we even rolled out eighty-four grand pianos playing Gershwin's "Rhapsody in Blue" while a three-hundred-member dance corps performed.

Peter Ueberroth reported he was standing beside Lord Killanin, the former head of the International Olympic Committee, when the eighty-four white grand pianos were rolled out playing "Rhapsody in Blue." He had attended every Olympics since 1948. He turned to Ueberroth and said, "This is simply the best I've ever seen." The musical portion of the program included classical music, Dixieland, marches, well-known songs from motion pictures—we were in Hollywood—big-band swing, Broadway music, and pop. And it also included Etta James.

When I began creating the show, I had never heard of Etta James. But, I received a copy of a letter she'd written to Mayor Bradley, asking for a chance to perform. Other people knew who she was—one of the greatest rhythm-and-blues singers in the world. Etta James, as I learned, had followed the path forged by so many great singers before her: on her way to the top of the music world, she had become a junkie. She became temperamental and walked out on bookings or simply didn't show up. Eventually, she ended up broke and suicidal—and saved herself through the power of prayer. She was looking for an opportunity to showcase her talent and sat down and wrote that letter to Mayor Bradley. After the mayor gave it to me, I asked Etta to come to my office. During our meeting she assured me that she was clean and intended to stay that way. We asked her to sing "When the Saints Go Marching In" at the ceremonies and she was a huge hit. She began getting club dates again. She released a CD and, eventually, was able to rebuild her career—and her life.

When the music ended, we did one of the great "card" stunts in history. The participating athletes marched into the stadium to be welcomed by President Reagan. The Olympic flag was carried into the stadium and four thousand "doves," actually white homing pigeons, were released. After that, the Olympic flame was lit by former decathlon champion Rafer Johnson. Then another Olympian, also to become a legend, Edwin Moses, recited the Olympic oath. Following that, in a salute to the ethnic diversity of the United States, two thousand Los Angelenos dressed in the native costumes of more than fifty countries appeared. For the finale, I had the entire cast singing special lyrics written for the lovely song "Reach Out and Touch (Somebody's Hand)" by its composers, Ashford and Simpson. And finally, the Olympic athletes marched out of the stadium.

It was a spectacular show. Words on paper can never adequately convey the excitement, the beauty, or the joy of this show. It was a tremendous success—but producing it meant solving more problems in a creative fashion than in any other project I had ever undertaken.

The problems began at the very beginning, in obtaining the Olympic flame, which would be used to light the torch. Traditionally, the flame is lit by sunlight on Mount Olympus, Greece, and carried by torch to wherever in the world the games are being held.

Getting the Olympic flame to Los Angeles involved intricate negotiations. Initially I was in charge of the torch run. I had suggested to Peter that perhaps we could raise money by selling "legs" of the torch run across America. Individuals or corporations would pay the Olympic Committee a fee for the honor of running with the torch over a measured distance. Peter came up with a better idea: we would charge for the honor of carrying the torch, but all moneys raised would stay in the local community. It was a wonderful concept; it ended up involving communities across the nation. The torch was carried nine thousand miles through thirty-three states by more than four thousand runners accompanied by thirty-four vehicles and one hundred support vehicles. We raised $10.9 million, which was distributed to local YMCAs, Boys and Girls Clubs of America, and the Special Olympics. About the only people who didn't think it was a good idea were some Greeks, who accused us of commercializing the Olympic ideal. In particular, the mayor of Olympia, where the flame was to be lit, was outraged. In an attempt to solve the problem, we offered to give some of the revenues to Greek charities, but the Greek committee refused to even discuss it. Basically, we were warned that if we insisted on selling rights to run with the torch, we would not be permitted to light it on Mount Olympus, the traditional location of the torch lighting.

Their protests lost a great deal of credibility when we looked at the

Olympic torch that had been carried for the winter games in Yugoslavia and noticed the name and logo of a Japanese sporting goods company was inscribed in its base. And when we looked at the torchbearers for the Moscow games, they displayed the logo for the same Japanese company on everything from their running shoes to their headbands. The mayor of Olympia said the only way we would get the flame would be to return every penny we had raised. Compromise did not seem possible. So Peter decided to steal the flame.

He sent a young student named Greg Haney to Olympia as part of a press planning junket. The student went to the top of Mount Olympus and used the rays of the sun to light a small flame in a jar with a gas cylinder in it. When he reached the bottom of the mountain, he used that flame to light a second flame, then carried both jars to the world headquarters of the IOC, where the authenticity of the flame was verified. Finally, Greg brought the flame back to the United States. As evidence that the flame had come from Mount Olympus, every step was photographed. We had the flame we needed.

Peter then called the mayor of Olympia and informed him that we had a flame, and if he was still unwilling to cooperate in an official flame-lighting ceremony, we would be pleased to tell the world how we'd obtained it—and then mentioned that the Greek team, which traditionally leads the parade of athletes into the stadium in the opening ceremonies, would, instead, march in alphabetical order, in the middle of the pack.

Within hours the mayor responded; the Greeks were looking forward to the official flame-lighting ceremony.

Just about every portion of the program was replete with problems. The mantra by which my staff lived for a year became my favorite saying: "It's not a problem if it can be solved by money." For example, at one Olympic games, when the pigeons were released, rather than flying to freedom, they had, instead, flown into the flame and were incinerated. To prevent any problems with our pigeons, we made a deal with the California Racing Pigeon Association and actually staged a race; our pigeon handlers released their birds, which circled the stadium and raced home. Safely.

One problem I could not possibly have anticipated turned out to be almost disastrous. I loved the Mylar balloons, for example, but once balloons are released, they are impossible to control. They fly wherever the wind takes them. To be safe we had to close the airport. No planes were allowed in or out of LAX for about an hour, until it was certain all the balloons had cleared the area. I had a big fight with the Federal Aviation Administration to make that happen, but eventually, they agreed to work with us. Some of the balloons traveled a long way; one of them flew cross-country and was found off the Georgia coast. Some of them didn't fly as far and, unfortunately, landed on power lines. Santa Anita racetrack lost all power. East Los Angeles was without power for four hours and missed the entire ceremony. Even ABC lost power for a second or so. Every few minutes I would get another terrible report about the damage caused by our balloons—and I knew hundreds of them were still flying all across southern California. Anything was possible. One balloon landed on a power line right next to our audio truck and shorted out all our power inside the coliseum. Fortunately, we had installed an expensive emergency generator system, which immediately kicked in, and nobody ever knew how close we'd come to disaster.

This wasn't only an outdoor spectacular, this was also a television show being broadcast around the world to billions of viewers. Everything had to be perfect. While getting eighty-four pianos to play "Rhapsody in Blue" simultaneously seems quite simple, it was, in fact, complicated. These pianos couldn't possibly be heard in the stadium, so we prerecorded several pianos and overplayed it on tape to sound like many more. The problem was that because light and sound travel at different speeds, the recorded sound of the piano playing would not be in sync with the actual playing in the coliseum. On television that would look awful, so we gave special cueing instructions to certain pianists and made sure the cameras shot only them. While they were out of sync with the rest of the pianos, on television the illusion was perfect.

Just when I thought I had covered everything, two weeks before the opening ceremonies a radical feminist attorney, Gloria Allred, filed for a restraining order to prevent us from opening the Olympics—because all of our pianists were men. I'm busy as hell and I find out I have to go to court. On my drive to the court to fight this attempt, I thought of my response: "Your Honor," I told the judge, "I cast this so it would seem as if each of these piano players were George Gershwin, playing his creation, 'Rhapsody in Blue.' If Mrs. Gershwin had written it, obviously, I would have used all women." The judge dismissed the restraining order.

The card stunt was my big surprise. It was an audience participation event with ninety-two thousand participants. I love card stunts, love them. In the opening ceremony at the 1980 Moscow Olympics, the Russians performed spectacular card stunts. They did moving images, they included thousands of changes. But they had used soldiers, so they had been able to rehearse for six months. My show director, Tommy Walker, and I realized we couldn't find thousands of people willing to rehearse for six months, but we really wanted to outdo the Russians. Then Tommy suggested, "Maybe we ought to have just one card stunt."

That's what we did. We decided what we wanted to do, then used computers to figure out how to do it. We put one-color vinyl cards under each of the ninety-two thousand seats in the coliseum with instructions in six languages, and on command, each person was asked to hold up his or her card and turn it over.

As this was as much a television show as a live spectacular, we had to work around commercials. To do the card stunt, we had to wait for the ABC network to finish its commercials. We waited . . . and we waited . . . and we waited. I was on the phone with Roone Arledge: "Roone," I asked him, "hurry up, please." He went to another commercial, then another. Finally, I told him, "Roone, I gotta go with it now," and then told Tommy to start the countdown. The entire stadium counted down from five . . . and at one turned over their cards to reveal the flags of every participating nation. It was spectacular, but ABC missed its instant creation. The network came back from the commercial to show ninety-two thousand people holding cards high and forming an array of bright flags. Fortunately, it was taped and replayed for the viewing audience.

One of the most complex problems we had to solve was where President Reagan would sit. For political reasons, he had to be visible, but his safety was paramount. Originally, we suggested that the president sit in one of the private boxes overlooking the arena, but because there was only one elevator down to ground level, the Secret Service rejected that idea. They would not allow the president to sit in a place that had only one escape route. Then they came up with what might have been the single worst suggestion of the entire Olympic Games. They wanted us to put a bulletproof glass bubble just off the field where the president could sit, visible to every spectator.

"That is the stupidest idea I've ever heard," I said in my most adamant producer's voice. "It would look ridiculous. It would be embarrassing, it just isn't going to happen."

A top agent of the Secret Service said nicely, "But we don't know where else he can stay."

"I'll tell you one place he isn't going to stay—in a bulletproof bubble on the field in the middle of my show."

Finally, presidential assistant Michael Deaver came to California to discuss the situation. I showed him an artist's conception of the bubble—and he thought it was as stupid as I did. Eventually, the Secret Service solution to their dilemma was to allow Reagan to sit in a private box. In addition to the elevator, they put a ladder down the front of the box so he could climb down to the next level and then be lead out through an audience exit. They also put a Secret Service agent in each aisle seat between the box and the audience exit.

What I didn't know is that whenever the president is seated aboveground, a thick piece of steel is placed under his chair, so that if a bomb goes off beneath the president, he will be protected. For some reason though, only the president sits on this shield. Gloria had this vision of a bomb going off and Mrs. Reagan going straight up into the air like a rocket while the president was totally unharmed.

While the preparations continued, so did the speculation about disasters. It seemed as if stories appeared in the papers every day detailing another horrible scenario: The entire city was going to be gridlocked by traffic. Prices throughout the city were going to be hugely inflated. Hidden taxes were going to cost the city a fortune. The city was going to be destroyed by terrorists' attacks. *Playboy* magazine ran one of the most irresponsible articles I'd ever read, basically predicting that terrorists were going to take over the city.

There were some threats, so both Peter Ueberroth and I were given extra protection. Early one morning, I was informed that police had detained four Mexicans who had been sitting near the entrance to my home.

The police had successfully captured my gardener and his three assistants, who had been waiting there for transportation.

With Los Angeles about to become the world's stage, and with memories of Munich in everybody's mind, law enforcement officials took every threat, even every rumor, seriously. The Los Angeles Police Department, the Secret Service, and even the FBI did a magnificent job preparing for any potential problems. About ten days before the show, I got an anonymous phone call informing me that one of our placard carriers, the women who walked in front of each national team with a card identifying that nation, was living with a terrorist. I immediately told security, then promptly forgot all about it. A few days later, one of our top security people came into my office and threw a series of nude pictures of a woman on my desk. This was our placard carrier. After the original phone call, security had discovered she'd lied on her application, claiming to be an American citizen when she was not. That got them nervous. Then they found out she was living with a suspicious character, a man with no obvious source of income who seemed to be living quite well—one of the hallmarks of a terrorist.

Their apartment was raided. The man turned out to be a small-time drug dealer. The woman was fired—not because of the nude pictures, but because she'd lied on her application. Although, admittedly, in my mind I envisioned the front page of the *National Enquirer* with the headline "Nudie Cutie Carries Placard at Olympic Games."

I had to deal with seemingly a million details. Producing miniseries such as *Roots* and *The Thorn Birds* had been complicated, but at least we had the luxury of time to solve the problems. All that was at stake here was the United States being embarrassed in front of 2.2 billion people—the largest viewing audience in history.

Personally, I felt the reputation of the entire Hollywood entertainment community was at stake. People throughout the world have come to expect spectacular events from Hollywood, and I felt that I had to deliver even more than was expected.

A week before the games, my friend legendary broadcaster Howard Cosell came into my office as I was finalizing my plans for the ethnically diverse group to carry the Olympic flag into the stadium. "Mr. Wolper," Cosell said, "I represent the Hispanic coalition of the city of Los Angeles, the largest ethnic population in this magnificent city, and we've noticed that you did not include a Hispanic among the flag bearers. Would you like to explain the reason for that to us?" I looked at my long, carefully planned list. Cosell was absolutely right, I'd completely forgotten to include a Hispanic. I added Olympic boxer Richard Sandoval and a second athlete and avoided another potential embarrassment.

During the Olympics, I was only able to attend one sporting event because I was busy day and night preparing for the closing ceremonies. I went to dinner with Howard Cosell, at Jimmy's restaurant. As we walked in, I realized that people were looking at me and all starting to applaud. It was such a wonderful moment. The people all standing up in the restaurant applauding me. After dinner, I sat next to Howard at the boxing matches as he broadcast them.

I was working on the ceremonies all day every day. My assistant Auriel Sanderson had stayed in my office at Warner Bros. to handle as much of that work as possible. Warner's had been completely cooperative when I told them I wanted to produce these ceremonies.

Gloria could not have been more supportive. For weeks before and during the games, I slept in hotels near my office and she never complained. Many things needed to be done at home and she simply took care of them without bothering me. Gloria and Auriel made it possible for me to concentrate on this task.

I wasn't being paid a penny for this year's work. In fact, Peter had established a firm policy that no one, absolutely no one, would receive free tickets. And he stuck to that firmly. I was in his office one day when George Shultz, the secretary of state, called about getting tickets. Peter told him that he would be happy to get him some tickets, but he needed to know exactly where to send the bill.

Gradually, all the details came together to make a show. Two days before the Olympics began, after 380 separate rehearsals, we had our first—and only—dress rehearsal. We went through the entire performance from beginning to end. I arranged for the members of our cast to invite their families and friends, so we had about seventy thousand people in the coliseum. Certain things became obvious: our "Singing in the Rain" number was ragged and I doubted it could be fixed in time, so I decided to drop it. One of the advantages of a four-hour show is that you can drop ten minutes and no one is going to object. No one'll even notice. Our choreographer, Ron Fields, pleaded to keep it in, but I said, "No, it's out of the show."

We solved several problems we found during the rehearsal. At one point, for example, I looked down upon a field covered by three thousand dancers wearing beautiful bright costumes—and I hated it. The different costumes detracted from the precision dance. The array of colors made it difficult to see that every single dancer was in step with every other dancer. I said in my most confident producer tone, "I want every person down there dressed in white—by tomorrow afternoon."

My assistants looked at me as if I were crazy. Where were they going to find three thousand white T-shirts in one day?

I didn't care. Pay whatever you have to, I told them, but get them. My reasoning was simple: if the ceremony was spectacular and I was a million dollars overbudget, nobody was going to notice that million. But if the ceremony was terrible, even though I had brought it in on budget, everyone would want to know how I could have wasted $9 million. Do it, I ordered, whatever it costs.

We bought every white T-shirt in southern California. If anyone in Los Angeles needed a white shirt for the next few weeks, he or she was out of luck. But we were successful, we got every dancer costumed in

white, enabling the spectators to see the beautifully symmetrical chore-
ography.

Perhaps the biggest problem we discovered during the dress rehearsal
was the sound system. Considering that much of the show consisted of
music, it was terrible. We had installed an entirely new audio system,
with speakers facing the audience, but as I walked around the field, I
realized it didn't work at all. It reminded me of announcements made in
the New York subway system. Each section could hear reverberations
and echoes from other speakers. Certain sections heard two speakers,
one slightly lagging behind the other. So, I told my sound people I
wanted them to install a new system.

We only have forty-eight hours, I was told.

I don't care, I said. Do it.

I think we can fix the existing system, I was told.

I don't want it fixed, I explained, I want it replaced.

But we only have forty-eight hours.

Then you've already wasted two minutes discussing it.

I never learned the technical details, but somehow they installed a
new system that worked perfectly.

With all my movies, I was able to tinker and edit until the moment
they were broadcast. This was a live show; we had one opportunity to
get it perfect.

During the program, I was sitting in a booth high above the stadium
floor. I had the very first cell phone ever put into use at my disposal. I had
a bank of phones connecting me directly to my main creative people and
the security department. Among those people were Tommy Walker, who
was actually directing the live show; Roone Arledge, who was in charge
of the broadcast for ABC; and Terry Jastrow, who was directing the ABC
TV show. Although I rarely take pills, about an hour before we began,
Nancy Tankel, the official nurse of the opening ceremonies, made me
take a Valium. It brought me down to a state of manageable insanity.

At the beginning of the ceremonies, I said to Tommy, "I'm Jewish
and you're Christian, so it's going to take the Son to get us through the
opening and the Father to finish it off. So, let's pray to both."

With all the attention to detail, with all the preparations, the problems
began even before the ceremonies started. Three minutes before we
were to begin, as one hundred thousand people slowly filed into the stadium, Ed Best, the head of Olympic security, came into my booth. I
assumed he was dropping by to say hello. "Don't get nervous," Best said,
"but there may be a bomb in the torch."

Don't get nervous? I looked across the stadium, and behind a wall, shielded from the spectators, I could see members of the LAPD bomb squad creeping toward the torch. During a second security sweep, with dogs, Ed explained calmly, a guard had noticed that a lock had been broken off the door leading to the torch tower. Somebody had gotten in there. Then he found a box with wires running from it into the tower itself.

Not a great beginning. After my experiences at Munich, the possibility that terrorists would try to disrupt the Olympics did not surprise me. But I had complete faith in our security people. The first thing I did was call the art director, Rene Lagler, on a private line and tell him there was a problem with the torch and we needed to find an alternative if it couldn't be lit. Lagler immediately went to work. I decided not to tell Rafer Johnson about it because I didn't want to make him more nervous than he was already.

The only person I needed to inform was Peter Ueberroth. He was sitting two seats away from President Reagan. I left my command post and went to his booth. As calmly as possible, I whispered to him, "Don't change your expression. Don't look startled when I tell you this because you'll get everybody crazy, but there might be a bomb in the torch. Security is taking care of it." Gloria was sitting in the president's box. When she saw me come in, she took one look at my face and knew something was terribly wrong—but she had to act as if she hadn't a care in the world. She put on an outstanding performance under enormous pressure.

Incredibly, I was so absorbed in the minute-by-minute details that I didn't have the time to worry about it. There was nothing more I could do, so I pretty much forgot about the bomb in the torch. About an hour later, Ed Best told me that the mystery had been solved; it wasn't terrorists, it was an ABC cameraman. He'd broken the lock because he couldn't reach a new camera position; the wires were electrical connections, and the empty boxes had contained a handheld camera.

President Reagan caused the next serious problem, although I'm certain he never knew about it. As 1984 was an election year, and this was the biggest stage in the world, the White House lobbied hard for him to have a substantial part in the ceremony. We fought them, insisting that we adhere to tradition. So, his role in the ceremony was limited to reading the statement, "I declare open the games of Los Angeles, celebrating the twenty-third Olympiad of the modern era." Few people realized it, but he said it backward. He was supposed to start with

"Celebrating . . ." It didn't matter, the games opened anyway. And I thought his way of saying it was better than the original.

But what we hadn't planned for was the Secret Service closing one of the main gates into the coliseum for the safety of the president and installing metal detectors at all the other entrances. It created monumentally long lines and short tempers. We needed that gate. We had planned to use it. Some members of our technical crew were locked outside without passes to get back in. Two thousand members of our cast were locked out, and tens of thousands of spectators were supposed to enter through that portal. Even Rafer Johnson was locked out after lighting the Olympic torch. In its zeal, the Secret Service practically caused a riot; people who could not get into the stadium began pushing at the open gates. It actually got pretty frightening for a few minutes as people who had paid a lot of money for tickets and couldn't get into the stadium got angry. I was advised to delay the beginning of the ceremony, but as we were broadcasting this show internationally, that was pretty much impossible.

It was a terrible headache and resulted in a lot of angry people, but somehow we managed to solve that problem. The ceremony itself went well: the rocket man flew, the birds survived, the dancers stayed in step, the sound system—with the exception of one speaker that was unplugged by a TV cameraman because it was bothering him—worked splendidly. I was most anxious about the torch lighting—even after we knew it wasn't going to explode.

Peter had chosen, with my agreement, Rafer Johnson, the 1960 Olympic decathlon champion from Los Angeles and a member of the L.A. Olympic Committee, to have the honor of carrying the torch up the coliseum stairs and lighting the Olympic flame. We were the only three people to know, although, admittedly, I might have given Gloria a big hint or two or six. We practiced in secret. Originally, Rafer was to run one lap around the track, then up the stairs to the platform from which he would light the torch. We had a few young collegiate runners try it, and they had great difficulty; it was too long a run and too steep a climb. They were short of breath before they reached the final turn. They could barely get up the stairs.

We shortened it considerably, but Rafer was still having difficulty getting up the ninety-two stairs to the torch. "I don't think I can do it, David," he told me with tears of disappointment in his eyes, "I'm not in shape."

"You can do it, Rafer," I told him. "You've gotta do it."

He began training at a high school stadium near his home, running up and down hundreds of stairs. Rafer was afraid his legs would cramp up, as they had on occasion when he was competing, and he wouldn't be able to complete his run. During one of his training sessions, for example, as I watched him, severe cramps in his legs prevented him from getting more than halfway to the top. But I knew Rafer, I knew his determination, so I remained confident he would be able to do it.

Just to be certain though, I arranged to have 1976 Olympic decathlon champion Bruce Jenner ready to meet Rafer halfway up the stairs, to help him carry the heavy torch to the top if he faltered. I had a lot of backups for this moment. For example, the stairs were raised hydraulically—but in case the electricity failed, I had four or five football players from a local high school ready to crank up the stairs mechanically. The Olympic torch was on top of the stadium; Rafer would light a tube well below. The flame would follow a path in the design of the five Olympic rings and finally light the torch. But, just in case something happened and the flame didn't reach the torch, I had someone inside the tower ready to light it. That torch was going to be lit!

Rafer arrived at the coliseum three hours before he was scheduled to appear and got dressed in my trailer. Jesse Owens's granddaughter Gina Hemphill carried the torch into the stadium to an original score by avant-garde composer Philip Glass. At the proper time, Rafer made his appearance. The crowd erupted because he is a popular man—and he took the torch from Gina. He climbed the ninety-two steps and lit the torch with absolutely no difficulty. Later, he told me that standing there, looking out at the spectators, it was so beautiful it nearly took his breath away.

My grand finale of the ceremonies was the "Reach Out" number. I loved the song. "Reach Out and Touch (Somebody's Hand)" had been written by Nick Ashford and Valerie Simpson and recorded by Diana Ross. I arranged for Ashford and Simpson to compose special lyrics for the opening ceremonies, and I had intended to ask Diana Ross to sing this song, accompanied by a thousand-voice church choir. But, I wanted to hear what it sounded like before approaching Diana Ross, so I asked the arranger, Earl Brown, to record it for me. For this recording, he pulled a woman named Vicky McClure out of the choir, a supermarket checkout clerk, and had her sing it. The recording was just beautiful. As soon as I heard it, I decided to use Vicky rather than a star. Apparently, Diana Ross was quite upset that someone else was singing her song on this international stage, but it was my choice.

I had a producer's dream: I didn't want my audience simply sitting and watching the participants, I wanted every person in the coliseum reaching out and touching—holding hands with the people sitting on either side. I wanted to create a love fest inside that huge, cold stadium. I've sat in enough audiences to know that people do not want to reach out and touch the complete stranger sitting next to them. I knew I had to overcome that reluctance. So, I told the lovely young women carrying placards that, as soon as the song started, I wanted them to grab the hands of the athletes on the field and hold them high in the air so everyone could see them—and the audience would follow.

Initially, we had intended to repeat the song three times, but I felt that wasn't enough time to create the emotional crescendo I needed. Ten times, I told Jack Elliott, our musical director, let's do it ten times.

The show had gone extremely well by the time we reached this grand finale. I knew it was either going to be a big letdown or a huge high. And as the choir started singing, something wonderful happened inside the Los Angeles Coliseum. My producer's dream came true. One hundred thousand people "spontaneously" joined hands and started singing along. On the huge screen in the stadium they showed a close-up of Olympic sprinter Evelyn Ashford, with tears of joy flowing down her face. People were singing and crying and laughing. It was the emotional outburst I'd been hoping to create. Vicky sang "Reach Out and Touch" for eleven and a half minutes.

Normally, at the conclusion of the opening ceremonies, the athletes march quietly out of the stadium as the spectators exit. I didn't want that ending. When the "Reach Out" number ended, I played some peppy dance music. When they heard that music, I had told my placard girls, they were to grab the hands of the athletes and start dancing. I knew everyone would have such a great time they wouldn't want to leave.

That's exactly what happened. The athletes stayed on the field thirty minutes after the ceremony ended. Spectators began clapping along with the music and wouldn't leave. It was as if Los Angeles were hosting a grand party.

The only way to end the celebration was to stop the music. When we finally turned it off, the athletes and the spectators began leaving the stadium. The opening ceremonies had been a complete success. Thousands of congratulatory telegrams began pouring in, from government and entertainment-industry leaders, and people I didn't even know. Among the reactions that will forever remain in my mind was a note from Quincy Jones, which read, "The Opening Ceremonies brought on two record breakers for me. The amount of tears that I cried and, for the first time ever, that I felt that patriotic." I have also kept and cherished an article written by a twelve-year-old girl, the daughter of a particularly difficult newspaper critic, who wrote in the *Times*, "I haven't cried so much and yet been so happy since *E.T.* Athletes from all nations joining hands together and singing along. A few minutes later everyone in the stands held hands and sang. Miraculously, we weren't really off-key when over 100,000 people are crying and singing all their emotions out, one hears an eternal peaceful sound . . . I hope the world heard us."

But most memorable of all was the telegram I received from ABC's Brandon Stoddard. After the success of *Roots*, he had told me that *Roots* would be on my tombstone. But, after the opening ceremonies, he wired, "Change the tombstone!"

The opening ceremony got the games off to a wonderful start. The mood of the city was tremendously upbeat. The Olympics became a celebration of civic pride. Not one of the dire predictions made about the games came true. Rather than massive traffic jams, if anything there was less traffic than usual because so many people had left the city, and many of those who had stayed to work used the special transit facilities. In fact, legend has it that one of the Rolling Stones wanted to attend the games, but had been warned by his manager that it would be a disaster and had gone on vacation. He was so angry that he missed this once-in-a-lifetime event that he fired the manager. Rather than sending prices skyrocketing, most businesses and restaurants welcomed visitors and most raised prices only slightly.

I wasn't really aware of what was going on in the city. As the athletes filed out of the coliseum, I was already hard at work on the closing ceremonies. Among several things I learned from these Olympics one thing stands out: one person should not produce both the opening and closing ceremonies. The details eventually run together. It's too much work for one person; although one of my staff, Ric Birch, successfully produced both ceremonies for the Sydney Olympics.

I had begun planning both ceremonies at the same time, although my objective was to evoke very different emotions. If the opening was to welcome the world to Los Angeles, the closing was to be a big party, a celebration for the Olympic athletes.

I wanted spectacular events. I wanted to create illusions that no one had ever seen before. Basically, I wanted to have a spaceship land and aliens get out. I decided to have a flying saucer appear over the stadium, communicate with people in the stadium, then land—and have aliens emerge from it. A lot of people did not share my enthusiasm; they believed flying saucers and spacemen had been done and overdone in movies. They told me it was an awfully corny idea, and besides, it would never work. Well, I didn't feel that way, I thought it would a spectacular surprise. If it worked, it would be out of this world.

I saw it in my mind, but making it happen was probably the most technically difficult task of the entire Olympics. I hired a special-effects company to create this illusion—and just as the Olympics began, it went out of business, leaving me with the responsibility for making this saucer fly. The original spaceship measured fifty feet two inches in diameter and weighed almost two tons. The plan was to have it carried by a long cable from a giant helicopter flying without lights. So, to spectators, it would appear that the spaceship was actually flying on its own power.

While the engineers called it *Starship Olympiad*, members of my staff referred to it as *The Aluminum Taco*. The spaceship was lifted into the air for the first time nine days before the closing ceremonies at a desolate spot out in Santa Monica. Many people believed it would never work— and they were right. I was sitting in my office when the phone rang and I was told that the ship had crashed. Specifically, I was told, "the taco had folded."

Crashed probably wasn't accurate. *Folded in half* would be more precise. Turned into a pile of aluminum junk might be another way of saying it. The spaceship was simply too heavy to be lifted; the exterior rings weighed so much it had collapsed in upon itself. Imagine a book open flat, then suddenly being closed; that's what had happened when we tried to fly with this saucer. When I went out to examine the wreckage on a Friday night, I lifted the cover—and I was looking at a metal mess. One of the chief engineers told me, "There's no possible way we could make this work in this form." He insisted that almost nothing could be done. This spaceship wasn't going to fly.

That was an interesting way of putting it. "Okay," I said, "if it can't be in this form, what else might it be." They began to see the possibilities. "The spacecraft can be anything our minds want it to be. Think about that, fellas."

The engineer then began explaining several different possibilities, and I realized they all had one thing in common. "All we really need are the lights around the outside," I said. "We don't need the body, no one can see the body anyway."

In addition to confidence, I had money. Contrary to warnings that the

Olympics were going to be a financial disaster, they were shaping up to be a huge financial success. Peter had told me, privately, during one of our regular breakfasts during the Games, that we were doing even better than anyone had hoped and said, "Spend whatever you have to to make the closing as spectacular as the opening."

I felt I could spend that. And maybe more. So I told this engineer that I didn't care what he had to spend, that ship was going to fly. As it turned out, we didn't have to build the entire flying saucer, we just needed the outer ring with blinking lights, sort of a lighted outline. Our flying saucer consisted of strobe lights, pulsating lights, reflectors, prisms, and a searchlight. While up close it actually looked a bit like a flying hula hoop, the lights were programmed to light sequentially, making it look as if the ship were actually moving. The ship weighed considerably less than the original and, in the initial tests, performed acceptably.

The following Thursday night I had them bring it to the stadium so we could see what it looked like and plan the flight. By doing that I knew I was taking a risk that people who saw it would give away the surprise. But not testing it would have been an even bigger risk. The plan was to raise it behind the coliseum, fly closer, and then put it down. We would then use bright lights outside the stadium to make it appear as if it had landed, and then an alien would appear on a platform visible to everyone in attendance.

We used a giant helicopter painted black that would fly without lights. There would also be two very visible "escort" helicopters, which would cover the clatter of the army helicopter. The lifting helicopter was huge, and when it took off near Figueroa Street during rehearsal, it created a windstorm that upended and blew away many of the small stands, on Figueroa, selling everything from hot dogs to Olympic pins. It blew away trash cans, merchandise, card tables, everything. It made a big mess—and it was going to cost these people a lot of money.

We were afraid these people would go to court and get an injunction to prevent us from taking off in a helicopter so close to a residential street, so we had one of our people meet with them and settle their complaints individually.

The illusion was terrific. We played with the lights for a couple of hours until it looked frighteningly realistic. While this was going on, we were rehearsing with our alien. At a UCLA-USC basketball game, several years earlier, I'd met seven-foot-nine-inch George Bell. When I needed an impressive figure to play the alien, I remembered him. He loved the idea. The alien costume, which was sort of an illuminated human being—a very, very big human being wearing a helmet—was sculpted to fit his body. So, our ship was ready and our alien was ready. The spaceship just had to hold together for one more flight.

The other problem I had to deal with was the fireworks display. When the Japanese Shipbuilding Industry Foundation decided to donate all the fireworks for the Olympics closing ceremony, I was happy to accept. My intention was to have a ten-minute-or-so performance near the conclusion of my program. But in their generosity the Japanese sent boxes and boxes and boxes of fireworks. Three thousand individual explosives. After looking at the shipment, Tommy Walker was impressed, telling me it included some wonderful fireworks—including the single largest firework he had ever seen. And then he said, "But, David, it's going to take at least twenty-five minutes to shoot them all off."

I didn't want to stop my program for twenty-five minutes. Fireworks are like ice cream; everybody loves a little, and nobody really loves too much. I wanted to do eight minutes of fireworks, maybe ten. So I called the chairman of the Japanese shipbuilding industry, Mr. Ryoichi Sasakawa, and told him that while we appreciated the generous donation, we had only allotted ten minutes to a fireworks display and I was returning everything we couldn't use.

Without intending to, I had created my own fireworks. The secretary of state, George Shultz, called to inform me that the Japanese government was upset. Apparently, I had insulted an important and powerful businessman. "Will you please use everything he sent you," Shultz asked.

"I can't," I explained, "it'll stop the program dead. It'll—"

"Please," Shultz repeated.

If the secretary of state tells you that the United States of America is in the middle of important negotiations, and your decision might affect the outcome, the correct answer is "I always wanted to use twenty-five minutes of fireworks."

I used twenty-five minutes of fireworks. We saluted every country ever to host the Olympics with fireworks. We saluted Los Angeles with fireworks. Every time somebody said a word—boom!—we shot another round. Admittedly, it was an awesome display visible to everyone in Los Angeles, ending with the single largest firework ever fired. And as I had predicted, it practically brought the program to a halt. Twenty-five minutes is a lot of fireworks.

But, we certainly did not insult Japan.

The most difficult aspect of the closing show was that we couldn't get into the coliseum until the night before because it was used for track-and-field events. So we had only hours to erect our giant stage and orchestra pit, install four huge scaffolded lighting towers, the fireworks, "dancing waters" equipment, and special effects. We rehearsed the entire installation on the athletic field at Aviation High School. The first time we assembled everything it took more than a day, which was unacceptable. But, we had a fabulous, dedicated crew, and they went through the entire exercise two more times and, each time, got it down within the time available to us.

But, we wouldn't know for certain that we really could do it until we really did it. This stage was a producer's nightmare—we only had one shot at getting everything perfect and we didn't have enough time to prepare for it.

The most important thing a producer can do to prepare is to put responsible people into positions of authority because, in the end, success or failure depends on those people. I'd hired FM Productions, a company that normally moves and sets up stages for rock-and-roll shows, to turn my concept into reality. At eight o'clock the night of August 11, the day before the close of the Olympic Games, the crew left Aviation High School. The setup was carried on forty-six twenty-two-foot-long flatbed trucks, escorted to the coliseum by LAPD ground and airborne units in a two-mile-long caravan. The crew began by laying two and a half acres of plywood over the track to protect it from the flatbed trucks. The crew worked through the night and into the next day to install the stage, finishing only hours before spectators began filing into the stadium.

Each ticket holder was handed a flashlight upon entering the coliseum. The spectators didn't know it at the time, but these flashlights were to be used to signal the spaceship—if it flew.

The Olympic Charter stipulates that each nation is to be represented by no more than six athletes at the closing ceremony, but so many athletes had remained in Los Angeles after finishing their competition that the IOC agreed to allow all participating athletes to march in the closing ceremony.

The closing ceremony began with the parade of national flags, followed by the athletes, who entered as a group rather than by nation. After the lowering of the Olympic flags, and some official speeches, the entertainment began. I literally held my breath waiting for the spaceship. The night before the engineers had christened the "ship" by breaking a bottle of champagne over it—and smashing one of the lights. While it had flown in rehearsal, during each flight something had gone wrong.

As we waited for the spaceship to approach, our alien, George Bell, was putting on his helmet at the top of the stadium, out of sight of the audience. And right on time, to the minute, the spaceship appeared over the rim of the coliseum, all its lights flashing. It was an incredible illusion, this spaceship was flying! It was an absolutely glorious sight. The crowd began screaming and cheering. Music filled the stadium. The spaceship signaled to the crowd—and in response, one hundred thousand people signaled back with their flashlights. The spaceship worked so well that Peter Jennings and Jim McKay, ABC TV commentators, couldn't figure out how the spaceship flew. If they couldn't figure it out, I am sure the audience just thought it was flying by itself. The spaceship began descending outside the stadium. As it did, a brilliant light blazed from the landing zone, and as seen through the great arches of the stadium, it made it appear as if the ship were landing. Everything was working beautifully. Seconds after the ship "landed," our alien appeared, spotlighted by bright white lights, at the top of the stadium. "I have come a long way," the alien said, and to the cheers of the crowd added, "and I like what I have seen."

It soared. It worked the one time it had to work better than it had ever worked before. People who had been less than enthusiastic about the entire concept, who thought it was corny or cheap, told me afterward that they had been enthralled by it. Among the night's highlights, it was *the* highlight.

After the spaceship came the fireworks, and more fireworks, and then even more fireworks. The Japanese must have been thrilled. Finally, Lionel Richie and three hundred break-dancers began singing "All Night Long." It was a rousing finish to the 1984 Olympics that became the party we had planned. Athletes and spectators were dancing on the floor of the coliseum and in the aisles. And then the athletes began dancing on our stage. It looked wonderful, but we were on the edge of a disaster. The stage had been built to support about three hundred people—and suddenly we had a thousand people up there dancing. Directly under the stage, at least one hundred lighting technicians were still working. I was terrified. If the stage collapsed, we were going to have some deaths and a lot of serious injuries. I was watching this in horror from my booth, banging on the window trying to get somebody's attention to get those people off the stage.

Finally, I had the public address announcer plead with the dancing athletes to get off the stage. When that polite request failed, the announcer became less polite and warned everybody to get off the stage because "it's going to collapse." Slowly, they got off the stage. The choir circled the stage and sang "Auld Lang Syne," we dropped thousands of balloons and dimmed the lights. The stadium emptied. It was done. The Olympics were over. A year's work was finished. I just sat there looking out over the coliseum. I was absolutely exhausted, but so proud, so very, very proud.

It took me several weeks to return to normal life. For others who had worked just as hard for just as long as I had, but had less exciting careers to which to return, the end of the games sent them into a deep depression. Having made so many films and seen close-knit production groups break up at the conclusion, I was used to this. The Los Angeles Olympic Committee provided psychiatrists to help those people make the transition. While I had been well known in the entertainment community, the Olympics made me a celebrity in Los Angeles. I immediately joined three country clubs, knowing that I had a brief window during which I was "hot," and I took advantage of it.

At a party after the final press conference, Peter honored me by giving me the Olympic torch, the torch that Rafer Johnson had used to light the Olympic flame. Affixed to it was a plaque that read "The spirit of the Games was ignited long before you received this torch. The glow would not have been possible or burned as bright without you."

I also received a wonderful gift from the great state of California—a personalized license plate reading 1USA. To me, that is pretty impressive.

For his work in making the Olympics a success, Peter Ueberroth received numerous awards, among them being named *Time* magazine's Man of the Year 1984. But to my great surprise and delight, I received the highest honor the entertainment community, my people, could bestow. One afternoon I received a phone call from my friend Dick Zanuck, who told me I was to receive the Academy of Motion and Picture Arts and Sciences' Jean Hersholt Humanitarian Oscar.

Few things surprise me. This stunned me. This award is given to an individual whose humanitarian efforts have brought credit to the motion picture industry. Rather than being given annually, it is awarded only when the committee believes a recipient has earned this honor. Among the winners have been Paul Newman for his charitable contributions and Audrey Hepburn for her work with the United Nations to aid the children of the world.

The night I received the Jean Hersholt Humanitarian Oscar was one of the most thrilling nights of my life. Gloria and I went to the ceremony with Mary and Mike Wallace. I had often heard others stand onstage and thank the people who had made it possible, but until I was standing there myself, I don't know that I truly appreciated that truth. I didn't do it myself. I produced it, I came up with some of the ideas, and I was the most ardent cheerleader and problem solver. But without Director of Ceremonies Tommy Walker, choreographers Ron Fields and Dee Dee Woods, Director of Production Ric Birch, Production Manager Barnett Lipman, Drill Team Director Kay Crawford, Choir Director Dr. Charles C. Hirt, Costume Designer Ray Aghayan, Band Director Dr. Arthur C. Bartner, Music Director Jack Elliott, Art Director Rene Lagler, Lighting Director Bill Klages, composers Marvin Hamlisch, Philip Glass, Dean Pitchford, John Williams, and Ashford and Simpson, and about twelve thousand volunteers, none of it would have been possible. I accepted full responsibility should anything have gone wrong and I'm certainly not shy about accepting the credit, but as every producer knows, without the right army marching close behind him, no battles can ever be won. I had a grand American army.

A funny volunteer story: One woman who volunteered wanted to be a driver. She was assigned to drive the president of the French delegation and other members to a reception in Bel Air. When she dropped them off, they asked her to wait; they'd only be about an hour. She said, "If you don't mind, I'd like to go home."

"We'd prefer you wait. Home is probably a long distance away, and we don't want you to go."

Her response was perfect: "I only live two doors down . . . over there."

As the story goes, they looked at her house and realized it was bigger than the one they were about to enter.

The end of the Olympics was not quite the end of our job. Contrary to the original fears that the City of Los Angeles would lose a fortune, we made a profit of $222,716,000. That's two hundred twenty-two *million* dollars, making it the most profitable sporting event in history. Sixty percent of the profits went to the U.S. Olympic Committee—which donated a third of that to the National Sports Federations—and 40 percent went to the Los Angeles Olympic Games Committee. We also left behind millions of dollars' worth of athletic facilities, among them an Olympic swim center at USC, a velodrome—a bicycle racing track—at California State University in Dominguez Hills, and a shooting range at California State University in San Bernardino. Almost two decades after the Olympics, our AAF foundation, formed after the Games to distribute our profits, annually awards monetary grants to sports organizations. I was the chairman for five years and remain chairman emeritus. The foundation has distributed more than $100 million and the bank account is still bulging.

The Los Angeles Olympics were a tremendous success, by any possible measurement. Tens of thousands of people benefited and will continue to reap the benefits for the foreseeable future. But for me, it remains a time and a place that I will never forget, a new area of show business and a memory I will always cherish.

THIRTY-NINE

I'M A YANKEE DOODLE DANDY

My feelings about producing
Liberty Weekend (1986)

For weeks after the conclusion of the Olympics, I continued to receive plaudits. I also received numerous offers to produce other live events, one of them from a Texas multimillionaire who offered me $500,000 to put on a great show for his daughter's wedding. I turned down all the offers. I had absolutely no interest in doing anything similar again.

Until Lee Iacocca called. On the Fourth of July 1986, the nation would celebrate the one hundredth anniversary of the gift of the Statue of Liberty from France. To mark that occasion, the Department of the Interior had refurbished the statue, cleaning it both inside and out, bathing it in new lighting and adding and restoring historical attractions at Ellis Island, the gateway through which had passed millions of immigrants who had transformed this nation. To celebrate the anniversary, Iacocca wanted to put on a one-day show that could be broadcast nationally and asked me to help plan it.

To me, it seemed more than the opening of the refurbished statue, it seemed to be a celebration of the core value that had made America great: the willingness to accept peoples from all over the world and give them the support they needed and the opportunities they craved to live a better life.

I love this country with all my heart. I am, simply, an old-fashioned patriot. My work has granted me the pleasure of exploring the history of the world, from the earliest cave dwellers, through all the wars, the lives of the greatest people who have lived, through the tragedies and triumphs of mankind. I know the facts. And I have never, never ceased to be astonished about the confluence of events that brought about the founding of this nation. I am not naive, I know about and have recorded, through my films, some of the worst things that have happened here. It is difficult ever to forget slavery or segregation or bigotry, but I can accept the past while still appreciating the greater successes we have enjoyed.

So, when I was offered this opportunity to celebrate our freedom, I not only accepted, I did the usual Wolper thing. Instead of staging a single show on the Fourth of July, I turned the rededication of the Statue of Liberty into an event. Liberty Weekend, I called it. A four-day national party to honor our heritage. The Statue of Liberty Foundation's original budget for the single-day affair was slightly more than $5 million. My budget, for the entire weekend, was $35 million. Obviously, we had different events in mind.

This really was a made-for-America event. In the four-day spectacular, I wanted to encompass as much of what we are as a people—while having a great time—as possible.

With the experience of the Olympics behind me, I assumed that I would be able to produce this show with a minimum of difficulty. I actually believed that.

The two events were as much alike as Los Angeles is like New York. I was born and raised in New York but have lived most of my adult life in southern California. I'm a Californian first by circumstances but much later by choice. The great differences between the coasts never became clearer to me than while I was creating and producing this show.

I began by laying out grandiose plans for the long weekend. I wanted Liberty Weekend to be a combination of patriotism and entertainment. The refurbished Statue of Liberty would be "unveiled" by President

Reagan the night of July 3. President Reagan would be joined by French president François Mitterrand. To mark that occasion we created something we called the Medal of Liberty, which we would present to twelve distinguished naturalized Americans during the opening ceremonies.

We would celebrate the Fourth of July with a parade of tall ships, which would include more than three hundred sailing ships, up the Hudson River and a concert, featuring pop stars, on the New Jersey side, which would conclude with the largest fireworks show in history of the Fourth of July.

The Statue of Liberty would officially be reopened to visitors by Nancy Reagan on July 5. Then we would stage a huge, free classical concert in New York's Central Park.

On the fifth and sixth we planned a conference entitled Liberty: The Next Hundred Years, which would encompass a series of lectures and discussions. We would bring together some of the leading historians, political scientists, journalists, politicians, educators, jurists, government officials, and philosophers to debate topics like free speech and the limits of privacy. We would close on July 6 with a sports event and a huge closing party at Giants Stadium in New Jersey.

It was an ambitious program. The initial problem I had to solve was visibility: just about everyone in the world was familiar with the Olympics; no one, except me and the few people I had recruited, had ever heard the phrase Liberty Weekend. I had to make this event, which existed only in my mind, seem like reality. To do that, I had to enlist the support of the media. If I could convince the media that this was an actual event, they would treat it that way. A lesson learned long ago came in handy here. Two important elements are necessary to interest reporters in an event: make it a must-see event and make it difficult to get access.

Over two weeks, I made numerous presentations to the most important newspapers, magazines, and television networks in the country. I told them about the weekend in great detail, showing sketches and sometimes making it up as I needed to, but I always concluded with an important admonition: You'd better file for your press accreditation early because accommodations on the island are going to be limited. You don't want to be left behind.

The president of the United States and the president of France! Big stars! Fireworks! The Statue of Liberty! The media didn't know whether it was real—but no one wanted to be stuck on Manhattan Island when all the action was taking place on Governors Island, the place for the best view of the Statue of Liberty. So, the frenzy for credentials started. I put Richard Perelman, who had been Olympic press chief, on the case. Within a month I had all the major news outlets, not only in the United States but throughout the world, committed to covering my weekend, which then made it much easier to convince stars to appear and raise money.

I put together a team consisting of the best people in the entertainment business, people I'd worked with at the Olympics and from other shows. Gary Smith and Dwight Hemion would produce and direct the opening show; Walter Miller would do the Americana Concert; Richard Heffner would take charge of the "Liberty conference"; David Griffiths and Kirk Browning would produce and direct the "classical concert" in New York; Tommy Walker would create the giant fireworks show; the final day, Sports Salute, would be produced by Linda Jonsson and Don Ohlmeyer; and the closing ceremonies would be produced and directed by Don Mischer. I began working with officials of the city of New York to make this all happen—and that's when I began to confront reality. I gave a complete presentation to city officials, the police department, the FBI, and the Secret Service. Everybody seemed enthusiastic. Then I followed up by contacting the New York Police Department to begin the actual planning for security and crowd control—and I couldn't get anybody to respond to my requests. Finally, I was told that the New York Police Department couldn't talk to me until I'd cleared everything with the mayor, with Ed Koch.

I'd met Ed Koch several times. He was a likable man who seemed reasonable. When I spoke to one of his assistants, she informed me politely, "I know you're having problems with the police department, Mr. Wolper, but before we figure out how to solve those problems, we need to know how we're going to handle the tickets for the mayor's office."

Tickets? At the Olympics, Ueberroth had handled it democratically—everybody paid equally. Apparently, the mayor had something else in mind. "The tickets will be handled by me," I said. "What can I do for you?"

"Well," she said, "I think the mayor is going to want a large block of tickets to the events."

"What is a large block?"

"Maybe a hundred for each of the ten events."

A thousand tickets? I was stunned into silence. Most of the events were going to be free. I was depending on revenue from ticket sales to the opening and closing ceremonies to cover much of my expenses. Because the opening ceremonies were being held on an island, I had only about ten thousand tickets to sell—and Mayor Edward Koch wanted a large batch of them. "Gee," I said, "the money really goes to the Statue of Liberty," and blah, blah, blah, blah.

"Of course we understand," she said, "but this is the way things are usually done in New York."

As soon as I agreed the mayor's office would get their tickets, I got a call from the police department to initiate preparations. As it turned out, this was only the beginning of my welcome to New York City. In Los Angeles, all the unions had been completely cooperative. We had to deal with only one person, Bill Robertson of the AFL-CIO, who served as the representative for all the unions. It's very different in New York, where each union local seems to run its own fiefdom. I needed to light my grandstand along the waterfront, for example, which would seat several thousand people and enable me to sell a lot of tickets to the parade of tall ships and the Fourth of July closing fireworks show. We put out requests for bids to light the grandstand and do all our electrical work. We estimated the price at no more than $100,000.

We got one bid. One bid, for $300,000. I didn't understand what had happened. "The other companies won't bid," my construction supervisor explained. "It looks to me like they're ganging up on us."

I had worked with many unions throughout my career. And I knew a guy, Neil Walsh, the official New York greeter, who knew a guy who had a brother-in-law who could maybe do something. Two days later, I got a phone call from a man who admitted, "Mr. Wolper, I'm a lighting guy. I got a business out in Brooklyn, in Sheepshead Bay. I gotta be honest with you, I just got out of prison, Sing Sing, and I'm trying to get this business going again. I can give you what you want if you'll give me a chance."

We sent him all the information and he came back several days later with a $130,000 bid, close to what we had estimated the actual price to be. When I spoke to him again, he said, "I know it's a little high. There's an extra twenty thousand to thirty thousand dollars in there that I need to solve this kind of problem."

I didn't ask for details. When I was satisfied he could actually do the work, I hired him. The work was done professionally and on time and for the price on which we had agreed.

It seemed that everything we tried to do caused another problem. What could be nobler than awarding medals to a dozen distinguished, living, naturalized Americans? But we received tremendous criticism, not for what we did, but for what we didn't do. The problems I had satisfying the diverse ethnic groups in Los Angeles were nothing, absolutely nothing, compared to the situation in New York. Our committee selected former secretary of state Henry Kissinger, astronaut Franklin Chang-Diaz, architect I. M. Pei, violinist Itzhak Perlman, journalist James Reston, psychologist Kenneth Clark, scientist Albert Sabin, industrialist An Wang, Elie Wiesel, Bob Hope, educator Hannah Holborn Gray, and composer Irving Berlin. What a distinguished group. Who could possibly argue with those selections?

To answer the most significant criticism—that no one of Irish or Italian descent was honored—noted historian Arthur Schlesinger, a member of the selection committee, wrote in the *New York Times*, "No one can conceivably deny the significant role that Irish- and Italian-Americans have played in our history, but the great wave of Irish and Italian immigration took place prior to World War I. It is, therefore, not surprising that most living Irish-Americans and Italian-Americans are American by birth, not naturalization."

Some people even complained that not a single American Indian was on our list—forcing us to point out that Indians are not naturalized citizens. It was finally resolved by setting up another award called the Ellis Island Award, which would be presented annually by a private organization after Liberty Weekend to outstanding sons and daughters of immigrants. Interestingly enough, I received that award from the organization.

I also envisioned a naturalization ceremony held simultaneously on July 4, in cities throughout the nation, at which many thousands of immigrants would become citizens of the United States. I envisioned thousands of people in the Los Angeles Coliseum raising their right hands and taking the oath of allegiance to our Constitution. I saw it so clearly in my mind. It was a beautiful sight.

Unfortunately, Judge Manuel Real, chief justice of the U.S. district court in Los Angeles, did not see it at all. He refused to hold the swearing-in ceremony in the Coliseum, the music center, or in any other open-air venue large enough. As one judge said, "Wolper's proposal was rejected . . . partly because a previous experiment at the Coliseum with a mass open-air naturalization was a complete disaster. . . . I hope we're doing our job in a dignified way with new citizens coming the way they should."

I could not have disagreed with them more. While certainly the ceremony should be dignified, becoming a citizen of the United States is a cause for great celebration. So, we held simultaneous ceremonies on Ellis Island, New York, and in Washington, Miami, St. Louis, and San Francisco, presided over by Chief Justice of the Supreme Court Warren Burger. Among the immigrants naturalized that day was Russian-born dancer Mikhail Baryshnikov, who went by boat from Ellis Island, where the ceremony took place, to Governor's Island, where he performed in our opening night show; his first performance as a new American citizen was dancing to the music of George Gershwin.

By this time, I knew more about fireworks than I had ever really wanted to know. I could talk fireworks with experts. I estimated the cost of the fireworks show I wanted to stage at about $4 million. The first corporate sponsor I approached was Macy's (where I had gotten a job wrapping Christmas packages as a kid), which, in addition to sponsoring New York's Thanksgiving Day parade, always sponsored a July 4 fireworks show in New York harbor. This time, Macy's executives decided they couldn't afford to participate at that price. While the French government donated the fireworks around the Statue of Liberty, Bloomingdale's and Abraham & Strauss sponsored the rest of my fireworks show.

I moved to New York and lived rent-free for eight months in a beautiful suite in the Towers of the Waldorf-Astoria, which was donated to the event by my friend Barron Hilton. While I was not paid a penny in salary for my work, I did receive living expenses. But, one morning, I was surprised to see a story in the *New York Times* reporting that I was receiving more than $400 a week in expenses and questioning my motives for producing the show. The reporter wondered, how much does it cost to eat each week?—then decided that we were hiding a salary in that payment.

I was as outraged as I have ever been in my life. Four hundred dollars a week? I have been a lucky man; I've earned a fortune doing exactly what I wanted to do. I had a magnificent home, I had an extraordinary art collection. My company was worth a considerable amount.

Four hundred bucks a week wasn't going to change my life. I love having the financial resources to completely enjoy life. But, spending eight months of my life away from my home for $400 a week was not financially beneficial to me. I was so insulted, I went with William May, the president of the Statue of Liberty–Ellis Island Foundation and a major New York real estate broker, to see the editorial board of the *New York Times*. I explained the situation to them carefully, pointing out that, if my motive had been to make a lot of money, this was not the job I would have taken. To be accused of lying about that, which the *Times* essentially had, was extremely hurtful to me. The board listened politely to my response to their story, then promptly ignored everything I'd said. They refused to retract a word.

In a few months, I had become more depressed in New York than at any other time during my life. The *Times* story, after having had to deal with the unions and the mayor's office, after having spent weeks meeting somebody with their hand out every time I turned around, was just too much. After another tough day, I came home and told Gloria to pack our bags. "Let's get the fuck out of here," I said. "Let's let them put on the show. This is just too goddamn much."

When I went to bed that night, I had decided to quit. For the first time in my life, I was going to give up on a project. I didn't like the feeling. I wasn't used to being defeated, and this was a defeat. Of course, it was the collective might of the city of New York, but still, it was a defeat. But, once I made the decision to leave, I knew it was the right one.

Until I woke up the next morning. I felt better the next morning. "Give it one more day," Gloria suggested. And we stayed to put on the show.

None of the major stars who appeared were paid either. For me, the major disappointment of the entire weekend was my musical hero Frank Sinatra. I had heard all the stories about how difficult he could be, but I knew that, with me, he would be different. At least I thought I knew. It all began when Lee Iacocca told me, "Sinatra has volunteered to be part of Liberty Weekend. Call Mickey Rudin and set it up."

Mickey Rudin was Sinatra's lawyer and close friend. "Frank wants to do it," Mickey Rudin told me. We agreed that he would appear in the opening ceremony to sing "The House I Live In," a beautiful song he'd sung in a World War II short film that had won an Academy Award, and then sing his city anthem "New York, New York" in the closing ceremony.

Thrilled does not begin to describe how excited I was. In addition to Sinatra and Baryshnikov, performers included Elizabeth Taylor, Gregory Peck, Whitney Houston, John Denver, Barry Manilow, Johnny Cash, Marilyn Horne, Zubin Mehta, Willie Nelson, Shirley MacLaine, Patti LaBelle, Liza Minnelli, and many more.

I met with Sinatra in his suite at the Waldorf Towers to go over some details. I was long, long passed being awed by celebrities, but I was still excited about meeting Sinatra. Two years earlier, I'd met his daughter, Nancy, and told her my story about chasing the truck carrying the sign, cutting off the head, hanging it over my bed, and Nancy had been so moved by my dedication to her father that she'd started crying.

When I met Frank, I couldn't wait to tell him about standing in line, chasing the truck, finding the sign from over the Paramount, and finally, "I took it home and hung it right over my bed!"

"Oh," he said, "do I exit to the left side of the stage or the right side?" That was my big story, a story I'd been telling for years, and he could not have cared less. I was so upset I was tempted to change the star of my story to Vic Damone!

We went through the details, he nodded in approval, and I left with some of my illusions damaged. It got worse. Two weeks before the show, Mickey Rudin called me: "Sinatra can't do the closing show. He's got to go somewhere that night."

"Well, naturally I'm disappointed, Mickey," I said, "but I can get someone else." I called Liza Minnelli, who agreed to sing "New York, New York."

One week before the show, Mickey Rudin called again: "Frank can't do the opening ceremony either."

"What are you talking about?" I said. "He's one of the stars of the show. It's only a week away."

"He's got something very important to do."

I didn't know what to say. "What's more important than a celebration of liberty?"

"Look, he just can't do it. I'll send you a letter that explains everything." The letter arrived a few days later. "Dear David," it read, "the sky is blue. The grass is green. The fence is yellow. That's why Sinatra canceled. Yours truly, Mickey Rudin."

It was the strangest letter I'd ever received. Naturally, I called Mickey and asked him what it meant.

"David, I can't give you any better reason than that. There is no fucking reason. He just doesn't want to do it."

I suppose if this had happened months earlier, before we had done all the publicity, before we'd sold millions of dollars' worth of tickets, I would probably not have been quite so upset. But I was stuck. I called Lee Iacocca and told him, as politely as possible, and admittedly it wasn't all that polite, that Sinatra had canceled, twice.

What do you mean canceled? Iacocca asked.

He's not going to show up at all, is what I mean, I explained.

There is a side to Lee Iacocca that most people have never seen. That day I saw it. He was even more angry than I was, assuming that is possible. Oh, yeah, he said, we'll see about that. Those were not his exact words. His exact words would not be printable.

Finally, Sinatra was delighted to sing at the opening ceremonies.

For Liberty Weekend, just as the Olympics, security was a prime consideration in everything we planned. We were bringing the president and Nancy Reagan to an island; the body of water surrounding us had to be secured. Just to make the situation a little more dire, several months before the opening ceremony the United States bombed the home of Libyan leader Qaddafi, who promised revenge. What could possibly be a bigger target than the one hundredth anniversary of the symbol of our liberty? That the president of the United States would be there was simply an added bonus.

Supposedly, security was even tighter than it had been at the Olympics. One day, I was walking on Statue of Liberty Island, where the lighting ceremony was to be held, being briefed by several security people, and as they told me about their elaborate precautions, I looked down at the harbor and noticed two guys fishing in a small boat. They were no more than twenty yards from the Statue of Liberty, guzzling beer, their radio blaring. "Where's all this security?" I wondered. "Look at those two guys. They could practically lob a bomb from there."

A member of the Secret Service leaned over and whispered, "David, they're ours." Security was extremely tight, from airplanes patrolling the night skies to frogmen in the water around the island making sure no unauthorized person got too close.

Just like at the Olympics, we had provided safe seating for the president. Initially, we decided that the Reagans would sit with President and Mrs. Mitterrand. Then we received a call from the White House explaining that President Reagan would prefer to sit separately from Mitterrand. The president would be bored sitting next to someone who doesn't speak English, I was informed. So, we gave each president his own box.

For most shows, lighting is important, but rarely is it the most important part of the show. For our lighting director, Greg Brunton, this was his dream. We were unveiling the Statue of Liberty from the cloak of night, and it had to be spectacular. This whole event was built around the rededication of the statue, and if it didn't look both new and completely unchanged, we would fail. It was a difficult lighting problem. One night they lit the statue for me using the regular lighting. It was not nearly spectacular enough. It wasn't bright enough, exciting enough, so we installed a $750,000 lighting system.

It was beautiful. It bathed the base of Lady Liberty in red, white, and blue and illuminated the statue itself standing in New York harbor, the torch of liberty held high and proudly. The Statue of Liberty stood etched in light against the dark night, as a welcoming beacon. For me, it was absolutely impossible to look at this statue and not try, briefly, to put myself in the position of one of the millions of immigrants who had given up everything he or she knew to come to America. How brave those people were, my ancestors, all of our ancestors. What was the night or day like when they came into this harbor and saw this statue for the first time? Thinking about it gave me goose bumps. I wanted to communicate that feeling.

People had been hearing about and reading about the refurbished statue for a long time. Most of them were curious to see what it looked like. We wanted to make the unveiling as dramatic as possible: President Reagan, standing on Governors Island, was going to press a button that would fire a green laser beam across the harbor. To the strains of "America, the Beautiful," the Statue of Liberty would be illuminated.

Assuming it all worked, of course. It is the nature of a producer to plan for those what-ifs of life. As the entire weekend was built around this ceremony, it would be more than embarrassing if this elaborate system failed—it would turn the entire event into a joke. To ensure that did not happen, we installed a backup system—that cost $250,000. That was a lot to pay so I could sleep soundly at night, but to me it was well worth it.

The three most important aspects of preparing for a live event of this magnitude are planning, planning, and planning. And then you have to be equipped to solve all those problems that you forgot to plan for. We were fortunate. Event after event proceeded exactly as we had hoped. The unexpected problems were easily solved; in fact, the only unpleasant moments of the entire weekend involved Frank Sinatra, my hero.

Sinatra did not want to do the show and continued to be difficult. There were at least two Sinatras: he could be the nicest, most generous human being you've ever met one minute, then turn around and become equally unpleasant. Countless people who had never met him had received checks because he'd heard they were in a desperate situation. You never really knew which Sinatra was going to show up. Two nights before the show, we had our dress rehearsal on Governors Island, the only land location that directly faces the Statue of Liberty. For this performance, we invited the families of the coastguardsmen—the residents of Governors Island—who had been working so hard the past few weeks. In the middle of the show, I got a call from Gary Smith, who was producing it. "Come down to the director's booth, please," he said. "Sinatra's going crazy."

Sinatra was furious. He hated to be kept waiting and we were keeping him waiting. "I gotta get out of here," he said repeatedly and somewhat more colorfully.

Trying to mollify him, I promised, "It'll only take a few more minutes."

"Why do I have to do a dress rehearsal?" he asked. "I know 'The House I Live In,' I've sung it a thousand times."

I tried to explain: "Frank, we've got all these Coast Guard people here and they're all big fans of yours. They're dying to see you."

Eventually he calmed down. He went through the rehearsal and got off the island as quickly as possible.

I hoped we had gotten through the most difficult moments with him, but unfortunately, I was wrong. That tirade was just a warm-up for the main event.

Weather is always the unknown factor. While we had made contingency plans in case of rain, we did not prepare for cold. And it was cold, the coldest July 3 it had been in many years. The temperature was slightly above freezing, which made an unpleasant situation even worse. On Governors Island we had erected a large tent that served as the greenroom, the waiting room for our celebrities before they went onstage. In addition to Sinatra, among many others waiting there that night were Gregory Peck, Elizabeth Taylor, Neil Diamond, Andy Williams, Ted Koppel. They couldn't have been nicer or more cooperative.

Sinatra got restless waiting to go on. Just to make things a little more uncomfortable, the Plexiglas window in the tent got fogged up because of the cold, so no one could see the Statue of Liberty. So, Sinatra got a knife and literally cut a hole in the tent—opening it up to the wind and the cold. As cold as it was in there already, it got worse.

Now everybody was freezing, but Sinatra was getting hotter and hotter. He's screaming, "What the fuck is taking so long with this show?"

He was being so obnoxious that, finally, Elizabeth Taylor stood up to him. "Come on, Frank," she said, "sit down. There's no sense leaving this island because everybody who is anybody is on this island tonight."

Sinatra would not be mollified. His performance was the usual Sinatra, meaning it was perfect, but as soon as he left the stage, he started again: "I'm getting out of here. How do I get off this island?"

There were several ways to get off that island at that moment: by the president's helicopter—which was reserved for Reagan and Mitter-rand—by ferry, or by private yacht. Frank Sinatra had a yacht waiting to take him back to Manhattan. However, only one dock was in use on Governors Island, and at that moment New Jersey governor Tom Kean's boat was tied to it. Sinatra's boat was waiting several yards offshore.

Sinatra told the state trooper on the dock, "Move this boat. I've got to get my boat in so I can get off this island."

To which the trooper replied, "I'm sorry, I can't do that, Mr. Sinatra. The governor told me to wait here until he returns."

Sinatra did not want to hear that. "I said move the fucking thing. Get it out of here so I can get off the island." When the trooper again refused to comply, Sinatra lost it, screaming at him like a madman. But the trooper continued to resist.

The show finally ended and Governor Kean arrived at his boat. Sinatra had savaged presidents, he certainly wasn't going to back down to a mere governor. It was a disgraceful scene. Finally, Governor Kean's boat started pulling away from the dock, the episode was about to end—but the governor had forgotten a passenger and had to return to the dock. People who were there thought Sinatra was going to die, he was so angry.

Finally, Governor Kean's boat left and Sinatra got his ride off the island.

When we gave the Medal of Liberty awards to our naturalized citizens, they sang Irving Berlin's "God Bless America." Berlin himself, one of our recipients, was too frail to attend. The next day, one newspaper described the ceremony as "corny." Later that afternoon my assistant Auriel Sanderson came running excitedly into my office to tell me Irving Berlin was on the phone. "I saw in the paper about your ceremony being corny," he told me. "I thought it was terrific. When I wrote 'God Bless America,' there were some critics who thought it was too corny. They're all gone, but the song is still here."

America's party was a jubilant success. The lights lit, the singers sang, the dancers danced; we welcomed thousands of new citizens to our nation and discussed and debated the elements of our democracy. Across the country more than 100 million people watched at least part of the celebration. Millions of people watched the parade of ships from the shoreline. Eight hundred thousand people attended our classical concert in Central Park, the largest live performance in the park's long history. We sold fifty thousand tickets to the closing show in Giants Stadium. And through it all, the Statue of Liberty shone magnificently.

We didn't quite earn enough money to pay all our bills, though. The final budget for the weekend, for what had started out to be a subdued $5 million, one-day event, was $35 million. We had staged eleven major events, attended by several million people, and charged for only the opening and closing spectaculars. We took in $30 million; so in reality, the cost equaled the original budget of $5 million. I tried hard to break even, financially, for the weekend, but I couldn't do it. I just couldn't do it. The unanticipated expense that put me overbudget was insurance for the fireworks. This was the greatest fireworks show in history—more than forty thousand fireworks had been burst in the air—and the insurance companies wanted nothing to do with it. Eventually, it cost us something like $2 million for insurance. We could have come a bit closer to breaking even if I had the revenue from the mayor's tickets, but even that money would not have been enough to put us in the black. A lot of unexpected items contributed to the deficit, but still, it was worth it. It was really worth it.

We had taken a moment to pay respect to our democracy. We'd partied, and I know, at times, tears of joy had been shed. I had worked on this event as long and hard as anything I'd ever done, and even with all the problems, it would be impossible to accurately describe the pride I'd felt. It was a weekend few people who participated in or watched will ever forget. Five million dollars seemed like a bargain to me and Lee Iacocca agreed.

Once again, I received countless congratulatory messages and several awards. The French government honored me with their highest award, the Legion of Honor, and I received a letter from President Reagan, which read in part, "Even with my past experience in show business, there are no words to properly thank you for that magnificent birthday party . . . an entire nation's heart was touched."

But, like any producer, I most remember my critics. After a four-day celebration that had included the unveiling, by light, of the Statue of Liberty, speeches by the president of the United States and the president of France, the swearing in of new citizens across the nation, the awarding of the Medal of Liberty to twelve distinguished naturalized Americans by Ted Koppel, and performances by several of the greatest entertainers of the century, I walked into the press tent to answer questions from reporters. The first question, for which, I admit, I was completely unprepared, was "Where were the Elvis Presleys, Mr. Wolper?"

It was almost enough to make a grown producer cry. Originally, we planned for the closing ceremonies a forty-five-second dance number featuring two hundred Elvis impersonators as part of a fifty-minute salute to American musical history. To report that it was disheartening to have that asked as the first question after the thrilling weekend we had staged would be an understatement. It didn't just miss the point, it missed the meaning of the entire event.

The day after the event, the *New York Post*'s front-page headline read, "Liberty Mogul: Never Again! Hollywood big passes the torch—forever." It had been an incredibly wonderful four days and a difficult eight months. And just to make sure that this was the last mammoth live project I produced, Gloria promised to hang that headline in our bedroom.

FORTY

MAY THE FORCE BE WITH YOU

The American Film Institute's 25th Anniversary celebration
(*l to r*): George Lucas, Martin Scorsese, President George Bush,
Steven Spielberg, AFI president Jean Furstenberg,
MPAA president Jack Valenti, and I

Actually, I wasn't done producing live events, just the type of massive project that dominated my life for months at a time. From that moment on, I agreed to produce only those things that sounded like fun. Surprisingly, Gloria and I have never been part of the Hollywood social scene. We're mostly stay-at-homes; we enjoy spending time with our family and closest friends. In fact, we're not really part of any organized social scene. I've been invited to the White House by just about every president since John Kennedy and have never accepted. Most of the events we attend are charitable dinners. So, when I was asked to produce one of those events, my basic rule was simple: Would Gloria and I want to go to this event?

With that standard in mind, I produced the twenty-fifth anniversary dinner for the American Film Institute in the Great Hall of the National

Building Museum in Washington, D.C. The AFI is an organization of moviemakers that truly celebrates film as an art form. The AFI has been the leader in preserving our motion picture heritage, and I serve, with pride, on its board. So, when asked to produce this gala evening, I agreed to do so. Besides, it sounded like a lot of fun.

To ensure that the evening would not be replete with speeches, we did a segment in which movie stars, directors, and political figures each read an appropriate and memorable line from a classic film. For example, the line I gave Dick Cheney, then the secretary of defense, was "May the force be with you."

The question was, what line should we give to the president of the United States, George H. Bush? I wanted him to look directly at Barbara Bush and say the classic line from *Casablanca* "Here's looking at you, kid." Several of the president's aides did not think it was appropriate, but I loved it. And when I approached the president about it, he loved it too. And while he was not the actor other presidents have been, his reading was fine.

Everybody laughed and applauded, but what they could not know was that I had arranged for the renowned critics Gene Siskel and Roger Ebert to review each participant's performance. Naturally they gave the president two thumbs-up. I seem to remember Siskel saying something before giving his review about not blowing dinner at the White House.

Two years earlier, I produced what was reviewed as the "biggest party in Hollywood history" at Warner Bros. studio. About three hundred performers who starred in Warner Bros. pictures, including President Ronald Reagan, attended a two-hour spectacular show. My buddy Steve Ross said, as he kissed me on the cheek, "It was like Liberty Weekend and the Olympics opening all rolled in one."

Unfortunately, so terribly unfortunately, the final big event I produced was a memorial tribute to my old high school classmate Steve Ross, who died in 1992 of prostate cancer. Steve Ross was truly a giant in show business, but more than that, he was simply one of the most beloved and giving human beings I had ever encountered. His friends in New York held a memorial service in Carnegie Hall. It was a remarkable tribute to him—and I was struck that a corporate executive could fill that legendary place. A month later at the Warner Bros. studios, I produced a memorial service, called "Celebrate His Life." We made a film about his life and I had speakers including Warren Beatty, Quincy Jones, Whoopi Goldberg, and Barbra Streisand. It wasn't a big production, but it was as difficult to produce as anything else I'd done in my life. I wanted it to be perfect for a man I'd known and loved and admired for a large portion of my life.

PART VII

Sunset

Golfing with astronaut Neil Armstrong (1992)

FORTY-ONE

THE TWENTIETH CENTURY, THE FINAL SHOW

With John Wayne

I don't know, specifically, when I began to think about retiring. But for a long time that was all I did about it—think about it. I was too busy doing those things I loved to do to stop working and find something I loved to do.

In truth, I had a difficult time stopping. I had too many ideas that needed to be turned into films. Fittingly, the last major project I completed was a documentary—and my subject was the summing up of the twentieth century.

I began working on this concept in the early 1960s, when I approached Paramount's Stanley Jaffe and Charles Bluhdorn, head of Gulf & Western, and tried to convince them to finance *The Encyclopedia of the 20th Century*. It remained on my list of projects for almost forty years. But I never gave up.

I pitched it many times to many people. In 1965. I made a deal with Harry Saltzman, who produced the James Bond pictures, and a major educational organization called Trimedia to make a twenty-hour *Ency-clopedia of the 20th Century of Sight and Sound.* Eventually, we decided it really needed to be seventy hours long. It was going to be done on the latest technology, super-8 cassettes. But Harry Saltzman never raised enough money to go ahead.

In the 1970s, I approached *Encyclopaedia Britannica* to convince them to jointly produce a visual encyclopedia. When that failed, I went to *Compton Encyclopedia.* That also failed.

Each time a new technology became available, I tried to find a sponsor for this package. Warner Home Video turned down my attempt to do it on home cassette in 1982. I tried again with different companies in 1986; in 1987, I had unsuccessful discussions with Pioneer for their new laser disc. I pitched it to Microsoft in 1990, and to other companies in 1992 and 1997. I nearly closed a deal with Coca-Cola. In the 1960s, my budget for twenty hours was $1 million. My budget in 1996 was $5 million for ten hours.

Finally, finally, in 1996, Warner Home Video put up $2 million and Warner International offered another million. I sold the ten hours to Turner to be broadcast on CNN, and Warner Bros. would distribute it on DVD and video and television around the world. To produce the program, I brought together many of the people who had started with me decades earlier, such as Bob Guenette, Bill Kronick, Marshall Flaum, Ed Spiegel, and Julian Ludwig. Originally titled *Great Events of the 20th Century,* we changed the title to *Celebrate the Century* when we made a deal with the U.S. Post Office, which was promoting its Celebrate the Century stamps program.

That gave me ten hours, the bare minimum needed to create this work. We had to cut out a lot of small wars to make it work. Then it occurred to me that we should produce *People of the 20th Century,* and I put together a $5 million deal for ten hours of programming. It had taken decades and had evolved from film to DVD, but finally I produced twenty hours—in two parts—of documentary history of the twentieth century.

But the concept of retiring still intrigued me. After having done so many different things in my career, almost everything I did began to feel repetitive. While the story we told in each miniseries was unique, for example, the production of each of them was similar. Over time, excitement became interest, became a job. I was never bored—with so much to do I didn't have the time to be bored—but I had learned how to hire people I trusted to do the finest job and step out of their way. In my own life, I needed new challenges.

I needed to find something that would engage my intellect as well as my passion. Fortunately, I found it. In my life I had fought against entrenched network executives, I had played a vital role in the history of documentaries, I had practically created the miniseries, and I had made award-winning motion pictures. I had probably produced more hours of quality television than anyone else in history, I had carefully built a renowned sculpture collection, I had found in Gloria the woman of my dreams, and I adore my life and seven grandchildren. I had helped raise three kids, each of whom had become a terrific person—but finally, I found the one thing that was more difficult than anything else I'd ever done before, the one thing capable of making me feel inadequate: golf.

I suspect it was one of the great philosophers who stated, for posterity, "Golf is the great equalizer." The truth is that we are all mortals—with the possible exception of Tiger Woods—when facing a golf course. I had played, on occasion, as a younger man, but only in my senior years, when I had the time, did I begin to truly appreciate the appeal of this game.

Golf pits each player against his greatest competitor—himself. Like the proverbial pot of gold, the perfect swing, the great shot, is always so tantalizingly close, yet remains so far away. I originally began playing golf when I was seventeen. I played mostly at Aldercress Country Club in New Jersey, which cost $200 to join and about a $10-a-month membership fee. Then I moved to California in 1951 and wanted to play—until I found out it cost $50,000 to join a golf club.

So I gave it up for forty years. When I started playing again I was sixty years old. Old enough to know better. I realized that, at my age, I was never going to be a great golfer, so my goal was to be the best golfer I was capable of being while enjoying the game. When I involve myself with a project, I dive into it as deeply as I can. I've never been satisfied to swim in the shallow, safe waters.

Which is how I came to own a golf course in the Napa Valley and to stage my own charity golf tournament.

I fell deeply in love with golf. A golf course was the one place in the world where I could truly relax. In business, I have been known, on occasion, to lose my temper just a bit, no more than a volcano bursts out of its peak, but unlike most people, I can relax completely when playing golf. Truthfully, there is no place in the world I would rather be than on a golf course. My philosophy of golf is simple: If I'm playing with Arnold Palmer or Jack Nicklaus and I hit a ball in the woods, under a tree, away from civilization, then I'm in serious trouble. But if I'm playing with my good friends, such as Richard Crenna, Grant Tinker, Mike Connors, Bud Yorkin, or Jack Valenti, with twenty or higher hand-icaps, it doesn't matter. No matter how many strokes I take, I still have a good chance to get on the green, get in the hole, and win.

My handicap is my overall ability. As an optimist might say, poor Tiger Woods, no matter how much he plays he can't get any better. But me? I have more room to get better than most people. But some shots I've made, I will never forget. On the par 3, ninety-eight-yard tenth hole at the Pacific Grove Country Club in Monterey, I had a hole in one. While most people might have used a 9 iron or a wedge on the hole, I carefully picked a 6 iron and attempted to punch it between sand traps onto the green. For those people who understand golf, the angle of each clubface determines the distance a properly hit ball should go. A 6 iron is used for much longer distance—usually. I hit the ball and it bounced and bounced and bounced and rolled right into the hole. Right into the hole! I couldn't believe it. My Napa friends Rod Stone and Dan Harberts, the people I was playing with, started cheering. They tossed their hats in the air. I was screaming and dancing. A hole in one!

Back at the clubhouse I filled in the forms necessary to receive a cer-tificate. And when I responded to the pro's question that I had used a 6 iron on the hole, my so-called friends started laughing. And kept laugh-ing until the pro said loudly, "I guess he used the right club."

That was the best shot. My worst shot is a little more complicated. It may not have been the worst shot ever struck, but it certainly has to rate high on the list of most unusual. I was playing in a foursome with two for-mer presidents of the United States Golf Association and TV-golf pro-ducer-director Terry Jastrow at the Seminole Country Club in Palm Beach, Florida. Using my 3 iron, I hit the ball squarely. It went on a low line drive about one hundred yards, then hit a palm tree. It ricocheted to the right and hit a second palm tree at a strange angle and started heading back toward me. Then it hit a third palm tree and went off to the left—rolling right back into the divot from which I'd hit it.

I don't believe in Bigfoot, I don't believe in the existence of aliens, and I certainly don't believe in the predictions of Nostradamus. And I know people won't believe in Wolper's Shot, but this happened. The ball traveled about one hundred yards forward, hit a tree, hit a second tree, hit a third tree, only to end up exactly where it started. I, certainly, had three reliable witnesses who will support that story.

As with everything else I do, when I started playing seriously, I got very serious about it. Within a brief time, I was asked to join the board of the United States Golf Association Foundation, a group responsible for releasing USGA funds to charitable organizations throughout the country. That's sort of like taking a buggy ride in Central Park and then being asked to ride in the Kentucky Derby. Obviously, the invitation had nothing to do with my skills, but after the Olympics, I was the hottest person in Los Angeles, which led to this invitation.

As a member of the board I collaborated with Bob Guenette to produce a film on the hundred-year history of golf in America, in addition to thirteen half-hour films on the nation's greatest golfers.

The best part of the job was the opportunity to play many of the great golf courses of America, from Augusta National to Pine Valley. One of the most appealing aspects of golf, to me, is that you never play the same venue. In tennis, no matter where you're playing your match, you're still playing on the same square. No one goes on vacation to play a great tennis court. Every football field has precisely the same dimensions. In baseball the bases are always ninety feet apart. But every golf course is unique. And because of the handicap system, no matter their skill level, anybody can play against anybody else.

Taking full advantage of my position, I traveled around the country with my instructor, golf pro Steve DiMarco, and either Richard Crenna or Robert Wagner. I found that playing in a foursome with a movie star and a pro golfer was a fine way to impress our host and to divert the attention of club members from my game.

In a commercial for an electric-razor company, its president proclaimed, "I liked the shave so much I bought the company." In my case, I liked golf so much that, in 1990, I bought the nine-hole Vineyard Knolls Golf Course in Napa Valley, right out of bankruptcy court. When Art Buchwald heard about this, he wrote, "Dave, I remember specifically you saying to me when we were at USC, 'One day I'm going to own my own golf course and I'd like you to become a member.' A warm feeling swelled up inside me and I responded, 'David you are full of shit!'"

As I learned, when you own your own golf course, people like Buchwald are always trying to be nice to you. I named each of the eighteen holes after a golfing friend of mine, so people can play, among others, Peter Ueberroth, Dinah Shore, John Argue, Merv Adelson, Mike Connors, Irwin Russell, James Woods, Ed Marinaro, Irving Karp, Peter

Barsoccini, Robert Wagner, Tom Poston, Rod Stone, Dan Harberts, and Richard Crenna.

I decided that, as long as I had my own golf course, I should have my own golf tournament. The Chrysler/David L. Wolper Tournament of Stars was a two-day event, in Napa; the public tournament was played the first day at Silverado County Club, which was followed by a celebrity show in the evening. On the second day, all the celebrities played privately on my course. I did it to raise money for the Boys and Girls Clubs of Napa. As a child I'd spent considerable time at a Boys Club in New York; my mother would drop me off there when she went to work with my father, and I always felt great gratitude to that organization. In the five years this tournament was held, we raised almost $700,000 for the construction of a new building for the club in Napa.

Among the celebrities who played in my tournament were three of the most private people I've ever known: Neil Armstrong, Sandy Koufax, whom no one ever sees, and Joe DiMaggio. Neil Armstrong doesn't even have an answering machine; if he doesn't answer the phone himself, you can't reach him. Joe DiMaggio didn't have a phone number; you have to reach him through his attorney. The first four years my celebrity team finished last. The fifth year, I was playing with Joe DiMaggio, Neil Armstrong, wine maker Michael Mondavi, and Basketball Hall of Fame's Rick Barry. DiMaggio was playing terribly, until Barry told him, "Joe, you're not finishing your swing."

The greatest hitter in the history of baseball was not following through. From that point on, he played extremely well; led by DiMaggio, we won the tournament.

But, of all the celebrities who accepted my invitation to play in this tournament, I remember most the response of former *Laugh-In* star Dick Martin. "Your tournament sounds like a lot of fun and you can count me in," he wrote. "The only thing that would change my mind would be if I get a job offer or a hard-on, neither of which seems likely."

Martin showed up.

While my love for golf has not diminished, neither has my true passion, telling the stories of history, nature, and extraordinary human beings. I seem to live my life now just one more project away from retirement. When you have spent your life as a producer, as I have, generating ideas and turning them into television programs or movies, it becomes almost impossible to stop. I can't train my mind to stop being curious, to suddenly cease being excited about new ideas. I still feel the energy of creativity.

Through more than four decades I've done thousands of films, both short and long, about our universe. My films have traced the history of civilization, explained how the world works, celebrated the famous and infamous, and recorded the moments in history that have shaped our lives. My films have educated, enlightened, and entertained. And as different as every film has been, my job has always been the same. I was the producer.

Producer. It's a specific title for such an amorphous job. I've spent my working life being one, but I've yet to adequately define it. Ben Benjamin, a respected network executive, once defined the producer as "a towel boy in a whorehouse," meaning that, while everybody else is busy having fun, the producer has to clean up after them. I call the producer the "man with the dream."

In filmmaking today, getting a producing credit is only slightly more difficult than getting a library card. In the halcyon days of moviemaking, the industry was led by strong, well-known producers, people who had a vision and understood quality—and the bottom line—such as Selznick, Goldwyn, Zanuck, Spiegel, and Walt Disney.

These men functioned as producers with complete control. Today that would be impossible. They would be dependent on the whims of the director or, particularly, the megastars, who have gained the power from their box-office appeal to have their demands, no matter how ridiculous they might sometimes be.

Perhaps the most complicated part of the producer's job was keeping the director and the stars under control without alienating them. There has never been a director who didn't want another take, another week on the schedule, two extra cameras, or an elephant painted purple. Traditionally, it had been the producer's job to recognize when the extra money would be spent productively, but to say a firm no the rest of the time. In television, where budgets are smaller and tighter, the producer still has this power; the networks depend on the producers. But, in the motion picture business it disappeared a long time ago. And with the advent of the $100 million box office and stars who can put behinds in seats, these stars have just about all the power. Films such as *Waterworld* get made because Kevin Costner, who has made some wonderful films, has the financial clout to make them happen, and no producer has enough studio backing to stand up and tell him when something is terrible or overbudget.

I have been successful as a producer primarily because I had the natural ability to recognize a good idea, whether it came from my mind, or someone else's. I could sell that idea; I worked as hard as I asked anyone working for me to work to bring it to fruition. I was not afraid to take risks to achieve quality, and maybe most important, I hired good people and gave them all the responsibility they could handle. I was always there in the background. I was never afraid to dive in and get dirty, but I had the good fortune to find great people and recognize their talent. And with my banking experience, I knew finance, so I could build a company.

I was the orchestra conductor who picked the music. I was the cook who mixed the ingredients. And I was the judge who made the decisions. I picked the people who worked for my documentary company. I picked the right people when I created the ceremonies at the Olympics. I picked the right people to make *Roots*.

I suspect not one of the hundreds of people who worked for a Wolper company would state that I was an easy person to work for; I wasn't. I demanded quality. I demanded people put in their best effort. But, what made that palatable to people with talent was that I respected them; I rarely tried to force my idea down someone else's throat. When the director, or the producer, and I were in conflict, rather than forcing him to accept my decision, we negotiated; we talked, we *hondled,* and somehow we reached a conclusion that left everyone satisfied, if not entirely happy. Compromise is the entire basis of society, so I knew I could live with it. I was the boss, but I didn't always get my own way, even when I was adamant. And looking back on an extensive body of work, I'm not sure I could point out a dozen places where that made a difference.

I'm spending a lot of time now at the David L. Wolper Center for the Study of the Documentary at the University of Southern California. In 2000, I donated my fifty-year collection of letters, contracts, publicity material, scripts, and film to the Cinema School of the university. As I was an old rat-packer, it was quite substantial. I saved everything. The center makes all this material available to students, scholars, and others. It's a joy to see students working at the center, using their computers to study the documents and screen the many films in the collection.

When I look back, I can still see myself in a beat-up old car carrying motion picture reels from brand-new TV station to brand-new TV station, trying to convince station managers to buy them. I can see myself trying to sell *The Race for Space* to the networks and trying to get my crew out of Czechoslovakia during the 1968 uprising. I can remember the arguments over Nat Turner and my own Indian wars. I can hear my friend

Alex Haley laughing gently at the enormous success of his story, or Jacques Cousteau trying to convince me that he needed more money for the *Calypso*. And I can feel the joy and the wonder as I watched *Willy Wonka* come alive in the body of Gene Wilder, and the overwhelming sense of pride as a thousand athletes danced gleefully on the infield at the opening ceremonies of the Los Angeles Olympics.

And after all of that, I have only one regret—I wish I were starting all over again. With all the new cable stations and satellite systems, for someone like me, that's an open market. I have so many ideas I can sell them. But, as I come to the end of my working days, I cannot express my feelings about retiring better than my hero George Washington did in a letter to the Marquis de Lafayette, February 1, 1784:

My Dear Marquis: I am become a private citizen on the banks of the Potomac, & under the shadow of my own Vine & my own Fig tree,— free from the bustle of a camp & the busy scenes of public life. I am solacing myself with those tranquil enjoyments.

—I am not only retired from all public enjoyments, but I am retiring within myself; & shall be able to view the solitary walk, & tread the paths of private life with heartfelt satisfaction.

—Envious of none, I am determined to be pleased with all; & this my dear friend, being the order of my march, I will move gently down the stream of life, until I sleep with my Fathers.

EPILOGUE

I vowed when I retired, finally, completely, and forever, that I was done making films. But on September 6, 1999, the television show *20/20* reported that grade-school history books in Texas included six lines about George Washington—and more than six pages about Marilyn Monroe. Shortly after, a poll revealed that while 55 percent of the American public knew Obi-Wan Kenobi said "May the force be with you," only 6 percent knew that George Washington was a general in the Revolutionary Army.

More evidence followed that we are doing a terrible job teaching our young people about the foundations of our democracy, that our kids are learning little about the roots of this extraordinary nation. Not one to think small, I decided I had to produce a fourteen-hour miniseries that I've tentatively titled *Life, Liberty, and the Pursuit of Happiness: The Making of America.*

But this is going to be far more than a history lesson. It's the story of one of the most dramatic periods in the history of mankind—sixteen years during which a handful of mostly young landowners and professional men, schooled in British tradition, mounted an unprecedented revolution against the most powerful nation on earth and created a form of government never before seen.

These were men like Washington, Thomas Jefferson, John and Samuel Adams, John Hancock, James Madison, Patrick Henry, Benjamin Franklin—towering figures whom providence had somehow put in the same place at the same time. Together, they altered the course of human history.

My first step was to form a citizens committee of important people who agreed with me that this project was vitally important. Among the members of this committee are former presidents George H. Bush and Gerald Ford, Senators Edward Kennedy and John Warner, Secretary of

State Colin Powell, Grant Tinker, Peter Ueberroth, Jack Valenti, and Mike Wallace.

Additionally, I formed a creative committee, people in the industry who would contribute their thoughts, their advice, and when needed, their status. Included in this group are Steven Spielberg, George Lucas, Ron Howard, Martin Scorsese, Robert Zemeckis, and Quincy Jones.

And naturally I put together a committee of the leading American historians to make certain we were historically accurate.

One of the things most people overlook about our revolution was how young our founding fathers were at this time. Jefferson was thirty-three years old when he drafted the Declaration of Independence. Marquis de Lafayette was twenty years old when he became a general in Washington's Revolutionary Army. James Madison was twenty-five in 1776; Alexander Hamilton was in his twenties. John Paul Jones was in his thirties when he became an admiral in the first American navy. This is a story about young people, and my desire, my intention, is to cast the leading young actors of today in these roles. These star actors will attract a wide audience of their peers to the exciting story of our history.

The events of September 11, 2001, brought this nation together as we have not been united in decades. It is the proper time to tell this story. Historical memory is essential if the next generations of Americans are to know and understand who we are as a people, what we stand for, where we came from. For me, the proper place to end my career is at our national beginning.

The ending of this miniseries could not be filmed if it weren't true. No one would believe it. On July 4, 1826, fifty years to the day that he had signed his creation the Declaration of Independence, eighty-three-year-old Thomas Jefferson died. Four hundred miles to the north, that same day, John Adams, the second president of the United States, who signed the Declaration and assissted in it writing, also lay dying.

Near noon, just before the time of Jefferson's death, Adams awoke and with great effort proclaimed, "Thomas Jefferson lives." Those were his last words. Both men died that day, the day known to historians as "a moment to God's hard command."

THE WOLPER FILMOGRAPHY:

1958–1999

(For additional information on the author go to www.davidlwolper.com)

WOLPER PRODUCTIONS—
DOCUMENTARY SPECIALS (58)

1958   Race for Space
1959   Project: Man in Space
1960   Hollywood: The Golden Years
1961   Biography of a Rookie
1961   The Rafer Johnson Story
1962   Hollywood: The Great Stars
1962   Hollywood: The Fabulous Era
1962   D-Day: June 6, 1944
1963   Krebiozen and Cancer
1963   The Passing Years
1963   The Making of the President, 1960
1963   December 7th: The Day of Infamy
1963   Ten Seconds That Shook the World
1963   The American Woman in the 20th Century
1964   The Rise and Fall of American Communism
1964   The Battle of Britain
1964   Yanks Are Coming
1964   Berlin: Kaiser to Khrushchev
1964   Trial at Nuremberg
1964   The Legend of Marilyn Monroe
1965   France: Conquest to Liberation
1965   Korea: The 38th Parallel
1965   Prelude to War
1965   Japan: A New Dawn over Asia
1965   007: The Incredible World of James Bond
1965   Let My People Go
1965   October Madness: The World Series
1965   Race for the Moon

1965   The Really Big Family
1965   The Bold Men
1965   The General
1965   Teenage Revolution
1965   The Way Out Men
1965   In Search of Man
1965   The Thin Blue Line
1965   Revolution in the Three R's
1965   Pro Football: Mayhem on a Sunday Afternoon
1966   The Making of the President, 1964
1966   Wall Street: Where the Money Is
1967   China: Roots of Madness
1967   A Nation of Immigrants
1967   Do Blondes Have More Fun?
1967   Sophia
1967   It's a Dog's Life
1968   The World of Horses
1968   Big Cats, Little Cats
1968   World of the Forest
1968   On the Trail of Stanley and Livingstone
1970   The Unfinished Journey of Robert F. Kennedy
1971   Say Goodbye
1976   The Unexplained: The UFO Connection
1976   Mysteries of the Great Pyramid
1978   Roots: One Year Later
1981   Hollywood: The Gift of Laughter
1992   Celebrations
1994   On Trial
1995   Golf: The Greatest Game
1998   Confirmation

DOCUMENTARIES—
SERIES AND SERIES OF SPECIALS (20 SHOWS—347 EPISODES)

1962–63   The Story of . . . (38)
1962–63   Biography (65)
1963–64   Hollywood and the Stars (31)
   1964   Men in Crisis (32)
1965–68
& 1971–75   National Geographic specials (27)
1965–66   The March of Time (8)
1967–68   The Rise and Fall of the Third Reich (3)
1968–72   Plimpton specials (7)

1967–68 The Undersea World of Jacques Cousteau (4)
1969 Untamed World (32)
1971–73 Appointment with Destiny (7)
1972–73 The Explorers (22)
1973 Men of the Sea (7)
1973–75 American Heritage specials (4)
1973–75 Primal Man specials (4)
1974 This Week in the NBA (20)
1974–75 Smithsonian specials (3)
1994 Heroes of the Game (13)
1998 Legends, Icons & Superstars of the 20th Century (10)
1999 Celebrate the Century (10)

MINISERIES
(14 SHOWS—108 HOURS)

1974–75 Sandburg's Lincoln (6)
1977 Roots (12)
1978 Roots: The Next Generations (14)
1979 Moviola (6)
1982 The Mystic Warrior (5)
1983 The Thorn Birds (10)
1985 North and South—Book I (12)
1985 North and South—Book II (12)
1987 Napoleon and Josephine (6)
1993 Queen (6)
1993 Heaven and Hell (6)
1996 The Thorn Birds: The Missing Years (4)
1998 A Will of Their Own (5)
1999 To Serve and Protect (4)

SPECTACULARS (14)

1976 Bicentennial of the United States
1984 Opening Ceremonies—1984 Olympic Games
1984 Closing Ceremonies—1984 Olympic Games
1986 Liberty Weekend
Opening Ceremonies: Relighting of the Statue
Opening Ceremonies: Operation Sail
American Music Concert
International Fireworks Spectacular
Statue of Liberty Ribbon Cutting Ceremony
Liberty Conference

International Classical Concert
Sports Salute to the Stars
Closing Ceremonies
1990   AFI 25th Anniversay Celebration of Tradition

THEATRICAL MOTION PICTURES (20)

1965   Fours Days in November
1967   The Devil's Brigade
1968   The Bridge at Remagen
1968   If It's Tuesday, This Must Be Belgium
1970   I Love My . . . Wife
1971   The Hellstrom Chronicle
1971   Willy Wonka and the Chocolate Factory
1972   King, Queen, Knave!
1972   One Is a Lonely Number
1973   Wattstax
1973   Visions of Eight
1973   Birds Do It, Bees Do It
1974   The Animal Within
1976   Victory at Entebbe!
1981   The Man Who Saw Tomorrow
1981   This Is Elvis
1988   Imagine: John Lennon
1994   Murder in the First
1996   Surviving Picasso
1997   L.A. Confidential

TELEVISION MOVIES (29)

1973   The 500 Pound Jerk
1974   The Trial of Julius and Ethel Rosenberg
1974   The Court-Martial of the Tiger of Malaya: General Yamashita
1974   The Court-Martial of Lt. William Calley
1974   The Morning After
1974   Men of the Dragon
1974   The First Woman President
1974   Get Christie Love
1975   Death Stalk
1975   I Will Fight No More, Forever
1976   Brenda Starr
1976   Collision Course
1981   Murder Is Easy

1982	Sparkling Cyanide
1983	Caribbean Mystery
1984	His Mistress
1987	The Betty Ford Story
1988	What Price Victory
1988	Roots: The Gift
1988	The Plot to Kill Hitler
1989	Murder in Mississippi
1990	Dillinger
1990	When You Remember Me
1991	Bed of Lies
1992	Fatal Deception: Mrs. Lee Harvey Oswald
1993	The Flood: Who Will Save Our Children?
1994	Without Warning
1995	Prince for a Day
1998	Terror at the Mall

ENTERTAINMENT SPECIALS—COMEDIES AND MUSICALS (14)

1966	A Funny Thing Happened on the Way to the White House
1967	A Funny Thing Happened on the Way to Hollywood
1967	Movin' with Nancy
1967	Beat of the Brass
1967	If My Friends Could See Me Now!—Shirley MacLaine
1968	Monte Carlo: C'est la Rose
1968	With Love, Sophia
1968	The Ice Capades
1972	Make Mine Red, White and Blue
1972	Of Thee I Sing
1974	Love from A to Z
1974	Yes, Virginia, There Is a Santa Claus
1974	Celebration: The American Spirit
1981	Small World

ENTERTAINMENT SERIES
(6 SHOWS—253 EPISODES)

1957	Divorce Hearing (39)
1974–78	Chico and the Man (88)
1974–75	Get Christie Love! (13)
1975–79	Welcome Back, Kotter (95)
1983	Casablanca (5)
1991	Best of the Worst (13)

DOCUMENTARIES—
POLITICAL AND CORPORATE (26)

1962   Governor Edmund G. "Pat" Brown of California,
       2nd term reelection campaign films
1962   Congressman Edward Roos Roybal of California campaign films
1963   Escape to Freedom (USIA)
1964   Democratic National Convention films:
       Quest for Peace
       A Thousand Days: A Tribute to John F. Kennedy
1964   And Away We Go!
1964   Governor Dan K. Moore of North Carolina campaign films
1965   Revolution in Our Time
1966   Governor Raymond P. Shafer of Pennsylvania campaign films
1966   Mayor John V. Lindsay of New York campaign films
1966   Destination Safety
1967   Men from Boys
1967   The Big Land
1968   The Dangerous Years
1968   California
1968   Los Angeles: Where the Action Is
1972   Here Comes Tomorrow: The Fear Fighters
1972   Republican National Convention films:
       The Nixon Years: Change without Chaos
       Nixon: Portrait of a President
       Pat Nixon: Portrait of a First Lady
1976   Senator Henry "Scoop" Jackson presidential campaign films
1985   Life at Warner Bros.: The Acting Career of Ronald Reagan
1990   Los Angeles bid film for 1991 Olympic festival
1992   Here's Looking at You, Warner Bros.
1993   Celebration of a Life: Steven J. Ross
1996   Warner Bros. Museum exhibit films

MAJOR PERSONAL AWARDS
AND HONORS

1950s

1959   San Francisco International Film Festival Grand Prize
        Producer, *The Race for Space*
1959   Academy of Motion Picture Arts and Sciences—Oscar Nomination
        Best Documentary Film
        Producer, *The Race for Space*

1960s

1963   Academy of Television Arts and Sciences—Emmy
        Television Program of the Year
        Executive Producer, *The Making of the President, 1960*
1963   George Foster Peabody Award
        Executive Producer, *Biography*
1966   City of New York Citizen of Honor Award
1966   Producers Guild of America
        TV Producer of the Year
1966   The National Association of Television Production Executives—
            Iris Award
        Man of the Year
1967   George Foster Peabody Award
        Executive Producer, *National Geographic*
1968   American Academy of Achievement
        Golden Plate Award

1970s

1972   The Academy of Motion Picture Arts and Sciences—Oscar
        The Hellstrom Chronicle
1973   St. Michael's College, Vermont, Honorary Degree
        Doctorate of Humane Letters
1973   The Society of Film and Television Arts of London
        Robert Flaherty Award

1973   Publicists Guild of America
         Television Showmanship Award
1973   Hollywood Chamber of Commerce
         Installation of Star on Hollywood Walk of Fame
1974   Anti-Defamation League
         Torch of Liberty Award
1974   Hollywood Foreign Press Association—Golden Globe
         Executive Producer, *Visions of Eight*
1974   La Cinémathèque Française—Film Retrospective
1976   American Revolution Bicentennial Administration National
             Bicentennial Medal
1977   George Foster Peabody Award
         Executive Producer, *Roots*
1977   Academy of Television Arts and Sciences—Emmy
         Executive Producer, *Roots*
1977   Television Critics Circle Awards
         Executive Producer, *Roots*
1977   NAACP Image Award
         Executive Producer, *Roots*
1977   Hollywood Foreign Press Association—Golden Globe
         Best Television Drama
         Executive Producer, *Roots*
1977   California Teachers Association
         John Swett Award
1978   USC Journalism School
         Distinguished Achievement in Journalism Award
1978   Academy of Television Arts and Sciences—Emmy
         Executive Producer, *Roots: The Next Generations*
1978   USC School of Performing Arts
         Distinguished Alumni Award

1980s

1983   Hollywood Foreign Press Association—Golden Globe
         Executive Producer, *The Thorn Birds*
1984   Hollywood Women's Press Club
         Louella Parsons Golden Apple Award
1984   The National Academy of Television Arts and Sciences International
             Council
         Founders Lifetime Achievement Award
1984   Academy of Television Arts and Sciences
         Special Award
         XXIIIrd Olympiad Opening and Closing Ceremonies, Los Angeles

1984   Caucus for Producers, Writers and Directors
        Member of the Year
1984   NAACP Image Award
        Opening Ceremony, XXIIIrd Olympiad, Los Angeles
1985   Academy of Motion Picture Arts and Sciences—Special Oscar
        Jean Hersholt Humanitarian Award
1985   University of Southern California General Alumni Association
        Asa V. Call Achievement Award
1985   Ministry of Culture, France
        Ordre des Arts et des Lettres
1985   Beverly Hills Chamber of Commerce
        Citizen of the Year Award
1985   *TV Guide*
        Lifetime Achievement Award
1986   Drake University Honorary Degree
        Doctor of Humane Letters
1986   New York City
        Big Apple Award
1986   People for the American Way
        Spirit of Liberty Award
1987   Daughters of the American Revolution
        Medal of Honor
1987   Freedoms Foundation
        Distinguished American Award
1988   The Boy Scouts of America
        God and Country Exemplary Award
1989   International Documentary Association
        Lifetime Career Achievement Award
1989   Inducted into Academy of Television Arts and Sciences
        Television Hall of Fame

1990s

1990   Producers Guild of America
        Lifetime Achievement Award
1990   Black Filmmakers
        Lifetime Achievement Award
1990   Republic of France
        The National Order of the Legion of Honor
1991   The Christopher Award
1992   The Ellis Island Congressional Medal of Honor
1993   Inducted into Boys and Girls Clubs of America
        Hall of Fame

1993   Martin Luther King Center
        The Trumpet of Conscience Award
1993   The Los Angeles Film Teachers Association
        Jean Renior Responsibility in Television Award
1995   Los Angeles Sports Council 100 Greatest Moments in Sports History
        Opening Ceremonies of the 1984 Olympic Games
1995   Thalians
        Lifetime Achievement Award
1996 USC School of Cinema-Television
        Mary Pickford Alumni Award
1996   USC Honorary Degree
        Doctor of Fine Arts
1998   Hollywood Arts Council "Charlie" Award
        Executive Producer, *L.A. Confidential*
1998   The National Association of Television Production Executives
        Education Foundation
        Lifetime Achievement Award
1999   Grand Marshal, 110th Tournament of Roses Parade
2000   Inducted into Broadcasters Hall of Fame
2002   Inducted into Event Industry Hall of Fame
        Champions Award, Oscar de la Hoya Youth Center

AWARDS PRESENTED IN THE NAME OF DAVID L. WOLPER

The Producers Guild of America:
The David L. Wolper Producer of the Year Award in Long Form Television
Awarded annually
International Documentary Association:
The David L. Wolper Student Documentary Award
Awarded annually

For complete information on Wolper programs, awards, and other references log on to www.davidlwolper.com.

THANK YOU ALL

No one person is responsible for the making of any film, in spite of the so-called auteur theory. Below are some of the producers, directors, writers, editors, composers, and executives who worked on many of my films and are responsible for their success.

Robert Abel
Dede Allen
Forest Allen
Nestor Almendros
John Alonzo
Ashford & Simpson
Stan Atkinson
Dennis Azzarella
Jean Baker
Peter Baldwin
Helmut Barth
Al Bell
Ben Bennett
Harvey Bernhard
Elmer Bernstein
Joseph Biroc
Guy Blanchard
David Blewitt
William Blinn
Paul Boorstin
James L. Brooks
Georg Stanford Brown
Warren Bush
Bill Butler
Chuck Campbell
William T. Cartwright
Marvin Chomsky
Nicholas Clapp
Eric Cohen
N. H. Cominos
Kevin Connor
Bill Conti

Stanley Cortez
Jacques-Yves Cousteau
Philippe Cousteau
James Crabe
Carmen Culver
Eric Daarstad
Frank Decot
Bea Dennis
Charles S. Dubin
Daryl Duke
William Edgar
Michael Eliot
Jack Elliott
John Erman
Scott Eyler
Don E. Fauntleroy
Jose Feliciano
Syd Field
Richard Fielder
Jerry Fielding
Charles B. FitzSimons
Marshall Flaum
Alan Folsom
Ian Fraser
Paul Freeman
Robert M. Fresco
Gerald Fried
Bud Friedgen
Chris Friedgen
Eliot Friedgen
William Friedkin
Tom Fuchs

Mort Garson
John Gilligan
Roger Gimbel
Philip Glass
Burt Gold
Ernest Gold
Herb Golden
Billy Goldenberg
Jerry Goldsmith
Dan Gordon
Alex Grasshoff
Walon Green
David Greene
David Griffiths
Sherman Grinberg
Robert Guenette
Andre Gunn
Jack Haley Jr.
Marvin Hamlisch
William Hanley
Curtis Hanson
William B. Hartigan
Jeffrey Hayes
James T. Heckert
Richard T. Heffron
Brian Helgeland
Dwight Hemion
Conrad Holzgang
James Wong Howe
Robert Human
Philip Hurn
Arthur Ibbetson

Tony Imi
James Ivory
Ruth Prawer Jhabvala
Jerry Johnson
Peter C. Johnson
Quincy Jones
Fred Karlin
Hyman Kaufman
Jack Kaufman
Alfred R. Kelman
Al Kihn
Greg Kinnear
Ernest Kinoy
George Kirgo
Buz Kohan
James Komack
Stanley Kramer
William Kronick
Robert K. Lambert
Alan Landsburg
Vilis Lapenieks
Steven Larner
Robert E. Larson
Stan Lazan
James Lee
Robert Leeburg
Michel Legrand
Malcolm Leo
Draper Lewis
Julian Ludwig
Kent MacKenzie
Henry Mancini
Delbert Mann
Stan Margulies
Alan Marks
Jacques Marquette
Laurence E. Mascott
Paul Mason
Andrew V. McLaglen
Chuck McLain
Ismail Merchant
David Meyers
Walter C. Miller
Don Mischer

Frieda Lee Mock
Arthur Morton
Gilbert Moses
Lyn Murray
Jeff Myrow
Lawrence E. Neiman
Ron Nelson
David Newhouse
Alex North
Nick Noxon
John Peer Nugent
Dale Olson
Albert Lloyd Olson
Joan Owens
Robert A. Papazian
Marty Pasetta
George Plimpton
Dean Pollack
Alan H. Presberg
Rudy Raksin
Al Ramrus
Mose Richards
Fritz Roland
Jeb Rosebrook
Philip R. Rosenberg
Barney Rosenzweig
Irwin Rosten
Herman Rush
Irwin Russell
Alan Sacks
Fouad Said
Terry Sanders
Kimberly Saunders
Laurence D. Savadove
David Saxon
George Schaefer
Walter Scharf
Lalo Schifrin
Arthur Schlesinger Jr.
Jim Schmerer
Howard Schwartz
Eric Sears
Michael Selegman
David Seltzer

Melvin Shapiro
David Shaw
Larry Shaw
Richard Shoppelry
Robert F. Shugrue
Sidney Skolsky
Michael Small
Bud Smith
Gary Smith
Bernard Sofronski
John Soh
Andrew W. Solt
Jeri Sopanen
Ed Spiegel
David Stevens
Theodore Strauss
Mel Stuart
Tom Tannenbaum
George Taylor
Jerry Taylor
Sandra Thomas
Joe Thornton
Jack Tillar
Neil Travis
Lawrence Turman
David Vowell
Malvin Wald
Tommy Walker
Nick Webster
Bernie West
John W. Wheeler
Theodore H. White
Joseph M. Wilcots
John Williams
Bud Wiser
Chris Wiser
Mark M. Wolper
Phillips Wylly
Roger Young
Mai Zetterling
Jerry Zietman
Vilmos Zsigmond

INDEX

Page numbers in *italics* refer to illustrations.